Exchange Rates and International Finance

Exchange Rates and International Finance

SECOND EDITION

Laurence S. Copeland
University of Stirling

ADDISON-WESLEY PUBLISHING COMPANY

Wokingham, England • Reading, Massachusetts • Menlo Park, California
New York • Don Mills, Ontario • Amsterdam • Bonn • Sydney • Singapore
Tokyo • Madrid • San Juan • Milan • Paris • Mexico City • Seoul • Taipei

Many of the designations used by manufacturers and sellers to distinguish their products are claimed as trademarks. Addison-Wesley has made every attempt to supply trademark information about manufacturers and their products mentioned in this book. A list of the trademark designations and their owners appears below.

Cover designed by Crayon Design of Henley-on-Thames and printed by The Riverside Printing Co. (Reading) Ltd.
Text designed by Lesley Stewart.
Typeset by CRB (Drayton) Typesetting Services, Norwich.
Printed in Great Britain by T.J. Press, Padstow, Cornwall.

First edition printed 1989. Reprinted 1990 (twice).
Second edition printed 1994. Reprinted 1995.

British Library Cataloguing in Publication Data
A catalogue record for this book is available from the British Library.

ISBN 0–201–62429–X

Library of Congress Cataloging-in-Publication Data applied for.

Trademark notice
IBM^{TM} is a trademark of International Business Machines Corporation
Lotus® and 1-2-3® are trademarks of Lotus Development Corporation
MS-DOS and Windows are trademarks of Microsoft Corporation
QUATTRO-PRO is a trademark of Borland International Incorporated

To the memory of Robert Copeland

Preface to the second edition

A number of changes have been made in this edition:

(1) Tables and graphs have been updated to cover the early 1990s instead of the late 1980s. Likewise, the potted history of the international monetary system in Chapter 1 has been updated to cover the collapse of the ERM.

(2) An explanation of the difference between bid and asked rates has been added to Chapter 1.

(3) An extra section (3.3) has been added to Chapter 3 to cover money market arbitrage, thereby generalizing the analysis of forward markets to cover borrowing and lending.

(4) A new chapter (10) has been added at the end of Part II. It covers the economics of currency unions, focusing mainly on the example of the proposed European union, but with sideways glances at a number of other instructive cases, not least the instances of monetary disintegration in what was the Soviet Empire.

(5) The other new chapter (14) explains the potential implications of non-linearity and complexity for exchange rates. In order to do so, it dwells at some length on the basic mathematics of chaos, using the standard phase portrait analysis of the logistic function à la Baumol and Benhabib. As such, the chapter may well provide a useful point of departure for the study of other markets where chaotic processes are suspected.

I am grateful to a number of people for comments on this edition. Before embarking on this edition, I received helpful comments and corrections from a number of readers on the first edition. I am extremely fortunate in having Sheila Dow as a colleague at Stirling. Her comments on an early draft of Chapter 10 (on currency unions) were invaluable. The publishers' own referees were thorough and painstaking in their comments on both the new chapters. Any remaining errors are probably due to my own stubbornness in not taking on board all their suggestions.

Laurence S. Copeland
June 1994

Preface to the first edition

'An economist is someone who, instead of telling us why the world is the way it is, tells us why it isn't the way his theories suggest it should be.'

Exchange rates play an increasingly important part in economic life. This is true of the public at large, of corporate management, of city financiers – and, of course, of treasury chiefs. Exchange rate fluctuations are nowadays part of the background of all our lives. The purpose of this book is to provide a guide to what the economics profession has to say about the causes and consequences of these fluctuations.

More than that, it is perhaps worth stating at the outset what this book is *not*. It is not a reference survey of the literature on international finance or, for that matter, on open economy macroeconomics. Nor is it a guide to the ins and outs of currency trading or to the esoteric detail of foreign exchange markets. Nor is it meant to be 'Teach Yourself International Macroeconomic Management' or the 'Practical Central Banker and Finance Minister'. Furthermore, the coverage of the institutional background is the absolute minimum for the exposition.

What the book *does* try to achieve is both more and less ambitious. The objective is to provide an explanation of what the economics profession has to say on a number of topics, chosen for their contemporary relevance rather than their importance in the history of economic thought. For that reason I have not covered the elasticity and absorption approaches, for example, decisions which may well appear perverse to some academic colleagues.

The orientation of the book is by and large away from the policy issues and towards the positive aspects of exchange rate determination, with a particular emphasis on the contributions of modern finance theory to our understanding of the subject (for example, efficient markets, risk premiums and so on).

Readership

The technical level has been kept as undemanding as possible. As far as the topics covered in the early chapters are concerned (purchasing power parity, interest rate parity, the monetary model) that poses no problem, so the material should be accessible to readers with little or no knowledge of mathematics and virtually no background in economics: first-year under-graduates, MBA students or interested market professionals. The later chapters are inevitably somewhat more demanding in terms of technical sophistication and will certainly be appreciated better by readers with a minimal proficiency in elementary calculus and, for the final chapter, some acquaintance with the basic concepts of statistics (variance and covariance and so on). These later chapters may well be of use to fellow academics from different specialisms looking for a quick overview of the state of exchange rate economics, as well as final year students.

Structure and content

The more advanced sections have been signalled by an asterisk, ★. In a few cases the starred sections are preceded by simplified versions of the analysis, so that an alternative to the 'high road' is provided.

Throughout the exposition the emphasis is on delivering the *intuition* behind the results. Rigour is available in abundance in the original liter-ature, references to which are provided at the end of each chapter. The same reasoning led to the decision to cover the empirical work briefly, with little attempt to explain research methodologies in any detail. To do so would in any case have presupposed an understanding of econometrics.

Instead, the aim in the sections on empirical results is to give a con-cise summary of what we know (or think we know) on the subject involved and some indication of which questions remain open. If the author's experience is typical, students and laymen often have difficulty in grasping *why* it is that the economics profession finds it so hard to answer questions like: does interest rate parity hold? is there a risk premium? are expecta-tions rational? Wherever possible I try to explain the main problems facing researchers, while at the same time trying not to forget that the overwhelm-ing majority of readers have no desire to lay the foundations of a career in academic research.

The book will have achieved its objective if, after reading any chap-ter, the student is able to understand the *economic argument* in an article on the same subject in one of the professional journals.

Acknowledgements

A number of people have helped in the production of this book. Colleagues Fred Burton and Martyn Duffy read chapters and offered helpful com-ments and gave much-needed support. Ronnie Macdonald waded through a draft of Chapters 10 and 11. Michael Artis not only read Chapter 11 but provided the vital encouragement at the outset, without which the book would never have been written. I am grateful to Addison-Wesley, particularly Sarah Mallen who had faith in the project and Allison King who has also showed the unfailing confidence in its prospects without which my determination to finish would certainly have flagged long ago.

Since the shortcomings that remain are the product of my own stubbornness, they must be my own responsibility.

Laurence S. Copeland
July 1989

A note on language
For reasons of simplicity the pronoun 'he' is used to relate to both male and female throughout the book.

At the time of writing both the EC and EU are in common use. To minimize confusion for the reader, I have standardized the text and used EU throughout the book.

Publishers' acknowledgements

The publishers wish to thank the following:

- The *Financial Times* for permission to reproduce Table 1.1 from the issue dated 7 July 1988, Table 1.2 from the issue dated 19 February 1993 and for permission to use data from issues published between 1976–86 to produce Figures 11.1 and 11.2.
- The Controller of HMSO for permission to reproduce material from *Financial Statistics, Economic Trends* (June 1992) in Table 1.3.
- Datastream International for permission to use data from various sources between 1972–93 for Figures 1.3–1.5, 2.1–2.4 and 8.5–8.10, and Table 1.3.

Contents

1

Introduction

■ Introduction

Until a few years ago, it might have been necessary to start a book like this by asking the question: why study exchange rates? and then giving an answer in terms of academic curiosity, the design of macro-economic policy, international trade and so on.

Nowadays, surely, there is no need to justify devoting a book to the subject. Exchange rates are no longer an arcane interest confined to a handful of economic specialists and traders. They are simply ubiquitous, to the point where it almost seems that whatever the subject under discussion – the outlook for the domestic or world economy, stock markets, industrial competitiveness at the level of the firm or the industry, even the outcome of the next election – the answer almost invariably turns out to revolve around the exchange rate. The days when exchange rates could safely be ignored by the vast majority of decision makers are long passed, and there is at the moment little prospect of them ever returning.

1

To some extent, the increased importance being attached to exchange rates is a result of the internationalization of modern business, the continuing growth in world trade relative to national economies, the trend towards economic integration (in Europe, at least), and the rapid pace of change in the technology of money transfer. It is also in large part a consequence of the fact that exchange rates are not only variable, but highly volatile. The attention given to them can be traced to the role they play as the joker in the pack: the unpredictable element in the calculations that could turn a profitable deal into a disastrous lossmaker, or make an attractive investment project into the albatross on the company's balance sheet, or push the cost of your family holiday way beyond your budget.

However, it would be dishonest to claim that the reader will learn from this book how to make reliable forecasts of future exchange rate movements. Neither the author nor anyone else really knows how to do that – and the chances are that anyone who *does* know how will never tell the rest of us. (Guess why!)

Instead, the objectives of this book are to enable the reader to understand:

(1) Why exchange rates change – at least, in so far as economists know why they do.

(2) Why it is so difficult to forecast exchange rate changes.

(3) How exchange rate risks can be hedged.

(4) What the main research questions are: what we know and what we do not yet know.

(5) How to evaluate critically the comments on the exchange rate found in the financial press, brokers' circulars and so on.

(6) What are the main issues of policy with respect to exchange rates – in general terms (floating versus fixed rates, international monetary reform and so on) and in particular instances (for example, the ERM membership controversy in the UK).

(7) How to interpret new research results.

Notice what is *not* claimed. The book will not enable the reader to embark on original research. To see why, take a quick glance at one of the technical references in the Reading Guide at the end of one of the later chapters. It will immediately be obvious that the prerequisites for undertaking serious research in what is already a well-worked area include:

(1)   A thorough knowledge of the existing literature on exchange rates.

(2)   A good grounding in general macro- and microeconomics.

(3)   A reasonable competence in the specialized applications of statistics to economic models, a discipline known as econometrics.

Now this book aims to provide a starting point for the first of these prerequisites. As far as the second is concerned, it tries to take as little for granted as possible, though inevitably some knowledge of economics has had to be assumed at various points in the book. Certainly, the coverage of topics outside the field of exchange rates can be nowhere near sufficient to equip the reader who wants to generate his or her own research results. As far as the third requirement is concerned, the decision has been taken to avoid almost completely any discussion of econometric issues or research results, and to limit the commentary to '... evidence was found to support the view that...' and so on. The reasoning behind what will appear to some readers a perverse decision is that covering the econometrics would make the book inaccessible to the many readers who lack the relevant background, while not really helping those who do, since surveys of the empirical literature are available in a number of different places (as will be made clear in the Reading Guide at the end of each chapter). In any case, after having finished the chapter here, the reader who can cope with econometrics should be in a position to go on and read the literature without hesitation.

Instead, the emphasis in this book will be on conveying *at an intuitive level* the main propositions in the literature. As a result, the reader with little economics background will be able to grasp propositions that would otherwise have been completely inaccessible. For the professional or academic economist coming to the subject fresh from other specialist areas and wanting to get to grips with the exchange rate literature in the shortest possible time, the coverage (particularly in the later chapters) is intended to offer a flying start.

This introductory chapter clears the ground for what is to come, starting with an explanation of what we mean by the exchange rate – bilateral, trade-weighted, spot or forward. In Section 1.2, we look in general terms at supply and demand in the currency markets, an exercise which provides the essential framework for analysing how exchange rates are determined. In the process, we see what is involved in fixing an exchange rate. The next section provides, for those readers who need it, an explanation of the balance of payments and its relationship to events in the currency markets. Section 1.4 looks at the conventional wisdom on exchange rates and the balance of payments – a worthwhile exercise if only because, for some purposes, what people believe to be true can be as important as the truth itself (even if we knew it). Section 1.5 contains a potted history of the international monetary system since World War II – essential to understanding the present situation in world financial markets. Section 1.6 gives an overview of the rest of the book, while the last two sections contain, as in all the other chapters, a Summary and Reading Guide respectively.

1.1 What is an exchange rate?

The first thing to understand about the exchange rate is that it is simply a *price*. Or, putting it the other way round, prices as we normally understand the term are themselves exchange rates: the UK price of this book is the exchange rate between a particular good (the book) and pounds sterling. Suppose that it is quoted as £20, which means a book sells for £20, or can be bought at that price. It changes hands at an exchange rate of 1 book = £20.

Notice, as far as the bookseller is concerned, that means 'money can be bought' at the rate of £20 per book. From the bookseller's point of view, the price of £1 is 1/20th of a copy of this book. If its price were £21, the shop would only need to supply 1/21th of a copy in order to earn a pound. So a *rise* in the price of the book, from £20 to £21, is the same as a *fall* in the price of money, from 1/20th to 1/21th of a book.

In the same way, an exchange rate of £1 = DM3.00 means that the price of a Deutsche Mark in UK currency is £(1/3.00) = £0.33. To a German, a pound costs DM3.00. In general, the exchange rate of currency A in terms of currency B is the number of units of B needed to buy a unit of A.

Unfortunately, while it is normal to talk of the (money) price of books rather than the (book) price of money, there is no *normal* way to express an exchange rate. Both £1 = DM3.00 and DM1 = £0.33 are acceptable ways of expressing the same exchange rate. Strangely enough, both the British and Germans *usually* choose the former. In general, the Continental Europeans and the Japanese tend to think of exchange rates as the price of foreign currency: *direct quotations*, in market jargon. The British (invariably) and the Americans (usually, though not always) prefer to think in terms of the purchasing power of the pound or dollar[1] respectively –

---

[1] To further complicate matters, it is common to refer to quotations against the dollar as either in European terms (that is, non-US currency per dollar) or American terms (dollar per currency). The reader, having been warned of the complications awaiting in the market, would be best avoiding them for the moment, by sticking with the conventions set out in this chapter.

nobody in currency markets seems very concerned to make life simple for the textbook reader (or writer)!

We had better make our choice here at the start of the book and stick with it. So:

> **Convention 1:** Throughout the analysis, the exchange rate (symbol S) will be defined as the domestic currency price of foreign currency. So a rise in S_t means a rise in the price of foreign exchange at the time t, hence a relative cheapening of the domestic currency, or a **depreciation**.
> Conversely, a fall in S implies a reduction in the number of units of domestic currency required to buy a unit of foreign exchange, that is, a rise in the relative value of the home country's money, or an **appreciation**.

The only exception is that, when we look at the facts (which we try to do after each new dose of theory), we shall sometimes talk in terms of dollars per pound, simply because it is so much more familiar. On all other occasions, we shall follow Continental practice, as in Convention 1 – which also happens to be much the more popular choice in the exchange rate literature.

1.1.1 Bilateral versus trade-weighted exchange rates

Suppose, one day, I hear the pound has depreciated against the US dollar – in other words, the price of dollars has risen. Does that mean the pound's international value has fallen? Or would it be more accurate to say that the value of the US currency has risen?

From a purely bilateral perspective, the two amount to the same thing. However, for many purposes, a two-country view is far too narrow. For example, suppose we wish to explain *why* the bilateral exchange rate has moved against the pound and in favour of the dollar. Plainly, if we have grounds for believing that it is the US currency that has strengthened rather than the pound that has weakened, we ought to look at developments in the USA rather than the UK to explain the change in the exchange rate, and vice versa if we believe the pound to have weakened while the dollar remained unchanged.

The problem is exactly the same as trying to explain a rise in the price of beef, say. Our first step ought to be to decide whether it is the *relative* price of beef that has risen, in which case the explanation is presumably to be found in changes in the beef market, or whether, on the other hand, it is the price of goods *in general* which has risen (that is, inflation), which would suggest a macroeconomic cause.

Notice that when the price of a single good or class of goods goes up, while all others stay the same, we say the price of beef or meat or whatever has risen. When the price of beef rises, *at the same time as all other prices*, we say the value of money has fallen.

In the same way, if the (sterling) price of dollars goes up, while the (sterling) price of all other currencies is unchanged, we say the US currency has strengthened. On the other hand, if all exchange rates move against the pound, the pound has weakened. The difference is not purely semantic. If the pound suddenly weakens against *all* other currencies, one would intuitively expect to find the cause in some change in the UK rather than the American or German economies, and vice versa if it is the dollar which has risen in value.

All of which should serve to illustrate why, for some purposes, it will suffice to look at the exchange rate between two countries only, while for other purposes this narrow approach could be completely misleading. So far, we have have only thought of exchange rates in a two-country context. To be more precise, we need the following definition:

> **The bilateral exchange rate** between, say, the UK and USA, is the price of dollars in terms of pounds.

So, what has been said is that a change in the UK–US bilateral exchange rate in favour of the dollar could be indicative of *either* a decline in the international value of the pound *or* a rise in that of the dollar, or both, of course. How can we be sure which? How can we get some indication of what has happened to the *overall* value of the pound or dollar?

One way would be simply to look at how both UK and US currencies have moved against the Deutsche Mark – which would involve looking at two bilateral exchange rates for the UK (£/$, £/DM) and two for the US ($/£, $/DM). To give a real-world example, look at Table 1.1, which is taken from the currencies page of the Financial Times of 7 July 1988, and shows cross rates – to be explained shortly – for the previous day.

The first row of the grid is easy to follow. It is simply the number of units of each of the ten currencies delineated across the top of the grid a pound would have bought on the day in question. So a pound would buy £1, or $1.713, or DM3.120, or ¥228.8 ... and so on. The first column, headed '£', shows sterling bilateral exchange rates as defined in Convention 1, that is, the price of the foreign currency (on the left) in pounds: a pound costs £1, a dollar costs £0.584, a Deutsche Mark costs £0.321 and so on – all of which are just the reciprocals of the numbers in the first row, of course.

Now look at the column headed 'DM'. The second entry down tells us a dollar costs DM1.821. Ask yourself the question: is this telling us anything we could not have worked out for ourselves from *either* the first row

Table 1.1 Exchange cross rates 6 July 1988.

6 July	£	$	DM	Yen	FFr.	SFr.	HFl.	Lira	C$	BFr.
£	1	1.713	3.120	228.8	10.50	2.590	3.515	2314	2.066	65.35
$	0.584	1	1.821	133.6	6.130	1.512	2.052	1351	1.206	38.15
DM	0.321	0.549	1	73.33	3.365	0.830	1.127	741.7	0.662	20.95
Yen	4.371	7.487	13.64	1000.	45.89	11.32	15.36	10114	9.030	285.6
FFr.	0.952	1.631	2.971	217.9	10.	2.467	3.348	2204	1.968	62.24
SFr.	0.386	0.661	1.205	88.34	4.054	1	1.357	893.4	0.798	25.23
HFl.	0.284	0.487	0.888	65.09	2.987	0.737	1	658.3	0.588	18.59
Lira	0.432	0.740	1.348	98.88	4.538	1.119	1.519	1000.	0.893	28.24
C$	0.484	0.829	1.510	110.7	5.082	1.254	1.701	1120	1	31.63
BFr.	1.530	2.621	4.774	350.1	16.07	3.463	5.379	3541	3.161	100.

Yen per 1,000: French Fr. per 10: Lira per 1,000: Belgium Fr. per 100

or the first column of the table? Obviously, we ought to have:

$$\text{Mark price of dollars} = \frac{\text{mark price of pounds}}{\text{dollar price of pounds}}$$

$$1.821 = \frac{3.120}{1.713}$$

(Ask yourself: what would happen if this relationship did *not* hold on any particular day?)

So most of the 100 numbers in the matrix are redundant. In fact, all the rates can be, and in practice actually *are* calculated from the nine exchange rates in the US dollar column. If we introduce the definition:

> **A cross exchange rate** is an exchange rate between two currencies, *A* and *B*, neither of which is the US dollar. It can be calculated as the ratio of the exchange rate of *A* to the dollar, divided by the exchange rate of *B* to the dollar.

we can then say that, given N currencies including the numeraire (the dollar), there will be $N(N-1)/2$ cross rates. In Table 1.1, we have $N = 10$ currencies, so there are nine (that is, $N - 1$) dollar rates, and $(10 \times 9)/2 = 45$ cross rates – the remaining entries are either ones or the reciprocals of the cross rates.

Now suppose that we were to look at the cross rates and find the pound has *depreciated* against the US dollar but *appreciated* against the mark. Is the net effect on the pound a rise (appreciation) or fall (depreciation) in its international value?

There is no completely adequate answer to this question. The nearest we can get to a satisfactory solution is to apply the same logic we use in dealing with changes in the domestic purchasing power of money. In situations where some (goods) prices are rising while others are falling, we measure changes in the price of goods *in general* by computing a price index.

In the same way, we can arrive at some indication of what has happened to the price of foreign currencies *in general* by looking at an index of its international value, defined as follows:

> **The effective or trade-weighted exchange rate** of currency A is a weighted average[2] of its exchange rate against currencies B, C, D, E ... and so on. The weights used are usually the proportion of country A's trade which involves B, C, D, E ... respectively.

Notice that the effective exchange rate is *multilateral* rather than bilateral. Furthermore, as is the case with the Retail Price Index, there is no meaning to be attached to the absolute level of the effective exchange rate – it all depends on our choice of base year. So, for example, the fact that the effective exchange rate of the pound stood at 75.5 on 6 July 1988 meant that its average value against the world's other major currencies was just a whisker above three-quarters its average level in the base year, 1975.

This is no place to discuss at length the question of when to use effective and when to use bilateral exchange rates. All that needs to be said is that the theoretical literature sometimes looks at the relationship between the economies of two countries, the domestic and the foreign, so that the conclusions naturally relate to the bilateral exchange rate. In other cases, it tries to explain the value of a single country's currency relative to other currencies in general, so that the obvious interpretation in terms of real-world data is the effective exchange rate. Nonetheless, even in the latter case, we can always handle the theory as though the exchange rate being determined is the one between the domestic economy and another all-enveloping country – the Rest of the World.

To simplify matters and clarify the exposition as far as possible, whenever the analysis takes place in the context of a two-country world, we shall keep to the following:

> **Convention 2:** Unless otherwise specified, the 'home' country is the UK and the domestic currency is the pound sterling. Likewise, the 'foreign' country is the USA, and the foreign currency the US dollar.

---

[2] In general, a weighted average of three numbers: X, Y and Z is calculated as:

$$w_1 X + w_2 Y + w_3 Z$$

where the weights w_1, w_2 and w_3 are proportions so that we have:

$$w_1 + w_2 + w_3 = 1$$

The reader may easily verify that what is known as 'the average' in everyday usage – the arithmetic mean, to give it its correct name – is simply a special case of a weighted average: one where the weights are all equal, and so can safely be ignored.

1.1.2 Spot versus forward rates

All of the exchange rates we have referred to so far have had one thing in common. They have all related to deals conducted 'on the spot' – in other words, involving the delivery of currency more or less immediately when the bargain is struck. In the jargon, we have been dealing with 'spot rates'.

However, there are many deals struck in currency markets that involve no immediate exchange of money. Contracts which commit the two parties to exchange one currency for another at some future date at a predetermined price – the forward or futures exchange rate, as the case may be – will play an important part in the later chapters of this book, and will be explained then. To avoid confusion, we shall stick to this convention:

> **Convention 3:** All exchange rates are **spot** rates, unless specified otherwise.

1.1.3 Buying versus selling rates

There is one more complication to deal with in looking at exchange rate quotations. It arises out of the fact that in the currency market, as in so many other markets, most transactions involve intermediaries who act as temporary buyers for agents wishing to sell and vice versa for those who want to buy. Of course, the intermediaries are not motivated purely by charity. In some cases, they may charge a fee or commission for the service of, in effect, matching buyers and sellers. For major transactions, however, the source of their profit lies in the gap between the price at which they buy a currency and the price at which they are able to sell it. As usual, there is specialized jargon to cover this situation:

> **The bid rate** for currency A in terms of currency B is the rate at which dealers buy currency A (sell currency B). **The offer** (or **ask**) **rate** is the rate at which dealers sell currency A (buy currency B). The (**bid/ask**) **spread** is the gap between the offer and bid rates.

For example, the Financial Times of 20 February 1993 contained the rates for the pound and dollar quoted in London shown in Table 1.2.

The top half of the table shows rates for the pound and the bottom half for the US dollar. Unfortunately, there is a possible source of confusion at the very outset. The column headed *Day's spread* has nothing to do with the spread between bid and ask rates. It refers to the range or spread between the highest and lowest rates reached for the currency in question during the day's trading. So, from the first entry in the column, we find that during trading in London on 19 February, the pound fluctuated

Table 1.2   Financial Times quotations for pound and dollar.

	Pound spot – forward against the pound					
19 February	*Day's spread*	*Close*	*One month*	*% p.a.*	*Three months*	*% p.a.*
US	1.4405–1.4625	1.4525–1.4535	0.36–0.34cpm	2.89	1.07–1.04pm	2.90
Canada	1.8150–1.8435	1.8255–1.8265	0.07pm–0.01cdis	0.20	0.08pm–0.06pm	0.15
Netherlands	2.6560–2.6830	2.6700–2.6800	⅜–½cdis	−1.96	1⅛–1½dis	−1.96
Belgium	48.65–49.10	48.80–48.90	18–14cpm	3.93	28–41dis	−2.82
Denmark	9.0470–9.1330	9.0875–9.0975	8–11½ordis	−12.87	25¼–30½dis	−12.26
Ireland	0.9675–0.9775	0.9740–0.9750	0.56–0.68cdis	−7.63	1.75–2.05dis	−7.80
Germany	2.3590–2.3850	2.3750–2.3800	⅜–½pfdis	−2.21	1⅛–1⅜dis	−2.10
Portugal	215.40–218.15	217.15–218.15	105–136cdis	−6.64	371–404dis	−7.12
Spain	169.15–170.75	170.35–170.65	103–133cdis	−8.30	313–349dis	−7.77
Italy	2249.75–2281.80	2280.00–2281.00	8–10liredis	−4.74	29–31dis	−5.26
Norway	10.0450–10.1400	10.0800–10.0900	1⅜–3oredis	−2.60	5⅝–7⅝dis	−2.68
France	7.9865–8.0640	8.0450–8.0550	3¼–3¾cdis	−5.22	10⅞–11⅜dis	−5.59
Sweden	10.9030–11.0750	10.9725–10.9825	1½–3⅞oredis	−2.94	6⅛–8⅝dis	−2.69
Japan	172.10–174.70	172.50–173.50	½–⅜ypm	3.03	1⅜–1⅛pm	2.89
Austria	16.58–16.81	16.69–16.72	1⅜–2½grodis	−1.48	5¾–7⅛dis	−1.63
Switzerland	2.1760–2.1980	2.1850–2.1950	¼–parcpm	0.68	⅜–⅛pm	0.46
Ecu	1.2145–1.2265	1.2215–1.2225	0.30–0.35cdis	−3.19	0.99–1.06dis	−3.36

Commercial rates taken towards the end of London trading. Six-month forward dollar 1.81–1.76pm.
12 Month 2.93–2.83pm.

	Dollar spot – forward against the dollar					
19 February	*Day's spread*	*Close*	*One month*	*% p.a.*	*Three months*	*% p.a.*
UK†	1.4405–1.4625	1.4525–1.4535	0.36–0.34cpm	2.89	1.07–1.04pm	2.90
Ireland†	1.4815–1.4985	1.4930–1.4940	1.45–1.25cpm	10.85	4.20–3.90pm	10.85
Canada	1.2550–1.2605	1.2560–1.2570	0.27–0.30cdis	−2.72	0.89–0.95dis	−2.93
Netherlands	1.8295–1.8530	1.8405–1.8415	0.74–0.77cdis	−4.92	2.23–2.29dis	−4.91
Belgium	33.50–33.80	33.65–33.75	15.00–17.00cdis	−5.70	46.00–52.00dis	−5.82
Denmark	6.2320–6.2830	6.2550–6.2600	6.00–10.00oredis	−15.34	20.00–26.00dis	−14.70
Germany	1.6240–1.6460	1.6355–1.6365	0.70–0.72pfdis	−5.21	2.12–2.15dis	−5.22
Portugal	149.15–149.60	149.50–149.60	118–123cdis	−9.67	365–377dis	−9.92
Spain	116.45–117.50	117.20–117.30	105–115cdis	−11.26	300–325dis	−10.66
Italy	1550.00–1570.00	1569.25–1569.75	9.60–10.40cdis	−7.65	31.50–32.50dis	−8.16
Norway	6.9165–6.9650	6.9375–6.9425	3.00–3.50oredis	−5.62	9.30–10.30dis	−5.65
France	5.5020–5.5525	5.5375–5.5425	3.65–3.85cdis	−8.12	11.70–12.00dis	−8.56
Sweden	7.5135–7.6315	7.5525–7.5575	3.60–4.20oredis	−6.19	10.50–11.50dis	−5.82
Japan	118.85–119.45	119.05–119.15	par–0.01ydis	−0.05	0.01–0.02dis	−0.05
Austria	11.4350–11.5240	11.5090–11.5140	4.20–4.55grodis	−4.56	12.60–13.70dis	−4.57
Switzerland	1.4970–1.5135	1.5075–1.5085	0.29–0.33cdis	−2.47	0.91–0.96dis	−2.48
Ecu†	1.1835–1.1950	1.1885–1.1895	0.60–0.59cpm	6.01	1.85–1.82pm	6.17

Commercial rates taken towards the end of London trading. †UK, Ireland and Ecu are quoted in US
currency. Forward premiums and discounts apply to the US dollar and not to the individual currency.

between a low of £1 = $1.4405 and a high of £1 = $1.4625, a range of 2.2 cents or 1.53 %[3] – one of the more turbulent days in the market, but by no means without precedent. Similarly, the rate against the Belgian Franc ranged from £1 = BF48.65 to £1 = BF49.10.

The next column, headed *Close*, shows the spread between buying and selling rates for the currencies at the close of trading in London that day. The dollar stood at $1.4525 bid and $1.4535 asked.[4] In other words, anyone selling dollars could expect to get a price of $1.4525, while buyers would have to pay dealers $1.4535, a bid/ask spread of $0.0010 or 1/10th of a cent, equivalent to about $700 on a million pound deal. On the other hand, for both the French and Danish currencies the spread was 100 points.

A point worth noting is that, since one can only *buy* one currency by simultaneously *selling* another, it follows that the ask price for currency A (in terms of currency B) is the reciprocal of the *bid*, not the ask price, for currency B (in terms of A). In other words, whereas in the absence of transaction costs, we can simply say that:

$$S(\text{£ per \$}) = 1/S(\text{\$ per £}) \tag{1.1}$$

this is no longer the case when we allow for the spread between bid and ask rates. Instead, if we write $S^b(\text{A}/\text{B})$ to denote the bid price for currency B in terms of currency A, $S^a(\text{A}/\text{B})$ for the ask price of B in terms of A, and similarly $S^b(\text{B}/\text{A})$ and $S^a(\text{B}/\text{A})$ are bid and ask for A in terms of B, then the following relationship holds:

$$S^b(\text{B}/\text{A}) = 1/S^a(\text{A}/\text{B}) \quad \text{and} \quad S^a(\text{B}/\text{A}) = 1/S^b(\text{A}/\text{B}) \tag{1.2}$$

One implication of this is that in practice the relationship between cross rates is not quite as simple as it was made to appear in Section 1.1. In fact, it turns out that cross rates can show inconsistencies in proportion to the bid/ask spreads on the currencies involved.

Obviously, dealers require a spread on all transactions, whether spot or forward. Typical spreads are between one tenth and one half of one per cent, with the larger margins applying to less frequently traded currencies,

---

[3] This may not seem very much, until it is realized that we are talking about a variation of nearly 2 % in one single day. As an annual rate (that is, if repeated day after day for a whole year) it amounts to an astronomic range. As it happens, according to the FT's commentary on the currency markets for the day in question, the pound fell in early trading after a bad night's trading in the Far East, and subsequently recovered to close the day at or near its high.

[4] In fact, this would tend to be quoted in the market (where brevity is at a premium) in the form $1.4175–85, or even just as 75–85.

where dealers may have to keep the currency they purchase on their books (that is, in stock) for far longer than the more heavily traded currencies.[5]

While there has been a little research on the subject of the spread, the topic is for the most part beyond the scope of this book. Instead, we shall regard the distinction between buying and selling rates as merely a technicality affecting precise calculations of the profitability of deals, but not in principle changing our conclusions regarding the basic mechanisms at work in currency markets. With the exception of Section 3.3, we shall ignore this complication from now on. In fact, we impose the following:

> **Convention 4**: Unless specified otherwise, all exchange rates, forward and spot, are to be understood as mid-market rates, that is, averages of bid and offered rates.

1.2   The market for foreign currency

What determines exchange rates? What factors can explain the wild fluctuations in currency values that seem to occur so frequently nowadays?

Answering questions like these will take up most of the book. However, at the simplest possible level, we can give an answer in terms of elementary microeconomics – one which is not in itself very illuminating, but provides an essential framework for thinking about exchange rates.

As with any other market, price is determined by supply and demand. Look at Figure 1.1(b), ignoring for the moment Figure 1.1(a) to its left. The upward-sloping supply and downward-sloping demand curves will look reassuringly familiar to anyone who has ever had any previous encounter with microeconomics. However, we need to be a little careful in interpreting them in the present case.

First, note the price on the vertical axis: it is the variable we are calling S, the exchange rate measured as the price of a dollar in domestic (UK) currency. On the horizontal axis we measure the quantity of dollars traded, because the dollar is the good whose price is measured on the vertical.

(Notice that, since the sterling price of dollars is the reciprocal of the dollar price of pounds, the vertical axis *could* have been drawn for $1/S$, the dollar price of pounds. To be consistent, we would have had to plot on the horizontal axis the quantity of *sterling* changing hands.

All of which serves simply to illustrate an obvious, but important point: in a bilateral context, *any supply of dollars is equivalent to a demand for sterling, and vice versa.* So the whole of the supply and demand analysis

---

[5] Of course, even for major currencies, spreads are far from negligible for small trades, as can be verified by consulting the table of tourist exchange rates published in the newspaper or displayed in the window of any bank or travel agent with a bureau de change. However, the impact of tourists' purchases and sales on the exchange rate is very small, so we concentrate on the activities of the large traders here.

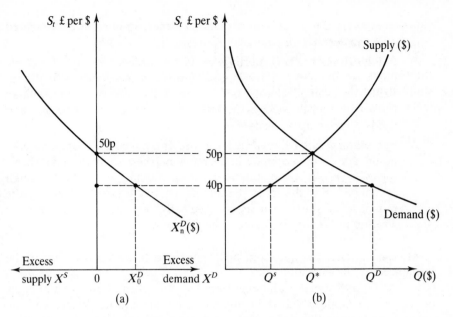

Figure 1.1　Supply and demand in the market for foreign currency.

which follows could be carried out in terms of the market for sterling instead of the market for dollars.[6])

Now consider the question: what is the motivation behind the demand and supply curves in Figure 1.1(b)? What kind of agents supply or demand foreign currency?[7] For present purposes, we can divide them all into one of three categories:

(1) **Exporters** supply goods to foreign buyers. In return, they either receive foreign currency directly, or are paid in sterling which has been purchased by the overseas importer with foreign currency. In either case, the net effect must be an associated *supply* of foreign exchange – dollars, if the exports were sold to the USA, or to any of the many other countries which use dollars for their foreign trade. Symmetrically, **importers** buy goods from foreign suppliers, paying with dollars bought for the purpose in the currency market, or occasionally with sterling, leaving the recipient in the USA or wherever

---

[6] It would be a worthwhile exercise for the reader to redraw Figures 1.1(a) and (b) in terms of the market for pounds rather than dollars.

[7] A trivial answer would be: foreign exchange traders, since the vast majority of currency transactions are carried out between professionals in the specialized currency markets in London, New York, Tokyo, Zurich, Frankfurt and so on. However, traders either act on behalf of other economic agents, in which case we prefer to deal with the actual decision makers rather than their representatives, or behave as principals in their own right, in which case they count as speculators or arbitrageurs themselves.

to convert the pounds into dollars. Hence, imports are associated with the *demand* for foreign currency.

(2) **Foreign investors** buy sterling so as to purchase assets like office blocks in the City, shares in UK companies or estates in Scotland. **British investors** exchange pounds for dollars so as to buy holiday homes in Florida, shares in IBM, or, perhaps via their pension funds, to snap up real estate in Texas.

(3) **Speculators** will be regarded for present purposes simply as economic agents who operate in currency markets so as to make themselves a profit from the activity of buying or selling foreign exchange.[8] For the most part, their activity takes the form of the purchase of short-term assets, typically deposits of one form or another in UK or US financial institutions.

Next, ask yourself the question: how will these three kinds of agents be influenced by the exchange rate?

As far as importers and exporters are concerned, there are a number of reasons to suppose that the demand for dollars will be greater and the supply smaller, the lower the price – in other words, the higher the relative value of the pound. The reason is that when the dollar is cheaper and the pound more expensive, a given sterling price of UK output translates into a higher dollar price. *Other things being equal*, this is likely to reduce the volume of exports from Britain and increase the volume of relatively cheap, dollar-priced imports. The net effect in the market for dollars must be to increase the demand and decrease the supply.[9]

A similar argument applies to what have been called long-term investors. It is not that exchange rates will necessarily be the dominant factor in their investment decision. All we can say is that the cheaper the dollar and the higher the value of the pound, the more dollars are required to buy any asset in Britain – hence, the less likely it is that the prospective

---

[8] A more precise definition of speculation will be given later in the book. For the moment, note that there is emphatically no intention whatsoever to make moral distinctions between speculators and non-speculators, or indeed to pass moral judgements on any type of activity carried on in the currency markets. It so happens that, in the author's opinion, there are no moral grounds for passing judgement, and even if there were, the fact would be irrelevant to the analysis.

All of which will probably not stop some readers from wanting to divide the currency markets into 'goodies' and 'baddies', the former consisting of the meek in spirit ('genuine' traders, that is, exporters and importers, long-term investors and so on – for the most part, multinational corporations), while the latter correspond to what were once called 'the gnomes of Zurich' – traders only interested in short-term gain; wealthy, cynical and, worst of all, foreign!

[9] This is not to say of course that the exchange rate will be anything like the only, or even the major factor affecting the volume of trade in the two directions – hence the qualification in italics, which will be familiar to readers who have had even the briefest encounter with elementary microeconomics. The subject is, in any case, one about which a lot more will be said later in the book, especially in Chapter 2.

investment will satisfy the decision criteria of the American investor, whether an individual or an institution. At the same time, a cheap dollar means UK investors and the institutions who manage much of Britain's wealth will find US assets attractively cheap to buy with sterling. The result must be that when the dollar is cheap and the pound relatively dear, at the lower end of the graph in Figure 1.1(b), the demand for dollars to buy US assets is great, and the supply, by Americans wanting to buy assets in the domestic economy, is small.

Finally, as we shall see, where speculators are concerned, the main consideration is prospective capital gain. Now there are a number of assumptions one could make about how they arrive at their forecasts of the likely capital gain, and we shall have a lot to say on this point in the course of the book. For the moment, if we ignore these issues and take speculators' expectations as *given*, we can say with some confidence that the higher the pound's international value, the less attractive it will be to hold, and vice versa.

In total then, whichever kind of agent we consider, the conclusion is the same: the lower is the price of dollars, S, the greater the demand and the smaller the supply. Conversely, when the dollar is expensive, there will be a smaller demand and greater supply. At some exchange rate – $1 = £0.50 in the diagram – the demand and supply will be equal. Below this equilibrium price level, demand is greater than supply, and above it, the opposite is true.

In Figure 1.1(a), excess demand is plotted, sloping downwards from left to right.

Now, of course, any demand and supply diagram can be redrawn in terms of excess demand alone. However, this approach is particularly appropriate in the present instance, because of the peculiar nature of supply and demand in the currency markets. In the textbook model of the market for a consumer good, supply is the outcome of the optimal behaviour of firms, while demand results from utility maximization by households. By contrast, in currency markets, not only is there a complete symmetry between the supply and demand – exporters and importers, inward investment and outward investment and so on – the agents involved on both sides are of broadly the same kind. In fact, one can go further and say *the suppliers and demanders will often be the very same individuals or institutions*.

This is unlikely to be true of exporters and importers, in the short term at least. By and large, exporters do not switch to importing when exchange rates are unfavourable, and vice versa.[10] Some types of investor

---

[10] Though in the long run, they may well switch sides. This is particularly true of multinational corporations (for whom a change from exporting to importing may simply involve diverting production from a subsidiary in the home country to one overseas) or indeed, of the international trading companies peculiar to the Far East.

can and certainly do switch from being buyers of a currency to sellers – particularly where the assets being bought are financial. Thus, a US mutual fund may be a net purchaser of shares in London when the exchange rate is $1 = £0.70, but a net seller out of its UK portfolio if the value of the pound rises to $1 = £0.40. What is certainly true is that the third category of agent in the currency market – the one we have called, for want of a better name, the speculator – is completely flexible, demanding dollars when he perceives the pound's value as too high, and supplying them when he thinks it is too low.[11]

Now it has become almost a truism to say that modern currency markets are dominated by speculators, whose trading volumes completely swamp those of other types of agent. It follows that, for all practical purposes, the distinction between supply and demand is irrelevant. There is no intrinsic difference between the two. We may as well think solely in terms of the *net* demand for a currency.

For this reason, much exchange rate theory can be seen as concerned only with the question of what determines the slope and position of the excess demand curve in Figure 1.1(a), rather than the underlying supply and demand curves in Figure 1.1(b).

1.2.1   Floating rates

Now consider Figure 1.2. Starting from an initial equilibrium at $1 = £0.50, suppose that for some reason or other the excess demand schedule rises, from X^D to $X^{D'}$ – whether as the result of an upward shift in the demand curve or downward shift in the supply curve is immaterial. The impact effect is to create an excess demand for dollars of X_1^D (at point B).

In practice, the excess demand for dollars (and associated excess supply of pounds) would manifest itself to traders in a build-up of their sterling positions beyond normal or desired levels, and a fall in their dollar holdings. Orders to exchange pounds for dollars would be greater in volume than orders to buy pounds with dollars. Given the speed with which currency markets move nowadays, traders would need to change the price immediately in order to be able to carry on doing business. The direction of the change is obvious. The excess demand for the dollar means that its price must rise, the excess demand for sterling dictates the need to reduce its relative price.

It follows that, in the absence of any impediment, the price of dollars will rise from $1 = £0.50, and carry on rising until the excess demand has

---

[11] Far from matching the free-wheeling 'cowboy' image of popular imagination, the speculator is most likely to be operating on behalf of an international bank which has reached the conclusion – with more or less help from the economic model on its computer – that the exchange rate is 'out of line'.

been eliminated, at the new equilibrium rate of $1 = £0.70. As we have seen, it is difficult to think of a reason why this process should not be very rapid indeed – more or less instantaneous, in fact.

Obviously, should there be an opposite change in market sentiment, pushing the excess demand schedule down to $X^{D''}$, the excess supply of X_2^D (at point A) would drive the dollar's relative price down more or less immediately to $1 = £0.40.

In this kind of regime, the exchange rate is determined by market forces alone. We define:

> **A completely flexible or (purely or freely) floating exchange rate** is one whose level is determined exclusively by the underlying balance of supply and demand for the currencies involved, with no outside intervention.

For the most part, we shall be concerned with the behaviour of floating exchange rates in this book. In fact, to avoid any possible confusion:

> **Convention 4:** Unless specified otherwise, the analysis assumes a freely floating exchange rate.

1.2.2 Fixed rates

Now it is not difficult to see why exchange rate fluctuations like those illustrated in Figure 1.2 are widely regarded as very damaging indeed for the economy of the country or countries concerned.[12] We are all familiar with the problems created for British tourists when there is a sudden change in the value of the pound. Of much more importance to the economy is the fact that exchange rate uncertainties make it very difficult for exporters and importers to enter into long-term commitments to supply or buy goods at a price fixed in advance. Worse still, the risk of unfavourable movements in the exchange rate adds to the uncertainties involved in international investment decisions: where to site new production facilities, which markets to expand into and which to abandon, and so on.

For example, a US motor manufacturer thinking of building a new plant will be faced with the problem that, given production costs in the two countries measured in pounds and dollars respectively, the new facility will be best sited in the UK if the pound's relative value is low, and in the USA if the dollar is relatively cheaper. The trouble is, the decision to build the plant has to be taken several years in advance, and in the interim the exchange

---

[12] Notice the potential asymmetry: volatility in the pound/dollar rate creates difficulties for many UK decision makers, but is in most cases of peripheral importance to their opposite numbers in the USA.

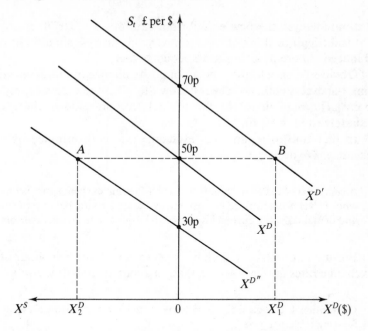

Figure 1.2 Shifts in the excess demand for foreign currency.

rate may change so as to make what looked the more cost-effective alternative completely uncompetitive by the time production starts.

From agreeing that exchange rate volatility is damaging, it is only a
short step to arguing that 'the government must do something'[13] – for
example, fix the exchange rate at an 'acceptable' level, whatever that may
mean. How can this be achieved?

One way would be to announce the fixed exchange rate, and impose
it by placing legal restrictions on dealings. For example, the authorities
could insist that, henceforth, all sales or purchases of foreign currency
must be made via the central bank only. Or, going further still, private
holdings of foreign currency could be banned altogether, or permitted only
with official consent.

Even today, restrictions like these are, sadly, more or less the norm
across the world – particularly in the developing countries, but often in the
industrialized world too. Their effect[14] is to make it possible for the

---

[13] A short step, though not necessarily a sensible one – after all, cold weather is often
damaging, but we only expect the government to help people live with the consequences, not
stabilize the temperature!

[14] Apart, that is, from distorting the real sector of the economy, fostering the creation of
'parallel' (that is, black) markets, with a consequent growth in criminal activity of one kind
or another and an erosion of respect for the law, as well as abridging the freedom of the
citizen in the countries in question – marginally, perhaps, by the restrictions themselves,
though much more seriously by the measures taken to enforce the restrictions.

authorities to peg the exchange rate without operating via the market. In the jargon, currencies subjected to controls like these are said to be *inconvertible* or *not fully convertible*.

However, where the authorities wish to fix the exchange rate while preserving convertibility, the situation is a great deal more complicated.

Suppose that the UK authorities wished to peg the pound/dollar rate at the level $1 = £0.50$. Obviously, as long as the supply and demand curves are in the same position as in Figure 1.1(b), there is no problem – the market rate is acceptable, and there is no need for the authorities to do anything but sit on the sidelines.

But, as we have seen, if market conditions change, and there is a sudden upward shift in the excess demand curve to X^D in Figure 1.2, the impact effect will be to create an instantaneous excess demand for dollars (excess supply of pounds) of $\$X_1^D$. If the market is left to its own devices – under a pure float – the upward pressure on the price of dollars will cause their price to be bid up to $1 = £0.70$ – in other words, a fall in the value of the pound.

How can the exchange rate be kept from moving? In order to prevent a depreciation, the government[15] could supply the additional dollars in order to satisfy the excess demand – or in other words buy up the excess supply of sterling, before its impact is felt in the market. If it does this, the market will remain in equilibrium at the fixed rate $1 = £0.50$. For all practical purposes, the authorities will have completely neutralized the shift in the underlying market excess demand schedule.[16]

If this seems simple, so it should. There is no difference in principle between fixing an exchange rate and fixing any other price. In order to fix the price of eggs, say, all that is required is for *somebody* – it need not necessarily be the government – to stand ready to enter the market, offering cash to buy up any excess supply that threatens to drive the price down, or supplying eggs to satisfy any excess demand that would otherwise cause the price to rise. The only prerequisite is a buffer stock – or,

---

[15] The task of actually operating in the currency markets so as to fix a country's exchange rate is usually assigned to another institution (often its central bank), which is not always strictly an arm of government. For example, while the Bank of England is an agency of Her Majesty's government, the US Federal Reserve Bank is independent of the federal government in Washington DC.

For our purposes, these subtleties are ignored, and at no point in the book will any attempt be made to distinguish between the policies and responsibilities of the government and the central bank.

[16] In fact, traders may not even be aware that the central bank has been operating in the market. Very often they may only observe 'business as usual', with brisk two-way trading and no tendency for positions to accumulate on either side of the market. Where the markets do get wind of intervention, it is often because the authorities intend the news to emerge.

Of course, in the end, it all 'comes out in the wash' – in the UK and USA, at any rate – with the publication of the monthly figures for the change in the reserves. But by then the information is of more or less historical interest only.

more precisely, two buffer stocks: one of eggs, for supplying when there is excess demand, and one of cash, for using when there is excess supply.

Put like that, it should be clear why governments prefer, by and large, to live with the vagaries of demand and supply in the egg market, rather than attempt to fix the price.[17]

Not only would the government have to bear the day-to-day cost of managing and financing a buffer stock of eggs, it would also have to deal with the perennial problem facing all such intervention systems: what happens when there are long periods of excess demand or supply? In the former case, it has to keep on supplying eggs to the market, so that at some point its buffer stock is likely to be exhausted. The latter case is slightly different. If it faces excess supply situations day after day, it will need to have access to a large stock of cash. For the monetary authority, printing additional money is always a feasible option – but it is impossible to reconcile with any monetary policy. Or more precisely, it means monetary policy has to be targeted on fixing the price of eggs![18]

Exactly the same type of problem arises in the case of a fixed exchange rate system, where the nation's reserves of gold and foreign currency act as the buffer stock. As long as short periods of excess demand for dollars (as at point *B* in Figure 1.2) alternate with periods of excess supply (point *A*), the system can be sustained. The central bank takes dollars into the reserves at times when the pound is strong and allows the reserves to run down at times when it is weak, so that over any period the level of the reserves is more or less steady.

However, if at some stage market sentiment should undergo a longer-lasting change, the reserves will be subject to a sustained rise or fall, depending on whether the new mood is in favour of the pound at the expense of the dollar, or vice versa.

There is an asymmetry here. If the pattern in the market is a sequence of excess demand situations (as at *B*, in Figure 1.2), the trend of the reserves will be downward. The situation is obviously unstable, since it carries the threat of complete exhaustion of the reserves, an event which the market will almost certainly anticipate, and thereby hasten.

On the other hand, there is nothing to stop the central bank printing money at zero cost to satisfy an excess demand for pounds (excess supply

---

[17] Except, that is, where the authorities are able and willing to impose a price by decree, as happened in the Communist bloc for example. In such cases what is needed is not a buffer stock, but either a docile populace willing to accept queuing as a way of life, or a secret police capable of preventing the market from reasserting itself – preferably both.

Notice that this scenario is simply the equivalent in the egg market of inconvertibility in the currency market – with about the same moral authority.

[18] Since originally writing this chapter, reality has caught up with this particular example in the form of the UK salmonella scandal at the end of 1988, when the British Government actually was forced to buy up a sudden excess supply of eggs in order to prevent the price falling.

of dollars) at points like *A* in the diagram – nothing, that is, as long as the government cherishes no other objectives for its monetary policy (for example, keeping its money stock constant, so as to prevent inflation).

The reader might be forgiven for thinking (along with many politicians and economic commentators) that it ought to be simple to sidestep this dilemma. After all, persistent excess supply or demand is, by definition, evidence of 'fundamental disequilibrium'. So, the argument runs, a fixed exchange rate regime is quite feasible, provided that the authorities make no heroic attempts to resist *long-run* changes in the equilibrium exchange rate. The prescription is simple: neutralize *temporary* excess demand or supply, so as to reduce the 'noise' in the system or if possible eliminate it altogether, but move the fixed rate up or down in response to *permanent* changes in equilibrium.

Unfortunately, in practice, it is usually impossible to distinguish between temporary and permanent disturbances to equilibrium *at the time they occur.*[19] A 'temporary' disturbance emerges unexpectedly, and as days turn into weeks, and weeks into months of disequilibrium, it gradually becomes apparent that the change in market sentiment is permanent, or at least far too long-lived to be resisted without either exhausting the reserves or leading to massive monetary expansion.

The difficulty is only slightly alleviated by the fact that fixed exchange rate systems are invariably operated in a somewhat less rigid fashion than is described here.[20] Typically, instead of announcing a completely fixed exchange rate, a 'parity value' is established, around which a pre-defined amount of variation will be permitted. For example, the UK authorities might decide to allow the pound to fluctuate freely within a band of 2 % on either side of the fixed rate of $1 = £0.50, that is, between a 'ceiling' level of $1 = £0.51 and a 'floor' of $1 = £0.49. This modification has the advantage of allowing the central bank more time to respond to market disequilibrium. On the other hand, it has the disadvantage that a currency which is seen to be bumping along its floor is even more obviously overvalued, and vice versa when it is pushed against its ceiling.

Although we are primarily concerned with floating rates in this book, we shall have more to say about the implications of operating a fixed exchange rate regime in Chapters 5 and 6.

---

[19] And often long afterwards too. For example, it is still unclear, even now, whether the rise in the dollar in the mid 1980s was, in fact, an equilibrium or disequilibrium phenomenon. What is clear, of course, is that it could never have been prevented by intervention in the currency markets alone.

[20] In practice, fixed exchange rate mechanisms tend to be highly complex arrangements, specifying in such detail the obligations and entitlements of the countries involved it would take a whole book to describe them fully. The objective here is, as always, simply to allow the reader to understand the general principles underlying the institutional arrangement.

1.2.3 Managed floating

From considering a fixed rate with fluctuation bands, it is easy to envisage a system, or rather a non-system, where the authorities manipulate the exchange rate to suit their own (usually unannounced) objectives,[21] sometimes intervening to fix the rate, sometimes staying on the sidelines. This type of compromise is known as a 'managed' or 'dirty' float. In fact, it characterizes the behaviour of most of the major exchange rates during the so-called floating rate era of the 1970s and 1980s. As proof, one need only cite the fact that the announced foreign exchange reserves of all the major countries fluctuated quite substantially over this period (see Section 1.4).

In general, then, exchange rate regimes could be classified by their implications for the foreign currency reserves. Under a pure float, the reserves are constant – in fact, there is no need for the monetary authority to hold any reserves at all. Under a managed float, the reserves fluctuate on a day-to-day, month-to-month basis, but around a broadly constant level. With a fixed exchange rate, however, the reserves must carry the full burden of adjustment to disequilibrium in the currency markets, and can be expected therefore to be far more volatile, probably exhibiting long swings up or down.

1.3   The balance of payments

Consider the problem of drawing up an account of all the transactions conducted between the UK and the Rest of the World (ROW). It would serve as a kind of index of the flow of demand and supply for the pound over any period. This is precisely the purpose of a balance of payments account.[22]

Table 1.3 presents a summary of the UK balance of payments for 1992.[23] The format of the account is set out in accordance with standard

---

[21] Obviously, this non-system has the dubious attraction that it maximizes the discretionary power of the monetary authority.

[22] More generally, the relationship of balance of payments accounting to the analysis of exchange rate determination is the same as that between national income accounting and (closed economy) macroeconomics or, for that matter, financial accounting and corporate finance theory.

[23] It must be emphasized that balance of payments accounts are subject to a margin of error that is wide even by the standards of economic data. It is highly likely that the 1992 accounts will be subject to drastic revision for some years to come, and when they are eventually allowed to settle down the final figures may well bear little resemblance to those given here, particularly as far as the capital account is concerned.

Table 1.3 UK balance of payments 1992 (summary form).

Current account	Credit £000m	Debits £000m	Balance £000m
A *Visibles*			
Exports	106.4		
Imports		120.0	
Total visible trade			−13.6
B *Invisibles*			
Services	31.0	27.4	3.6
Interest, profits and dividends	72.4	66.1	6.3
Transfers	n.a.	n.a.	−5.1
Total invisible trade			4.8
Current account balance: A + B			**−8.8**

Capital account	Assets £000m	Liabilities £000m	Balance £000m
Direct investment	−9.4	10.3	0.9
Portfolio investment	−33.4	20.5	−12.9
Bank lending	−25.4	23.8	−1.6
Non-bank non-government lending	−15.9	35.3	19.4
Official reserves (asset increase −)			3.6
Balancing item			−0.6
Capital account balance	**−84.1**	**89.9**	**8.8**

international conventions, with the current account in the top half, followed by the capital account.

1.3.1 The current account

As the name implies, the current account covers transactions which create no *future* claim in either direction, involving simply an exchange 'here and now'. The account is itself divided into two halves, dealing with visibles and invisibles.

Visibles

The visibles account ('merchandise account' in the USA), as the name suggests, covers all current transactions between the UK and the ROW involving the purchase or sale of *goods*[24] for *current*[25] purposes. In practice, this coincides for the most part with items cleared through customs, so that reasonably accurate data is available within a few weeks of the end of the month in question. As can be seen from Table 1.3, exports of goods amounted to well over £100bn in 1992, while imports totalled £120bn, leaving a visible trade deficit of £13.6bn.

Invisibles

The invisibles account is exactly the same in concept as the visibles account, with the obvious difference that it deals with cross-border transactions involving the purchase or sale of intangibles.

Now, just as in a domestic context there is no meaningful economic distinction between transactions in services and transactions in goods, the same is true in balance of payments terms. In the same way the American importer of Scotch whisky has to buy sterling with dollars, so the US Public Broadcasting System has to do the same in order to buy the rights to screen British TV productions. Conversely, a British company assembling US-designed aircraft has to buy dollars to pay for the service it imports in the form of a production licence from the USA, so that the effect is qualitatively the same as if it had imported the aircraft in complete form.

The services account covers the whole spectrum of international transactions like these. In the case of the UK, the major invisible items are tourism (in deficit) and insurance, shipping and banking (all three heavily in surplus). The result is a very substantial surplus: Britain sold services to a value £3.6bn greater than those it bought from the ROW.

The item labelled 'Interest, Profit and Dividends' is sometimes known as 'capital service'. The idea is easy to grasp. In so far as British

---

[24] As someone once described them: items which hurt when you drop them on your toe!

[25] There is an uneasy compromise here between what is feasible and what is ideally desirable. Strictly speaking, if the distinction between transactions on current and capital accounts is to be preserved, imports of durable goods (for example, motor vehicles, aircraft, computers) ought to be treated as the purchase of assets rather than imports of (consumer) goods, and similarly for exports of durables. However, as is often the case with data on domestic aggregate consumption, separating the two is impractical.

In the context of the balance of payments, the result is that if a British firm purchases a piece of equipment in the USA and brings it into the UK, it is deemed to have imported on current account. On the other hand, if for any reason the equipment remains abroad – leased back to its original owners or used by the British company for its operations in the USA or elsewhere outside the UK – then the purchase, if it is picked up at all by the statistics, will be included in the capital account. From our standpoint, all that matters is that in both cases, the result of the transaction is (a) an addition to the UK's productive capacity and (b) an increase in the net demand for foreign currency by sterling holders.

capital is employed by foreigners, payments made for its use are earnings of the UK economy, and vice versa. For example, if IBM rent a house in England to accommodate their executives, the rent payment to the (British) landlord represents the export from the UK of housing services, and furthermore serves to swell the demand to exchange dollars for pounds. Less obviously, the interest earned by a British company on its deposit in a New York bank amounts to a payment by Americans for the use of British-owned funds – again, an export of capital services. Similarly, profits or dividends earned by UK residents or British-registered companies from their holdings of shares in US companies count as exports from Britain, imports by the USA, and vice versa.

Obviously, other things being equal, the balance on capital services will be greater (that is, more positive) the larger the domestic country's capital stock. The latter, *in the international context*, is the country's net asset position *vis-à-vis* the ROW. The more the country has accumulated (net) claims on foreigners, the greater is likely to be the (net) flow of income it receives from overseas as payment for the use of its assets.

For example, the Industrial Revolution in Britain generated wealth which was to a large extent invested overseas: in development projects in the Empire, in building railways in the Americas, in developing oil fields in the Middle East, and so on. The result was to create a situation where the UK had a very large surplus on capital service. Conversely, during the same years, while the US economy was developing fastest, it sucked in capital from the ROW, particularly Britain, so that it ran a deficit on capital service – paid for largely by exports of its raw materials.

During the first half of this century, that balance was more or less reversed, as economic growth in the UK decelerated and the volume of savings diminished, a trend exacerbated by the two world wars. The outcome was that, by the 1970s, Britain had all but ceased to be a net creditor nation, while for over a generation the USA had enjoyed by far the strongest net asset position in the world.

As most readers will be well aware, this situation has undergone a very rapid reversal in the last decade or so. On the one hand, Britain has had the benefits of North Sea oil revenues, combined with a more rapid growth rate and, for most of the 1980s, a respectable savings rate, so that the UK's net asset position has been rebuilt. Hence, the surplus of over £6bn on this item in 1992. On the other hand, the perennially low rate of private saving in the USA has been exacerbated in recent years by massive federal deficits, so that by the time of writing, America is almost certainly the most indebted nation in history. One result is that the US current account deficit is likely to be swollen for years to come by the payments required to service the enormous stock of dollar assets bought by foreigners in order to finance the deficits of the recent past.

The final item in the invisibles account – unilateral transfers – is relatively unimportant for the UK. It consists of unrequited payments made to the UK by foreigners, and vice versa – in other words, payments made without any specific offsetting transfer of goods or services such as gifts, subscriptions to international 'clubs' of one description or another (EU, IMF, UN agencies and so on), aid donations and so forth.[26]

The importance of trade in invisibles can be judged from the fact that total invisible exports amounted to well over £100bn – almost exactly the same as visible exports.[27] Furthermore, the surplus of £4.8bn made a sizeable contribution to covering the deficit on visible trade.

Current account balance

The overall current account surplus (or, in the present case, deficit) is for many purposes the most important single figure in the balance of payments. There are a number of ways of expressing what it signifies. From one perspective, it serves as an indicator of the balance of demand and supply within the domestic economy. So the fact that the UK current account was in deficit to the tune of £8.8bn indicates the scale of excess demand for goods and services in the British economy over the period.

Putting the matter slightly differently, it is easy to show[28] the current account deficit is identically equal to the total saving net of investment in the economy – public plus private sector. Hence, in the same way that an individual who saves over any period adds to his net worth, a country running a current account surplus accumulates net assets, and one running a deficit reduces its assets or increases its liabilities. In 1992, then, the UK's net credit position in the world deteriorated by £8.8bn.

In fact, looking at the bottom line of the current account, there are two points worth noting. First, consider the scale of the total flows through the account: well over £200bn in each direction. Given the figures

---

[26] For some countries this item is far from negligible, relative to the balance of payments as a whole. For example, most of the countries of Southern Europe have substantial foreign currency income in the form of remittances from emigrants working abroad to their families at home. Some developing countries have considerable receipts of aid which come under this heading. Likewise, reparations paid by Germany after the world wars appeared as transfer payments in the German balance of payments and as credits in those of the recipient countries.

[27] The difference between the two figures is well within the margin of error. In fact, it is quite likely that the statistics on trade in invisibles are underestimates, something which cannot be said to the same extent of the figures for exports and imports of goods.

The scale of the trade in services is, on reflection, not surprising, given that nearly two-thirds of the UK's GNP originates in the services sector of the economy.

[28] See the chapter on the circular flow of income or national income accounting in any economic principles textbook, or Section 5.1.1 of this book.

for 1992,[29] the two-way trade on current account was equivalent to over three-quarters of gross domestic product (GDP). Secondly, the current account *balance* is a tiny quantity – under 2% – relative to the scale of the gross flows in each direction. It follows that what looks like a dramatic improvement or deterioration in the current balance can result from a purely marginal change on the credit or debit side of the account.[30]

1.3.2 Capital account

How far did this reduction in the UK's net assets take the form of an increase in the debts owed by the UK public sector to the ROW? Or did it mainly take the form of an increase in private sector liabilities? To what extent did it involve, instead, the running down of UK assets overseas? Were the assets involved short term or long term? Financial or non-financial? Portfolio assets or direct holdings?

In principle, the capital account gives the answer to all of these questions. In practice, however, the data are grossly inaccurate and in any case very difficult to interpret. For that reason, the net amounts have been presented in Table 1.3 under only five headings, so as to give the reader a flavour of the kind of difficulties involved.

The first and second categories are best explained together. The difference between direct and portfolio investment is that the latter refers, as the name implies, to assets purchased purely as additions to international portfolios of equities, property, bonds and so on – mainly held by financial institutions of one kind or another. Thus, the UK's £13bn deficit on this item is probably indicative of the fact that American and Japanese financial institutions bought far larger quantities of UK equities and gilt-edged securities for their investment portfolios than did UK pension funds, unit trusts and life assurance companies over the year.

On the other hand, direct investment in the UK occurs when, for example, a foreign company increases the scale of its operations in the UK, either by buying a British company or expanding an existing subsidiary, or, for instance, when a foreign resident buys a home in London. In principle, direct investment occurs when the asset buyer takes a managerial interest in the assets purchased. In practice, however, the distinction between this item and portfolio investment is somewhat nebulous. There are many cases where the difference between portfolio and direct

---

[29] About £600bn for the UK's GDP at market prices (average estimate).

[30] Or, indeed, from a relatively tiny error in the statistics themselves.

investment is more or less arbitrary, often based more on convention than on any broadly justifiable criterion.[31]

The next two headings cover net lending by agencies other than the UK Government: first banks, then individuals and institutions other than banks. Note the volume of bank lending – around £25bn in both directions. This suggests transactions in short-term financial instruments – Certificates of Deposit, Eurocurrency deposits, Treasury Bills and so on, as well as trade credit – was on a scale smaller than the flows on visibles or invisibles account. However, these figures are a gross underestimate, for a number of different reasons.

Firstly, many (perhaps the majority of) transactions under these headings pass through channels which are more or less unmonitored. Secondly, the vast majority of movements across the exchanges are unrecorded in the *annual* balance of payments figures because they are simply too short term. As long as a transaction is reversed during the year in question, it will never need to be recorded.[32] At any rate, the Bank of England estimated the volume of currency traded through the London market at around $300bn *per day* in 1992. Even allowing for the fact that much of the trade would have involved currencies other than the pound, it still seems probable the daily turnover in sterling would have been on a scale of several billion dollars per day.

The most important item in the capital account is the one labelled 'official reserves'.[33]

---

[31] For example, suppose that (American company) A buys 10 % of the equity of (UK company) B in a 'dawn raid' on the London Stock Market. Does that count as portfolio or direct investment in the UK? Presumably, if it increased A's holding in B to 51 % (in other words, if A previously owned 41 %) then the answer would be unambiguous, since for all practical purposes (that is, in terms of control of the target company), it would be as good as 100 % ownership. But what if A's move had only raised its stake in B to 30 %?

In fact, international conventions for balance of payments presentation fix an arbitrary cut-off point at 30 %. But this is clearly unsatisfactory, especially when one takes account of the fact that shares and even real estate are often purchased via nominee holdings, which make it almost impossible to sort out true ownership patterns.

It is worth pointing out that capital account presentation used to focus much more on the distinction between 'short' and 'long-term' investment than it does today. The case for this distinction rested on the assumption that long-term investment was inherently less sensitive to market sentiment with respect to the currency than short-term investment, which in the limit was nothing more than so-called 'hot money'. This distinction was probably never clear enough to warrant separating the two types of investment in this way even in theory, let alone in practical statistical terms.

[32] For comparison, imagine trying to work out how far someone had travelled during the year, simply by comparing his location on 31 December with his position on 1 January!

Note that, while monthly current account statistics are compiled for the UK and USA, in neither country is capital account data published more often than quarterly.

[33] The official reserves figure given here includes a small additional item: transactions in other (that is, non-reserve) assets and liabilities of central government.

As we saw in Section 1.2.1, in a pure float this item would be identically zero – by definition, the reserves are constant under a regime of pure floating, leaving the exchange rate free to move so as to generate a capital account balance just sufficient to offset the current account deficit or surplus.

On the other hand, if the exchange rate is to be prevented from moving, the burden of adjustment must fall on the official reserves. The fact that the Bank of England's reserves changed during the year is proof that the exchange rate was being managed. In fact, in September 1992, the UK was a member of the European Monetary System (see Section 1.5.4) and, as such, had a fixed exchange rate for three-quarters of the year. In the light of the tumultuous events surrounding Britain's exit from that system, a fall in the reserves of only £3.6bn is quite small.

The balancing item of £0.6bn is an error term. It arises because, by definition, the balance of payments must balance: the measured deficit (surplus) must be equal to net asset sales (net asset accumulation) during the period, in exactly the same way an individual's spending in excess of his income must be identically equal to the increase in his liabilities or decrease in his assets.

However, since the data on current and capital accounts are collected from completely independent sources, any inaccuracies show up in a non-zero overall balance, which by convention is presented as a separate item of the size and sign required. The small balancing item of £600m for 1992 is only one and a half per cent of the flow through the current account – a highly satisfactory degree of accuracy, by the standards of economic data.

Unfortunately, for reasons that are not yet clear, 1992 was an exceptionally good year from this point of view. For example, in 1984, 1985 and 1986, the balancing item amounted to £5.0bn, £4.5bn and an amazing £12.2bn respectively – figures so large as to dwarf the current account balance and raise questions about the value of the whole exercise.[34]

---

[34] It is usually assumed that the main source of inaccuracies lies in the capital account. However, other evidence suggests there may well be enormous errors in the current account data too.

For example, as long as there is no trade with Mars, then the sum total of all the world's current account balances must obviously equal zero – one country's surplus must be another's deficit. Unfortunately, instead of adding up to zero, the world's current account has in recent years been in apparent deficit by as much as $60bn – a staggering figure greater, for example, than West Germany's surplus during the 1980s. If this under-recording were shared out in proportion to each country's proportion of world trade, the UK's current account position would have been transformed throughout the 1980s into one of embarrassing robustness.

1.4   The DIY model

In a well-known series of lectures,[35] David Henderson referred to what he called the 'do-it-yourself model', as a useful summary of the conventional lay 'wisdom' – the common sense, man in the street's misguided view of how the economy works.

The exchange rate is perhaps not as obviously a subject for amateur economists as, say, the rate of inflation or unemployment. Nonetheless it is quite possible to define an 'economic correspondent's' model, one which seems to lie behind the opinions of media commentators, politicians and intelligent laymen – if not *quite* the man on the proverbial Clapham omnibus. Perhaps instead of a DIY model, it ought to be called a mongrel model, since it contains elements of a number of models found in the typical undergraduate syllabus in the 1960s – when many of today's commentators were economics students.[36]

The DIY model of the exchange rate consists, at the minimum, of the following propositions:

(1) *The higher the level of economic activity and/or the more rapid its growth rate, the lower the value of the domestic currency and/or the greater the current account deficit.* The proposition is rationalized by the argument that, at high levels of activity, the demand for imported consumer goods is high, other things being equal, and the incentive for domestic producers to export rather than sell on the home market is reduced. Furthermore, cost pressures build up in the domestic economy when output is buoyant, thereby eroding the competitiveness of local production (see Chapters 5 and 6).

(2) *Devaluation improves the competitiveness of the devaluing country's output, thereby increasing its current account surplus or reducing its deficit* (see Chapter 5).

(3) *The higher are interest rates in any country relative to the Rest of the World, the greater the value of its currency* (see Chapter 3 and beyond).

In each case, these propositions will be shown to be not strictly wrong, but certainly incomplete and usually misleading.

---

[35] The BBC's 1985 Reith Lectures, published in *The Listener*, from 7 November 1985 onward.

[36] It owes most to the orthodox Keynesian models current at that time, which is ironic in the light of Keynes' own famous and prophetic comment at the end of his General Theory that:

'Practical men, who believe themselves to be quite exempt from any intellectual influences, are usually the slaves of some defunct economist.'

Perhaps an analogy from outside economics would be useful here. Consider the following proposition: strenuous activity often triggers heart attacks.

As it stands, it may well be supported by the facts. Nonetheless, the statement is potentially misleading, since it ignores the more fundamental causes of heart attacks (smoking, obesity and so on). Furthermore, if we base our forecasts on the proposition, we will be hopelessly wrong (for example, we will expect to see marathon runners dropping like flies), and as a basis for policy decisions, it seems to imply we should stop all exercise immediately!

1.5 Exchange rates since World War II: a brief history

It will help to provide a backdrop to some of the discussion in later chapters (especially Chapters 2, 5 and 6) if we take a very brief look at the post-war history of the international monetary system. In particular, the reader may be puzzled by the willingness of the industrialized world's governments to tolerate floating exchange rates, with all the difficulties and uncertainties they introduce into decision making in both private and public sectors. The answer is to be found in the evolution of currency markets since 1945.

1.5.1 The Bretton Woods System: 1944–68

The world of international economic policy making at the end of World War II was dominated by two preoccupations: first, to facilitate the reconstruction of European economies, and second, if possible, to prevent a return to the competitive devaluations and protectionism that had characterized the 1930s. To that end, the British and American governments established the International Monetary Fund (IMF), which was intended to police a system of fixed exchange rates known universally as the Bretton Woods system, after the small New Hampshire ski resort where the agreement was signed in 1944.

Under the Bretton Woods system, countries undertook two major commitments: first to maintain convertibility and secondly to preserve a fixed exchange rate until unambiguous evidence of 'fundamental disequilibrium' appeared, at which point they were expected to devalue or revalue, as the case may be – in other words, announce a new ('fixed') parity. Convertibility turned out to be more a pious intention than a realistic objective – it was always more honoured in the breach than the observance, with only the USA among the major economic powers ever permitting full freedom of capital movements.[37]

As far as fixity of exchange rates was concerned, however, the Bretton Woods system was a success. Changes in the major parities were few and, when they did prove unavoidable, tended to be relatively small scale, at least by comparison with the wild swings that have taken place in the 1970s and 1980s. Until the process of breakdown began, in the late 1960s, there were only really two marked trends: the decline in the value of the pound, with two devaluations, in 1948 and 1967, and the rise of the Deutsche Mark, as the German economy recovered and the competitiveness of US trade decreased.

The Bretton Woods system worked on a principle known as the Gold Exchange Standard, which amounted to a kind of nineteenth century Gold Standard by proxy. Under this arrangement the USA operated a fully-fledged Gold Standard – in other words it pledged to keep the dollar price of gold fixed irrevocably (at the price of $35 per ounce), by standing ready to exchange gold for US currency on demand via the so-called Gold Window.[38] Notice that the requirements for fixing the dollar price of gold are similar to those for fixing the dollar price of foreign currency – the will and the resources to exchange dollars for gold or vice versa *in whatever quantity market conditions may demand.*

Other countries then fixed their currencies in terms of dollars, devaluing or revaluing as necessary in order to counteract disequilibrium, whether it was deemed to originate in their own deviant behaviour or in that of the USA. In other words, the USA anchored the system as a whole, by virtue of the fixed dollar price of gold. Other countries then had to accommodate themselves by changing their exchange rates when required.

1.5.2   The breakdown of Bretton Woods: 1968–73

Much has been written about how and why the Bretton Woods system broke down. For present purposes, and in view of the fact we have yet to look at even the simplest model of exchange rate determination, it will suffice to explain the breakdown in terms of the elementary supply and demand framework covered in Section 1.2.2. Broadly, the net demand for

---

[37] Broadly speaking, from about 1958 onward, the major European currencies offered current account convertibility – that is, were freely usable for financing trade – but were either completely unavailable or subject to serious restrictions where the purchase or sale of foreign assets was concerned.

[38] Though, strictly speaking, this amounted to less than full convertibility, since only banks were allowed access to the Gold Window. Neither in America nor Europe were private citizens allowed to hold gold. It is interesting to speculate how much sooner the system would have broken down if private holdings of gold had been permitted.

dollars shifted downward progressively throughout the 1950s and 1960s, for the following reasons:

(1) The parities established at the outset (including the gold price) reflected the world as it was at the end of the war, with the USA overwhelmingly the world's major economic power, possessor of virtually the entire stock of gold, and with industries that for the most part faced no international competition at all. As the rest of the industrial world recovered, the initial parities were bound to become increasingly inappropriate. In the event, they did so to an extent which could hardly have been foreseen, particularly as the process was exacerbated by the relatively sluggish rate of growth in US productive capacity, compared to the rapid expansion in the continental European economies and the explosive growth in Japan.

(2) Instead of the deflation, which had been feared by the participants at the original Bretton Woods conference, the 1950s and 1960s witnessed steadily accelerating worldwide inflation – slow, at first, but quite rapid from about 1967 onward. This had the effect of raising the price of all commodities other than gold, leaving gold increasingly undervalued in terms of all the major currencies.

(3) What was probably the decisive factor in bringing about the collapse was the willingness of the US authorities to print money in the second half of the 1960s so as to finance war on two fronts: domestically, on poverty (the Great Society), and overseas, on North Vietnam. The result was, on the one hand, to make the dollar seem overvalued relative to other hard currencies, particularly the Deutsche Mark, whose value was protected by the ultra-conservative monetary policies of the Bundesbank. On the other hand, in so far as monetary expansion pushed up the dollar prices of other goods, including raw materials, it made $35 per ounce of pure gold look more and more of a bargain offer.

(4) With diminishing economic hegemony came a weakening in the political and moral force of the USA. In particular, the Gaullist French administration recognized no obligation to refrain from hoarding gold, and began an ostentatious programme to substitute gold for dollars in its reserves, further increasing the excess supply of US currency and excess demand for gold.

(5) As with all fixed exchange rate regimes, the more they are expected to disintegrate, the greater the pressure on them.[39] Thus, as the

---

[39] Recent years have seen the growth of a literature analysing mathematically the process whereby fixed exchange rate regimes collapse. Its starting point is the insight that the market will not look passively on as a country's reserves run out. Instead, it will anticipate the point at which the reserves are exhausted, and in the process hasten the collapse. The literature is somewhat technical, and is related to the work on price bubbles covered in Section 12.5.

prospect of breakdown came ever closer, buying gold – preferably with borrowed dollars – became more and more of a one-way bet, since there was every prospect of being able ultimately to sell the gold at a profit, and repay the debt in devalued US currency.[40] That, in turn, increased the demand for gold and supply of dollars, so that it became possible to extrapolate to the point at which Fort Knox would be emptied.[41]

In the event, the disintegration came in stages, starting in 1968 with the inception of an unofficial free market in gold, from which central banks were barred. What this meant was in effect a two-tier gold price, which had the effect of making absolutely transparent the extent to which the official price of monetary gold was unrealistic. Putting the matter differently, it made it possible to calculate the extent to which dollar holders were subsidizing the USA.

The system finally broke down on 15 August 1971, when President Nixon announced the closing of the Gold Window. After a six-month hiatus, there followed an attempt at patching up the fixed exchange rate system, known as the Smithsonian Agreement, which increased the price of gold from $35 to $38 and set a new, more realistic grid of parities in terms of the dollar. Unfortunately, as was perhaps inevitable, the Smithsonian System was never more than a museum piece, and broke down in under 12 months, mainly as a result of upward pressure on the Deutsche Mark.

It should be pointed out that, while the end of the Bretton Woods system was entirely a matter of *force majeure*, it did nonetheless come as the culmination of more than 20 years of debate within the economics profession over the relative merits of floating compared to fixed exchange rates. In the 1950s, while the fixed exchange rate system was at its most robust, the advocates of floating were relatively few, though they included the formidable figure of Milton Friedman. In the late 1960s, however, as national inflation rates began to diverge and the inconsistencies in Bretton Woods became increasingly obvious, floating appeared more and more attractive as a possible solution to the problems created by the incompatible macroeconomic policies of the major industrial countries.

In particular, the argument that a floating exchange rate country behaves like a closed economy (for reasons to be explained in Chapter 5)

---

[40] Something which is often forgotten by people discussing the merits of fixed exchange rates is that even a relatively small probability of a devaluation (or revaluation) may be enough to attract a speculator, *if the chance of an adverse movement can be totally discounted*, as it often can under fixity. The one-way bet situation is usually exacerbated by the fact that governments often delay parity changes, particularly devaluations, until far too late.

[41] In fact, even as early as 1960, foreign central bank holdings of dollars were estimated to be greater than the US stock of gold, valued at the official price of $35 an ounce.

Figure 1.3 Exchange rates against the US dollar 1973–92.

seemed convincing to many economists. A corollary of this view was that fears that floating exchange rates would be highly volatile were largely groundless.

1.5.3 The floating rate era: 1973 to date

The period since the beginning of 1973 has been characterized by a number of attempts to reinstate fixed exchange rates, all of which have failed for one reason or another. However, apart from the EMS period (see the following section and Chapter 10), the major rates have floated to a more or less managed degree for the whole period, as can be seen in Figure 1.3.

The floating exchange rate era has certainly not delivered anything approaching the degree of stability its advocates had hoped to see. Ever since the end of the initial 'honeymoon' period in the mid 1970s, currency

Figure 1.4 Effective exchange rates (trade-weighted) 1975–92.

values have been subject both to wild day-to-day fluctuations and to long-run swings into apparent over- or undervaluation. In general, the period has been dominated by the dollar's cycle: initial decline during the mid 1970s, followed by resurgence to a peak in 1985 and decline since then and to date (see Figure 1.4). Notice the amplitude of the movements in the dollar's trade-weighted value, from a low point of 86% of its 1975 level in 1978 to a peak of 41% above it in 1985 – and, of course, the variation in bilateral exchange rates was even greater (as can be seen in the case of the pound from the comparison in Figure 1.5).[42]

On the other hand, when account is taken of the shocks to the world's financial markets over the period, it becomes clear that no

---

[42] The graphs also mask the variability because they plot annual average exchange rates. End-of-year data, for example, would exhibit greater variability. Of course, higher frequency data would show still more variation.

Figure 1.5 The pound (bilateral and trade-weighted) 1975–92.

straightforward comparison of the fixed and floating exchange rate periods can reasonably be made: the 1970s and 1980s have been far more turbulent in a number of respects than the Bretton Woods period.[43]

---

[43] No attempt is made here to cover the debate on the merits of floating versus fixity (recently rejoined in the UK, with fixed rate fans wearing EMS colours). The interested reader should see the references in the Reading Guide.

Readers ought to be warned, however, that there is more at issue than simply the desirability or otherwise of fixed rates. It is also a question of the feasibility of fixing exchange rates. Too often, the debate centres on the first question alone, ignoring the second. If fixity is unachievable then its attractiveness is irrelevant. This author suspects that there is no force on earth which could have anchored the major dollar exchange rates in the 1980s, given the domestic macroeconomic policies pursued by the protagonists, particularly the USA. Of course, proponents of fixed rates argue for coordination of domestic economic policies. But that is a political issue, related more to Utopian visions of world government than to economics. Many of these issues appear again in the discussion of currency unions in Chapter 10.

The main features of the floating exchange rate period so far have been:

(1) A large US current account deficit, reaching well over $100bn by the end of the 1980s, whose domestic counterparts were a very low savings ratio in the private sector, and federal overspending of the same order of size as the external deficit (the so-called 'twin deficit' problem). By contrast, both Japan and West Germany enjoyed large surpluses for most of this period.

(2) Two massive increases in the price of crude oil, engineered by the (OPEC) cartel – in 1973–4 and 1979. Broadly speaking, the first shock was accommodated by the fiscal and monetary policies of the oil-importing countries, and therefore led to accelerated inflation. The second shock, by contrast, was not accommodated, and was associated with a short, sharp recession in the USA and a more pro-longed slump in Europe. The consequent decline in relative oil prices since 1984 has attracted far less attention, partly because it has been masked to some extent by the fall in the value of the dollar (in which oil prices are fixed). Nonetheless, its impact on world financial markets, though indirect, has probably been substantial, particularly via its effect on the stability of the US banking system.

(3) A deepening, and as yet unresolved, international debt crisis. The massive OPEC oil surpluses of the 1970s and early 1980s had found their way, in large part, into short-term deposits in Western commercial banks, whence the latter had 'recycled' them into (mostly dollar-denominated) loans to governments of Third World countries ('sovereign loans'), particularly in Latin America. However, for reasons that are not yet clear, as inflation decelerated in the early 1980s, nominal interest rates stayed high.[44] The consequent high

---

[44] For readers unfamiliar with this very important distinction:
The nominal interest rate for example for 12 months, is the interest rate actually observed at any time, for 12 month riskless loans. **The real interest rate** is the nominal interest rate less the inflation rate the market expects will apply over the 12 month life of the loan. In other words, we have, by definition:

$$r^N \equiv R^e + \dot{p}^e$$

where the left-hand side is the nominal rate, R^e is the real rate and the final term is the expected inflation rate. So, for example, a nominal interest rate of 12% might be observed when the market requires a real rate of 2% on loans of 12 months and expects the relevant inflation rate to turn out at 10%. Equally, the same nominal rate could be the outcome when the real rate in the market is 7% and the expected inflation rate is 5%. Obviously, in the absence of inflation, the nominal rate would equal the real rate.

We can therefore say that, in the absence of taxation, the real rate is the return on a loan after allowing for the effect of inflation on the value of the debt. Alternatively, the nominal rate at any time reflects the amount needed to compensate the lender for the decline in the value of money and still give a return equal to the real rate.

real interest rates combined with the rising exchange rate of the dollar and other aggravating factors (falling primary product prices, political instability and so forth) all served to create a situation where a large number of countries were unable to service their debts. The effect of insolvency on a global scale is still being felt in financial markets.

(4) The problems of sovereign lending were further exacerbated by a crisis in the US financial system, on a scale which is not yet fully clear at the time of writing. Whatever the root cause or causes, the symptom is a growing number of failures among banks lending to Latin America, the local US agricultural sector, high-cost oil producers and so on and, perhaps most serious of all, increasing insolvencies in the Savings and Loan (that is, housing loan) sector.

(5) A perceptible acceleration of post-war trends in terms of the balance of economic power. By the mid 1980s, Japan was in most respects the world's largest trading nation (though the EU is the major trade bloc). Japan is also the greatest creditor nation. In many respects – the scale of its equity market, its financial institutions and the funds they manage – it has come to dominate the world's financial markets. In the last decade or so, however, this trend has been somewhat overshadowed by the rising importance of the other East Asian economies: Hong Kong, Singapore, Taiwan, Thailand, Malaysia and, above all, China.

(6) Much greater international capital mobility, brought about by technological advance, increasing internationalization of commerce and industry, and deregulation of capital markets in all the major financial centres.

(7) Greatly increased volatility in most financial markets – whether as a result of the developments already mentioned or for other reasons is not yet clear. The volatility of currency markets will be a recurring theme of this book. But it should be borne in mind that increased, in some cases unprecedented, volatility also characterized other financial markets – most spectacularly, equity markets in the period surrounding the worldwide stock market crashes of October 1987, and lesser sharp falls in the years since then.

(8) As a result of the last two developments mentioned, the 1980s and 1990s have seen an astonishing expansion in the trade in derivative financial instruments. Not only has there been a vast increase in the volume of trade in existing derivative securities: that is, forward and future contracts. The last few years have also witnessed the introduction of a bewildering variety of new instruments, in particular a large and still-expanding range of different types of option contracts:

options on spot rates, options on forwards, bond options, stock-index options and so on. With the increasing variety of available instruments has come increased sophistication on the part of the more important agents in currency markets, particularly multi-national corporations, for whom the Treasury Department is nowadays expected to hedge a large proportion of its currency risk and possibly generate a profit too.

For all these reasons, there is no justification for the glib conclusion that floating exchange rate regimes have somehow failed to deliver the tranquillity promised *ex ante* by their advocates. In any case, as is plain from the demise of the EMS as well as from numerous previous experiments, fixed exchange rates are simply not an achievable objective, other than in very limited circumstances.

1.5.4 The European Monetary System 1979–93[45]

In 1979, the member countries of the EU[46] with the exception of the UK fixed the values of their currencies against each other in a so-called parity grid, specifying central rates for each exchange rate, along with maximum ranges of fluctuation. During the early years, the EMS had two major advantages. In the first place, it involved only two major currencies, the DM and the French Franc, of which the former carries far more weight in international trade and finance. By comparison, the other currencies were relatively minor, so that the central exchange rate was overwhelmingly the franc/DM rate. Secondly, this key exchange rate was kept stable to a great extent by capital controls in France, as well as some of the other countries in the system.

Even with these advantages, there were strains, most notably in 1981 when the new socialist government in France was initially unwilling to accept the constraints of EMS membership. As the worldwide recession took hold in France, it tried to reflate the French economy. The resulting devaluations of the franc (in 1981–83) made the constraints plain for all to see, and no country subsequently attempted to 'go it alone'.[47]

---

[45] In theory, the so-called exchange rate mechanism described here was only one component of the EMS. However, since it was by far the most important feature of the system, we follow common practice in this chapter, using the EMS to refer to the exchange rate mechanism alone.

[46] On 1 November 1993 the Maastricht Treaty came into force and created the European Union. At the time of writing both the EC and EU are in common use. To minimize confusion for the reader, I have standardized the text and used EU throughout the book.

[47] Though there was another franc devaluation in 1986.

As so often seems to happen in financial markets, what appears inevitable ultimately happens, but not necessarily at the expected time. In the late 1980s, the EMS seemed to be becoming more and more stable, thanks to a broad consensus on the need for coordinated monetary policy and a consequent convergence of inflation rates and, to some extent, interest rates across the EMS. A future of permanently fixed exchange rates leading to full monetary union appeared to beckon.

A number of developments at the end of the 1980s proved fatal, however.

(1) The removal of the remaining restrictions on capital movements into and out of France meant the franc was for the first time completely exposed to changes in market sentiment.

(2) The entry of the UK on 8 October 1990, the culmination of years of increasingly frantic lobbying, introduced another major currency into the system, as well as an economy with a post-war history of (by European standards) highly volatile financial markets.

(3) The last straw which broke the system's back was the reunification of Germany in the early 1990s.[48] The burden of raising standards of living in the former Democratic Republic to equality with those in the West caused the German budget deficit to mushroom. Given the refusal of the Bundesbank to contemplate printing money to finance the additional expenditure,[49] the effect was to raise German high interest rates, and hence those of other EMS countries – even those which were impeccably conservative in their fiscal policies. As the business cycle turned down in the aftermath of the late 1980s boom, the burden of high interest rates became increasingly onerous.

The EMS disintegrated in two stages. The first crisis resulted in the departure of the UK and Italy on 16 September 1992. The final agony

---

[48] Of course, it is a matter of conjecture whether the system would have survived without the geopolitical upheavals that occurred at the end of the 1980s. It is the author's view that fixed exchange rate systems are as prone to accident as they are to death from natural causes. On this view, if it had not succumbed to the problem of the German budget deficit, some other *deus ex machina* would no doubt have wrecked the EMS. Thus, if the UK had joined the EMS at its inception in 1979, it seems highly doubtful that it would have proved possible to keep sterling within its permitted limits in the face of the upward pressure generated by the oil price rise in 1980 and 1981.

[49] The situation was exacerbated (albeit to an extent which cannot be quantified) by the fact that the German currency was being widely used in the newly liberated countries of Eastern Europe. This meant that the growth rate of the German money stock probably substantially underestimated the degree of monetary stringency over the period.

came nearly a year later, when the French authorities gave up the battle to prevent the franc falling below its floor against the DM.[50]

1.6   Overview of the book

The remainder of the book is divided into three parts.

Part I deals with the important preliminaries, with two chapters on the basic arbitrage relationships in an open economy, starting with the goods market (Chapter 2), then the market for securities (Chapter 3). Chapter 4 covers the macroeconomic foundations for exchange rate determination, extending the basic aggregate supply and demand model to accommodate an external sector. Most readers will be familiar with some of the material in these chapters, in which case they may choose to skip this part of the book. In any case, it may be convenient to be able to refer back to it during later chapters.

In Part II, we get down to business, with an examination of a number of well-known models of exchange rate determination, starting with the very simplest examples of the genre, the flexible price monetary model (Chapter 5) and the fixed price Keynesian model (Chapter 6), and going on to analyse a more complicated extension which takes account of the fact that goods and labour markets (the 'real sector') are slower to react to disturbances than are financial markets (Chapter 7). Chapter 8 introduces two additional complications in the form of markets for domestic and foreign currency bonds. Chapter 9 concentrates on the phenomenon of currency substitution in situations where economic agents are free to hold foreign as well as domestic money balances. Finally in this block, Chapter 10 discusses some of the issues relating to currency unions, with particular reference to the proposals for European Monetary Union.

The third block, Chapters 11 to 14, contains more difficult material. The unifying theme of these chapters is exchange rate uncertainty: its implications for the market and for individual economic agents, and how to modify our earlier conclusions to cope with it.

Chapter 11 deals with the meaning and implication of the concepts of rational expectations and market efficiency. Both play a large part in the succeeding chapter, which relates these ideas to the volatility of currency markets. Chapter 13 sees a change of scene, with attention focusing on individual behaviour under uncertainty, as we look at the way the market rewards risk-bearing. The following chapter looks at the possible implications for exchange rates of non-linearity, and in particular of the class of processes usually called chaotic.

---

[50] Strictly speaking, the system remains in operation, with 15 % rather than 1 % fluctuation bands – which means it is alive in the same way as the parrot in the famous Monty Python sketch.

The final chapter stands on its own. It concludes the book by looking at some of the issues – theoretical, empirical and institutional – not touched upon in the book, as well as listing some of the many questions about exchange rates left unanswered in the research literature to date.

■ Summary

- A **bilateral spot exchange rate** is simply the price of foreign exchange (dollars) measured in units of domestic currency (pounds). For some purposes, we need to look at a broad index of the value of a currency, measured against a basket of other currencies – the effective or trade-weighted exchange rate.

- In the market for foreign currency, the demand is smaller and the supply greater when the price rises. This is because, when the foreign currency, the dollar, is relatively expensive (the pound relatively cheap), imports and foreign investments are less attractive and, given market expectations, so is speculation on a rise in the price of dollars. Conversely, exporting and investing in the UK are more profitable than at a low dollar price.

- Under a **pure float**, the exchange rate is determined by demand and supply, so that spontaneous (in the jargon – endogenous) fluctuations in supply or demand schedules are reflected in variation in the exchange rate. Under **fixed exchange rates**, the authorities are committed to preventing any variation in currency values. In the absence of controls on transactions in foreign exchange, they can only achieve this by direct intervention in the market, to buy up excess supplies of pounds with dollars, when necessary, and conversely, to supply additional sterling when there is an excess supply of dollars. Fixing the exchange rate therefore implies surrendering control of the domestic money stock. A system where the government intervenes at its own discretion is known as a managed or dirty float.

- **The balance of payments** is an account of the flow of demand and supply for the domestic currency over a year or quarter. **The current account**, covering visibles and invisibles, deals with the country's flow of net earnings from overseas, resulting from sales of goods and services less purchases thereof. The difference between current sales and purchases is the current account surplus or deficit. **The capital account** keeps track of changes during the period in the country's net assets (assets less liabilities). It shows how the deficit was financed (by net asset sales) or the surplus allocated to net asset purchases. Under a floating exchange rate regime, the capital account consists entirely of endogenous capital movements. Under fixed exchange rates (or dirty floating), there will be an exogenous item: changes in the total of **official reserves**, resulting from intervention by the authorities in the currency markets.

- In the popular view (the **do it yourself model**), the pound is weaker and the balance of payments more likely to be in deficit when national income is high and interest rates low.

- The post-war history of the international monetary system consists of two phases, the first being the fixed rate era, known as the **Bretton Woods** regime, which broke down in 1971, and the floating rate period since then. For reasons that are not yet clear, floating rates have proved extremely volatile, with violent short-term fluctuations and longer-run swings to apparent over- and undervaluation characterizing all the major currencies, including the dollar. Among the notable features of the international financial scene in recent years have been: the US 'twin deficit' problem, two OPEC oil shocks in the 1970s and a steeply falling price in the 1980s, a gathering crisis in international and US domestic debt, the rapidly increasing importance of Japan and concomitant decline in the relative weight of the USA in world markets – all accompanied by an unprecedented degree of volatility and rapid innovation, both in the technology of executing transactions and in the range of financial instruments actually traded.

READING GUIDE

The subject matter of Sections 1.2 and 1.3 is amply covered in most textbooks about economic principles, all of which also provide more than enough microeconomic background material, for example, Begg, Dornbusch and Fischer (1987). For more detail, see specialized texts like Kindleberger and Lindert (1978) or Grubel (1977). Section 1.1.3 is a little different in orientation. A fuller coverage is given in most international financial management texts, which typically also explain more of the jargon of the currency markets.

The trouble with books on the institutional background is that they date very quickly, as a result of the speed with which trading patterns in currency markets evolve nowadays. They are also frequently rather personalized in their approach – as may be the treatment here, too. Good examples are McKinnon (1979) and Williamson (1983), both of which contain excellent accounts of the Bretton Woods years. Perhaps the most useful guide to the intricacies of foreign exchange market operation is Grabbe (1986), which also starts with a fuller history than is given in Section 1.6

above, and will be of particular interest to any reader wanting more detail on the mechanics of the EMS.

For a summary of the facts of floating exchange rate life that need explaining, see Mussa (1979). Running commentaries are available in a number of different places, for example, the Bank of England Quarterly Bulletin.

The references to the debate on the relative merits of fixed versus floating rates in Section 1.6.3 may be difficult for the reader to understand at this stage. It might be worth looking back at these passages after reading Chapters 2 and 5. At any rate, the classic statement of the case for floating exchange rates is Friedman (1953). Dunn (1983) argues against floating. On the economics of the EMS, see the readings in Artis (1984).

Part I

The International Setting

The next three chapters cover some very important preliminaries, setting the scene for what is to follow in Parts II and III. We start in Chapter 2 by looking at the price of goods and services in an open economy, and introduce the concept of Purchasing Power Parity (PPP), which plays a vital part in many theories of what determines exchange rates. The implications of capital mobility for interest rates are considered in the next chapter, where we encounter another parity relationship – Interest Rate Parity. In the process, we explain what is meant by a forward exchange rate. The final chapter in this part gives an overview of the textbook aggregate demand and supply model, extended to take account of the fact we are dealing with an open economy.

2

Prices in the Open Economy: Purchasing Power Parity

■ Introduction

In one form or another, Purchasing Power Parity (PPP) doctrine is
almost as old as paper money itself. In fact, it has been traced back as
far as sixteenth century Spain. Its revival in modern times, however,
is attributable mainly to the work of the Swedish economist, Gustav
Cassel, in the period between the two world wars.

Today, while there are severe doubts about how well it holds in
practice, an understanding of the basic notion of PPP is essential if we
are to be able to get to grips with more sophisticated models of
exchange rate determination. That is why we choose to cover it first,
starting in Section 2.1 with what is perhaps the most fundamental law
in economics, the law of one price, and introducing you, via a number
of examples, to some very important ideas such as arbitrage,
transaction costs and so on. In Section 2.2, we go on to consider the
law of one price in the international context. Section 2.3 contains a
useful digression: a simple exposition of what is meant by a price
index. It can easily be skipped by anyone who is already familiar with

the basic concept. Section 2.4 introduces you to PPP proper, and the chapter ends with a consideration of the relevance of PPP in the light of the facts about post-war inflation rates.

2.1   The law of one price in the domestic economy

In the context of the domestic economy, the **law of one price** states simply that:

> If two goods are identical, they must sell for the same price.

This looks a harmless, uncontroversial enough statement. It is in fact, just the kind of blindingly obvious statement that sceptics complain about in economics. However, the same sceptics would almost certainly change their tune if they were to consider the implications of the law of one price. On the contrary, they would probably dismiss economics as a collection of very dubious propositions indeed!

In order to illustrate the kind of issues involved, let us take a look at a number of more or less everyday examples to which we can refer back in later sections.

Example 1

Imagine that Michael Jackson is giving a concert at Wembley Stadium in London, a fortnight from now. All the tickets have been sold at face value through the usual distribution channels across the country, but excess demand has created a black market, operating outside ticket agencies, in pubs, on street corners, in discos and in the classified ads columns of local newspapers.

Now suppose that you are told that tickets for seats in a particular part of the stadium are on offer on the black market in Birmingham for £50. What would you expect an identical ticket to cost in, say, Manchester? By the law of one price, the answer has to be £50, and, in practice, under these circumstances, you probably would find tickets of the same category on sale at more or less the same price in different towns.

Why would this tend to be the case? To see why, ask yourself what would be likely to happen if the law did not hold in this example. Suppose, for argument's sake, that the price of a ticket were £5 lower in Manchester than in Birmingham. Then anyone in Birmingham who wanted to go to the concert would buy their ticket in Manchester, while no one in Manchester would buy in Birmingham. So, sellers in Birmingham would be unable to sell any tickets as long as there were any on sale cheaper in Manchester.

You may object that in reality ordinary Michael Jackson fans in Birmingham would be unlikely ever to find out that tickets were on offer at a lower price on a street corner in Manchester, or in the small ads pages of Manchester newspapers.

That is almost certainly true. At the very least, it might take some days or even weeks before word reached Birmingham, by which time it would be too late – the big day would have come and gone!

Do we then conclude that the law of one price might well break down in this, the first case we have examined?

We might do so, were it not for the well-known fact that there are people who make a living out of exploiting just such situations. What they do is to watch out for price divergences like these. In the present case, they would simply buy up as many tickets as they could in the cheap location (Manchester) and sell them immediately in the dear location (Birmingham). In the process, they would be doing three things: making a tidy profit for themselves, driving up the price of tickets in Manchester from £45 and driving down the price in Birmingham from £50. On each ticket they trade a profit is made that is equal to the price differential. The larger the price differential, the greater the profit and hence the greater the incentive to trade. As they bid up the price in Manchester and push down the price in Birmingham, the gap narrows and their profit falls from £5 per ticket to virtually nothing, so that the incentive to trade is progressively reduced. Obviously, the process tails off and stops altogether when prices in the two cities are brought into equality at some price between £45 and £50, say £47. At this point, profit opportunities have been exhausted.

People who make a living by trading rock concert (or football match) tickets on the black market are usually called 'touts' or 'scalpers', though touts also operate in the black market in another way. More generally, and more relevant to the subject matter of this book, the process of moving goods from one market to another so as to take advantage of a price differential is referred to as arbitrage, and those who make a living in this way are called arbitrageurs. As we shall see, they have a number of important roles to play in the currency markets, and in fact throughout the financial sector of the economy, so the following definition is given here for future reference:

> **Arbitrage** is the process of buying or selling something in order to exploit a price differential so as to make a riskless profit.

The word 'something' is intentionally vague. For the present, we are concerned with arbitrage in goods and services, but in Chapter 3 we shall be concerned with arbitrage in securities. The expression is a completely general concept and is also frequently encountered in markets for equities, commodities and currencies themselves.

Now let us return to our example, and consider the following question: given the existence of arbitrageurs, albeit in the somewhat unsavoury form of ticket touts, are there any factors which could prevent the law of one price prevailing?

Lack of information has been ruled out as unlikely, simply because the touts will make it their business to know about any price differentials that exist. Their livelihood depends on them keeping their 'ears to the ground'. They specialize in gathering this type of information.

Similarly, they are unlikely to be hampered very seriously by the actual cost of trading. The costs might involve a few trips between the two cities carrying their precious cargo, possibly the price of a small advertisement or two, no doubt some long-distance phone calls, some postage, a few drinks to close valuable deals and 'oil the wheels', and so on.[1] However, these costs are likely to be small, probably negligible, relative to the value of the transactions involved.

As we shall see in subsequent examples, the costs of actually transacting will not always be so insignificant. For now, it will be useful to have a definition to hand:

> **Transaction costs** are all the costs associated with a transaction, over and above the cost of the good which actually changes hands.

As a specialist trader in large blocks, the scalper's transaction costs are minimal. A scalper who knows that a consignment of, say, 100 tickets can be bought and sold with transaction costs of only £10 will still be able to exploit the £5 per ticket price differential between Manchester and Birmingham. The profit from the purchase and sale of 100 tickets is shown in the calculation in Table 2.1.

Obviously, profit is reduced by the amount of the transaction cost (£490 instead of £500), but the deal is nonetheless well worthwhile. Notice that the profit per ticket sold has fallen from £5 to £4.90. Why? This is because while the selling price of each ticket has remained the same, the all-inclusive cost of the average ticket has risen by the amount of the transaction cost *per ticket*, that is, £0.10 (= £10/100).[2]

---

[1] Note that an important element in these expenses is likely to be the cost of actually collecting information on price divergences.

[2] Of course, as the example should make clear, there are substantial cost savings to be made by trading in large quantities. The cost of arbitrage in blocks of a thousand tickets is likely to be far less per ticket than for a block of only one hundred, because most of the components of the transaction cost, particularly those involved in information gathering, are likely to be the same irrespective of the size of the deal. In the jargon of microeconomics, there are substantial economies of scale to be exploited in arbitrage, and this fact explains why it pays for some individuals or agencies to specialize in the activity.

Table 2.1   The ticket tout's profit.

Costs:	
Buy 100 tickets in Manchester @ £45 each = total outlay of:	£4500
Transaction costs (buying + selling):	£ 10
Total cost	£4510
Revenue:	
Sell 100 tickets in Birmingham @ £50 each = revenue of:	£5000
Profit:	
Revenue less total cost	£ 490

As arbitrage proceeds, however, we have seen that the price differential is progressively reduced. At what point will arbitrage no longer be profitable? In the absence of transaction costs, the answer was: when the price differential was completely eliminated. Will this still be true, now that we are allowing for the fact that simply buying and selling involves a cost?

Looking at the calculations in Table 2.1, it is plain that our previous conclusion has to be modified to read: arbitrage will cease to be profitable when the price differential is no greater than the transaction cost per item. Instead of ending up with a situation where a price of £47 reigns in both towns, the arbitrage process will come to a halt when the price differential has narrowed to £0.10. You can see this for yourself if you repeat the calculation with a price of £47.10 in Birmingham and £47 in Manchester. You will find that at these prices arbitrage profits are zero.

For future reference, we will describe this equilibrium in symbols as follows:

$$P^B = P^M + C \tag{2.1}$$

where P^B is the price of a ticket in Birmingham, P^M is the price in Manchester and C is the transaction cost.[3]

Before going on to look at a very different example, there are one or two more points worth noting. Notice that our conclusions relate to the

---

[3] Strictly speaking, Equation 2.1 ought to be written as an inequality:

$$-C^* \leqslant P^B - P^M \leqslant C$$

where C and C^* are the transaction costs of arbitrage from Birmingham to Manchester and vice versa. Assuming the costs are the same in both directions, then the price differential cannot exceed C. For simplicity, we assume it is as great as is permitted by this relationship.

price of tickets outside London, where the concert is to be held. Since London fans have so much shorter a distance to travel, it could reasonably be expected that the demand for tickets will be greater at any price level there than in the provinces. Does this mean the price in London will be higher than elsewhere in the UK?

A moment's consideration will show that, under our assumptions, we can rewrite Equation 2.1 with P^L on the left-hand side (that is, the price in London). In general, throughout the country, arbitrage will have 'smoothed out' the price variations that might otherwise exist due to localized excess demand (or supply) situations.

To see what loose ends remain in our analysis of this example, let us briefly recap. It was concluded that it would be unrealistic to expect price equality to prevail, because of the existence of transaction costs. Taking them into account, however, led us to the conclusion that the modified version of the law of one price in Equation 2.1 could be expected to assert itself, thanks mainly to the activities of ticket touts specializing in arbitrage operations.

Now, are there any other factors we have neglected that may prevent even our modified law of one price from asserting itself? One obvious 'fly in the ointment' is the unfortunate fact that ticket touting, whatever its economic benefits, is more or less illegal. In fact, legal barriers to arbitrage are not uncommon, even in much less racy sectors of the economy, particularly those sectors involving international trade and investment. Their effectiveness in preventing arbitrageurs from trading varies enormously, depending on the nature of the commodity, the type of market, the seriousness with which law-breaking is treated and so on. In the present case, it seems the legal barriers would probably have very little effect – the law of one price would almost certainly prove stronger than the law of the land.[4]

As a matter of fact, we can claim to have taken at least some account of the legal barrier to trade in our Equation 2.1. Our transaction cost, C, will be substantially affected by the fact that the business deals involved may amount to a crime. Perhaps, for example, the choice of relatively expensive marketing channels (selling in pubs, small ads and so on, and in small batches of ones and twos) is dictated by the need to evade the long arm of the law. Perhaps the £0.10 per ticket also includes an element of reward for the risks of arrest and subsequent fine by the courts, or it may even incorporate an allowance for legal costs.

An important point to note is that risk of arrest is the *only* risk involved. In a pure arbitrage transaction, there are no trading risks in the normal sense. The arbitrageur takes the opportunity of a near-riskless profit. Arbitrageurs can be regarded as selling their tickets in Birmingham

---

[4] In any case, it appears that ticket touting is actually on the margins of legality depending on all sorts of conditions of sale, contract terms and so forth.

almost at the same time that they buy in Manchester, so that their actual trading risk is zero. The absence of risk is a distinguishing feature of arbitrage.

Because arbitrage involves no trading risk it might seem that there is always likely to be a ready supply both of arbitrageurs and of funds to finance their operations. As the present example illustrates, however, this will not always be the case. Reputable financial institutions will not be willing to make loans to ticket touts, even though they stand to make a riskless 'killing'. This is not simply because the funds are required for an illegal activity. Even if they can invent a 'respectable' reason for wanting an advance, ticket touts will probably not be in good enough standing with their bankers to be able to raise very large loans. The possibility arises, then, that the law of one price could be frustrated simply by the fact that the supply of arbitrage funds is too small to eliminate the price differential.

Mention of borrowing and lending raises the question of interest rates. Ought there to be an interest charge included in our transaction cost term, C? (Note: the answer has nothing whatever to do with the question of whether a ticket tout borrows or uses his own funds as working capital. Why not?)

In principle, there is no interest cost to pure arbitrage for the same reason there is no risk: if buying and selling are instantaneous, the working capital needed is nil. In practice, there may be a cost of financing stocks of tickets for, say, one day prior to sale, but we shall regard this as negligible.

Finally, it will be helpful if we use this example to compare and contrast the two classes of market agents who have already been mentioned with a third type of agent. Recall that we introduced the arbitrageur into the story only after concluding that the price in different towns was unlikely to be equated simply by the interaction of bona fide Michael Jackson fans who are buying tickets with the concert organizers who are selling them. Does this mean their activities are completely irrelevant to the determination of market prices?

Certainly not. The interaction of what we could call normal traders – fans wanting to attend the concert, and the organizers supplying the seats – these are the ultimate determinants of the equilibrium, 'central' (say, London) price. We can then think of the operations of arbitrageurs fixing the Manchester and Birmingham prices in the way we have analysed in this example.

In cases like this, however, the equilibrium price may also be affected in the short run by the activity of a different species of ticket scalper – one who holds on to tickets *in expectation of higher prices later*. From now on, we shall use the following name for this form of enterprise:

> **Speculation** is the activity of holding a good or security in the hope of profiting from a future rise in its price.

Notice that, unlike arbitrage, speculation is inherently risky, since the price rise may fail to materialize. The speculator-tout buys tickets and holds on to them so as to sell them when 'the time is right' – typically, outside the stadium immediately before the concert starts. He backs his judgement. If however, he miscalculates, and there turns out to be an excess supply on the day of the concert, he loses money.

To summarize, in any market, we may potentially have three different kinds of agent at work:

(1) Traders (in our example, the fans, whose tastes condition their demand, and the organizers, whose costs determine the supply).

(2) Arbitrageurs (the touts who exploit local price variations).

(3) Speculators (scalpers who hold on to tickets in the hope of making a 'killing').

Though we shall deliberately ignore the moral and legal distinctions between the activities of these three classes of market agents, we shall often have cause to treat them separately in our analysis of other markets in Chapters 3, 6 and 7. The theoretical distinctions are clear. However, we must not forget, particularly when thinking about policy measures, that *in practice* it is often virtually impossible to separate the different classes of transactors. In our example, there may be no feasible way to tell the tout from the 'genuine' rock music fan, let alone the arbitrageur-tout from the speculator-tout. Certainly, a legally-convincing distinction may be elusive, which is precisely the problem faced by law enforcement agencies.

This case has been analysed in some depth because it illustrates many of the issues surrounding the functioning, or non-functioning, of the law of one price, as well as providing a first encounter with some of the concepts which are central to the material in the rest of the book. The remaining examples will be dealt with more briefly, starting with:

Example 2

The down-to-earth subject of this example is the price of potatoes. Could the price in Manchester ever deviate from the price in London? Plainly, this is a straightforward application of the modified law of one price, as in Equation 2.1. The transaction cost, C, may be quite substantial in this case, simply because potatoes are costly to move from one end of the country to the other. Provided that we allow for this fact, and make sure we are looking at the same quality of potato in each case, we are likely to find that prices in the two cities are very close to each other.

Notice that the question of where the potatoes have been grown is irrelevant. Note also that we need not rely on the existence of arbitrageurs. (Anyway, whoever heard of potato arbitrageurs?) As long as retailers are competitive, they are likely to keep price deviations within the margins set by the costs of transporting potatoes. Or, to put the point another way, genuinely competitive distributors (wholesalers or retailers) will themselves act as arbitrageurs.

Example 3

Take a typical manufactured good, for example, a folding umbrella made in Germany. Can we be sure that its price will be uniform across the UK?

At first glance, you might think the answer was no – the price even varies from shop to shop in the same town. That's why we 'shop around', isn't it?

Not really. We shop around for two reasons mainly. Firstly, because we like to compare different makes of goods and secondly to compare different models produced by the same manufacturer. However, *the law of one price only relates to identical goods.* Where manufactures are concerned, products made by different firms are rarely, if ever, regarded as identical. Even though the objective differences may be small, products are almost always differentiated in the minds of consumers, if only as a result of the efforts of the advertising industry. So the fact that two products with different labels do not carry the same price tag has no bearing whatever on the law of one price.

Even so, don't prices vary even for genuinely identical goods – same model, same producer, same label? Yes, they do if we look in different shops. Why? The reason lies in large part in the fact that a shopper buys not only the umbrella but also the services of the retailer who sells it. If the shop itself supplies a retailing service which is above average in prestige, or in convenience, or in friendliness, or helpfulness or whatever, it will be able to sell its service at an above average price, which will take the form of a premium on some or all of its wares. The umbrella will cost more if bought in a smart city store than in an unprepossessing discount warehouse out in the suburbs. Likewise, try buying one at four o'clock on a Sunday morning when it is pouring down. If you can find anywhere to buy one, do not expect a bargain!

The failure of the law of one price in the case of a typical manufactured good, like an umbrella, may for these reasons be only apparent. If we are sufficiently strict in defining identical goods, we may well conclude that the law of one price holds reasonably well.

Example 4

Compare the price of houses in the North (Manchester) and the South (London). Where do you start? How can we find two genuinely identical houses in two different cities? Even if we are careful enough to choose a given type of house for comparison (say, semi-detached, three bedrooms, garage and so on), we cannot avoid the problem that a house in Manchester is simply *not* the same asset as a house in London. The difference is attributable in the first instance to local market conditions. However, it is sustained by one obvious fact: houses cannot be moved from one end of the country to the other. The transaction cost is not simply high, it is infinite – at least in the short run.

Since arbitrage has to be completely ruled out in this case, does it follow that the price of houses in the two locations can diverge without limit forever? There is no clear answer to this question, but it is certainly possible that there exist forces likely to prevent prices diverging indefinitely. At some point, the relative price of housing in Manchester will become so cheap it will start to attract Londoners whose work situation allows them to move. People may even start to commute from Manchester to London so as to exploit the cheap housing in the North. On the other hand, builders will be tempted to divert resources from other areas, particularly cheap housing areas, to sites in London, thereby increasing the supply and reducing the excess demand.

In the long run, therefore, there may well be a kind of law of one price operating even here, the only difference being that, in this case, it is the relative price of houses in the two locations which is kept constant, at a level where prices in London are, say, 1.75 times higher than those in Manchester for otherwise comparable accommodation. Even then, remember that we are only forced to talk in terms of a relative price because of the fact that we are comparing two commodities which are intrinsically different anyway.

For a final example, a totally different item, but with similar conclusions applying:

Example 5

A haircut. To avoid the problems of comparability that we have already encountered in previous examples, it had better be a 'standard' haircut, of the kind favoured by old-fashioned men, like the author.

Remember, first of all, that nothing in economics relies on a distinction between the market for goods and the market for services. For the purposes of economic analysis, it makes no difference at all whether we are talking about a tangible, visible good or an intangible, invisible service. This fact should be borne in mind throughout the book.

Now, can the price of a haircut in London deviate from that in Manchester? Plainly, the answer is yes, and substantially so. Even if demand is similar, the cost of the main hairdressing inputs (wages, rent and so on) is greater in London, so the supply curve is further to the left.

As before, arbitrage in the normal sense is obviously ruled out, so that the short-run price differential can be enormous. This fact has led many writers in the international economics literature to describe services like hairdressing, motor vehicle repairing, plumbing, medical services and so on as well as some goods (like houses), as **non-traded goods**. For future reference, let us introduce the following definition:

> **Non-traded goods** (or **non-tradeables**) are items (usually services) for which inter-regional price differentials cannot be eliminated by arbitrage.

Notice that the definition does not refer to goods, if any such exist, for which price differentials can *never* be eliminated. All we mean is goods which, for sound practical reasons, cannot be moved from place to place so as to exploit price differences. As we saw in the previous example, and as is plainly true in the case of haircuts, there may well be other, less direct mechanisms than arbitrage which will ultimately drive London and Manchester prices into equality. For anyone who is not completely bald, haircuts figure in the cost of living in the same way as housing does, and in the long run there may well be forces tending to eliminate price deviations over broad categories of services, as we shall see in Chapters 5 and 7. Nonetheless, since arbitrage is impossible, haircuts and so on must be regarded as non-traded goods, and the law of one price cannot be expected to apply.

Put differently, we can say the transaction cost in the case of a haircut is near-infinite – not in absolute terms, as was the case with houses, but because, relative to the cost of the commodity itself, it amounts to several hundred or thousand per cent (that is, the cost of travelling between Manchester and London, relative to the price of the haircut itself). With this sort of argument in mind, we could view the vast range of goods and services produced in a modern economy as spanning the whole spectrum from most to least tradeable. At one end would be homogeneous commodities with negligible transport costs (financial assets, tickets for rock concerts and so on) and at the other end would be personal services, real estate and so forth.

Now that we have examined in some detail a number of examples of the working or non-working of the law of one price in a closed economy context, moving over to the open economy will turn out to be quite simple.

2.2 The law of one price in the open economy

In this section, we have the task of answering the same kind of questions as in Section 2.1, with one vital difference. What if the two cities involved are not London and Manchester, but London and New York? What changes have to be made in our conclusions?

There turns out to be only one significant change required, and it will be encountered as soon as we return to our first example.

Example 1a

The Michael Jackson concert again. An enterprising New York travel agent is selling tickets for the concert – mainly to attract customers for his cut-price trips to London. If you make him an offer though he will sell the concert tickets separately. How will the price that he can sell them for compare with the price of £50 which rules on the free (that is, black) market in London?

The first and most obvious point is that, in the window of the New York travel agent, the price will not be shown in pounds at all. It will be in dollars, of course. We cannot directly compare the price in London and New York in the way that we could compare the price in London and Manchester.

Let us be a little pedantic about the reason why we cannot compare prices on opposite sides of the Atlantic. Strictly speaking, it is *not* just because the UK and USA are two different countries. It is because they use different currencies. Quite frequently there are situations where countries, for one reason or another, share a common currency, officially or unofficially.[5] Where two countries do indeed share a common currency, we can compare prices directly, and for purposes of the law of one price, we may as well be dealing with a closed economy.

Where there is no common currency, however, we have to translate dollar prices into pound prices or vice versa, so as to allow us to make a comparison. It is a problem familiar to anyone who has ever been on holiday abroad. Unfortunately for our purposes, holidaymakers often buy their foreign currency, traveller's cheques and so on before setting out on their trip, so that they do not always see the connection between the two relevant prices: the price of the goods they buy abroad and the price of the currency.

Now put yourself in the position of an enterprising London ticket tout who has just heard from some American tourists that tickets are on sale at, say, $100 each in New York. Is it worth making a transatlantic call to order tickets for resale in London? For every ticket he wants, he will have to buy $100, then send the US currency to New York. Let us ignore transaction costs for the moment. (When all is said and done, if it doesn't pay to do anything when we ignore transaction costs, it certainly won't pay when we take account of them!)

---

[5] In the modern world, inflation is the most frequent explanation of this phenomenon. The Israelis for example, coped with triple-digit inflation in the early 1980s by quoting all 'big-ticket' prices such as houses, cars and so on in US dollars. And, of course, US dollars are widely used alongside local currency in Canada.

The best way to look at this deal is to regard it as involving what we might call a 'compound purchase': first, buy the dollars, then use the dollars to buy the tickets. In the closed economy context, we exchange domestic money directly for goods. When buying from another country, we *first* have to exchange domestic money for foreign money, *then* exchange the foreign currency for the foreign goods.

In this example, the price paid by the London tout for US dollars is, of course, the sterling/dollar exchange rate. For convenience, we repeat here our definition of the exchange rate:

The exchange rate is the price of a unit of foreign currency, measured in units of domestic currency.

Remember from Section 1.1.1, that our definition is 'the other way round' from the way that we in Britain are used to seeing the exchange rate quoted. Instead of the dollar price of pounds (for example, $1.25 = £1), we are following the practice of most other countries which is, units of domestic currency per unit of foreign currency ($1 = £0.80, and so on).

The advantage of doing things this way round should be clear when we work our way through the arithmetic of our imaginary international arbitrage in concert tickets. Whenever you undertake a 'compound purchase', buying an item for cash, then using that item to buy a second, the overall price you will have paid will be the product of the two prices. In the same way, the sterling price that the London tout will have to pay for the New York tickets will be the product of the price of each dollar and the dollar price of the tickets.

Suppose, on enquiry, that the exchange rate turns out to be $1.00 = £0.80. In other words, the price of a dollar is 80 pence. Obviously, it will cost 100 times 80 pence (£80) to buy the $100 asked for by the New York travel agent for each ticket. The £80 is the result of the following calculation:

(sterling price of a dollar) *times* (dollar price of a ticket) = sterling price of a ticket

If we use the letter S to denote the exchange rate (remember that this is defined as the pound price of a dollar) and P^{NY} for the price in dollars advertised in New York, then the overall price to a Londoner is SP^{NY}.

We have now found out how to translate foreign prices into domestic currency prices. To put it differently, we have converted ticket prices into a common currency. Sterling was chosen because we were putting ourselves in the place of a Londoner, who was only interested in his profits measured in pounds, for the obvious reason that almost all of his spending was in pounds. As will be made clear, we would reach exactly the same conclusion if we looked at things from the American point of view.

You will be glad to know that we have now finished the most important task in this section. From now on, it will be downhill all the way. All we need do is apply exactly the same logic to our translated prices as we did in Section 2.1 to our UK domestic prices.

Will it be worth paying £80 for a ticket from New York? Certainly not – they can be bought for £50 in London, remember? What is more, as soon as New Yorkers find out that they are better off waiting to buy tickets when they get off the plane in London, the demand in New York will tail off. In fact, there is every chance that an enterprising competitor of our American travel agent will steal a march, by jetting over to London and buying a consignment to take back to New York. For each ticket wanted, the competitor will need to buy £50. Each pound will cost $(1/0.80) = 1/S$ dollars that is \$1.25. The total outlay will be: \$1.25 × 50 = \$62.50 per ticket. It follows that, if we continue to ignore transaction costs, the competitor can afford to undercut the competition by \$37.50.

We can shorten the story somewhat, thanks to our analysis of the closed economy example. At some point, it is likely that the forces of normal trade and probably of arbitrage as well will eliminate profit opportunities. This will have been achieved when the price in New York stands in such a relation to the price in London that, when translated into a common currency the two prices are equal: in other words, when the price in New York has fallen to just \$62.50 (assuming the New York market is, in this case, negligibly small relative to the market in the UK, where the concert is actually taking place).

To represent the equilibrium symbolically, look back at Equation 2.1. Replace P^B and P^M by P^L and P^{NY}, the London and New York prices. Now, on the left-hand side we have the London price (in pounds). On the right-hand side, we must have the equilibrium New York price (in dollars) times the price of a dollar which is, \$62.50 × 0.80 = £50.00, or $P^{NY} \times S$. For good measure we will add the transaction cost, C, just to remind ourselves that in practice there will be room for some divergence from the strict law of one price, so we have:

$$P^L = SP^{NY} + C \tag{2.2}$$

as our open economy version of the law of one price.

All the other points made in the closed economy example follow in obvious fashion. There is one significant extension that needs to be made, however, and it relates to the activities of speculators in the present context. It is simply this: if there are a significant number of tickets in the hands of New Yorkers, then the London speculator runs an extra risk, over and above the one borne by the speculator in a closed economy context. Not only must he gamble on the underlying demand for tickets, but he must also take a chance on the exchange rate. For example, suppose in the last few days before the concert, the dollar weakens (that is, the price of a dollar falls). Since that will initially raise the equilibrium New York price, it may damp down demand by Americans and reduce the total demand for tickets even though nothing has happened to affect the popularity of the concert itself. We shall not follow up the implications of this fact at the moment, though we shall have cause to refer back to it in Chapters 8 and 13.

We now proceed to examine the remaining examples from the previous section, starting with:

Examples 2a and 3a

Let us take the two cases together, potatoes and umbrellas. Can we simply apply Equation 2.2, without further ado? Obviously, transport costs are likely to be even higher in an international than in an interregional context. Is that the only difference between the open and closed economy as far as this example is concerned?

It is not, because, in addition to the difficulties involved in trading goods within a country, there will usually be man-made, or rather government-made barriers to cross-border trade.

In the first place, there will often be tariffs, which are a barrier to trade that are familiar to most tourists under the name of customs duty. A general definition would be as follows:

A tariff is a tax levied on goods crossing an international border.

Nothing has been or will be said in this book about the method used to calculate the size of the tariff payable on goods. Suffice to say, the level of tariff varies with the importing country, the broad category of goods, sometimes also with the destination of the goods, as well as a host of other factors. The calculation is sometimes so complicated as to be incomprehensible to all but dedicated industry professionals. (An example of this occurs with the imports of wines and spirits into the UK.)

The question of the impact of a tariff on the price of a good is one that would fill several chapters in a history of international trade theory. For our purposes, we need only note that it represents another factor likely to drive a wedge between foreign and domestic prices. Strictly speaking, where it is levied at a flat rate per unit, it can be regarded simply as inflating the value of our transaction portmanteau term, C. More frequently, it consists of a more or less *ad valorem* tax, in other words one levied in proportion to the price per unit.

In the case of agricultural products, particularly, there may be other barriers to international trade. Some countries impose quotas which are more or less rigid limits on the quantity of a good that may be imported or, occasionally, exported.

Nor is this all. If you try carrying potatoes through UK customs, you may encounter more problems than simply a slipped disc. There are actually prohibitions on bringing into the UK a variety of agricultural products, animals, domestic pets and so on. These non-tariff barriers, as they are called, are sometimes put in place in order to protect the health of a country's human or non-human residents. There are also restrictions on the import of manufactured goods of certain types: dangerous toys, weapons and so on, as well as on the export of strategic goods, art treasures and so forth. Often the restrictions amount to little more than red tape, especially for the large firms who conduct most of the world's international trade. On other occasions, they amount to an intentional or unintentional trade blockage, designed specifically to prevent the law of one price from asserting itself in the way described in the closed economy case.[6]

We can conclude, then, that the simple relationship described by Equation 2.2 is likely to hold only as an approximation. It is a reasonably accurate one for some goods but a very distant one for others. If these are our conclusions with regard to traded goods, what can we expect of non-traded goods?

Examples 4a and 5a

In the case both of housing and of services like haircuts, the closed economy arguments apply with somewhat greater force. As with interregional trade, it would be overstating the case to argue that the law of one price will always be completely inoperative. For example, many UK estate agents advertise homes in foreign holiday resorts such as Spain, Florida and so on alongside their domestic properties. Now obviously a holiday home on the Gulf of Mexico is hardly a substitute for the typical semi-detached house in a London suburb. Nonetheless, *at the margin*, it may well compete directly with a holiday home in a UK resort (fortunately, not everyone likes the sun!). These kinds of considerations may place a limit on the degree to which prices can deviate internationally, even for housing.

Remember also that, in the case of so-called non-tradeables, the man-made barriers to trade such as tariffs, quotas, red tape and so on are

---

[6] A notorious example occurred when the French authorities relocated customs clearance facilities for imports of 'cheap' Japanese video cassette recorders from a large Paris office to a small, patently inadequate provincial one. The resulting queues, delays and so on amounted to a non-pecuniary tariff intended to deter importers, while at the same time avoiding the political problem of having to defend the imposition of an overt tariff increase.

often fewer than for tradeables.[7] That being the case, the only obstacles are usually the physical ones which apply equally in a closed economy. It follows that the price of a service like a haircut in New York may turn out to be nearly as close to the price in London as it is to the price in Los Angeles.

In the end, the question of how closely the (international) law of one price fits the facts cannot be settled by theory. Ultimately, the answer can only be found by examination of the evidence, in other words by a careful comparison of prices of individual goods and services across different countries. Surprisingly little research has been carried out in this important area, so that it is difficult to arrive at a firm conclusion.

However, it is probably significant that three major studies carried out during the 1970s arrived at the following unanimous conclusions:

(1) In the post-war period, there appears to have been very little correlation between prices of identical goods in different countries at any particular moment.

(2) Not only were the price differences quite wide, they also persisted for long periods.

On the other hand, more recent research has cast some doubt on the way that prices were observed in these studies, and suggests that the law of one price might turn out to be quite robust in an international context.

One can only conclude that the issue must be regarded as remaining open, pending further investigation. Fortunately, the scope for research is almost unlimited, since the population from which all the studies draw their sample is potentially vast, almost infinite in fact (all the different products times the number of countries in the world).

It is worth finishing with a warning about a specious argument often encountered in discussions of the law of one price and indeed, in many other areas far removed from international trade issues, or even from economics. In the present case, it goes something like this: 'It is a fact that only a tiny percentage of sales of this type of good (or service) involve exports (or imports). So it follows that there can be very little relationship between prices at home and abroad.'

To see why this argument is invalid, imagine that the death penalty was introduced for the crime of drunken driving (as it once was in the

---

[7] It is interesting to speculate why this is the case. No doubt in some cases the volume of cross-border trade is regarded as too small to warrant government interference. In other cases, it is probably more a result of the fact that trade in services is, for some reason or other, less politically sensitive than trade in manufactures. Thus, for some reason beyond this author's understanding, the majority of British and American politicians seem convinced that a nation's economic prowess requires it to have a large positive balance on trade in motor vehicles, but see nothing wrong with a deficit on tourist services – the outcome, presumably, of an unholy marriage between mercantilism and Stalinism!

USSR). And suppose that it worked. Now consider the following argument: 'There were no executions last year, so the new "get tough" policy on drinking and driving must have failed completely.'

It is obviously nonsense. In the same way that the threat of the death penalty presumably deterred drivers from drinking, the 'threat' of losing markets to foreign competition, particularly when enterprising arbitrageurs are around, may well have a decisive impact on prices *without any trade taking place at all.*[8] From this point of view, it might be preferable to talk of 'tradeables' and 'non-tradeables', rather than 'traded' and 'non-traded' goods.

2.3 A digression on price indices

So far, we have been concerned with the price of individual, identical goods. If we are to make any progress, however, we are going to have to turn our attention at some point to the price of goods in general, in other words to the general price level. In order to do that, we will have to introduce the concept of a price index. In doing so, no attempt will be made to go into details – they are in any case readily available elsewhere (see the references at the end of this chapter. Readers who are already familiar with the concept of a price index are invited to skip this section).

First, for future reference, a definition:

> **A (consumer) price index** is a weighted average of individual product prices, with weights determined by expenditure shares.

To see why we need a price index, imagine the following scenario. You open the newspaper one day to read these sensational headlines:

> **Price of salt to double! petrol also up by 3 %!**

As soon as you recover from the shock, you want to know what this means for your cost of living. Clearly, just because the price of salt has doubled, it does not follow that your cost of living has doubled. How can we take simultaneous account of the fact that the price of salt has gone up by 100 % and the price of petrol by 3 %, while everything else has remained unchanged?

---

[8] For an example of what happens when people fall into this particular logical trap, one could not do better than to look at the US and UK car industries. A generation ago the same specious argument was widely used in both countries to support the view that foreign prices (especially those for Japanese and German cars) were irrelevant, since imports were a negligible proportion of sales anyway. Those were the days!

One answer would be to take a simple (that is, unweighted) average of the price increases:

$$(100\% + 3\%)/2 = 51.5\%$$

or perhaps:

$$(100\% + 3\% + 0\%)/3 = 34.33\%$$

in recognition of the fact that the price of everything else besides salt and petrol has stayed constant.

Both answers are highly unsatisfactory. The first calculation gives us a figure which is halfway between the price change for salt and that for petrol, thus implying that each of the two prices is equally important, an assumption which is obviously nonsensical. Why? *Not* because salt is somehow less of a necessity than petrol, nor is the opposite true of course.

To see why these calculations are absurd, look at the second of them. Where does the 3 in the divisor come from? A moment's thought will show that it is totally arbitrary. It is not simply *one* other good whose price has remained unchanged, it is *all* other goods. In that case should the divisor be 3, or rather 30, or 3000 for that matter?

In general terms, the calculations are misleading because they contain the hidden assumption that all products, or product categories, are equally important. For most purposes, however, they are *not* all equally important, particularly when we are concerned to answer a question like: how great an increase in my salary, or pension, or student grant do I require in order to compensate for this latest round of price increases? Imagine your employer's reaction if you show them these newspaper headlines and tell them that it means you need a 51.5% rise to compensate.

The way economists (and nowadays governments) deal with this problem is by weighting the price increase for each individual product by a fraction equal to its proportionate contribution to the average household's total expenditure. Now it so happens that most governments in industrialized countries find that they need to collect information on how households spend their income for a variety of different reasons, apart from compiling a retail price index. It is, in principle at least, a relatively simple affair to use this information to compute budget shares for most of the goods and services in the typical family's shopping basket. Once the weights have been calculated, they can be updated at reasonable intervals (annually, in the UK). Using these weights, information gathered during any month on prices in shops, restaurants, pubs and so on can rapidly be translated into a price index.

For example, in the article which follows the newspaper headlines the newspaper's economic affairs correspondent warns readers that the grave news in the headlines amounts to a rise in the cost of living of 0.25% (or, one quarter of one per cent) or in the jargon, it will add a quarter point to the retail price index. The way the calculation is arrived at is by looking at the official statistics to find the weight attached to each of the two goods. Suppose weights of 0.1% for salt and 5.0% for petrol are found (which are more or less the correct figures for the UK). Then the calculation is simply:

$$(0.001 \times 100\%) + (0.050 \times 3\%) = 0.1\% + 0.15\% = 0.25\%$$

Notice that, although its price rose by so much less than that of salt, the relatively small petrol price increase contributes more to the rise in the index than does the doubling in the price of salt. Note, also, that there is a hidden third term in the calculation which is the one for all other prices. It has been suppressed, because it would read:

$$(0.949 \times 0.0\%) = 0.0\%$$

The weight on 'all other goods' is calculated as $(1.0 - 0.001 - 0.050)$, since the sum of all the expenditure proportions must be unity. In other words, the newspaper correspondent has implicitly assumed that all other prices will remain constant.

That is not all that has been assumed, however. It has also been taken for granted that expenditure shares will remain constant. Now this is a very reasonable assumption to make in the circumstances of our imaginary example, but the same will not always be the case. In 1979, for example, when world crude oil prices were raised almost overnight by 200%, it was only too easy to take that year's expenditure weights for petrol of 3.3% and extrapolate to the conclusion that the cost of living in the UK would rise by $0.033\% \times 200 = 6.6\%$, and many commentators who ought to have known better did just that. In the event, of course, the *quantity* of petrol consumed fell drastically across the industrialized world, so that the ultimate rise in the cost of living was far less than this calculation would suggest.[9]

Those readers familiar with the microeconomics of consumer demand theory will recognize the problem as one relating to the household's budget line. When the price of one good increases, the budget line pivots inward, making the household worse off. How much worse off? That depends on whereabouts along the budget line the household operates – the more it consumes of the good whose price has remained constant, the less important is the increase in the price of the other good. In the limit, if it does not consume the good whose price has risen anyway, the household is completely unaffected, so we ought to allocate a weight of zero to it in our index calculation.

There is a snag, though. When we talk about where the household operates along the budget line, do we mean *before* or *after* the price increase? Since the post-increase equilibrium will usually involve a fall in

---

[9] In fact, by 1981, UK consumption had fallen by about 20% in volume terms from its 1979 level – a repeat of what had happened in the two years following the 1973 OPEC price rises.

consumption of the good which has been marked up in price, and rise in consumption of the other good, the expression 'where the household operates' is ambiguous. For small price changes, for example a 3 % rise in the price of petrol, we can ignore the problem, but not when the price rises by 200 %.

A lot of theoretical and empirical work has gone into the analysis of this question, without any practical solution being in sight. For our purposes, it will be sufficient to note the following conclusion: that as long as price index weights remain fixed, price level comparisons will only be valid for small price changes.

One final point needs to be made with respect to the concept of an index. Our definition refers to an average price, whereas all our numerical examples referred to price changes. The reason is that no unambiguous meaning can be attached to an average of prices for different goods. What meaning can we attach to the statement that the average of the price of salt and the price of petrol was £10 in February 1986? Apart from anything else, the figure will be unit-dependent, in other words if you use the price of a litre of petrol instead of a gallon, you will substantially change your price average.

If, instead, we look at percentage rates of price increase, we will be dealing with common units (per cent) and the weighted average will have an obvious interpretation, which is the rise in the price of the typical good or service during the period in question.

We then face another problem: it is a rise in price, but since when? A price which has fallen by 2 % in the past year may have fallen by 60 % in the last two years but *risen* by 400 % over the last ten. The only solution to this particular problem is to bear in mind that the choice of the period to be used for comparison, called the **base period**, is always arbitrary. Depending on the use to which the index is put, you may get a completely different impression if you change the base period.[10] (Note that, by convention, the value of the price index for the base month or year is usually set equal to 100.)

Subject to all these caveats, there is no reason in principle why an index cannot be compiled to keep track of movements in the price of any commodity or set of commodities. For our purposes, we shall confine ourselves to considering the general level of prices. This means, in practice, the Retail (or consumer) Price Index (RPI), which is based on a sample of prices in shops and other retail outlets, and the Wholesale (or producer) Price Index (WPI), which measures prices 'at the factory gate'. The former measures prices from the point of view of the household sector, including indirect taxes and distributors' margins and so on and covers all goods and services in the typical consumption basket, whether imported or

---

[10] A fact which, in the case of share prices, is widely exploited by unit trust salesmen.

domestically produced. The WPI, on the other hand, is intended to be a guide to the underlying price level of inputs coming into, and output leaving the firms in the corporate sector of the economy.

2.4   Purchasing power parity

Now, at long last, we are in a position to be able to understand the notion of Purchasing Power Parity (PPP). The basic proposition will be seen to be very simple, though its ramifications are potentially much more complex. We shall build the theory by putting together the components we have assembled in Sections 2.2 and 2.3.

To start with, suppose that we are dealing with two countries, the UK and USA. Assume transaction costs such as transport, tariffs and so on are negligible, so that the law of one price applies to all goods and services consumed. Under these circumstances, let us rewrite Equation 2.2. Instead of the superscripts L and NY for London and New York, we shall nominate one country, the UK, as the 'home' country, and leave its variables unsuperscripted, with asterisks as superscripts for the other, 'foreign' country.

Now, remembering that C is zero, because we are assuming away transaction costs, we have:

$$P_i = S P_i^* \qquad i = 1 \ldots N \tag{2.3}$$

Notice the Ps have acquired subscripts, to show that they relate to the good or service number i. We had no need of a subscript in Sections 2.1 and 2.2 because we were always referring to a particular case of a specific good. Now that we have introduced the notion of a price index, we have to distinguish carefully between individual and general price levels. Equation 2.3 states that the law of one price holds with respect to the relationship between the domestic and foreign prices of good number i. We happen also to be assuming that Equation 2.3 holds with respect to *all* the goods (and services) consumed in the two countries. So, if there are N such goods, Equation 2.3 could be repeated N times over, with a different subscript each time, which explains the term $i = 1 \ldots N$.

Now ask yourself the question: what can be said about the price index for the domestic country (UK) compared to that of the foreign country, for example the USA?

In general, not much – unless we make an additional assumption. One possibility would be to assume *the weights used in compiling the respective price indices are identical*. In other words, suppose that, for each one of the N goods, we can say that its share in total US expenditure (and hence its weight in the US price index), is exactly the same as its share of UK expenditure. Under these circumstances, we can be confident that

Equation 2.3 will apply equally to the general level of prices, so that we can write:

$$P = S P^* \tag{2.4}$$

where P and P^* (without a subscript) refer to the home and foreign country's price index respectively.

This is the simplest possible version of the PPP hypothesis, and we shall return to it a number of times in one form or another throughout the rest of this book. To be more precise, Equation 2.4 is a statement of what is sometimes called the **absolute purchasing power parity** doctrine, which amounts to the following proposition:

> The general level of prices, when converted to a common currency, will be the same in every country.

The remainder of this chapter will be spent exploring its implications, its shortcomings and its ability to explain the facts.

Notice that we are dealing with a theory that predicts equality between national price levels translated, via the exchange rate, into a common unit of account. Nothing has so far been said about the mechanism that brings about this result. Now the drift of this chapter so far might seem to offer an obvious answer to this question. After all, if the prices of individual goods are aligned according to the law of one price, either as a result of arbitrage or the normal competitive trading processes, then it is to these forces one should look for an explanation of how PPP asserts itself. According to this microeconomic view, then, the PPP hypothesis is a natural consequence or a by-product of the law of one price, reflected at aggregate level.

This however, is by no means the *only* way to arrive at a PPP equilibrium. It is equally possible to argue in favour of what we might call a *macroeconomic* approach, one that was hinted at indirectly in Sections 2.1 and 2.2. Suppose, instead of the prices of individual goods and services being equated internationally, it is the general price levels themselves which are brought directly into the relationship predicted by PPP. Those readers who have done some macroeconomics before now may well be familiar with simple models of how the price level is determined in a closed economy; in any case, the subject will be covered in Chapter 4. For present purposes, let us simply assume each national price level is determined by that country's macroeconomic policy in the same way it would be if the economy were completely closed. Then, given these independently determined national price levels, the exchange rate could move to satisfy PPP.

There are three points to note about this macroeconomic view of PPP. Firstly, notice that it amounts to treating Equation 2.4 as one that determines the exchange rate. In fact, it is a simple version of what we shall later call the monetary model of the exchange rate (see Chapter 5).

Secondly, it follows that this scenario presupposes a floating exchange rate. In periods when the exchange rate is fixed, either PPP fails to work, or it is assumed to function in a different way, which is precisely the subject of the so-called monetary model of the balance of payments, also covered in Chapter 5.

Thirdly, note that, in principle at least, this approach does not rely on the law of one price. However, it might still apply, even if there were wide divergences between countries in the price of individual goods and services. As was suggested in Section 2.2, even if there is no mechanism to equate the price of, say, haircuts internationally, there may well be forces generating a broad equality between the cost of living in different countries.

In a sense, then, we would not require the law of one price to hold in each and every case – it might never hold for any good or service, and as we saw, the existing evidence is far from reassuring. It would be sufficient that upward deviations from the law of one price in the case of one good were offset by downward deviations in another case. For example, as between the UK and USA, it might be that relatively high prices for some UK services (hotels, restaurant meals and so on) are compensated for by relatively low prices for clothing, healthcare and so forth.

Notice also that, on this interpretation, we do not require equally-weighted price indices. What we do require is no less restrictive, however: that if one good with a weight of 1% is *over* priced by 50%, contributing $(0.01 \times 50\%) = 0.5\%$ to the general price level, there has to be another good contributing exactly -0.5%, for example, one carrying a 5% weighting *under* priced by precisely 10%. This may seem unlikely, but, as with the law of one price, its plausibility or otherwise is ultimately an empirical question. In other words, the proof of the pudding is in the eating!

One final point about the interpretation of PPP. We have chosen to approach the subject by way of the 'real world' concept of a price index, for the essentially pedagogic reason that it is one with which the reader should be familiar and one that is going to crop up in Chapters 5 and 7. But this is not the only way PPP can be viewed. At the very least, most economists would agree that none of the published price indices is anything like a perfect measure of the appropriate price level for PPP purposes. In part, the shortcomings may be the same ones that make the retail price index, for example, an imperfect measure of the cost of living: problems of accounting for differences of quality between products, problems of sampling prices actually paid, rather than listed prices, and so on. In other cases, the shortcomings may be of the kind that are really only significant in an open economy context, like the fact that different tax regimes and differing degrees of provision of public goods make international cost of living comparisons highly questionable.

Since it is virtually impossible to remedy these deficiencies, you may have concluded by now that PPP is a dead duck, in advance of looking at the evidence. Apart from being premature, the judgement is also misguided, for the following reason. Even if there does turn out to be little empirical support for PPP, it is at least possible that, because we are dealing with price level measures which are so imperfect, PPP is in fact alive and kicking in the real world. In other words, Equation 2.4 may be completely valid, but only with the 'true' price level variables which are *unobservable*, and is only very distantly related to what we actually observe, that is, the *published* UK and US price statistics.

In that case, you may think PPP is untestable, because it relates to unobservable variables, and not of much 'practical' use either, for the same reason. As we shall see in Chapter 5, that conclusion does not necessarily follow. If the true price levels (in other words the ones that are relevant to PPP) are in fact related to other observable variables, then the PPP hypothesis becomes fully operational. Of course, that does not make it any more likely to be true.

Whether true or not, PPP is an important benchmark for the analysis of exchange rate movements, particularly in so far as they impinge on international competitiveness. If the general level of prices is a reasonably accurate index of the cost of production in a country, and this is almost certain to be the case, then the ratio of price levels for any two countries will serve as a measure of relative competitiveness.

Notice that if PPP could be relied on to obtain at all times, competitiveness measured in this way would not only be constant, it would in some sense be equalized across different countries. No country would have a price advantage over another, at least in terms of the broad spread of goods and services represented by the general price level. In practice, as we shall see, international competitiveness has been far from constant in the post-war world. For this reason, economists often wish to measure deviations from PPP, and the concept most often used for this purpose is the so-called real exchange rate:

> **The real exchange rate** is the price of foreign relative to domestic goods and services. Formally, it is measured by:

$$Q = SP^*/P \tag{2.5}$$

Notice that an alternative interpretation would be to say that it amounts to the exchange rate as we have so far understood it (that is the *nominal exchange rate, S*), corrected for relative prices, P^*/P.

If PPP holds, then the value of Q ought in principle to be one, as you can see from Equation 2.4. In practice however, no meaning can be attached to the absolute size of Q, for the same reason that the absolute level of a price index is meaningless, as we saw earlier in this chapter in Section 2.3.

To see that this is the case, suppose that at some point in time the UK price index is 200, while the US index stands at 250 and the exchange rate is £0.80 = $1.00. (Check that PPP holds and $Q = 1$ for these figures.)

Now recall that the choice of base year for an index is completely arbitrary. Choose a different base period for an index ('rebase it') and you will always end up with a different figure, unless by chance the index in the new base period is the same as in the old. So rebasing either or both of the price indices in our example will disturb the apparent equilibrium. Moreover, it will not help to base both UK and US price indices on the same period, as all that does is to arbitrarily set both price levels to equality (at 100).

For this reason, it makes more sense to think in terms, not of price levels, but of rates of change. In this form, the **relative purchasing power parity hypothesis** states that:

> One country's inflation rate can only be higher (lower) than another's to the extent that its exchange rate depreciates (appreciates).

To reformulate our PPP Equation 2.4 in terms of rates of growth requires a little elementary calculus. First, take logs of Equation 2.4. Using lower case letters to denote logs, this gives us:

$$p = s + p^* \tag{2.6}$$

Now if we take the derivative of a natural logarithm, we arrive at the proportional rate of change, that is $d(\log P) = dp = dP/P$ and so on. In the present case, differentiating in Equation 2.6, we have:

$$dp = ds + dp^* \tag{2.7}$$

This equation only says that the home country's inflation rate, dp, will be equal to the sum of the foreign inflation rate, dp^*, and the rate of currency depreciation, ds.

It might be more illuminating, perhaps, to rewrite Equation 2.7 as:

$$dp - dp^* = ds \tag{2.8}$$

which says that the domestic country can only run a higher rate of inflation than the foreign country if its exchange rate falls *pro rata*. One way of interpreting this relationship is simply as an extension of the familiar idea that, when prices rise, the value of money falls. The more rapidly prices rise, the faster the value of money falls. In a two-country context, the more rapidly prices rise in the home economy *relative to the foreign country*, the more rapidly domestic money loses its value relative to foreign money or, the more its exchange rate depreciates.

Notice that the reformulation in terms of rates of change avoids all the difficulties of choosing a base for the price index. There is no problem in defining unambiguously the rate of inflation or the rate of exchange rate depreciation – at least, no problem of the kind involved in making the absolute PPP hypothesis operational. That is why, although absolute PPP often figures in theoretical models, it is only relative PPP that can actually be tested by an examination of the evidence.

Before going on to do just that, there is one important loose end to be tidied up. When discussing the law of one price, it was freely admitted that allowance would need to be made for transaction costs such as transportation, tariffs, non-tariff barriers and so on. Surely these costs ought to figure somewhere in our PPP equations, if PPP follows from the open economy version of the law of one price?

Rather than deny this obvious fact, the economics literature copes with the problem in one of the following ways:

(1) For some purposes, where nothing very important hinges on the way it is specified, economists have tended to use the unadorned versions of absolute or relative PPP, as in Equation 2.4 or Equation 2.7 on the grounds that transaction costs are small enough to be negligible.

(2) If not negligible, it could be argued that most of the main elements in the total cost of trading vary in proportion to the value of the goods in question. For example, as already noted, tariffs are often charged *ad valorem*, transportation charges may frequently be related to the value of goods shipped and items like insurance premiums will almost invariably bear some more or less fixed relation to price per unit.

This being the case, if we make the assumption that all these costs are proportional to price, it is easy to see that they will not figure at all in our relative PPP Equation 2.7. Look back at the steps on the way from Equation 2.4 to Equation 2.7. Retrace them, starting with an absolute PPP equation modified to take account of transaction costs:

$$P = K(S P^*) \qquad\qquad (2.4')$$

where K is a constant, greater or less than unity, covering the total cost of conducting international trade. As before, take logarithms:

$$p = k + s + p^* \qquad\qquad (2.5')$$

From here, it is easy to see that we end up with the same result for relative PPP as before, simply because when we differentiate Equation 2.5, the cost term will disappear. (Remember that the derivative of a constant like k is zero.) Intuitively, the reason is that under these circumstances, transaction costs have the same effect as a once-over rescaling of prices – they have no effect on the (relative) rate of inflation itself.

(3) For a more agnostic view, if neither of the previous assumptions is acceptable, one possibility is, as we shall see, to fall back on an equilibrium real exchange rate, usually one that obtains only in the long run. Obviously, this amounts to assuming that relative PPP applies in some kind of steady state, with deviations permitted in the short run.

(4)   Finally, we could make use of the distinction already introduced between traded and non-traded goods to reformulate PPP in terms of tradeables alone. In other words, divide the economy into two sectors: one to which PPP applies, and another where prices are determined domestically. While this approach has the advantage of providing a degree of realism, it has the drawback already noted – that, in fact, it may well be that a rigid division of the economy into traded and non-traded goods sectors is no more realistic than the original assumption that all goods are potentially tradeable.

Ultimately, as has been mentioned on several occasions, the question of the acceptability or otherwise of PPP can only be resolved by an examination of the evidence, to which we now turn.

2.5   Purchasing power parity – a look at the facts

The volume of published research on PPP is vast, and it has generated a broad consensus on a number of important points. Looking at post-war experience in the industrialized countries, the general conclusions can be summarized as follows:

(1)   In the short run, deviations from PPP are so frequent as to be more or less the norm. As we shall see, they are also very substantial and almost certainly too great to be explained away by international differences in the methods used to collect statistics.

(2)   There is not even much sign of a tendency towards PPP in the long run. All that can be said is that the long swings in real exchange rates which have characterized the 1970s and 1980s have eventually been reversed, so that long periods of overvaluation relative to PPP have invariably been followed by long periods of undervaluation. As a result, the times when PPP has obtained have been few and far between and, with the benefit of hindsight, look like chance encounters on the way from one extreme disequilibrium to an opposite one of more or less equal scale.

(3)   In terms of volatility (about which we shall have a lot more to say in Chapters 5, 7 and 11–13) it is unquestionably true that exchange rates have varied far more than prices. Look back at Equation 2.8, which shows how an exchange rate moves according to the relative PPP doctrine. On the left-hand side is the relative inflation rate. Now relative inflation rates between industrialized countries vary somewhat from year to year. A 5% gap may narrow to, say, 3% or 4%, or possibly widen to 6% or 7% or even 10% by the time a year has elapsed. But when we look at exchange rates, we find fluctuations of this magnitude, 1% or 2% or more, *within the space of a single day's trading*!

There is only one exception to these otherwise negative conclusions. If we look at situations of very rapid ('triple digit') inflation, notably in Brazil, Argentina, Chile and Israel in recent years, we find PPP maintained to within fairly narrow margins. Not surprisingly, the same is even more true of hyperinflations, that is, inflation at astronomic rates (Germany in 1923–4 being the classic case). The reason seems to be that in this type of 'hothouse' environment, the cost of being wrong about any price is potentially so great that agents are forced to invest considerable effort and expense in gathering information. Furthermore, there tends to be a progressive collapse in the kind of institutional and legal arrangements that in normal times serve to make prices sticky, such as long-term contracts, price controls and so on. In particular, attempts to fix the exchange rate are soon swamped. The end result is that both prices and the exchange rate move smoothly along their PPP paths.

To illustrate the extent to which PPP appears to have broken down in the industrialized countries, look at Figures 2.1 to 2.4. The first two

Figure 2.1 Real exchange rates 1973–92 (consumer prices).

Figure 2.2 Real exchange rates 1973–92 (producer prices).

figures show the way that real exchange rates have fluctuated over the years since 1973, relative to the base value in 1980.

First, notice that there is a considerable degree of similarity in the pattern for the five countries (United Kingdom, Switzerland, France, West Germany and Japan). This reflects the fact that all the exchange rates have moved in broadly similar fashion relative to the dollar. Thus, all five appreciated to some extent against the dollar in the late 1970s, then depreciated sharply in the 1980s as the US currency rose to a peak in 1985, since when, of course, it has reversed its rise and gone into an unprecedented decline. As a result, what we see in the figures reflects a combination of developments specific to the country in question with, at the same time, developments affecting the relative value of the US dollar.

Second, and most important of all, notice the amplitude of the fluctuations in what should, under PPP, be flat graphs. For example, the pound appreciated (in other words, UK competitiveness fell relative to the USA) by about a third in real terms between 1976 and 1980 (from 150 to 100). From that point onward, the pound then fell by around 60%, and has since found its way back to about its 1980 level. The other currencies were only slightly less volatile.

Figure 2.3 Purchasing power parity exchange rates 1976–92 (consumer prices).

In fact, Figures 2.1 and 2.2 could almost be said to track the movements in *nominal* exchange rates shown in Figure 1.3 of Chapter 1, a feature which merely serves to illustrate the point made earlier on that, except for highly 'deviant' inflation rates, exchange rates fluctuate to an extent that swamps variations in relative price levels.[11]

Figures 2.3 and 2.4 present the facts in a different form. What is labelled there the PPP exchange rate is the nominal exchange rate against the US dollar required to preserve the same *real* exchange rate (that is, the same level of competitiveness) as in 1980. In other words, it is the (1980) nominal exchange rate adjusted for changes in the price ratio. In

---

[11] Furthermore, this statement becomes even more obviously true when we examine higher frequency (for example, quarterly or monthly) data. The data used in the charts is also biased in favour of PPP in so far as it relates to average exchange rates over the year. End-year or mid-year rates would be considerably more volatile whereas, by contrast, taking averages over a whole year tends to smooth out some of the fluctuations.

Figure 2.4   Purchasing power parity exchange rates 1976–92 (producer prices).

Figures 2.3 and 2.4, the PPP exchange rate is shown as a ratio of the average spot rate actually observed over the year in question (times 100). Thus, when this ratio is above 100, the exchange rate is 'overvalued' relative to the dollar – assuming it was at its PPP level in the base year, 1980.

It is tempting to conclude that the pattern reflects long swings around a PPP equilibrium, in other words, the hypothesis already mentioned: that PPP is a long-run phenomenon, with disturbances being eliminated only over a number of years. The trouble with this interpretation is that it is hard to see any evidence of the real exchange rate 'settling down' to a long-run level. To put the matter somewhat differently, while the cycles of over- or undervaluation do tend to reverse themselves eventually, there is no sign that the the process of correction stops when equilibrium has been reinstated, a fact which has led some economists to conclude that exchange rates have an inbuilt tendency to overshoot, as we shall see in Chapter 7.

Because 1980 represented a peak in the pound's value relative to the dollar, the graphs tend to suggest it was undervalued for the rest of the period. If we had taken 1976 as our base year, we would have reached the opposite conclusion – which only goes to show how hard it is to arrive at a firm conclusion as to the true value of a currency, even using a criterion as simple as PPP.

We can summarize the evidence by saying that there is no obvious tendency towards purchasing power parity. It is not even clear that producer prices fit the hypothesis any better than retail prices, which may be a sign that the distinction between traded and non-traded goods emphasized by some researchers is not very important in practice. The conclusion has to be either that both types of price index are inadequate for present purposes or that PPP holds only in the very long run – too long, in fact, to be apparent over a decade – or, of course, that PPP never holds other than by chance.

Of course, researchers have investigated PPP at much greater depth than can be attempted here. On the basis of their reading of the evidence, some economists have in recent years come to the conclusion that changes in real exchange rates are actually random: in other words, that at any point in time, far from tending to return to some long-run equilibrium level, the best forecast one could make would be for the real exchange rate to remain constant. However overvalued a currency may appear to be relative to its PPP level, it is as likely to rise as fall in subsequent periods.

This theory is one to which we shall return in Chapters 11 and 12. For the moment, we simply note that it implies that PPP is of little use in modelling exchange rates.

2.6   Conclusions

We have seen there are persuasive reasons for supposing that, in principle at least, purchasing power parity ought to be a reasonable approximation. Unfortunately, the facts would appear to indicate otherwise. Why?

One plausible explanation that has already been mentioned is the possibility that PPP applies to the true, unobservable price levels. If we instead look at what factors determine price levels in a domestic context (particularly the money stock), then PPP will dictate what *ought* to be the relationship between them and the exchange rate. This is precisely what we shall do in Chapter 5.

However, it appears more likely the true explanation is to be found in the importance of speculative influences in currency markets. Given the scale and volatility of capital account movements in the 1970s and 1980s relative to the comparatively small (and stable) flows of international trade in goods and services, it seems hardly surprising the conditions for current account equilibrium have not been satisfied.

Indeed, the other side of the same coin is the persistence of massive current account surpluses and deficits, and their relative insensitivity even to quite substantial changes in the exchange rate. Because the capital account has been very much the tail that wags the dog in the floating rate era, we shall have very little to say in this book about the factors that influence international trade patterns.

■ Summary

- The *law of one price* states that two identical goods must sell for the same price. In the context of the domestic economy, if we allow for *transaction costs*, this relationship can be expected to hold, because it pays entrepreneurs to exploit any price divergences which emerge temporarily, by buying large quantities of the good in the cheap market and selling it immediately in the expensive market, until the price differential is eliminated. This form of riskless trading is known as *arbitrage*. By contrast, *speculation* involves buying something in the hope of being able to resell it later at a higher price.

- The importance of transaction costs will vary from good to good. In some cases, they are a negligible factor, and the law of one price might be expected to hold almost exactly. In others, transaction costs drive a substantial wedge between prices in different markets. In the extreme case (*non-traded goods*), transaction costs are so high relative to the price that arbitrage becomes prohibitively expensive.

- In an open economy context, the law of one price states that two identical goods must sell for a price that is the same when translated into a common currency. In order to translate the price in terms of one country's money into the price in terms of another's, one needs to make use of the relative price of the two currencies or the exchange rate. Hence, the open economy version of the law of one price states that the domestic price of a good must be equal to the foreign price multiplied by the domestic currency price of foreign exchange.

- The barriers to international trade and the transaction costs involved are likely to be, for the most part, of the same nature as those in domestic markets, but will usually be more substantial. In particular, there will freqently be *tariffs* (which are taxes on cross-border trade) as an additional obstacle to arbitrage.

- In order to measure the level of prices in general, rather than the price of individual goods and services, we need to use a *price index*, which is simply a weighted average of the component prices, with weights corresponding to the relative importance of each product in total expenditure.

- Under certain circumstances, what is true of the prices of individual goods and services in different countries will also be true of the level of prices in general. In other words, (*absolute*) *purchasing power parity* (PPP) will apply, that is, the level of prices in the home country will be equal to the product of the foreign country's price level and the exchange rate, measured as the (domestic currency) price of foreign exchange. Depending on our interpretation of the PPP mechanism, this may or may not presuppose among other things that barriers to trade, including all incidental costs, are negligible.

- In practice, since no meaning can be attached to the absolute level of a price index, it is sensible to consider the PPP hypothesis as it relates to *changes* in price levels (inflation rates). Then *relative purchasing power parity* states that two countries' inflation rates will diverge by the extent of the change in their bilateral exchange rate.

- Deviations from PPP, where they occur, will normally be associated with changes in a country's relative competitiveness. For that reason, it is often useful to look at the *real exchange rate*, which is the (nominal) exchange rate corrected for changes in relative prices.

- Examination of the facts suggests that PPP has rarely applied in the post-war period, at least as far as the industrialized countries are concerned. It seems that PPP only really applies when one of the countries has an inflation rate which is so high that price adjustments become more or less continuous and the cost of deviating from PPP is therefore prohibitive.

READING GUIDE

Much of the research on PPP and the law of one price is quite easy to understand without very much mathematics or econometrics.

The most detailed modern work on PPP is Officer (1976). Influential research has been published by Kravis and Lipsey (1971) and Katseli-Papaefstratiou (1979). Magee (1978) dissents from the view that PPP does not hold, attributing apparent deviations to inaccurate price measurement. Two studies supportive of PPP, for the 1920s at least, were published by Frenkel (1978) (1980a). On the other hand, the same author charted the 'Collapse of PPP During the 1970s' (1980b).

Though somewhat out of date by now, it is still worth reading Mussa (1979), which attempts to summarize the facts on PPP, as well as on other aspects of exchange rate movements.

The idea that changes in the real exchange rate are essentially random is due to Roll (1979), though see also Adler and Lehmann (1983).

3

The Financial Markets in the Open Economy

■ Introduction

In Chapter 2, we saw how the fact that an economy was open to trade with other countries meant that there were certain relationships that could be expected to apply between domestic and foreign prices, though we also found that, in reality, they rarely hold very closely. In this chapter, we shall look at the markets for financial assets rather than goods, and at the relationships one can expect to find linking domestic and foreign asset prices.

We have already looked at one good that had some of the properties of a financial asset: tickets for a rock concert are like assets, in so far as they yield a future return, in the form of entertainment, and also because, being easy to transport and more or less homogeneous, arbitrage is likely to go a long way in order to eliminate price differentials.

Here, we shall be concerned with a more conventional asset. For simplicity's sake, let us pick a single, standard security and stick with it throughout the chapter. The best asset to choose for present purposes will be a 12-month time deposit, that is, a deposit for a fixed term of one year, paying an annual interest rate at maturity and nothing before then. We shall ignore other short-term assets in order to highlight the relationship between the UK and US interest rates on this standard type of deposit.

We shall be concerned with the alternatives open to a representative investor[1] with a large stock of wealth in liquid form. In fact, the investor could actually be a bank or multinational company with liquid funds. In any case, the choice with which we shall be concerned is between two otherwise identical deposits, one in a UK bank, the other in a US bank.[2] For the most part, we shall view the alternatives as seen from the UK, though symmetrical arguments will apply to US-based investors. We shall also assume that there are no barriers to international transfers of funds, an assumption that is fairly realistic as far as today's currency markets are concerned, and that our investor is exempt from all taxes that might affect the choice of where to deposit.

3.1   Uncovered interest rate parity

To start with, put yourself in the position of a UK resident on 1 January with some funds that he wishes to leave on deposit for one year on the most favourable terms possible. It will simplify matters without changing our conclusions if we assume that the amount involved is just £1. We shall compare two alternatives (call them the UK and the US strategies, respectively) in terms of the sterling return they promise. As an aid to understanding the mechanism involved, we shall make use of Figure 3.1 and Table 3.1, which deal with the general case in terms of symbols, side by side with the numerical examples in Tables 3.2 to 3.4.

---

[1]   We are using the word 'investor' to denote an institution or individual with wealth available for allocation to one or more forms of asset holding. This is the way that the term is used in business life, and indeed the way that it is used in finance. For the benefit of those who have followed a basic macroeconomics course however, this is precisely the way the term 'investor' should not be used. In the jargon of macroeconomics we are concerned here with a 'saver', or with an institution acting on his behalf.

[2]   We shall discuss the choice as though it involved actually depositing in Britain in pounds or, alternatively, in America in dollars. In practice, it is nowadays quite simple (and legal) for a British citizen to take sterling to a high-street bank anywhere in the UK and ask to open a deposit in US dollars, and similarly for US citizens. For the most part, in doing so, the retail banks are simply acting as intermediaries – channels through which the man in the local high street can have access to another country's money market. In other words, the UK citizen's pounds, when used to open a dollar deposit in a bank somewhere in England usually end up by one route or another in a New York financial institution – without the Briton either knowing or caring when or how the transfer takes place. However, the doubting reader may work through an imaginary scenario to convince himself that the conclusions reached in this chapter would be unchanged if we dropped the fiction that the respective deposits are made directly in the UK or USA.

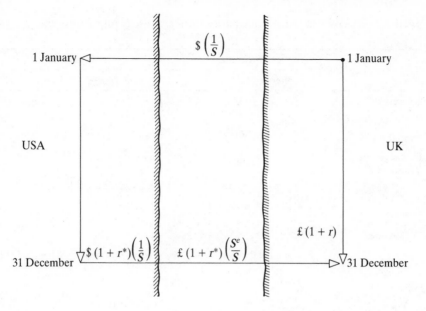

Figure 3.1   Uncovered interest rate parity.

3.1.1 The domestic strategy

If the appropriate UK interest rate (expressed as a decimal) is r, then £1 deposited for 12 months in a UK bank will have attracted £1 $\times r$ of interest by the end of the period. The £1 will therefore have 'grown' to:

$$£1 + (£1 \times r) = £(1 + r)$$

by 31 December, as we can see from the downward pointing arrow on the right-hand (UK) side of Figure 3.1 (or in the middle column of Table 3.1). Note that this outcome is available with complete certainty. The only possible risk would be of bank failure, and we shall rule out that eventuality as being too improbable to be worth considering.[3]

For example, if the interest rate in the UK is 5% per annum (or 0.05), then £1 will earn £0.05 of interest, so that the end-of-year value of the deposit will be £1.05, as we can see from the middle column of Table 3.2.

---

[3] It is sufficient simply to assume that the probability of the UK bank defaulting is the same as that for the US bank. In reality, deposits in both countries are guaranteed by the monetary authorities – de jure in the USA, de facto in the UK.

Table 3.1 Uncovered interest rate parity – general case (assuming no risk premium).

	UK strategy		US strategy	
	Action	*Yield*	*Action*	*Yield*
1 January				
12 month interest rate		r		r^*
Available for deposit		£1		£1
Exchange rate (£ price of $)				£S
			Buy $ @ £S each:	$(1/S)$
	Place on deposit:	£1	Place on deposit:	$(1/S)$
31 December				
	Liquidate deposit:	£$(1+r)$	Liquidate deposit:	$(1+r^*)(1/S)$
Expected exchange rate (£ price of $)				£S^e
			Convert back to £ *sell* $ @ £S^e each:	£$(1+r^*)(S^e/S)$

Conclusion: If £$(1+r) > $ £$(1+r^*)(S^e/S)$: *deposit* in UK
If £$(1+r) < $ £$(1+r^*)(S^e/S)$: *deposit* in USA
If £$(1+r) = $ £$(1+r^*)(S^e/S)$: *equilibrium*

The alternative, on the other hand, is a little more complicated:

3.1.2 The foreign strategy

This consists of the following three operations: convert the pound into dollars, then deposit the dollars with a US bank and, finally, at the end of the year convert the proceeds back into sterling. To calculate the return to this strategy, follow the route round the other three sides of the rectangle in Figure 3.1, or down the right-hand column of Tables 3.1 and 3.2:

Stage 1

Convert the £1 into dollars so as to 'cross the Atlantic' to the USA (the top arrow in Figure 3.1). One pound buys $1/S$ dollars, so this is the amount available for deposit with the US bank.

Table 3.2 Uncovered interest rate parity – case 1 disequilibrium (assuming no risk premium).

	UK strategy		US strategy	
	Action	*Yield*	*Action*	*Yield*
1 January				
12 month interest rate		5%		6%
Available for deposit		£1.00		£1.00
Exchange rate (£ price of $)				£0.50
			Buy $ @ £0.50 each:	$2.00
	Place on deposit:	£1.00	Place on deposit:	$2.00
31 December				
	Liquidate deposit:	£1.05	Liquidate deposit:	$2.12
Expected exchange rate (£ price of $)				£0.60
			Convert back to £ *sell* $ @ £0.60 each:	£1.27

Conclusion: *deposit* in USA

For example, if the exchange rate is $1 = £0.50, our investor will have $2.00 available for deposit in the US bank (Table 3.2, right-hand side).

Stage 2

Leave the balance on deposit in America for 12 months. How much will it earn? That will obviously depend on the US interest rate, which we will call r^*. So $1/S$ left on deposit at the US interest rate r^* will earn $(1/S)r^*$ by the end of the year. Hence, the deposit will, by the end of the year, have grown to $(1 + r^*)1/S$.

Continuing our numerical example, if the US interest rate is 6%, the $2.00 deposited will have grown to $2.12 by 31 December.

Before moving on to the final stage, note that from the standpoint of our imaginary UK investor, the *dollar* proceeds of depositing in the USA are known in advance, on 1 January. All the elements in the calculation of the dollar returns can be taken as known at the start of the year, when the choice of where to deposit is made. The US interest rate is known, in the same way the UK rate was known. The exchange rate at which dollars can be bought for Stage 1 is equally available, on application to any bank or currency dealer.

Table 3.3 Uncovered interest rate parity – case 2 equilibrium (assuming no risk premium).

	UK strategy		US strategy	
	Action	*Yield*	*Action*	*Yield*
1 January				
12 month interest rate		25%		5%
Available for deposit		£1.00		£1.00
Exchange rate (£ price of $)				£0.50
			Buy $ @ £0.50 each:	$2.00
	Place on deposit:	£1.00	Place on deposit:	$2.00
31 December				
	Liquidate deposit:	£1.25	Liquidate deposit:	$2.10
Expected exchange rate (£ price of $)				£0.60
			Convert back to £ *sell* $ @ £0.60 each:	£1.25

Conclusion: *equilibrium*

Now the crucial point in understanding the process is not to forget that the next stage takes place 12 months later than the first two. What concerns our UK investor is the sterling value of the deposit. This is obviously true if the investor is a UK resident. However, even if he is a member of the international jet set, with a life-style that involves spending in more or less equal amounts in all the major currencies, or if, more prosaically, he is treasurer of a multinational corporation, *it is only by converting into a common currency that a valid comparison with the domestic deposit strategy can be made*, and we are assuming the common currency is the pound sterling.[4]

Stage 3

On 31 December, liquidate the US deposit and convert the proceeds from dollars into sterling at whatever happens to be the exchange rate on the day in question.

---

[4] It would be a useful exercise for the reader to try replicating Tables 3.1 to 3.4 for the case of a US investor, or possibly for a Japanese faced with the choice between depositing in London or New York.

Table 3.4 Uncovered interest rate parity – case 3 equilibrium (assuming no risk premium).

	UK strategy		US strategy	
	Action	Yield	Action	Yield
1 January				
12 month interest rate		15%		5%
Available for deposit		£1.00		£1.00
Exchange rate (£ price of $)				£0.40
			Buy $ @ £0.40 each:	$2.50
	Place on deposit:	£1.00	Place on deposit:	$2.50
31 December				
	Liquidate deposit:	£1.15	Liquidate deposit:	$2.63
Expected exchange rate (£ price of $)				£0.44
			Convert back to £ *sell* $ @ £0.44 each:	£1.15

Conclusion: *equilibrium*

Now, as of 1 January, that exchange rate is unknowable. All the investor can do to arrive at a decision is to make his own forecast of the exchange rate that seems likely to prevail at the end of the year. Call this forecast of the end-of-year exchange rate: S^e.

Given his forecast of the exchange rate at which it will prove possible to convert the dollars back to sterling, we can close the circle, or rather, the rectangle in Figure 3.1. A dollar will buy £S^e on 31 December, if the investor's guess turns out to be correct. So the $\$1/S(1 + r^*)$ which the investor will have on 31 December if he decides to follow the US deposit route will buy £$(1 + r^*)S^e/S$ when converted back into sterling (in mid-Atlantic, on the bottom arrow in Figure 3.1).

In terms of our numerical example, if the investor expects the sterling exchange rate to have deteriorated to £0.60 = $1, the investor will be able to convert his dollar deposit of $2.12 into £1.27 (the bottom line of Table 3.2).

3.1.3 Equilibrium: the bottom line

We are now in a position to compare the attractiveness of the two strategies. What should we expect to find? Remember that we are dealing with deposits of the same kind, for the same period, in banks of the same type.

Can we then apply the law of one price and conclude that the return from the two strategies must be equal in equilibrium, otherwise arbitrage profits will exist?

Not quite. Recall that, from the point of view of the UK resident, the domestic strategy is riskless. It requires no forecasting, no guesswork, no danger of unpleasant surprises. The calculated return does not rely on expectations which may turn out to be wrong, possibly by a large margin.

The US deposit strategy, by contrast, involves making a guess about the future exchange rate which is a hazardous business at the best of times. To this extent, the US deposit is not the same asset as the UK deposit. In general, we might expect economic agents either to avoid running risks or, more likely, to demand a reward for doing so. We shall have more to say on the general subject of risk later in the book, especially Chapter 13, but at this stage it is worth introducing one or two concepts which will enable us to sidestep the problem without ignoring it altogether. First:

> **The risk premium** is the reward, usually in the form of an anticipated excess return, that an economic agent gets in order to persuade him to bear risk.

Why do agents usually require an incentive in order to undertake risky projects? The answer given by economic theory relies on the nature of people's preferences when faced with choices between uncertain prospects. It is assumed that, for the most part, individuals prefer riskless to risky investments, other things being equal. This feature of preferences is what explains why risky investments usually yield a higher return than riskless ones. Not that tastes are always such that people demand a risk premium. There are some instances where agents seem content to run risks for no reward, or even in some cases to pay for the privilege of bearing risk. The following definitions are useful in this context:

> **Risk averters** are economic agents who require a (positive) risk premium in order to persuade them to hold risky assets. By contrast, **risk lovers** are willing to pay a premium for the privilege of bearing risk, while **risk neutral** agents are willing to do so in return for a zero risk premium.

For the most part, one would expect to find that people are averse to risk, at least in their attitudes to purely economic decisions. Nonetheless, allowing for uncertainty in economics makes analysis very difficult indeed, which is why we are going to defer any consideration of the problems associated with risk until Chapter 13. For present purposes, we shall make the following simplifying assumption:

> From now on and until further notice, we shall be assuming that economic agents are broadly risk neutral.

Notice this means we are assuming they are, on balance, neither risk averters nor risk lovers – they are indifferent between an investment yielding a completely secure return, on the one hand, and one offering the prospect of an identical return on average, but with the possibility of a much higher or lower return, on the other. In other words, we assume they are concerned only with average returns.

For the moment, we shall suspend consideration of how realistic this asssumption is in practice, and note only that it allows us to ignore the risk premium. In the present case, it permits us to jump to the following simple conclusion about the relative attractiveness of UK and US deposits:

> In equilibrium, the domestic and foreign strategies will have to yield the same sterling return.

In other words, in equilibrium the investor must be indifferent between deposits in the two countries. Otherwise, if returns were not equal, our investor would be faced with a 'one-way bet'. Given the investor's expectations, and that he is risk neutral (that is, indifferent to risk), the question of whether to deposit in the UK or the USA will have a clear-cut answer, and it will be one shared by anyone who holds similar expectations. If there is anything approaching a consensus in the market, then, there will be a flood of investment either into or out of the UK banking system, depending on which of the two strategies has the higher pay-off.

Look at the bottom line of Table 3.2. The US alternative yields £1.27 while the UK deposit pays only £1.05. Plainly, under these circumstances no one would deposit in the UK. Given the level of the exchange rate and its future expected value, and given our assumption of risk neutrality, either the UK interest rate must be higher or the US interest rate lower for depositors to be indifferent between the two alternatives.

In general, then, for equilibrium (that is, a situation where there is, on balance, no tendency for funds to move into or out of the UK from the USA, and vice versa), we require that the return from depositing £1 in the UK, $£(1 + r)$, be just equal to the return on a US deposit, $£S^e/S(1 + r^*)$. The steps in the reasoning are summarized in Table 3.1. As can be seen from the bottom line of Table 3.1, equilibrium requires that the following relationship hold:

$$(1 + r) = (1 + r^*)S^e/S \tag{3.1}$$

Now with a little manipulation, this equation can be rewritten in a simpler form. First, notice that the term S^e/S has a simple interpretation: the numerator is the exchange rate expected to prevail at the end of the year, and the denominator is the actual exchange rate at the time the decision is being made, that is, 1 January. Hence, the ratio of the two, S^e/S, will be greater than one if the price of foreign currency is expected to have risen by 31 December. For example, if the exchange rate is expected to be 50% higher by the end of the year (in other words, if the price of foreign currency, S, is forecast to rise by half) the ratio S^e/S will be 1.50. It therefore makes sense to use the following redefinition:

$$S^e/S \equiv 1 + \Delta s^e \tag{3.2}$$

where Δs will be referred to as the rate of depreciation (of the domestic currency) or the rate of increase in the price of foreign currency over the period in question, with, as before, the superscript 'e' to remind us that in the present case, we are concerned with the *expected* rate of depreciation.

Now use Equation 3.2 in place of S^e/S in Equation 3.1, and multiply out on the right-hand side to give:

$$(1 + r) = (1 + r^*)(1 + \Delta s^e) \tag{3.3}$$
$$= 1 + r^* + \Delta s^e + r^* \Delta s^e$$

Notice, first, that we can subtract one from both sides. Next, consider the final term, $r^* \Delta s^e$. It is the product of two rates: the rate of interest and the expected rate of depreciation. Unless we are dealing with a case of very rapid deterioration in a currency (in a hyperinflation, for example) this cross-product term is likely to be 'of the second order of smallness', and as such, can safely be ignored.[5] We are left with:

$$r = r^* + \Delta s^e \tag{3.4}$$

This is the form in which the **Uncovered Interest Rate Parity condition** (UIRP) is normally stated. In words:

> The domestic interest rate must be higher (lower) than the foreign interest rate by an amount equal to the expected depreciation (appreciation) of the domestic currency.

The reasoning should by now be clear. First, look back at the numerical examples.

In the example in Table 3.2, the price of a dollar is expected to rise from £0.50 to £0.60, that is, the pound is expected to depreciate at the rate $(0.6/0.5 - 1.0) = 0.2$, or 20%. If UK and US interest rates were equal, no economic agent, wherever domiciled, would keep his wealth in the UK if there was the alternative of depositing in the USA. In order to persuade

---

[5] In fact, the reader who attempts to check the results in Tables 3.3 and 3.4 – a computer spreadsheet program like Lotus 1-2-3 is ideal for the purpose – will find that the results have been 'fiddled' so as to satisfy Equation 3.4! For example, the last figure in Table 3.3 should be £1.26 (2.10 times £0.60) not £1.25. The difference of one penny is precisely the cross-product term: the rate of depreciation times the US interest rate, 0.20 times 5% = 1p.

the economic agent to hold pounds, the interest rate on sterling deposits would have to be higher than on dollar deposits by 20 %, so as to compensate for the fact that repayment at the end of the year is in devalued currency (as in Table 3.3).

Conversely, suppose the pound had been expected to appreciate against the dollar. Then no UK resident would have wished to deposit in the USA (and every US citizen who could do so would want to hold sterling deposits) – unless the UK interest rate were low enough to neutralize the attraction of being repaid in currency that had risen in value over the year.

The reasoning behind the interest rate parity relationship has been covered in somewhat exhaustive detail, not only because it will have an important part to play in some of the models we shall be examining in Chapters 7–12, but also because it has important implications in its own right. To see what some of those implications are, look back at Equation 3.4 and ask yourself the question: which of the three variables involved is exogenous, and which endogenous?[6] To put the question more simply, what causes what? Do increases in the expected rate of depreciation cause the UK interest rate to rise or the US rate to fall? Or do changes in the interest differential, $r - r^*$, cause expectations to change?

The answer to each of these questions depends on the structure of the economic model we choose to believe, and we shall have a lot more to say on these issues in Part III of the book. For the moment, however, it is worth sketching an *ad hoc* answer that will provide a first insight into the linkages between the different national capital markets.

At a casual level, if we take the expected rate of depreciation first, one would guess that operators in foreign currency markets form their own view, or use the services of professional forecasters. Whether arrived at formally (by using the tools of economics, statistics and so on) or informally (by guesswork, casual impressions, rumour or astrology), these predictions are unlikely to be amenable to direct influence by the authorities. There is no way in which a government or central bank can decree a change in agents' expectations. From a policy point of view, they may as well be taken as given, at least in the very short run.

What of the US interest rate? As far as the British authorities are concerned, the level of US interest rates is simply a fact of life, a feature of the environment which they must accept and to which they must accommodate their policy. This is a consequence of the obvious fact that the UK is a

---

[6] For those unfamiliar with this particular piece of jargon, variables endogenous to any relationship are ones that are assumed to be determined by the relationship or model in question. On the other hand, an exogenous variable is one whose value is taken as a datum, because its value is assumed to be determined outside the model, that is, by some other relationship which is beyond the scope of the analysis being undertaken or even, in some cases, beyond the scope of economics altogether.

small economy relative to the USA (notice that the converse is not necessarily true).

   We have reached the conclusion that, viewed from the UK, both of the terms on the right-hand side of Equation 3.4 may be taken as given. It follows automatically that the left-hand side, the domestic UK interest rate, must be given. A small country, like the UK, cannot control its own interest rates. Given the state of expectations, its interest rates are determined on the money markets of New York or, possibly, in the corridors of power in Washington.[7]

3.2   Covered interest rate parity

The process of moving capital around so as to exploit uncovered interest rate differentials, along the lines described in Section 3.1, is often loosely referred to as arbitrage. If we are to be consistent, however, we cannot do the same here. Look back at the definition of arbitrage given in Section 2.1 of Chapter 2 – the crucial words are 'riskless profit'. Although we sidestepped the issue by assuming risk neutrality for purposes of deriving the UIRP condition, there is no avoiding the fact that, in practice, making a deposit in a foreign country involves risk. It is, therefore, an activity more like speculation than arbitrage.

   It so happens that there is one way of eliminating all risk from a transaction like the one dealt with in Section 3.1. To see what is involved, recall first that, for the UK resident, the risk in depositing in the USA originates in the uncertainty surrounding the future exchange rate, S^e. The dollar proceeds of the US strategy only become available for reconversion to sterling on 31 December. As of 1 January, when the decision has to be made, the would-be depositor is forced to hazard a guess as to what that rate will be at the end of the year.

   Look back at the first of the numerical examples (Table 3.2), and ask yourself how much would be yielded by a deposit in the USA if the exchange rate on 31 December actually turned out to be, not £0.60 = $1.00, but rather £0.45 = $1.00. Under those circumstances, even the 1 % higher interest in the USA would be insufficient to compensate for the fall in the relative value of the dollar, and the outcome would be, not only less

---

[7] It is on the basis of considerations such as these that some people in the UK and other European countries charged the USA with keeping world interest rates at what they regarded as damagingly high levels in the 1980s. There is, of course, far more than this to the question of whether world interest rates have been 'too high' in recent years, and if so, why. For the most part, the issue lies beyond the scope of this book. However, the point is raised in the text at this point simply to illustrate the relevance of interest rate parity to questions of national and international economic policy.

attractive than holding a sterling deposit, but an actual loss on reconversion to UK currency. (Of how much?)

Now consider the following remedy: instead of waiting 12 months to reconvert the dollar proceeds of a US deposit to sterling, enter into an agreement with another economic agent to exchange the dollars for pounds in advance. (Remember that the depositor knows at the outset exactly how much US currency he will have for conversion on 31 December, because that depends only on the interest rate on dollars quoted on 1 January). The agreement will of course specify an exchange rate at which the dollars will be converted to pounds in 12 months' time, and that rate will not normally be the same as the exchange rate prevailing on transactions conducted immediately (or 'on the spot'). The following jargon is used in currency markets:

> **The spot (exchange) rate** is the rate figuring in agreements to exchange one currency for another more or less immediately.

In other words, we have until now been dealing with the spot rate, as we always will be, unless we explicitly specify otherwise. On the other hand:

> **The (1-, 3- or 12-month) forward (exchange) rate** is the rate which appears in contracts to exchange one currency for another 1, 3 or 12 months in advance of the actual transaction.

Notice that no currency actually changes hands between the parties to a forward contract at the time it is signed. All that happens is that both parties contract to exchange one currency for another, at the specified forward rate, at some time in the future (the 'maturity date').[8]

---

[8] In reality, things are not quite so simple. For a start, forward contracts are usually conducted through foreign currency dealers, who are specialist intermediaries, in other words who make it their job to match agents who wish to buy a currency forward with those who wish to sell it at the same maturity. Not only will they charge a commission but they will also quote differing rates for buying and selling ('bid' and 'offer' rates). They may also insist on a 'margin' from a would-be buyer of a forward contract, that is, a sum of money 'up front' as a guarantee of the individual's ability to cover any loss on the deal.

As far as the maturity date is concerned there is no reason in principle why there should not exist a market in forward contracts of all maturities – from one day, up to one century. In practice, a high-volume market exists only at maturities of 30 and 90 days, and then only in the major 'hard' currencies.

Similarly, there is no reason in principle why forward contracts should not be traded in any type of goods or services. In practice, explicit forward contracts exist only across a narrow range of mostly financial assets. Nonetheless, implicit forward prices often play a part even in the most mundane transactions. For example, it is not unusual to see items like houses and foreign holidays offered at a 'guaranteed' price to buyers willing to commit themselves immediately to a 'forward' contract.

Note that a forward contract is almost, but not quite the same thing as a futures contract.

Returning to our example, suppose the depositor in Case 1 of Table 3.2 is able to sell the dollar proceeds of his US deposit 12 months in advance, on 1 January. Furthermore, let us suppose that he is able to do so using the exchange rate entered in Table 3.2 as the expected rate, that is, $1.00 = £0.60 (we shall have more to say later about whether the forward rate will in fact be equal to the expected rate). Exactly the same procedure is followed as before, the only difference being that, on 31 December, instead of taking pot luck in exchanging his dollars in the spot market, the depositor is able to enjoy the benefit of the forward contract, which allows the depositor to force the other party to the contract to buy the dollars at the rate agreed at the start of the year.

Put in that way, the advantage of the deal ought to be plain. It is not that the return is any greater than the £1.27 yielded by a spot transaction, because we are assuming the forward rate is exactly the same as the rate the depositor expected to see prevailing in the spot market on 31 December. Rather, the advantage lies in the fact that, using the forward market, the depositor can *guarantee* a return of £1.27. In other words, the transaction can be made completely riskless – the whole deal is 'wrapped up' on 1 January, at a known US interest rate and a known forward rate. In this sense, the investor is 'covered' or insured against the risk in the interest rate arbitrage process.

Notice that, by 'locking in' the exchange rate via the forward market, the depositor is insured against any nasty shocks – but in doing so the chance of benefiting from any pleasant surprises is sacrificed. Not only does a forward purchase serve to hedge against a lower dollar value than anticipated, it also means giving up any additional profit that might have been made.

As far as the market as a whole is concerned, since we are now dealing with riskless transactions (arbitrage in the proper sense of the word) it is even less likely that a gap between the sterling yield on UK and US deposits could persist for any length of time. In other words, this time we *can* conclude that the return from depositing in the USA must be the same as that from depositing in the UK, irrespective of whether potential depositors are risk neutral or not. Thus, the law of one price can legitimately be invoked.

In the same way that we derived Equation 3.1 by assuming the dollars were converted (spot) at the rate expected to prevail on 31 December, S^e, we now allow for them being sold in advance on 1 January at the 12-month forward rate available at that date. For present purposes, where there is no possibility of confusion over the maturity date, let F denote the forward exchange rate (that is, the sterling price of US dollars) prevailing on 1 January for US currency to be 'delivered' on 31 December.

Then, since all other features of the transaction are unchanged from the previous section, we can simply write F in place of S^e in Equation 3.1 to give:

$$(1+r) = (1+r^*)\frac{F}{S} \qquad (3.5)$$

as the precise form of our covered arbitrage condition. Again, we can manipulate the formula to yield a more intelligible relationship by rewriting F/S, as follows:

$$\frac{F}{S} \equiv 1+f \qquad (3.6)$$

where f is defined as follows:

> **The forward premium (discount)** is the proportion by which a country's forward exchange rate exceeds (falls below) its spot rate.

In Case 1 of Table 3.2, for example, if \$1 = £0.60 is the 12-month forward rate prevailing at the start of the year, when at the same time the spot rate is \$1 = £0.50, it follows that there is a forward premium of 20% on dollars (and a forward discount on sterling), because dollars to be delivered in 12 months cost 20% more than dollars to be delivered 'on the spot' so, rewriting Equation 3.6:

$$f \equiv \frac{F}{S} - 1 = \frac{0.60}{0.50} - 1 = 0.2 \qquad (3.7)$$

In general terms, then, we can rewrite our equilibrium condition by following the same steps as in the previous section, this time with f in place of Δs^e:

$$(1+r) = (1+r^*)(1+f) \qquad (3.8)$$
$$= 1+r^* +f +r^*f$$

As before, we would expect r^*f to be of the second order of smallness, so that we end up with:

$$r = r^* +f \qquad (3.9)$$

This is the normal formulation of the **Covered Interest Rate Parity hypothesis** (CIRP), which states that:

> The domestic interest rate must be higher (lower) than the foreign interest rate by an amount equal to the forward discount (premium) on the domestic currency.

3.3 Borrowing and lending

At this point, it is worth pausing for a moment to adopt a slightly different perspective on the arbitrage process discussed in this chapter so far. Let us go back to the example in Table 3.2. The UK and US interest rates are 5% and 6% respectively, and the exchange rate is expected to change from $1 = £0.50 to $1 = £0.60 over the next 12 months. In each of our hypothetical scenarios, the individual was assumed to have a sum of money in pounds (in fact, just £1) available for investment. While this simplification may have helped to make the process easier to understand, it also had the effect of making the power of arbitrage mechanisms appear weaker than it actually is.

Suppose our hypothetical investor had no money available for deposit either in the UK or USA. Does this rule out the possibility of profiting from arbitrage? Plainly, no. As long as the investor can borrow pounds, he can exploit any opportunities offered by deviations from interest rate parity. To see how, go back to the numerical example illustrated in Table 3.2, and rework the calculations on the assumption that the investor borrows £1 on 1 January.

The result is that making a deposit in the USA generates a profit of £0.22 per £1 borrowed, whereas the UK deposit simply breaks even (remember we are ignoring transaction costs both for borrowing and lending and for currency conversion). This outcome should come as no surprise. It is clearly no more than would have been expected from the computations in Table 3.2.

For present purposes, however, it is useful to view the process in terms of the investor's asset position in each currency, which is precisely what has been presented in Table 3.5.

As far as the first step is concerned, in borrowing pounds the investor deliberately incurs a liability in sterling. Currency market jargon is helpful here:

> An investor who has **a liability (an asset)** denominated in a specific currency is said to have **a short (long) position** in that currency.

So the investor starts by taking a short position in sterling.

Now as far as the UK strategy is concerned, depositing the proceeds of the loan creates an asset denominated in pounds too, that is, a long position in sterling of exactly £1. The *net* effect is to leave the investor with a balanced position in pounds. Moreover, this net zero balance is maintained throughout the year, as the value of the long position increases with the accumulating interest on the deposit and the size of the debt simultaneously rises at the same rate.

By contrast, the US strategy involves converting the £1 to dollars and depositing it in the USA, thus creating a long position in dollars. Now

Table 3.5 Uncovered interest rate arbitrage with borrowing.

	UK strategy		US strategy	
	Action	Yield	Action	Yield
1 January				
12 month interest rate		5%		6%
	Borrow	£1.00	Borrow	£1.00
Position taken	short sterling (£1.00)		short sterling (£1.00)	
			Buy $ @ £0.50 each:	$2.00
	Place on deposit: i.e. lend	£1.00	Place on deposit: i.e. lend	$2.00
Position taken	long sterling (£1.00)		long dollars ($2.00)	
Net position during year	**nil** **(long – short = 0)**		**(short £1.00)** (long $2.00)	
31 December				
	Liquidate deposit:	£1.05	Liquidate deposit:	$2.12
			Convert back to £ *sell* $ @ £0.60 each:	£1.27
	Repay loan:	£1.05	Repay loan:	£1.05
Net profit		**£0.00**		**£0.22**

while it is true that initially, on 1 January, the two positions offset each other – the investor's long position in dollars and short in sterling are both valued at exactly £1 – the situation of exact balance will not be sustained. If the dollar weakens in February, say, the value of the investor's dollar holding will decline while the sterling debt increases.

In other words, the risk associated with the uncovered arbitrage transaction arises from changes in the net position as exchange rate fluctuations alter the value of the position in the two currencies. The problem never arises in the case of the UK strategy because the two positions – borrowing and lending, short and long in pounds – are perfectly matched. Any change in the value of the pound will have offsetting effects on the value of the short and long positions respectively.

Here, we are assuming the exchange rate ends the year at $1 = £0.60, which means the value of the long position in dollars appreciates to £1.27 by the time it is liquidated, while the short position has risen as a result of accumulated interest on the borrowing to only £1.05, leaving a net profit of £0.22.

Before going on to look at covered interest rate parity from this perspective, there are a number of lessons to be drawn from the computations in Table 3.5:

(1) It pays to borrow (be short in) a depreciating currency and lend (be long in) an appreciating currency.[9]

(2) Since speculation can be achieved by an agent who actually owns no sterling, UIRP does not need to rely on the existence of UK depositors with international perspectives and an inexhaustible supply of funds. In fact, the representative investor/arbitrageur need be neither a UK nor a US resident. Typically, in fact, the agent in question will be a multinational financial institution based in London or New York or one of the major currency trading centres of Continental Europe or the Pacific Basin.

(3) Currency risk arises whenever an investor's net position in a currency is non-zero. When a long position is matched by an equal and opposite short position in the same currency, the investor is said to have a (fully) hedged or covered position in the currency.

Consider hedging the arbitrage in the present example. We saw in the last section that this can be achieved by the simple expedient of selling the dollar proceeds of the US deposit on the forward market on 1 January. The impact on the investor's asset position is traced out in Table 3.6.

The otherwise unbalanced position at the start of the year which introduced the element of risk into the US strategy disappears, because the investor who covers in the forward market has zero net exposure throughout the year. This outcome is achieved as a result of the fact that the forward contract can be viewed as involving two simultaneous transactions: a claim against the counterparty to collect pounds (hence, a long position in sterling) and a commitment to deliver dollars (a short position in dollars). Together, the two transactions undertaken in signing the forward contract offset precisely the initial short position in pounds and long in dollars that arose when the investor borrowed sterling to deposit in the USA. We can therefore add the following conclusions to those we have already deduced in this section:

---

[9] This obvious point applies not only to currencies. For example, where they can, oil companies borrow dollars and promise to repay lenders in crude oil when they expect the (dollar price of) oil to fall on world markets. Similarly, stock market traders aim to be long in shares which rise in price and short in those which fall. They therefore hope to own and/ or lend shares about which they feel bullish and borrow those about which they feel bearish.

Table 3.6   Covered interest rate arbitrage with borrowing.

	UK strategy		US strategy	
	Action	Yield	Action	Yield
1 January				
12 month interest rate		5%		6%
	Borrow	£1.00	Borrow	£1.00
Position taken	short sterling (£1.00)		short sterling (£1.00)	
			Buy $ @ £0.50 each:	$2.00
	Place on deposit: i.e. lend	£1.00	Place on deposit: i.e. lend	$2.00
Position taken	long sterling (£1.00)		long dollars ($2.00)	
			sell $/buy £ forward @ $1.00 = £0.60	$0.60
Position taken			long sterling (£1.00) short dollars ($2.00)	
Net position during year	**nil** (long – short = 0)		**nil** (long – short = 0)	
31 December				
	Liquidate deposit:	£1.05	Liquidate deposit:	$2.12
			sell $ @ £0.60 each:	£1.27
	Repay loan:	£1.05	Repay loan:	£1.05
Net profit		**£0.00**		**£0.22**

A forward sale of *x* dollars against *y* pounds (a forward purchase of *y* pounds with *x* dollars) is equivalent to lending (being long in) the present value of *y* pounds and borrowing (being short in) the present value of *x* dollars.[10]

Viewed from this point of view, the CIRP relationship between spot and forward exchange rates and interest rates is less surprising. The

---

[10] The present value of a cashflow of, say, $5000 arising 12 months from now is that sum which, if deposited immediately, will yield just $5000 with accumulated interest at the end of the year. In other words, it is the value of a future sum of money in terms of its worth at the present time, allowing for the fact that wealth in the future is of less use than wealth here and now and must therefore be discounted to an extent measured by the appropriate interest rate. For present purposes, the interest rate used should be the rate on 12 month deposits in the currency in question, that is, US dollars.

commitment to exchanging future claims (borrowing and lending) in the two currencies via the forward market must result in the same pay-off as exchanging current claims in the spot market. Hence, any difference in the exchange rate at which the two transactions occur must reflect differences in the interest rates on the two currencies.

Putting the matter in hedging terms, the proceeds of the dollar deposit could be hedged without recourse to the forward market by borrowing $2 at the start of the year, converting to sterling on the spot and leaving the £1 on deposit for 12 months. At the end of December, the £1 will have grown to £1.05 – just enough to repay the initial loan – and the $2 borrowing on which $2.12 will be owed can be repaid from the original deposit in the USA.

Clearly, however, what is being described here involves no more than putting the original borrowing/lending mix into reverse, thereby *unwinding* the original position so as to eliminate the risk. It so happens the type of exchange of claims described here is very common in currency markets, under the following guise:

> **A (plain) currency swap deal** involves two parties in the exchange of
> principal and interest payments on a loan in one currency for principal
> and interest payments in another currency.[11]

3.4   Covered interest rate parity – the facts

In the last three sections, the covered and uncovered interest rate parity conditions were derived by identical routes, using the same examples modified very slightly. In formal terms, the results were, not surprisingly, very similar, as you can see from Equations 3.4 and 3.9. However convenient it may be to approach the two relationships in parallel, as we have done here, it is important to emphasize the differences as well as the similarities between covered and uncovered parity. In this section, we shall compare them and, in the process, have a first encounter with the important concept of market efficiency.

The first thing to notice is that the covered parity condition is unlike most of the relationships in elementary economics, in so far as it relies on very few assumptions about the behaviour or tastes of the agents operating in the market. We do not require that agents maximize utility, we make no assumptions about how they form expectations and, as already noted, since the transactions involved are riskless, we need say nothing about their attitude to risk. All that is required for covered interest rate parity to hold

---

[11]   There are in practice a number of other wrinkles in the details of currency swaps. For example, swaps typically commit the two parties (usually large companies or financial institutions) to exchange interest payments over a number of years. (See the references in the Reading Guide.)

is that three rather weak (and to some extent overlapping) conditions apply.

First, there must be sufficient speculation funds available – in other words, one or more potential arbitrageurs with access to enough free resources to drive the respective rates into equilibrium. By 'free', we mean not only liquid, in the normal 'domestic' sense of the term, but also unconstrained by restrictions on international capital movements.

Second, we need the foreign exchange markets, spot or forward, to be organized, with well-defined and well-publicized rates freely available to a group of informed traders who are committed to exploiting any profit opportunities that crop up. In fact, these conditions are almost certainly fulfilled in the markets for the main hard currencies, where a number of financial institutions and specialist foreign exchange traders, as well as the Treasury departments of multinational companies make it their business to watch for profit opportunities that appear temporarily on the banks of visual display units in their trading rooms.[12]

Third, we need it to be true that transaction costs are low enough to be negligible. Otherwise, the possibility arises that rates may deviate from CIRP to the full extent of trading costs. Again there is every reason to suppose that, in this type of highly competitive environment, dealing costs will be extremely small, particularly for the large, professional participants responsible for most of the trading – which is why we have ignored them so far in our theoretical treatment.

Nonetheless, if we wish to proceed to examine the evidence on interest rate parity, we cannot continue to neglect the issue of transaction costs altogether. In fact, as far as covered interest rate parity is concerned, most researchers interpret the question to be investigated as follows: has the gap between international interest rate differentials and the respective forward premium been within the bounds one would expect to find, given the size of dealing costs?

In other words, where (as is usually the case) Equation 3.5 does not hold precisely, is the difference between the left and right hand sides of the equation too small to represent an unexploited profit opportunity, after allowing for transaction costs? In formal terms, the question is whether the following inequality is satisfied:

$$|(1 + r) - (1 + r^*)\frac{F}{S}| < c \qquad\qquad \textbf{(3.10)}$$

where c is the cost of carrying out the transaction, and the left-hand side is the absolute value (that is, ignoring the sign) of the gap between UK and US interest rates, adjusted for the forward premium.

---

[12] In particular, financial markets are nowadays characterized by a considerable volume of so-called 'program trading', that is, trading triggered automatically by computers programmed to generate buy or sell orders whenever an arbitrage relationship like Equation 3.9 is violated.

The key question, then, relates to the scale of the relevant dealing costs. Estimating costs might appear to be a simple task. In practice, there are a number of complications. For example, do we restrict our attention to arbitrage using 'own' (that is, unborrowed) funds, or do we also consider the transaction costs of borrowing in the UK in order to lend in the USA, when US interest rates are above their forward parity level?[13]

Fortunately, differences over the measurement of transaction costs have not prevented a fair measure of agreement emerging on this issue. In a major study of the subject, Levich (1979) concluded that:

> 'Overall, the evidence supports the view that . . . there are few unexploited opportunities for risk-free profit in covered interest arbitrage.' (p. 49)

The evidence to which Levich refers relates to the years 1962 to 1975, a period of broadly fixed exchange rates, and certainly very different from the environment of the 1980s and 1990s. If anything, the progressive liberalization of international financial markets in recent years is likely to have tied interest rates even more closely together. Indeed, in cases where interest rates have deviated from CIRP during the 1960s and 1970s, there seems every reason to suppose the cause to have been exchange controls, actual or threatened.[14]

3.5 Efficient markets – a first encounter

If CIRP seems to fit the facts reasonably closely, what of UIRP? It might appear that we can proceed directly to an examination of the evidence in support of this condition too. Unfortunately, there is an immediate obstacle to this approach. Look back at Equation 3.4 and ask yourself the question: are all the variables observable? The answer is plainly no. The expected rate of depreciation is certainly not an observable variable – expectations are not easily quantified, and they are in any case inherently subjective.

This is not to say there are no assumptions one could make about the nature of market expectations – there are any number of superficially plausible guesses one might make about how agents forecast exchange rate movements. For example, one might formulate a hypothesis that the

---

[13] See Section 3.3 of this chapter. A related question concerns which of the alternative routes arbitrageurs choose to take, and, in particular, whether they operate on the spot or forward markets. See Deardorff (1979) for a discussion of these and related issues.

[14] See Aliber (1973). It is nonetheless surprising to see that the Bank of England was still reporting a covered differential between interest rates on Eurodollar and UK local authority deposits of up to one quarter of 1 %, and even higher for interbank sterling deposits. The transaction costs on large deposits must surely be far smaller than this.

market always expects the same rate of depreciation in any period as it experienced in the previous period. Or, by contrast, one might postulate that it always expects any change in the rate to be reversed in the next trading session, or that it expects an outcome which is some kind of moving average of the outcomes for the last three days, or five days, or three months, or instead of any of these mechanistic rules, one might hypothesize that, as a (very) rough approximation, the market always guesses correctly what the actual change in the exchange rate will be.

Any assumption that allows us to substitute an observable, quantifiable data series for the term s^e in Equation 3.4 will serve to extricate us from the impasse of not being able to test the UIRP condition; this is subject to one major drawback, however, which we shall henceforth refer to as the joint hypothesis problem. To understand the nature of the difficulty, consider a simple example. Suppose we made the rough-and-ready assumption that the market always expects the existing exchange rate to stay unchanged over the next period, in other words assume (*temporarily*) that $s^e = 0$. Looking back at the UIRP condition, Equation 3.4, we would have in that case:

$$r = r^* \tag{3.11}$$

If, relying on this assumption, we then examined the two interest rate series and found there to be significant deviations between the UK and US rates, could we then conclude that UIRP was not supported by the facts? Obviously not – the failure of the data to accord with Equation 3.11 could be explained *either* by the fact that UIRP does not hold *or* that our assumption about how market expectations are formed is at fault, *or both*. In other words, we would be simultaneously testing a theory about the relationship between observable variables (interest rates) and a theory about how the market arrives at its predictions or expectations. That is, we would be testing a joint hypothesis.

For this reason, we shall defer any attempt to consider how well the facts accord with uncovered parity until Chapters 11 and 12, by which stage we shall be in a position to take fuller account of expectations, as well as of the determination of the risk premium. For the moment, it is worth simply taking note of the fact that we have made our first encounter with the ubiquitous problem of market expectations.

There is an important link between uncovered and covered interest parity, and it is one which involves the concept of market efficiency. Recall that, in introducing the idea of hedging in the forward market in Section 3.2, the assumption was made that the forward rate on 1 January was equal to the spot rate expected to prevail on 31 December. In order to illustrate what was meant by covered arbitrage, some value for the forward rate had to be assumed, and the expected spot rate was certainly convenient, since it allowed us to use the same numerical examples in both cases.

Look back at the formal analysis in Equations 3.5 to 3.8. Nothing there required us to have $f = s^e$ (or $F = S^e$). Covered interest parity could therefore still apply, even if we did not have the forward rate equal to the expected spot rate.

Nonetheless, it is obvious from comparing Equations 3.4 and 3.9 that the condition $f = s^e$ is far from arbitrary. In fact, since Equations 3.4 and 3.9 together imply that $f = s^e$, it is obvious that covered and uncovered parity cannot *both* apply unless we also have equality between the forward rate and the expected spot rate. Putting the matter differently, as long as we continue to assume risk neutrality, if the forward rate is not equal to the expected spot rate, then either covered or uncovered parity has broken down, or both.

Now consider for a moment the situation of an individual market agent who, on 1 January, confidently expects the spot rate at the end of the year to be at a level different from the one currently obtaining for forward foreign currency. Suppose, for example, that the 12 month forward rate is $1.00 = £0.50, and he is quite convinced that the rate at the end of the year will be $1.00 = £0.60.

If he is confident in his judgement, he will see himself as having the opportunity to profit by a simple transaction in the forward market. All he need do is 'buy dollars forward', in other words sign a contract to buy dollars at the end of the year at the current forward price of £0.50 each, which he is so convinced will seem a bargain price on 31 December. If he is correct in his forecast, then 12 months later, when he fulfills his promise under the terms of the forward contract to buy the dollars at £0.50 each,[15] he will be in a position to resell them immediately at the end of year price prevailing in the spot market, £0.60 each – a profit of £0.10, or 20% per dollar bought.[16]

Of course, this strategy is risky, so if the investor is not risk neutral, he will require a risk premium to persuade him to undertake the transaction, and £0.10 per dollar may not be sufficient. However, if we maintain the fiction that investors are risk neutral, we can say that anyone who expects the spot exchange rate at some future period to be different from the forward rate currently quoted for that period can profit by 'backing his judgement', that is, by speculating.

If we can generalize the argument to the market as a whole, or in other words, if we can treat the market as if it were a single individual,

---

[15] Notice that he cannot back out of the deal. Having taken on the forward contract at the start of the year he has no choice but to buy the dollars at the specified price even if, in the event, he turns out to have guessed wrongly (say, if the pound appreciates to $1.00 = £0.40 by 31 December). This is precisely the difference between a forward contract and an option. The advantage of buying an option rather than a forward contract is that it confers the right (the 'option') to deal at the pre-specified price, without any obligation.

[16] In fact, the usual contract size is £25,000.

then it follows that equilibrium will entail a forward rate equal to the consensus view of the future spot rate. Otherwise, there will be a net excess demand or supply of forward exchange, which will itself tend to move the rate towards its equilibrium level. We shall henceforth make use of the following definition to describe this situation:

> **Unbiasedness** applies when the (3-, 6- or 12-) month forward rate is equal to the spot rate that the market expects to see prevailing when the contract in question matures.[17]

What we are talking about here is a particular example of a very general concept indeed: market efficiency.[18] For the moment, we shall take the opportunity to introduce the following definition:

> **Efficient markets** are ones where prices fully reflect all the available information. There are, therefore, no unexploited opportunities for profit.

The definition seems a little vague, and, in a sense, so it should. What are we to understand by 'fully reflect' all information? That depends on the model of the market in question, and its properties. By contrast, unbiasedness is a very clearly defined state, and is in that sense a special case of market efficiency. Unbiasedness implicitly assumes a particular market model, one where the following conditions apply:

(1) There are an adequate number of well-funded and well-informed agents in the currency markets, with broadly similar views about likely future developments.[19] Market prices are well-defined.

(2) There are no barriers to trade in the markets (that is, no exchange controls) and no costs to dealing (no transaction costs).

(3) Investors are risk neutral.

---

[17] This is not quite complete as a definition of unbiasedness. It also ought to be the case that market expectations are, on average, correct predictions of the future spot rate. However, we defer consideration of these questions until Chapter 11.

[18] The notion of market efficiency was originally developed by researchers in finance, particularly Eugene Fama. It has become so well established that it nowadays crops up quite frequently in stock-market commentary in the newspapers. As you will have already noticed it forms the subject matter of Chapter 11.

[19] The vagueness is again intentional. It can be shown that, under certain circumstances, we do not need all market operators to share exactly the same view of the future exchange rate. We can also have some investors better informed than others. Again, these issues are beyond the scope of the discussion at this point.

■ Summary

- If we consider the typical investor faced with the choice between holding a dollar deposit in America or a deposit in pounds in Britain, what will concern him will be the difference between UK and US interest rates, after allowing for any expected change in the exchange rate over the period of the deposit – the **uncovered interest differential**.

- If investors are *risk neutral*, and all share broadly the same expectations, equilibrium will require that the uncovered differential be zero: that is, that the gap between UK and US interest rates be *just equal* to the consensus view of the likely change in the exchange rate over the relevant time period (uncovered interest rate parity). Otherwise funds will flood out of one of the countries and into the other.

- Since a British investor, for example, can eliminate the currency risk involved in depositing in the USA by the device of contracting to sell the dollar proceeds on the forward market, it follows that riskless profits will accrue to international interest rate arbitrageurs *unless* covered interest rate parity is obtained. In other words, the law of one price requires that, in equilibrium, the gap between UK and US interest rates be *just equal* to the difference between the forward and spot exchange rates at the date when the decision is taken (the forward premium or discount).

- If both covered and uncovered parity holds it follows that the forward rate must be equal to the market's expectation of the future spot rate. It is possible to list a number of superficially plausible assumptions which would imply just this proposition, even without recourse to interest rate parity conditions.

READING GUIDE

On the theory of covered interest rate parity, the classic work is Tsiang (1959). More recently, influential work has been that of Aliber (1973), Frenkel and Levich (1975) and Levich (1979). See also Deardorff (1979).
    Taylor (1987) on CIRP is meticulous, but still easy to read.
    For references on UIRP see Chapter 11.

4

Open Economy
Macroeconomics

■ Introduction

So far in this part of the book, we have been dealing with international linkages between macroeconomic variables. As such, we have looked at these relationships in isolation – the so-called partial equilibrium approach. In this chapter, we step back from the fine detail to consider the overall context within which open economy relationships operate to determine the exchange rate.

The general equilibrium model here will look familiar to most readers, since it is simply an extension of the closed economy aggregate supply and demand framework found in most modern undergraduate textbooks. Nonetheless, an understanding of this apparatus is essential to what follows in Chapters 5, 6 and 7, when it will be used to present three important models of exchange rate determination.

We start in Section 4.1 with an introduction to the open economy version of the *IS–LM* model of aggregate demand. It will be seen that, as far as the *IS* curve is concerned, allowing for the openness of the economy involves introducing an additional shift variable, the real exchange rate. The *LM* curve needs no modification at all to accommodate a floating exchange rate. With a fixed exchange rate, however, allowance needs to be made for the endogeneity of the money stock, a task which is undertaken in Sections 4.2.2 and 4.2.3.

The remainder of the chapter is concerned with the aggregate supply curve, in its classical and Keynesian forms. It is assumed here that openness makes no difference to the supply side of the economy model,[1] so the analysis is identical to that found in macroeconomics texts.

4.1   The *IS–LM* model of aggregate demand

4.1.1   The *IS* curve

In an open economy, the national income identity can be written as follows:

$$y \equiv C + I + G + B \tag{4.1}$$

where y is (real) national income, C and I are expenditure on consumption and investment, respectively, G is net government purchases of goods and services, and B is the surplus on the current account of the balance of payments:

$$B \equiv exports - imports \tag{4.2}$$

that is, the excess of the country's exports over its imports.

If we subtract C, I and B from both sides of Equation 4.1, we have:

$$Savings - I - B \equiv G \tag{4.3}$$

where we have made use of the fact that savings are, by definition, income less consumption.

Now Equation 4.3 is simply an accounting relationship: as it stands it can tell us nothing about what determines the level of aggregate demand. In order to reach any conclusions about the determination of aggregate demand, we must make some assumptions about what factors actually impinge on the components of aggregate demand.

Start with saving which, for simplicity's sake, we can identify with the unspent income of the household sector.[2] What kind of elements are likely to have the most significant impact on the household's savings decision? As far as the individual household is concerned, it seems obvious

---

[1] See the Reading Guide for references to research on the implications of openness for aggregate supply.

[2] In reality the corporate sector saves by not distributing profits. We shall ignore this fact, without running any risk of it affecting our conclusions.

that the higher its income, other things being equal, the more it will save.[3] Aggregating households, then, total private sector saving is likely to depend positively on the (planned) level of economic activity.

However, that is not all. At any given level of income, it seems probable that a rise in the level of interest rates in the economy will stimulate savings. This is likely because, when interest rates are high, the incentive to save (or refrain from consuming) is great, and vice versa when interest rates are low. In fact, the interest rate can be viewed as the premium set by society on present relative to future consumption. At a zero interest rate, one might expect saving to drop to zero.

Investment spending by the corporate sector[4] will depend on a comparison of the cost of funds for the purchase of equipment and so on with the profits to be expected from the investment. Now although in practice this calculation is bound to be hedged in with uncertainties surrounding the prospective cash flows to investment projects, there is one statement that can be made with reasonable confidence: other things being equal, the higher the interest rate in the economy, the greater the cost of capital, and hence the less likely it is that any given prospective investment will appear profitable to the decision maker. In general, therefore, aggregate investment will vary inversely with the interest rate.

Notice we have concluded that savings will increase as interest rates rise, while investment falls, so that the difference (savings less investment) will be *positively related* to interest rates.

Government spending will be taken as exogenously given – determined outside the model by factors (political, social, technological and so on) beyond the scope of a mere economist. That is not to say we assume it never changes. On the contrary, we shall be very much concerned with analysing the effect of a change in fiscal policy. We are only saying that we shall not be concerned with questions of *why* or *how* fiscal expenditure changes.

Finally, but most important of all for present purposes, we come to the current account of the balance of payments. What are likely to be the main influences here? Among the many factors which affect the demand by UK residents for other countries' products and, conversely, the demand by foreigners for goods from Britain, there is almost certain to be one overriding consideration: the competitiveness of domestic relative to foreign output.

In a way, the issue is one which has already been covered in Chapter 2, where the PPP hypothesis was discussed, compared with the facts and

---

[3] Notice, it is not being claimed that, as a household's income rises, it will actually save a higher proportion of its income, though that may also be a reasonable conjecture. All that is being asserted here is that its savings will be greater in absolute terms the higher its income.

[4] For simplicity, we assume investment is an activity exclusive to firms which means ignoring investment by other sectors of the economy.

appeared to fail. It was concluded there that, whether because of deficiencies in the way that price indices are calculated or because different countries produce different goods or because of the failure of the law of one price, PPP did not apply other than in the very long run. At the same time, it was also argued that it would be grossly implausible to go to the opposite extreme of supposing trade volumes to be completely unaffected by relative prices.

Consider a compromise to take account of the obvious fact that, invariably, the composition of one country's exports differs from that of another, so that country A's exports are only an imperfect substitute for those of country B. For example, the UK exports very little in the way of agricultural products, whereas a significant proportion of US exports consist of wheat, rice, soya beans, fruit and so on and thus cannot be said to compete with UK output. Moreover, as was pointed out in Chapter 2, even where similar types of good are concerned, product differentiation means that direct, head-on competition in international trade is quite rare: a *Cadillac* is by no means a perfect substitute for a *Jaguar*, nor Bourbon for Scotch. Even where international trade in services is concerned, *Dallas* is not the same soap opera as *Coronation Street*, nor Disneyworld the same kind of attraction as Tower Bridge.

The conclusion reached in Chapter 2 was that indirect international competition between imperfect substitutes would mean that purchasing power parity would not necessarily be obtained as an equality at all times, but that, instead, *there would be an equilibrium price ratio fixed by the market at any moment*. In other words, there is an equilibrium relationship between the price of Bourbon and the price of Scotch, which is not necessarily one of equality. It might be, for example, that one bottle of Scotch equals one and a half bottles of Bourbon. If the price of Scotch were to rise to double that of Bourbon, consumers in both countries would switch in increasing numbers to Bourbon.

What this implies for price levels in general is that it is relative competitiveness, that is, **the real exchange rate**:

$$Q \equiv \frac{SP^*}{P}$$

which determines the state of a country's current account. Recall that the numerator of Q is the price of foreign (that is, US)-produced goods, measured in pounds. The greater is Q, therefore, the more competitive is domestic output. It follows that, *at higher levels of Q, the current account surplus is likely to be greater (or the deficit smaller) than at low levels*.

There is one other macroeconomic factor likely to influence the current account balance. Just as consumption of domestically produced goods and services rises with national income, the same is bound to be true of expenditure on imports, at a rate determined by the country's *marginal propensity to import*. The higher the income, the smaller is likely to be the surplus (or greater the deficit) on external trade, *other things being equal* – in other words, at any given real exchange rate. Notice that symmetry requires *our* (UK) exports to be greater when *their* (US) national income is higher, so that our external balance depends on the level of economic activity in the USA – which is one of the major channels through which booms and slumps spread from one country to its trading partners. However, since US national income is very much exogenous to a model of the UK economy, we ignore this relationship here.

We now look back at Equation 4.3, and incorporate our conclusions about how the components of aggregate demand are determined. To keep the analysis simple, suppose the relationship takes the following simple form:

$$by + zr - hQ = G_0 \qquad (4.4)$$

where b, z and h are behavioural parameters, the coefficients of the 'unknowns' in the equation, and are all positive. The first term on the left-hand side summarizes the dependence of savings and imports on the level of economic activity, the second incorporates the positive relationship between interest rates and the private sector's saving net of its investment and the third represents the current account as a function of the real exchange rate. On the right-hand side is the exogenous policy variable, G, fixed initially at the level G_0.

Now Equation 4.4 represents the equilibrium condition in the goods market. In other words, it shows the relationship that must hold between the three variables, y, r and Q, for there to be no excess demand for goods and services.

We shall proceed by taking a given value of Q, say Q_0, allowing us to rewrite the equation as follows:

$$by + zr = G_0 + hQ_0 \qquad (4.5)$$

which reduces it to a relationship between y and r, for the given values of G and Q on the right-hand side.

Obviously, there are an infinite number of possible combinations of y and r that satisfy Equation 4.5. Consider plotting them on a graph, with r on the vertical axis and y on the horizontal.

Start by picking any arbitrary value for the interest rate, say r_0 (Figure 4.1), and ask yourself the question: at that level of the interest rate, what would have to be the level of national income, if we were to have equilibrium in the product market? The answer is, of course, given by the value of y that solves Equation 4.5, when r takes the value r_0. If that value is y_0, then the combination (r_0, y_0) at the point A in Figure 4.1 is the first point we have found on the curve we set out to plot. In other words, one possible solution of Equation 4.5 is given by:

$$by_0 + zr_0 = G_0 + hQ_0 \qquad (4.5a)$$

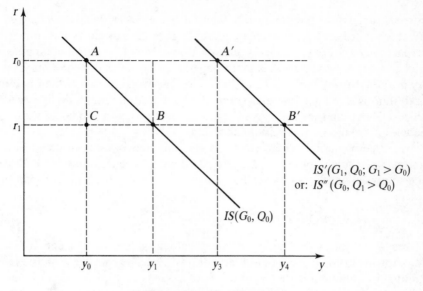

Figure 4.1 The *IS* curve.

To generate more points on the curve, we simply repeat the process, starting from a different interest rate, say r_1, lower than r_0. Now, at r_1, the term zr_1 will be smaller (remember that z is positive, as are all the parameters) so, at the previous value of y (that is, y_0), the left side of Equation 4.5 will be smaller than before, and hence smaller than the right-hand side. In terms of the economics, at the lower interest rate the volume of saving will be smaller and the volume of investment spending greater than at A. Therefore, since A was an equilibrium, with saving net of investment just sufficient to finance the given deficits in the public and external trade sectors of the economy (as in Equation 4.3), net saving must be inadequate at the point C. In other words, there must be an excess demand for goods and services. The crucial point is that the *additional savings will only be forthcoming if the level of national income is greater than y_0, say, y_1.* B will be the next point on our locus of solutions to Equation 4.5 if it happens to be the case that by_1 is just great enough to offset the impact of the lower value of zr (that is, zr_1), so as to leave the left-hand side unchanged. In that case, y_1 will be the level of economic activity which stimulates a flow of savings sufficient to offset the otherwise reduced level of net saving associated with the lower interest rate so that Equation 4.5 is satisfied at point B by:

$$by_1 + zr_1 = G_0 + hQ_0 \tag{4.5b}$$

We see from this argument that the curve we are plotting, which is universally known as the *IS* curve, will be downward sloping, always associating lower levels of the interest rate with higher levels of y.

Note, however, the exercise we have just undertaken involved seeking solutions of Equation 4.5, for a *given value* of the right-hand side of the equation, $G_0 + hQ_0$. For this reason, we have taken care to label the *IS* curve with the values of G and Q to which it relates. Obviously, an increase in net government spending, G, would make this term larger. So also would a rise in the real exchange rate, Q (that is, a real devaluation) since, as we have already seen, h will be positive, reflecting the fact that the UK current account will have a larger surplus (or smaller deficit) the more competitive are British prices relative to those of the USA. Conversely, a lower value of Q will reduce the right-hand side of Equation 4.5, by making UK output less competitive.

Now consider the effect of an increase in the right-hand side of Equation 4.5 on the solution values for r and y. For example, go back to the interest rate r_0 and repeat the question: what would have to be the value of y if we were to have equilibrium in the product market at this interest rate, now that the right-hand side of Equation 4.5 has increased? With a larger right-hand side, the left-hand side of the equation will need to be greater than before. In other words, where previously we saw that y_0 was the answer to our question, making the left-hand side into $by_0 + zr_0$, we must now have a greater value of y, say y_3. Similarly, when the interest rate is at the lower level, r_1, equilibrium now requires y_4 instead of y_1.

The logic of these conclusions is easy to follow. The right-hand side of Equation 4.5 is the sum of the public sector deficit and the foreign sector surplus. This represents the total finance required out of net saving by the domestic private sector. An increase in that requirement can only be satisfied by a change in y and/or r that serves to increase net savings in the economy. The change could be a *rise* in y, stimulating greater saving by households, or a *rise* in r, which would have the same effect but which would also cause a fall in investment by the corporate sector, or a rise in both.

We conclude that the *IS* curve will shift to the right whenever there is any change which increases the right-hand side of Equation 4.5, whether a rise in net government spending, G, or an improvement in UK competitiveness (increase in Q).

Before proceeding, we summarize our conclusions about the open economy *IS* curve.

(1) The (open economy) *IS* curve is a downward-sloping line joining all combinations of the interest rate and the level of income, such that the flow of net savings is sufficient to cover the total financing requirements of the public and foreign sectors.

(2) It is drawn for given values of net government spending, G, and the real exchange rate, Q. Any increase in either G or Q or both will shift the *IS* curve outwards.

4.1.2   The money market

We now turn to a consideration of the conditions necessary for equilibrium in the money market.

Before we go ahead, however, there is an important question to be settled: what do economists mean by the term 'money'?

The problem arises from the fact that 'money' is another of those words like 'demand', 'supply', 'scarce' and a number of others which are used both by economists to mean something very precise and by non-economists to refer vaguely to something rather imprecise. Readers who are unfamiliar with the distinction will find it difficult to understand what is meant by concepts like the 'demand for money', because in layman's terms money is often just a synonym for wealth or even, on occasion, for income.

From now on, we shall restrict ourselves to using the word 'money' in the way that economists do:

> **Money** refers to the asset or assets which are commonly used as a means of payment.

In other words, money is the name given to the assets used to finance transactions such as to pay for goods and services, to discharge debts and to make loans.

There are a number of things to notice about this definition. In the first place, nothing has been said about which assets actually *are* used as a means of payment, for the simple reason that this will vary from country to country and from one period to another. In medieval Europe for example, gold and silver were the only widely-accepted means of payment. Nowadays, at least in the industrialized countries, transactions are conducted using either coins or banknotes or, most frequently, by cheque or electronic funds transferred directly between bank accounts.[5] In the latter case it is the actual bank deposits which serve as the means of payment.

Notice also that this definition does not exclude the possibility that money assets may have other important properties, in addition to their usefulness as means of payment. Typically, money will also serve, to some extent at least, as a store of value, particularly in situations where short-

---

[5] It should be noted that, even in industrial countries, there can arise situations where the normal means of payment are no longer universally accepted, either as a result of bank failures or, more frequently, as a result of a lack of confidence in the internal or external purchasing power of the currency. In such circumstances, the spontaneous response may be to return to a commodity money (cigarettes, gold, silver and so on), as in the German hyperinflation of 1923 or, in some cases, to adopt a foreign currency as an unofficial means of payment (for example, Israel in the early 1980s). The latter phenomenon is known in the literature as 'currency substitution', and its implications will be examined later in Chapter 9.

term considerations are paramount. However, this feature of money is, of course, one it shares with all other assets (this is precisely what we mean by the word 'asset') so it can hardly be used to distinguish money from non-money assets. In fact, money is a small part of total wealth, both for typical individuals and for the economy as a whole.

In the context of wealth in general, it is not only the case that money has, to some extent at least, the same property as other assets, that is, its usefulness as a store of value. The opposite is also true: other assets may to a greater or lesser degree share the essential characteristic of monetary assets, functioning as a means of payment. Obviously, some assets (for example, real estate, capital equipment and so on) are virtually useless for conducting transactions. On the other hand, many short-term financial assets other than bank current account deposits are so easily realized, so 'liquid', as to be strong candidates for inclusion in the definition of money, for example, deposits in building societies (Savings and Loan associations in the USA), and time deposits in banks.

Not surprisingly, a number of different operational definitions can be and are used in practice: the narrowest, known as $M0$ or the monetary base is currency in circulation, $M1$ which is simply $M0$ plus demand deposits and broader still, $M3$ which includes time deposits.[6] How far one should stretch the definition of money to embrace near-money assets is essentially an empirical question, and not one that is directly relevant to the subject of exchange rate determination. Nonetheless, in so far as the reader may, on occasion, find it a help in understanding what follows, it is worth specifying more or less arbitrarily a particular measure of the money stock. That being the case, it is suggested that all statements in this book about the demand for or supply of money be interpreted as relating to the total of currency in circulation plus demand deposits ($M1$ in the official statistics) unless otherwise specified.

The demand for money

Perhaps no subject in macroeconomics has received as much attention from researchers as the demand for money, so what follows can only be a greatly simplified overview of this vast literature. (See the Reading Guide for further references.)

Start with the following fundamental (and deceptively simple) question: why do people hold money? Why not hold all one's wealth in the form

---

[6] For the sake of simplicity the definitions given here ignore a number of the less important financial instruments. For a detailed description of how these aggregates are computed in the UK, where $M4$ and $M5$ money supply definitions have recently been introduced, see the *Bank of England Quarterly Bulletin*, May 1987.

of other, non-money assets? Remember that currency earns no interest at all, and neither, until very recently, did cheque accounts.[7]

The answer obviously relates to the special qualities of money already mentioned. Other assets can be used to execute payments, but nowhere near as easily as money. No other asset can offer as attractive a collection of characteristics as money: near-universal acceptability, portability, storability. Money as an asset is easily realized (that is, converted into other assets) and its value, though variable, is usually a lot easier to assess than it is for other assets, with the result that the transaction costs of using money are lower than for other assets. In general, to use an expression which summarizes all these features, we say money is the most *liquid* of all assets.

It follows that, in holding a proportion of their wealth in the form of money, people are able to enjoy the advantage of liquidity. The greater their money balances, the more of this intangible, unmeasurable, but very real benefit they enjoy. The less they hold, the more frequently they have to realize other assets such as stocks or bonds, life insurance policies, real estate and so forth so as to pay for transactions.

We can state, then, with complete confidence that *liquidity is always an inherently desirable property*. The statement is virtually a truism. Why then do people ever choose to hold illiquid assets? Why not hold all wealth in its most liquid form – money?

The obvious answer is that non-money assets offer a counter-attraction to the liquidity of money. In exchange for the sacrifice of liquidity, non-money assets offer as compensation a return, which appears in a number of different guises: interest (on savings deposits, for example), yield (on bonds), dividend and, possibly, capital gain (on shares), rent (on property), and so on. Sometimes the reward for illiquidity is completely intangible – like the psychological benefit in the peace of mind given by risk insurance, or the satisfaction of owning a prestige make of motor car. In other cases, it may be an 'own' return, like the benefit of having a roof over one's head, which is part of the return on house ownership, or the cooling services yielded by an air conditioner. In the case of physical assets, the returns are often part pecuniary, part non-pecuniary. A

---

[7] Until, say, the early 1970s, it was almost universally true that demand deposits earned no interest. In fact, there was some debate in the profession as to whether one could regard this as an intrinsic feature of money or whether it was simply a result of the way the banking system had developed, the monopoly power of banks, low inflation rates and so on. During the last decade or so the increased competition in banking, combined with higher inflation rates, has led to a situation where explicit interest payments are frequently made to holders of demand deposits.

What is even more common, however, is implicit interest on cheque accounts. This involves paying interest by the back door: offering depositors 'free' banking by refunding any charges they would otherwise incur for normal banking operations, like cheque clearance, use of automated teller machines and so on. This amounts to paying interest in kind – the bank pays its customers in units of its own output, banking services. Economists refer to this type of arrangement as the payment of an 'own rate' of interest.

painting hanging in one's home for example, may yield an intangible return every time one sees it. It may also yield a capital gain when sold. Similarly, a house may yield pecuniary and/or non-pecuniary benefits.

Note that, since there is a rental market for houses and for many consumer durables, it is possible to put a reasonably accurate value on the services they yield simply by seeing how much people are willing to pay in order to rent them.

In general, then, illiquidity is rewarded by the return on an asset. There is another way of putting the same point: liquidity involves sacrificing the return that could have been earned by holding a less liquid asset. In particular, holding money means sacrificing the return that could be earned on non-money assets. In the jargon of monetary economics:

> **The opportunity cost of holding money**[8] is the return that could have been earned by holding a less liquid asset than money.

Notice that, in principle at least, there are as many possible measures of the opportunity cost as there are non-money assets. In particular, in an open economy context, the alternatives may include foreign securities or currency, as we shall see in Chapters 8 and 9.

We can now see the broad outline of how the demand for money mechanism works. On the one hand, economic agents need a stock of money balances in order to transact efficiently. The more transactions they want to conduct, the more money they would like to hold, other things being equal. On the other hand, holding one's wealth in the form of money involves a sacrifice, in the form of a foregone return. The choice as to how much money to hold involves a trade-off between the benefit in terms of transactions convenience and the opportunity cost.

So we have a theory which says that, broadly speaking, the demand for money will be greater the larger is the volume of transactions and will be smaller the higher is the return on non-money assets. All that remains at this stage is to make the theory operational by specifying, if possible, observable macroeconomic variables to act as indicators of the volume of transactions and of the opportunity cost.

Take the volume of transactions first. A transaction, for present purposes, is any activity where money normally changes hands – either in exchange for goods and services, or in exchange for repayment at a later date.

Consider the relationship between transactions and the level of economic activity. Macroeconomics uses as its index of economic activity the aggregate known as national income, which includes only those transactions involving the generation of value added. National income thus

---

[8] In general, opportunity cost is the term used by economists to refer to the cost of a resource, viewed as the loss incurred by not employing it in its best alternative use.

excludes, among other things, purchases of raw materials, loans, gifts, government transfers, gambling, and so on, because they involve no net output in the domestic economy. However, all these activities are likely, at some stage, to involve the transfer of money balances, and they are all therefore potentially relevant to the demand for money. Nor is that the only problem.

Even where transactions are properly associated with national income, factors like money transfer technology, established payment practices, the structure of the economy and so on are likely to influence the relationship between the number of transactions in the economy and the use of money balances. For example, other things being equal, the more infrequently employees are paid, the higher their *average* money balances will need to be.[9] Similarly, any change in the acceptability of near-money assets or in the efficiency with which money balances can be used (because of increased availability of credit cards for example) would also be likely to affect the demand, for any given volume of transactions.

It follows that we can neither take national income as an infallible indicator of the volume of transactions, nor rely on a completely fixed relationship between transactions and the demand for money.

However, suppose that the structure of the economy is fairly stable over some period. In particular, suppose that the kinds of institutional and technological factors that determine the way money is used in the economy are fairly stable, and that the structure of the various industries is such that the volume of transactions bears some stable relationship to national income. It may then be reasonable to assume that there would be a stable relationship between the level of economic activity and the volume of transactions.

If we ignore the opportunity cost argument for the moment, what we have arrived at is a relationship between the demand for money and national income which could be summarized as:

$$M^d = k\,Y \qquad k > 0 \tag{4.6}$$

where M^d is the demand for money and Y is national income, both measured in *nominal* terms,[10] and k is a positive parameter.[11] The reason why M^d and Y are both defined in nominal terms should be obvious. Other things being equal, one would expect, say, a 10% increase in the real volume of transactions to have the same effect on the demand for money

---

[9] To see why, compare two employees, one paid monthly, the other paid the same annual salary once a year. Suppose they both spend their income at a smooth rate throughout the year. The monthly paid employee would have an average balance over the year equal to one half the monthly wage, while the second employee's average money balance would be one half the annual wage or six times the monthly wage.

as a 10% increase in the price level at which the transactions are conducted. In fact, if we define:

$$Y \equiv Py$$

which just says nominal income, Y, is by definition the product of real income, y, times the price level, P, at which it is traded, then we can rewrite Equation 4.6 as:

$$M^d = k\,Py \tag{4.7}$$

This formulation is known as the Cambridge quantity equation. The quantity theory, of which it is one version, was the orthodox approach to what we now call the demand for money until well into the present century. It is characterized by a concentration on the role played by the volume of transactions, to the exclusion of any other variables, in particular the return on non-money assets.

The corollary of ignoring the return on other financial assets is that we implicitly assume that economic agents choose between money and goods in general, not between money and near-money assets. In this sense, Equation 4.7 is over-simplified. Nonetheless, there will be occasions in the next chapter (Sections 5.1 and 5.2) when it will be convenient to make use of this formulation, because of its simplicity and because, very often, it is sufficient as it stands to generate important insights.

Before moving on, notice that by dividing both sides of Equation 4.7 by P, it can be rewritten as follows:

$$\frac{M^d}{P} = ky \tag{4.8}$$

which is for some purposes a more useful way of looking at the quantity equation.

The left-hand side is the demand for real money balances, in other words the quantity of purchasing power the agents in the economy wish to

---

[10] The distinction between nominal and real values is very important. A real variable is one which measures a physical quantity or volume of goods or services. A nominal variable is one which is valued in money terms. So a nominal value rises when prices rise and falls when they fall, while a real variable only changes when the quantities it measures change.

In practice, real variables are computed by taking the values we actually observe – which are always nominal magnitudes – and 'deflating' them by an appropriate price index. For example, if Y is nominal national income and P is the relevant price index (called, in this case, the 'GNP deflator'), then real income, also known as income in volume terms, is given by: $y = Y/P$.

[11] Strictly speaking, k is the product of two factors of proportionality: one relating national income to the volume of transactions, the other relating the demand for money to transactions. In fact, k is the reciprocal of what is known as the (income) velocity of circulation.

The demand for money is presented here in linear form, for simplicity. In fact, researchers nowadays tend to favour a demand for money equation that is linear in logs.

hold in the form of money. The right-hand side is the constant k times the real income generated in the economy. Now if, as was often assumed by the classical economists, the level of economic activity can be regarded as fluctuating more or less randomly in a fairly narrow region around its long-run equilibrium level, it follows that the right-hand side of Equation 4.8 must be reasonably stable, and hence the demand for real balances must equally be stable.

To see why this is so important a conclusion, consider the effect of an increase in the money supply in this context.

Equilibrium in the money market involves a situation where the demand for money is equal to the supply. So, in the aftermath of an increase in the stock of money by, say, 10%, equilibrium can only occur when the demand has risen by the same amount.

Now look back at Equation 4.8. With the right-hand side broadly constant, the demand for real balances must, as we have seen, be more or less fixed – once the dust has settled, at least. And the demand for *real* balances will only be constant if the 10% rise in the demand for *nominal* money, M^d, is offset by an increase of equal proportions in the price level, P, thereby keeping the ratio M^d/P constant. In other words, each increase in the money supply generates an equiproportionate rise in the price index.

Not only that, but the converse is also true: in a quantity theory world, no increase in the general level of prices can occur without an accommodating rise in the money stock. Hence Milton Friedman's famous assertion, albeit on the basis of a far more sophisticated version of the quantity equation, that 'inflation is always and everywhere a monetary phenomenon'. With the real demand fixed, the real money stock must be pegged, which in turn means the numerator and denominator must move in parallel.

The power of these conclusions all stems from one critical simplification which is the assumption, already mentioned, that agents choose between holding money and goods, rather than between money and bonds (or long-term deposits, or savings accounts and so on). It follows that money balances can only be reduced by spending, creating a direct transmission mechanism from excess money supply to additional demand for goods, which, with output fixed, must drive up the price level. Conversely, excess demand for money can only be satisfied by reducing spending on goods and *not* by selling other financial assets. Hence excess demand for money is directly associated with excess supply of goods, as agents in aggregate attempt to replenish their balances. The result must be a fall in goods prices, on average at least.

It turns out that these conclusions all have to be modified as soon as we take account of the opportunity cost of holding money.

In order to decide how to measure the opportunity cost, one has, in principle, to decide first what are the relevant assets competing with money for a share in economic agents' portfolios. Again, at this theoretical level, any or all other assets are potential candidates such as savings deposits, bonds, stocks and shares, real estate, or even consumer goods held as inventories (assuming they are not perishable). Much research and not a little controversy has centred on this issue, but it is for the most part not directly relevant to exchange rate determination,[12] so we shall not open up this particular can of worms, that is, this complex and largely uninvestigated topic.

Instead, make the following assumption: suppose that whenever the return on one non-money asset goes up by 1 %, all the other rates of return do the same, other things being equal. This is not as unrealistic an assumption as it might at first appear. Broadly speaking, the difference between the yield on, for example, government long-term securities and the same kind of paper issued by a private sector company is determined by factors unrelated to macroeconomics, so there is no reason to expect it to change simply because interest rates in the economy rise. In general, if the relative liquidity of the various assets is unchanged one would expect the returns they offer to stay the same. In fact, changes in the returns on different assets are so closely correlated that it is very difficult in practice to identify a separate impact on the demand for money for more than two assets.

The advantage of making this assumption is that, if it holds good, it makes little difference which rate of return we choose in order to measure the opportunity cost of holding money. The simplest way to proceed, then, is to take an interest rate which is easily observable (the yield on Treasury Bills, for example) and refer to it from now on as *the* interest rate. If we do that, we can modify Equation 4.8 as follows:

$$\frac{M^d}{P} = k\,y - l r \qquad k,\, l > 0 \tag{4.9}$$

The equation now expresses our contention that the demand for real balances will increase with the volume of transactions, but decrease with the opportunity cost, as measured by the interest rate, r.

Notice that our simple quantity theory conclusions about the impact of money supply changes no longer apply, unless interest rates can be assumed to remain constant, which is unlikely.

Moreover, if over some period the price level can be regarded as constant, an increase in the nominal money supply must amount to a rise in the value of real balances in the economy, and this in turn must cause an increase on the right-hand side of Equation 4.9. Again, if changes in real

---

[12] Broadly speaking, Keynesian monetary theory tends to emphasize substitution between money and other financial assets (typically bonds) while monetarists are more inclined to concentrate, at least in theoretical argument, on the margin between money and real assets, like physical capital or consumer goods. In practical applications (that is, empirical work) these issues have proved hardly worth the controversy. (See Laidler.)

The only aspect of this question relevant to exchange rates is, as has already been mentioned, the possibility that the appropriate opportunity cost involves foreign assets (see Chapters 8 and 9).

income are ruled out this must imply a *fall* in *r*, so as to reduce the damping effect of the opportunity cost on the demand for real balances.

We can summarize the implications of this more sophisticated demand for money equation as follows. It states that the impact of an increase (or decrease) of *x*% in the supply of money will be *either* to cause the price level to rise (fall) by *x*% if the interest rate is unchanged, *or* to push the interest rate down (up), if the price level is constant, *or some combination of the two*, that is, a price change of less than *x*% in addition to an interest rate change.

The government budget constraint and the money supply

In order to understand how the supply of money is determined, it will be helpful to start by making a detour to consider the mechanics of government budget finance.

Suppose that in some year the government decides to spend more than it receives in tax revenue. In other words, suppose the government wants to run a budget deficit. How can it finance spending in excess of its tax revenues?

Essentially, the answer to this question is that just like you or I a government can only live beyond its means (that is, spend more than its income) by reducing its net assets, in other words by borrowing from others, thereby increasing its liabilities, or by running down its accumulated assets ('borrowing from itself', so to speak). Since governments rarely have much in the way of accumulated assets with which to finance spending[13] we shall assume any budget deficit is financed by borrowing of one form or another. Let us summarize this fact in the following identity:

$$G - T \equiv \text{the budget deficit} \equiv \text{total government borrowing}$$

where *G* is government expenditure on goods and services during the year and *T* is government tax revenue during the year.

Now there are many different forms in which a government can borrow, as indeed there are for an individual, depending on whether the borrowing is long or short term, secured or unsecured, indexed or unindexed, in negotiable or non-negotiable instruments and so on. With one vital exception we shall not be concerned with the particular form government borrowing takes.

The single exception is that governments have one borrowing option open to them which is not available to the ordinary individual: they can

---

[13] Though they invariably have enormous physical assets they are rarely willing to use them to finance budget deficits, except as part of privatization programmes undertaken, ostensibly at least, for different reasons altogether.

Incidentally, readers in the UK will note that, for once, British jargon is particularly appropriate in referring to the budget deficit as the public sector borrowing requirement.

issue, via the agency of the central bank, a kind of security which the public is willing to accept as money. The fact that some of the state's liabilities are universally acceptable in order to settle debts between parties outside the government sector gives the authorities another degree of freedom, an additional avenue for financing overspending which is not open to any other agency.[14]

In recognition of this fact, we can rewrite the identity, breaking down the right-hand side into components that reflect government borrowing in money and non-money terms:

$$G - T \equiv \Delta MB + \Delta B^s$$

where MB is the quantity of currency in existence, B^s is the quantity of non-monetary government debt in existence ('bonds')[15] and Δ is, by convention, an operator denoting the change in a variable over any period.

This identity is usually given a special name:

The government budget constraint is the identity that expresses the fact that all government spending over any given period must be financed either by taxation, by issuing currency or by issuing non-money securities (typically, long-term debt, called from now on 'bonds').

Although it is an identity, in other words a truism, the government budget constraint is important because it summarizes the necessary relationship between fiscal policy, affecting net expenditure on the left-hand side of the equation, and monetary policy, determining the way spending is financed on the right-hand side.

Armed with an understanding of the broad outline of the government's funding problem, we can now proceed to a consideration of the money supply mechanism.

The supply of money in an open economy

The first thing to notice about the supply of money is that it is not really a supply at all – at least, not in the sense we use the term in elementary microeconomics. What we mean by the supply of money is nothing more than the quantity of money in existence in the economy at a particular point in time. It is not very helpful for present purposes to think of money actually being *supplied* to the market. Rather, think of the supply process as being simply a mechanism whereby the stock of money (currency plus demand deposits) gets determined.

---

[14] The power to print money is referred to as seigniorage.

[15] From now on, we shall use the term 'bonds' as a shorthand to refer to all non-monetary financial instruments issued by the authorities.

It turns out that, in order to understand the process, we need to take a look at the structure of the banking system. The fine detail of the institutional framework is, for most industrial countries, bewilderingly complicated, and characterized by all sorts of peculiar features, some attributable to legal or regulatory constraints, others to custom and practice. To make matters worse the whole subject is often shrouded in a fog of esoteric jargon.

We shall avoid most of the complications by dealing with the banking system in broad outline only, avoiding much of the fine detail or relegating it to footnotes which the reader can safely ignore without losing the thread of the argument.

One notable simplification made here and throughout the book, with the exception only of Chapter 9, is to ignore foreign holdings of domestic currency. As far as money supply control is concerned it is hard to see why foreign holdings of sterling balances should create a problem. Certainly, any difficulties caused are likely to pale into insignificance beside those resulting from demand instability – or even beside the problems the authorities have created for themselves in the past.

Look at Figure 4.2, which lays out in schematic form the balance sheets of two kinds of institution.

The first balance sheet is for a central bank such as the Bank of England, the Federal Reserve Bank of the USA, the Bank of Japan or the Bundesbank in West Germany.[16]

Now, although it is the linchpin of a country's financial system, most people's only perception of their central bank is as the issuer of the banknotes they use. Certainly, serving as the bank of issue is an important function,[17] but it is by no means the only one performed by the central bank. In the first place, the central bank has the job of holding the nation's reserves of gold and foreign currency[18] – hence the first entry on the asset side in the table, labelled *FX*. Second, and most important of all, the central bank differs from a commercial bank in having one large customer,

---

[16] What's in a name? Not a lot, in this instance – neither the Bank of Scotland nor even the Royal Bank of Scotland, nor the Bank of America are central banks, whatever their names may suggest.

[17] But not one that is always the exclusive preserve of the central bank. The Scottish commercial banks for example, are permitted to issue their own banknotes. They do so, however, under licence to the Bank of England. For our purposes here, we shall ignore such complications and assume the central bank is the sole issuer of currency.

[18] A point to note with regard to jargon: in the context of the open economy the reserves can be taken to refer to the reserves of gold and foreign currency. However, as we shall see shortly, in the context of domestic banking we often need to refer to a very different type of reserve, the precautionary cash (that is, domestic currency) reserves kept by commercial banks in their vaults. Since it is only in the present section that any possibility for confusion could arise, the convention will be followed in this chapter and throughout the rest of the book that 'the reserves' when unspecified always means the stock of gold and foreign currency held by the central bank.

Central bank

Commercial banks

Consolidated banking sector

Assets		Liabilities	
Gold and foreign currency reserves	FX	Currency in circulation: $MB - MB^b =$	MB^p
Domestic credit: $L + LG =$	DC	Deposits of public	D
Money supply: $FX + DC =$	M^s	Money supply: $MB^p + D =$	M^s

Figure 4.2 The balance sheet of the banking system.

the government, to whom it is forced to provide the main banking services of facilitating transactions and, inevitably, providing credit.[19]

At this point, we are back to the question of how the government funds its deficit spending, but this time we concentrate on the mechanics of the process. Suppose a government decides to spend £100m, without raising any additional taxation. Suppose, furthermore, that it intends to do so without borrowing from the non-bank public – in other words, it is determined to avail itself of the option to increase the money supply in order to pay for its spending. The first step in the process involves the government approaching the central bank for a loan, which is granted more or less automatically. In return, we can think of the treasury being compelled to sign IOUs, promising to repay the central bank at some uncertain future date. These IOUs (government securities) are then locked away in the vaults of the central bank.

This transaction is represented on the asset side of the accounts by the item 'Lending to Government', consisting of the accumulation of government securities held by the central bank. The form the loans take is the printing of currency, which can then be used by the government for its additional expenditure. Notice that currency printed counts as a *liability* of the central bank, though neither the Bank of England nor the Federal Reserve Bank is actually obliged to redeem banknotes in any meaningful sense at all.[20]

Notice, also, that it is the supply of *currency* that is increased when the government borrows in this way from the central bank, not the money supply in any but the narrowest sense. The notation ΔMB in the government budget constraint refers to the change in the quantity of currency issued or, as it is sometimes called, base money.

However, this is not the only way the monetary base can be changed. Just as you or I sometimes borrow in order to spend (or consume), we also may, on occasion, take a loan so as to buy another asset. In effect, we voluntarily take on a liability (the loan) in order to purchase an asset such as a house perhaps, or some shares, or a partnership in a

---

[19] The word 'forced' probably overstates the case somewhat, at least for some countries. Suffice to say that the degree of independence of the central bank depends entirely on constitutional considerations and/or custom and practice in the country in question. The whole issue of the feasibility and desirability of central bank independence is an extremely vexed one, and is related to a number of questions regarding monetary and fiscal policy which will crop up at various points in what follows.

For present purposes we shall treat the central bank as simply an arm of government, so that transactions between it and the rest of the government are a purely formal, bookkeeping exercise.

[20] Under the old Gold Standard, banknotes could in principle be exchanged for gold on demand, though by the time the system collapsed (in August 1971, in the case of the USA), the right to do so was restricted almost exclusively to foreign central banks. British banknotes still carry the meaningless legend: 'I Promise to pay the Bearer the Sum of . . .', signed, it should be noted, not by a minister or government official, but by the cashier of the Bank of England.

business. In the same way, the government sometimes borrows in order to spend, as we have seen already, but may also at other times decide simply to raise a loan from the central bank in order to buy assets. Typically, the government may use the loan to buy back its own IOUs (mainly gilt-edged securities or bonds) from their holders among the non-bank public.

In the jargon of central banking, this type of activity is known as an *open market purchase* to distinguish it from transactions conducted 'behind closed doors', that is, between the government and the Bank of England.

As far as the impact on the monetary base is concerned, the effect will be to cause an expansion just as if it had used the loan to finance increased spending. Conversely, the government could decide to reverse the process, by issuing debt 'unnecessarily' so as to raise cash direct from the non-bank public (an open-market sale). If it subsequently spends the proceeds, the effect on the monetary base is nil. If, on the other hand, it uses the proceeds so as to repay its debts to the central bank (reducing *LG*), it effectively retires money, reducing *MB*.

Now consider the commercial banking sector.[21] Start this time on the liabilities side of the balance sheet. There is only one major item here, deposits by the public with the banks, *D*. Clearly, your deposit with the bank in the high street is an asset to you. However, it must equally be a *liability* of the bank, since it represents an obligation on the part of the bank to repay a fixed amount on demand.[22] Thus, that part of the money stock which consists of demand deposits is in fact a liability of the commercial banking system.

What do banks do with the funds deposited with them by the public? If they are to be able to pay any interest on deposits, or indeed cover their costs,[23] they must put the funds deposited with them to work. The way they achieve this is, of course, by lending, mainly to corporate borrowers, though often also to private individuals. At any rate, the important thing to note is that these loans constitute *assets* of the banking system, since they are obligations by the non-bank sector of the economy to repay debts to the banking sector.

---

[21] A commercial bank is best thought of as the kind of financial institution with which we are all familiar: the retail or 'high street' bank, which takes deposits from the public at large and lends the proceeds to local businesses. For present purposes we can safely ignore the existence of the 'wholesale' banks, discount houses and other quasi-banks as unnecessarily complicating factors.

[22] Only in the case of demand deposits (that is, current or checking accounts). For time deposits ('deposit accounts') and the like, the balance may not have to be repaid on demand. However, in order to keep matters simple we shall restrict our attention to demand deposits, as is consistent with the definition of the money stock we chose at the beginning of Section 4.1.2.

[23] The costs of running a bank are covered in two ways: through explicit charges and through the gap between the interest rate the bank earns on its assets and the rate it must pay on its deposits (which is often zero in the case of cheque accounts).

Now it would be very helpful, from the bank's point of view, if it could put out on loan every last penny it received on deposit. Unfortunately, it would also be grossly irresponsible, since it would be left with nothing in the till with which to repay depositors who wanted cash. As far as the public is concerned, it is on the understanding that they can liquidate their deposits for cash on demand that they agree to deposit in the first place. An inability to meet a demand for cash would almost certainly precipitate a crisis of confidence and a 'run on the bank'. Prudence requires, therefore, that a significant proportion of the funds deposited with the banks be held as a cash reserve in order to cover demands for withdrawals.[24]

Hence, the first item on the asset side of the commercial banks' balance sheet, MB^b, which represents precisely these precautionary reserves. Currency in the commercial banks' vaults is kept at a manageable level by regular trips to deposit cash at the central bank – hence the armoured vehicles cluttering up the roads outside our high street banks. By convention, no balance sheet distinction is made between the currency actually in a commercial bank's till at any moment and the amount it has available on deposit with its bank, the central bank. The total cash reserve is the commercial bank's share of the monetary base, MB^b in the figure.

The bottom third of the figure contains a consolidated balance sheet for the banking sector as a whole, commercial banks plus central bank. To see how that is derived, we need to write the balance sheets of the central bank and the commercial banks respectively as equations. First the central bank:

$$FX + LG \equiv MB$$

Then the commercial banks:

$$MB^b + L \equiv D$$

Now if we add the two balance sheet equations, we get:

$$FX + MB^b + (LG + L) \equiv MB + D$$

---

[24] Not only prudence. In some countries, and at times in the UK, the authorities have fixed the proportion of cash the banks are required to hold, not because they mistrusted the banks' judgement but as an alternative means of controlling the volume of bank lending. In other words, instead of controlling the quantity of cash in existence, they control the ratio of cash to loans.

Another complication we shall ignore is that banks are often allowed to include some types of highly liquid earning assets (for example, Treasury Bills) in their precautionary reserves. Another fact of banking life over which we draw a veil is that, in addition to making provision for the repayment of deposits to normal, solvent customers, banks also have to set aside a reserve in order to cover 'bad debts'. Finally, we also choose to ignore the possibility that banks can (and do) issue shares and use the proceeds to expand their balance sheets.

The term in brackets represents the total of the consolidated banking sector's lending, both to the government and to the private, non-bank sector. It is known as *domestic credit, DC* for short. If we rewrite the equation making use of this definition and also taking MB^b away from both sides, we get:

$$FX + DC \equiv (MB - MB^b) + D$$

On the right-hand side, in brackets, we have the total monetary base, MB, *net* of that part which is in the coffers of the banks themselves, MB^b. Obviously, currency not in the banks must be in circulation with the non-bank public. Call this part of the monetary base, MB^p. Thus, we can rewrite our equation as:

$$FX + DC \equiv MB^p + D$$

The right-hand side now consists of the total of currency in circulation plus deposits in the banks – which is precisely how we defined the money stock at the beginning of Section 4.1.2. We can therefore conclude that:

$$FX + DC \equiv M^s \tag{4.10}$$

In words: the money supply is identically equal to the sum of the domestic credit generated by the banking system *plus* the value of the country's reserves of gold and foreign currency held at the central bank.

There are a number of points worth noting about this very important equation. Notice that it is an *identity*, in other words, a relationship which is true by definition. It cannot be disputed or disproved. What, if anything, does it tell us? If we regard the left-hand side as showing the ultimate process by which the money stock is generated or backed, it tells us that every unit of domestic money must originate *either* in lending by the banking system (domestic credit) *or* in the reserves of foreign money. In terms of an expansion of the money stock, it says each additional unit of domestic currency must have been generated by an expansion of domestic credit or, alternatively, by an increase in the reserves of gold and foreign exchange.

Now these two kinds of asset are qualitatively different. For present purposes, the essential difference is in the way they are created. As far as domestic credit is concerned, it is all directly or indirectly amenable to control by the home country's monetary authorities. To see this is the case, look back at its two main components: central bank lending to the government and commercial bank advances to the non-bank sector. The former is self-evidently within the control of the authorities – it is determined by the government's budget constraint in conjunction with any central bank open-market operations that may be undertaken.

As far as commercial bank lending is concerned, the situation is not quite as clear-cut.[25] Recall the discussion of how commercial banks were forced to keep reserves broadly in proportion to their liabilities. This amounts to saying that their lending is constrained by the available reserves of cash. We shall assume that, either by virtue of its control of the quantity of base money printed, or via its ability to fix, legally or otherwise, the relationship between commercial banks' lending and their till money (that is, the ratio MB^b/L), the authorities can determine the total domestic credit in the economy, DC. In other words, we shall assume domestic credit is an exogenous, policy variable.

By contrast, we cannot possibly regard the foreign exchange reserves as a policy variable. For one thing, the Bank of England cannot print US dollars or Deutsche Marks to put in the reserves – that is the prerogative of the Federal Reserve and the Bundesbank respectively.

To understand this important distinction recall what was said about the function of the reserves in Chapter 1. They represent a buffer stock of international money available, when necessary, to purchase the domestic currency so as to support the exchange rate. Their size is determined by the accumulation of gold and foreign currency bought by the central bank on previous occasions to support other countries' currencies relative to the domestic.

Changes in the reserves therefore come about as a result of imbalances between the endogenous demand and supply in the currency markets. If there is an excess supply of the domestic currency (that is, excess demand for the foreign currency), a fall in the domestic country's exchange rate can only be prevented by using some of the reserves to buy the domestic currency, thereby satisfying the demand for foreign money. Conversely, the reserves will increase when there is an excess supply of foreign currency which must be bought with domestic money in order to prevent an appreciation.

Two conclusions follow. First, and most obviously, there is no point in a country hoarding reserves if it does not intend to peg its exchange rate. At the very least, if it is content to see its exchange rate determined in the freely operating currency markets, it need never use its reserves. Second, since the balance of payments accounts represent, at least in principle, an analysis of the flow supply and demand in the currency markets, a deficit

---

[25] In fact, in a closed economy context, control of domestic credit is all there is to money supply control. Nonetheless, there have been long, acrimonious debates about how far it is possible to control the money stock, even in a closed economy. The issues, which revolve around the minutiae of the institutional arrangements for control of the banking system, need not concern us here. It should suffice to say that it is certainly possible to imagine a banking system such that control of domestic credit would be possible to 100% accuracy. Whether it is desirable to have such a system is another matter, as indeed is the question of whether domestic credit can be controlled under the regimes actually in force in, say, the UK or USA today.

in those accounts will need to be offset by reductions in the reserves, and vice versa for a surplus. Thus, whatever factors determine the balance of payments also determine the change in the reserves.

To see the importance of these conclusions, go back to our open economy money supply identity, Equation 4.1, and rewrite it in terms of discrete changes:

$$\Delta FX + \Delta DC \equiv \Delta M^s \tag{4.11}$$

The change in a country's money supply is identically equal to the sum of the change in the volume of domestic credit issued by its banking system *plus* the change in its stock of international reserves.

Now, if the country's authorities either have no reserves or choose not to use them, in other words if they are happy to see the value of their currency determined in world markets, then the first term in Equation 4.11 is always zero, and changes in the domestic money stock originate exclusively in domestic credit expansion or contraction. Putting the point in terms of the balance of payments account, under these circumstances the balance for official financing is kept at zero.

It follows from all this that we can rephrase the definitions given in Chapter 1:

A (pure or cleanly) floating exchange rate regime is one such that the balance of payments for official financing is identically zero, because the monetary authority either holds no foreign currency reserves or never uses them to intervene in currency markets.

This is not all, however. Since, in this case, any changes in the money supply are entirely due to domestic credit expansion or contraction, we can add the following to our definition of a floating exchange rate:

Under a floating exchange rate, the domestic money stock only changes as a result of changes in the lending behaviour of the domestic banking system. Since the volume of lending can be controlled by the authorities, so can the money stock. In this sense, the money supply is a policy instrument at the disposal of the home country's monetary authority.

By contrast:

A fixed exchange rate regime (including a '**managed**' or '**dirty**' float) is one such that the balance of payments for official financing is *not* identically zero, the surplus or deficit being covered by the domestic monetary authority's use of the foreign currency reserves to intervene in currency markets.

The implications of fixed exchange rates for the money stock have already been mentioned in this section.

Under any form of fixed exchange rate, the domestic money stock may change *either* as a result of a change in the volume of bank lending *or* as a result of a change in the foreign currency reserves (that is, a balance of payments deficit or surplus for official financing) *or both*. Since the change in the reserves cannot be *directly* controlled by the domestic monetary authority, neither can the change in the domestic money stock.

It follows that, under a fixed exchange rate regime, the money supply cannot be regarded as a policy variable, but instead will be an endogenous variable determined by whatever factors influence the balance of payments.

In a nutshell then, under a floating exchange rate regime, the balance of payments surplus and the consequent increase in the reserves are fixed at zero, making the money supply exogenous and leaving the exchange rate to be determined endogenously by market forces. Under fixed exchange rates, the balance of payments, the change in the reserves and in the money supply are all endogenous. Only the change in the exchange rate is exogenously fixed at zero.

It follows that, in an open economy context, the term 'monetary policy' has two different meanings. Under floating exchange rates monetary policy means exactly the same thing it does in textbook models of a closed economy, that is, the management of the money supply. By contrast, under fixed exchange rates, monetary policy means control of the banking system's lending – in other words, what we have called domestic credit.

The LM curve

Equilibrium obtains in the money market when demand is equal to supply. Combinations of income and the interest rate consistent with equilibrium are plotted along the *LM* curve.[26] Looking back at Equation 4.9, this means when:

$$\frac{M^s}{P} = \frac{M^d}{P} = k\,y - lr \qquad k, l > 0 \tag{4.12}$$

where we bear in mind what was said in the last section about the determination of the money supply and its relationship to the exchange rate regime.

Now, if the money stock is fixed initially at the level M_0^s, Equation 4.12 is a single equation in *three* unknowns: r, y and P. To proceed, *take a*

---

[26] So called because it joins points at which the money stock is equal to the demand for money, originally denoted with the letter L, in deference to Keynes' name for it: liquidity preference.

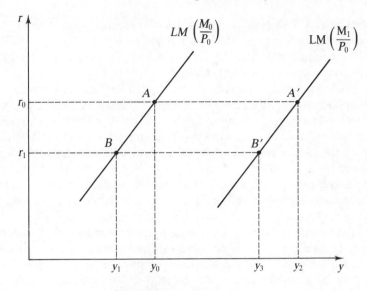

Figure 4.3 The *LM* curve.

given level of prices, say P_0. If we do that, we are left with the equation:

$$ky - lr = \frac{M_0^s}{P_0} \qquad k, l > 0 \tag{4.13}$$

as the condition necessary for the money market to be in equilibrium – in other words, for the demand for money to be equal to the supply.

Notice that Equation 4.13 now has the same general form as Equation 4.5, the equation of the *IS* curve. The right-hand side is given, as before, and we can again generate the equilibrium conditions by picking an interest rate at random and asking ourselves the question: if the interest rate is r_0, what must be the level of y if the money market is to clear? The answer, y_0,[27] is the first point we have located on our *LM* curve, because it is the first combination of r and y we have found that generates a demand for money just equal to the given supply (the point A in Figure 4.3).

Now consider a lower interest rate, r_1. The implication of a lower interest rate is a smaller penalty for holding non-interest-bearing assets, and hence less of an incentive to economize on money holdings. It follows that, at r_1, the demand for money would be greater than the supply at the previous level of activity, y_0. Equilibrium therefore requires the lower interest rate to be offset by a lower level of activity, so as to damp down the demand for money for transactions purposes, and thereby compensate for the reduced incentive to make money balances 'work harder'. It follows

---

[27] Not, of course, the same y_0 as in Figure 4.1.

that money-market clearing requires a lower interest rate (like r_1) to be associated with a lower level of real activity (like y_1).

We conclude that the *LM* curve drawn for a given level of real money balances must be upward sloping.

As before, consider a change in the right-hand side of Equation 4.12. Clearly, an increase in the supply of real money balances could come about as the result of a *rise* in the nominal money stock or a *fall* in the price level at which it is valued. In fact, as we saw, the impact of, say, a 10% rise in the numerator, M^s, would be identical to that of a 10% fall in the price index, since it would have an identical effect on the ratio M^s/P. Anything that leaves the ratio unchanged, for example a 25% increase in *both* the nominal money stock and the price level, will have no effect on the *LM* curve.

From whatever source, an increase in the real money stock will mean that previous equilibrium combinations of r and y are now associated with an excess supply of real balances. At any given interest rate, say r_0, there will have to be a compensating change in order to increase the demand. Clearly, this must mean a higher level of activity than at the previous equilibrium. y_0 will no longer be associated with a high enough transactions demand. An income level like y_2 will be required. Putting the same argument somewhat differently, at any level of activity (and associated transactions demand) the larger real money stock makes possible a lower interest rate, because it reduces the required equilibrium opportunity cost of money holding.

We can summarize our conclusions about the *LM* curve as follows.

(1)   The (open or closed economy) *LM* curve is an upward-sloping line joining all combinations of the interest rate and the level of income, such that the demand for real money balances is exactly equal to the supply.

(2)   It is drawn for given values of the nominal money stock, M^s, and the price level, P. Any increase in the ratio M^s/P, whether associated with a rise in the nominal money stock, M^s, or a fall in P, will cause an outward shift in the *LM* curve and vice versa in the case of a fall in M^s or rise in P.

4.1.3 Aggregate demand

Figure 4.4(a) combines the *IS* and *LM* curves so as to generate a unique solution to the two simultaneous Equations 4.5 and 4.13. In other words, the value of y at A, y_0, is the answer to the question: what would be the equilibrium level of income if government fiscal spending amounted to G_0, the money supply were set at the level M_0^s, the price level were P_0 and the real exchange rate were Q_0.

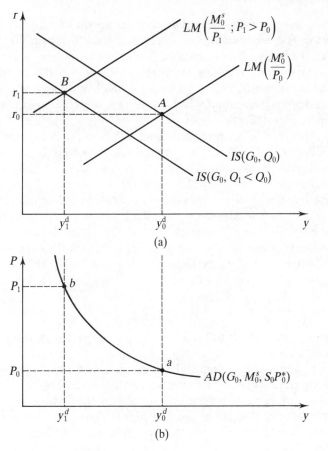

Figure 4.4 Derivation of the aggregate demand curve.

However, the term 'equilibrium income' has to be interpreted with care in this context. It means nothing more than 'the level of income consistent with equality between planned spending and income, on the one hand, and also consistent with equality between the demand for money and the supply, on the other'. While this may seem quite a mouthful, it is not yet sufficient for a complete equilibrium. What is missing is some consideration of how the output y_0 relates to the productive capacity of the economy – it might, for example, be way beyond maximum potential output levels. Conversely, it might be so low as to imply mass unemployment of labour and/or capital.

These considerations lie behind the determination of the aggregate supply schedule, which will be dealt with in Section 4.2. For the moment, in recognition that the value of y that corresponds to equilibrium in the *IS–LM* model may not be the output actually produced, we shall refer to it as aggregate demand, denoted y^d.

Now ask yourself the question: suppose that aggregate demand is greater than the economy's productive potential – what is likely to happen? The intuitively obvious answer is that the price level will rise – and, on this occasion, the intuition is correct. How will a rise in the price of goods and services affect aggregate demand? The answer is given by the aggregate demand schedule, which plots how aggregate demand changes as the general price level changes.

In Figure 4.4(b), aggregate demand is plotted against the price index, taking G, M^s and SP^* as given. Hence the equilibrium at A in the *IS–LM* diagram is associated with the point on the aggregate demand curve labelled a.

The remainder of the points on the aggregate demand schedule are derived simply by varying the price index upward or downward from P_0. Take, for example, the higher price level, P_1. As far as the *LM* curve is concerned, we have seen that a higher price level reduces the value of the given nominal money stock, because it must be the case that:

$$\frac{M_0^s}{P_1} < \frac{M_0^s}{P_0}$$

if P_1 is greater than P_0. It follows that the *LM* curve for P_1 is further to the left (that is, higher up) than for P_0.

What about the *IS* curve? The only effect of a higher price level on the *IS* curve arises via the international relative price term, Q. *Other things being equal*, and, in particular, assuming neither the nominal exchange rate nor the foreign price level change, the higher domestic price level reduces the competitiveness of UK production, pushing the *IS* curve downward and to the left.

Since both shifts are to the left, the outcome must be a lower level of aggregate demand, say y_1^d instead of y_0^d.[28] Plotting the outcome on to the bottom diagram we conclude that the aggregate demand curve will be downward sloping, for given values of the money stock, fiscal expenditure, the nominal exchange rate and the foreign price level.

The aggregate demand curve AD_0 was drawn for given values of G, M^s and SP^*. Now consider the effect of changes in each of these variables in turn.

At any given price level an increase in the nominal money supply will, as we have seen, shift the *LM* curve outwards, moving the equilibrium down the *IS* curve to the south-east, in the direction of higher aggregate demand and lower interest rates. It therefore follows that it will shift the aggregate demand curve outwards, accommodating higher demand at all price levels.

---

[28] And, almost certainly, a higher interest rate, since the effect of the upward shift in the *LM* curve is unlikely to be offset by the downward shift in the *IS* curve.

An increase in net government expenditure has effects that are similar, but not identical. As we have already established, a fiscal expansion shifts the *IS* curve outwards, other things being equal, so that the new equilibrium involves a higher level of both the interest rate and aggregate demand in the economy. The greater the rise in interest rates, the smaller the increase in aggregate demand. On the one hand, interest rates have to rise so as to persuade agents to economize on money balances so as to finance the new, higher volume of transactions. On the other hand, the more interest rates rise, the lower the level of private sector expenditure in the new equilibrium. To the extent that the net outcome is a smaller increase in demand than would have taken place if interest rates had remained unchanged, private sector expenditure is said to have been **crowded out** by the additional government spending.

Most important, consider the effect of an increase in SP^*, the home currency price of foreign products. At any given domestic price level, P, an increase in SP^* translates directly into a rise in $Q = SP^*/P$, in other words, an improvement in UK competitiveness. This is the case whether the change is brought about by a rise in S (sterling devaluation) or in P^* (foreign inflation). Hence, a rise either in S or in P^* leads, via the increase in Q, to a rightward shift in the *IS* curve and consequent rise in aggregate demand, other things being equal. The aggregate demand schedule is therefore moved to the right by the change.

To summarize our conclusions about the aggregate demand curve:

(1) The aggregate demand curve shows how the level of income that clears the goods and money markets (that is, the equilibrium level of income in the *IS–LM* curve context) varies as the (domestic) price level changes. It is downward sloping because as the domestic price level rises, other things being equal, the real money stock is reduced in value and also the competitiveness of UK output falls, at given levels of S and P^*.

(2) The aggregate demand curve is drawn for given levels of government spending, G, the nominal money supply, M^s, the nominal exchange rate, S, and the price of foreign output, P^*. An increase in any of these variables will shift the schedule outward, since they will induce greater aggregate demand at any domestic price level.

4.2 Aggregate supply

The exposition given here of the underpinnings of the aggregate supply curve is brief in the extreme. A fuller explanation taking account of the possibility of short-run output variations can be found in almost any undergraduate macroeconomics textbook.

As a starting point in the derivation of the aggregate supply curve, assume that the quantity of equipment, plant and machinery and so on (the economy's capital stock) is given at any moment in time. The implication is that, with one factor of production fixed, output depends only on the manpower employed.[29]

Now consider the situation in the labour market.

4.2.1 Flexible prices

A profit-maximizing firm will demand labour up to the point at which the value of its marginal product is just equal to the money wage,[30] that is, up to the point where the last man-hour adds just as much to revenue as it does to costs. If marginal product diminishes as labour utilization increases and if employers are competitive in the labour market, then, subject to the usual provisos with respect to aggregation conditions, the demand for labour across the economy will be a decreasing function of the nominal wage at any given price level.

For example, at the price level P_0, the demand for labour will be given by the downward-sloping line labelled $n^d(P_0)$ in Figure 4.5(a).

Clearly, if the price level were 20% higher, firms would seek to employ the same amount of labour at a money wage 20% greater than previously because, other things being equal, the marginal man-hour would result in a proportionately greater addition to revenue than previously. Hence, the demand curve would shift vertically upwards so as to associate with any given employment level a nominal wage 1.2 times higher.

On the other hand, households are presumed to be intent on choosing a utility-maximizing combination of work and leisure. If they are able to do so *in freely competitive labour markets*, they will offer their services up to the point at which the monetary benefit (in terms of consumption) they derive from the last man-hour supplied, as measured by the wage rate, is equal to their subjective assessment of its leisure value.[31] The marginal utility of leisure can safely be assumed to increase as the number

---

[29] Ignoring other 'textbook' factors of production such as land, managerial expertise and so on. Notice also that employment ought, in principle, to be measured in man-hours of homogeneous labour.

[30] Strictly speaking, the product wage. We assume the distinction can be ignored, at least at the aggregate level. We also make all the usual assumptions necessary to guarantee a downward-sloping marginal physical product curve.

[31] Viewed either as the marginal utility of leisure or (the negative of) the marginal disutility of work. We assume leisure is, in the jargon of microeconomics, a normal good.

Figure 4.5 Derivation of the classical aggregate supply curve.

of hours worked rises and leisure time is reduced. It follows that, at any price level, the quantity of man-hours supplied will be an increasing function of the nominal wage, as can be seen from the line marked $n^s(P_0)$ in Figure 4.5(a).

Again, at a higher price level $P_1 = 1.2P_0$, any given money wage buys 20% less consumption. The household will therefore be in equilibrium supplying any given number of man-hours at a money wage 20% higher than before.

At the initial price level, the combination of a downward-sloping demand for labour with respect to the nominal wage and an upward-sloping supply of labour guarantees a unique equilibrium level of employment, $\bar{n}$, and a corresponding real wage, $\bar{w}_0 = \overline{W}_0/P_0$. Following the accepted jargon, we shall call these market-clearing values the equilibrium or *natural* real wage and rate of employment.

At the higher price level $P_1 = 1.2P_0$, as can be seen at point B in Figure 4.4(a), the equilibrium money wage is 20% higher, but *both the real wage and the level of employment are unchanged.*

If the labour market clears with employment equal to $\bar{n}$, what will be the level of output? Given the level of the total capital stock, the quantity of equipment per worker will be given, at any employment level. Assuming a given state of technology, it follows that the productive capacity of any quantity of labour will be determined. The functional relationship between the quantity of labour utilized and the output produced is normally called the short-run production function (Figure 4.4(b)). In particular, the employed labour force, $\bar{n}$, will produce the output, $\bar{y}^s$, which we can, in turn, regard as the equilibrium or natural level of real national product.

Now what does this analysis imply for the aggregate supply function? Recall that, symmetrically with the aggregate demand schedule, we are looking for the relationship between aggregate supply and the price level in the economy.

It is plain from what has already been said that the price index has no part to play in determining equilibrium output, since both the demand for labour and the supply depend on the *real* wage. As long as the corporate sector's demand for labour and the household sector's supply are both unaffected by price level changes (as long as neither side suffers from money illusion) the aggregate supply curve will be a vertical line at the level $\bar{y}^s$, so that the actual output produced in the economy will be independent of the price level (Figure 4.4(c)).

Notice the implication: if there is no connection between the price level and aggregate supply, the latter cannot determine the former. It follows that the price level must depend on aggregate demand alone. In other words, any of the factors which have been shown to shift the aggregate demand curve upwards cause the price level to increase, and vice versa for a price level decrease.

One point which should be absolutely clear from this brief analysis is that the role of price and wage flexibility is absolutely critical. If money wages rose by more (or less) than 20% as the price level rose from P_0 to P_1, the outcome would be an increase (or decrease) in the real wage and consequent fall (rise) in employment and output. Everything hinges, therefore, on the smooth functioning of the labour market.

Now since a faith in the ability of markets to adjust rapidly to shocks is the hallmark of Classical economics,[32] we conclude:

> The Classical or flexible-price aggregate supply curve is vertical at the long-run capacity output level of the economy. This is because, as the price level fluctuates up or down, the money wage adjusts to keep the real wage constant. Hence employment and output never vary, and the price level itself is determined by aggregate demand.

4.2.2 Fixed prices

Now consider what would happen if money wages were fixed.

This situation might arise in a number of ways. It could be regarded as the very short-run reaction to a sudden change in the price level – after all, money wages can hardly respond overnight. In fact, wages may be fixed over a longer horizon by the existence of employment contracts, explicit (in other words, written) or implicit (unwritten, but nonetheless binding). In many cases, the contracts might be between employers and employees represented by trade unions, in which case the mechanism for adjusting money wages is likely to be even more cumbersome.[33]

In any case, the implication is that the *effective* labour supply curve is horizontal at the current fixed money wage, $\overline{W}_0$. Assuming firms continue to react to price changes in the way described in Section 4.2.1, it follows that employment and output are no longer constant (Figure 4.6). A rise in the price level is associated with a fall in the real wage and a consequent increase in employment from $\overline{n}_0$ to $\overline{n}_1$ and output from $\overline{y}_0^s$ to $\overline{y}_1^s$. The result is the upward-sloping aggregate supply curve labelled $AS(K)$ in Figure 4.6(c).

In the limit, if wages form the bulk of the corporate sector's costs, or if non-labour costs are constant, competitive producers will never raise prices. Firms will react to higher demand for their output by simply taking on more labour at the fixed money wage and scaling up production at constant unit costs. The outcome will be a completely flat aggregate supply curve.

Now nobody believes this scenario to be the complete truth about aggregate supply in the long run as after all, it would imply that a policy of

---

[32] Known nowadays as New Classical economics.

[33] It is not our concern here as to why or how money wages might be fixed. The original Keynesian view was that money wages were not so much constant as 'downward invariant', that is, incapable of being pushed down, even in the aftermath of price deflation, but quite easily pushed upward. This asymmetrical money illusion was held to be, at least in part, a cause of the mass unemployment of the 1930s.

Figure 4.6 Derivation of the Keynesian aggregate supply curve.

demand expansion (for example by printing money) could lead to a permanent increase in employment and output. Nonetheless, the account given here will serve as a conveniently simplified description of a commonly-held view of aggregate suppply in the short run, one we shall henceforth refer to as Keynesian or fixed price.

We conclude:

> The Keynesian or fixed-price aggregate supply curve is flat at the currently given price level, reflecting the fact that demand fluctuations are associated with equal and opposite variation in the real wage. Hence, with fixed prices, employment and output are demand-determined.

With the price level fixed in this scenario, we need only concern ourselves with aggregate demand and the position of the *IS* and *LM* curves – which, as we shall see in Chapter 6, is exactly the focus of the Mundell–Fleming model.

4.2.3 A compromise: sticky prices

If the flexible wage model seems an implausible description of the very short-run reaction of labour markets, while the fixed wage alternative is equally unrealistic as a description of long-run behaviour, consider a compromise between the two extremes.

Suppose the assumptions underlying the Keynesian model apply to the short run, while wages and prices are completely flexible in the long run, as in the classical model. In other words, suppose the aggregate supply curve is flat in the immediate impact phase, but gets steeper as time elapses, ultimately becoming vertical in the steady state equilibrium.

According to this scenario, the economy passes through three phases in the aftermath of a disturbance. Take for example the case of an increase in demand from AD_0 to AD_1 (Figure 4.7).

The impact effect is felt purely on output and employment. Workers willingly supply more labour at the going wage, whether because they are unsure how long the increased demand will persist, or because they are bound by fixed wage contracts, or simply as a result of very short-run inertia. The economy therefore moves more or less immediately from point E to A, with an increase in output from $\bar{y}_0^s$ to y_1^s.

As time passes, however, contracts (implicit or explicit) are renegotiated, and money wages are progressively bid up as employers seek to increase output. In turn, the corporate sector recoups the rise in labour costs by raising output prices, thereby giving added impetus to the wage inflation, as households seek to increase their pay to take account of the higher cost of living. The adjustment phase is therefore characterized by rising prices and falling output, as the aggregate supply curve tilts toward the vertical. At each stage of the adjustment process, we can think of the economy being in a temporary equilibrium like B in the diagram, with output at y_2^s still above its initial long-run level, and the price index somewhat higher, at P_2.

Figure 4.7   The sticky price aggregate supply curve.

Eventually, the economy reaches its long-run steady state at *C*, where all real quantities are back where they started. The price level is at its new long-run level of $\bar{P}_3$, but since the money wage has increased pro rata, the real wage and hence employment are unchanged. Output is back at its natural level.

We can summarize this model as follows:

> The sticky-price model of the supply side of the economy is one where the aggregate supply curve is instantaneously flat, becoming steeper as time passes and eventually vertical. It follows that the reaction to an increase in aggregate demand involves initially an expansion in output with no inflation. As time passes, the price level rises and output falls back toward its long-run level.

This compromise provides the background to the Dornbusch model, which will be the subject of Chapter 7.

4.3   Conclusions

For those readers who are familiar with the basic textbook model of the closed economy, this chapter will have contained only two new features.

First, the introduction of the real exchange rate into the *IS* curve. The higher the real exchange rate, the more competitive is domestic output on world markets, and hence the greater the demand in the economy, other things being equal.

The second innovation is in the treatment of the determination of the money stock. Under a fixed exchange rate regime, the money supply is no longer a policy variable, because, as we saw, it contains a component which is the direct counterpart of the country's foreign currency reserves. Since the latter are clearly not within the direct control of the *domestic* monetary authority, it follows that the money stock can no longer be regarded as simply a policy lever which can be operated at will by the Governor of the Bank of England or the Chancellor of the Exchequer.

With the end of this chapter, we can now proceed to the analysis of models of exchange rate determination, the subject matter of Part II of the book.

■ Summary

- The open economy *IS* curve links combinations of the interest rate and income consistent with equilibrium in the market for flows of goods and services. It is downward sloping. Increases in the real exchange rate (real devaluation) or in government net expenditure cause it to shift to the right.

- *Money* means the asset or assets which are usually used as means of payment. For most purposes, it consists of currency in circulation *plus* demand deposits (cheque accounts).

- *The supply of money* is equal to the sum total of the domestic credit created by the central bank in its lending to the government and the commercial banks by their advances to the public, *plus* the country's reserves of gold and foreign exchange, if any.

- Increases in the supply of money can arise from policy decisions to permit increased domestic credit or from growth in the reserves. The latter are the result of maintaining a fixed exchange rate under conditions of balance of payments surplus. It follows that, under a fixed exchange rate, changes in the money stock are not necessarily the result of policy decisions. Only under a freely floating rate is the money stock an exogenous variable, since, in that case, the whole of the money stock (or at least, the whole of any change in it) consists of domestic credit.

- *The demand for money* is to be construed as the demand to hold a stock of purchasing power in the form of monetary assets. It is therefore a demand for real balances. As such, it will be greater, other things being equal, when national income is higher, since then the volume of transactions to be financed is larger, and it will be smaller the higher are interest rates in the economy, because higher rates of return on non-money assets mean a higher *opportunity cost of holding money*.

- The *LM* curve links combinations of income and the interest rate consistent with equilibrium in the money market. It is upward sloping. An increase in the real money stock, whether originating in one of the components of the nominal supply or in a fall in the price level, causes the *LM* curve to shift to the right.

- The aggregate demand curve shows how the *IS–LM* equilibrium value of national income ('aggregate demand') varies as the price level changes, holding everything else constant. Since, at higher price levels, a given stock of nominal balances represents a lower real money supply, the aggregate demand curve slopes downward.

- On the supply side of the economy, the demand for labour is a downward-sloping function of the money wage, at any given price level.

- If households are concerned only with the real value of any wage offer, their labour supply will be homogeneous in prices and wages. If all prices adjust smoothly, it will follow that the level of employment and output are constant, other things being equal, and in particular independent of the price index. Hence the (Classical) aggregate supply curve is vertical.

- If households behave as though subject to money illusion – whether as a result of long-term contracts, or inertia, or misinformation, or simply delays in reacting – real wages will not be invariant, and hence both employment and output will fluctuate as the price level changes. Hence the (Keynesian) aggregate supply curve will be upward sloping. In the limit, it could well be horizontal.

- It could be argued that the classical aggregate supply curve is a plausible picture of the long-term behaviour of the economy, while the Keynesian version relates to the short term. A compromise would therefore be to take the aggregate supply curve as flat in the immediate term, pivoting upward as time passes in the aftermath of a demand disturbance, until ultimately the economy returns to its steady state along the vertical long-run supply curve.

READING GUIDE

The closed economy aggregate demand-supply framework is covered in practically all modern textbooks, though the extensions given here are harder to locate. A good elementary exposition, especially of aggregate supply, is to be found in Parkin and Bade (1988). Alternatively, see Artis (1984), particularly on the open economy aggregate demand model.

The approach taken to the demand for money in this section is by no means the only one possible, nor even the most plausible in some respects. Interested readers, and for present purposes that includes all those with ambitions to progress beyond this book in the study of exchange rates, would be well advised to consult Laidler (1985) on the demand for money, and the more important references given therein.

There are a number of channels through which the external sector might impinge on the supply side of the economy – for example, via a cost of living index with a significant import component. However, the result of incorporating these linkages is usually to complicate matters very substantially. The adventurous reader with sufficient mathematical background might like to look at the different approaches taken by Daniel (1982), Bruno and Sachs (1982), Marston (1982) and Copeland (1983).

Part II

Exchange Rate Determination

Having covered the preliminaries, we are now in a position to progress to looking at some models of exchange rate determination. We start in Chapter 5 with the simplest (and oldest), the monetary model, which is founded on the assumption that prices are completely flexible, so that PPP obtains at all times. By contrast, Chapter 6 examines a model which takes the price level as absolutely fixed, and allows for variations in national income. The Dornbusch model (Chapter 7) offers a compromise with sticky prices and financial markets which compensate in the short run by over-adjusting. The last two chapters of this part concentrate on a richer specification of the menu of assets: domestic and foreign bonds are included in the portfolio balance model (Chapter 8) and the implications of allowing for domestic holdings of foreign currency are examined in Chapter 9. Finally, Chapter 10 looks at the question of optimal currency zones, a topic in applied exchange rate economics that seems likely to dominate international affairs for the remainder of the 1990s.

5

Flexible Prices:
The Monetary Model

■ Introduction

There are a number of reasons why we choose to look at the monetary model first. For one thing, it was the earliest approach to explaining the related phenomena of exchange rate variations, on the one hand, and the balance of payments, on the other. It also had a brief renaissance in the early 1970s. More importantly, it represents an obvious benchmark for comparing the other approaches to modelling exchange rate determination, many of which themselves grew out of the monetary model. Finally, while it is completely inadequate in explaining the wild day-to-day, month-to-month gyrations seen in recent years, it nonetheless provides some useful insights into the broader picture of long-run trends.

What we now call the monetary model is rooted in an approach to the balance of payments that dates back at least as far as the work of David Hume in 1741. It will be seen to consist of two basic building-blocks: the purchasing power parity relationship that is familiar from Chapter 2, and the demand for money, which was covered in Chapter 4.

In the first section, these two relationships will be incorporated in a particularly simple version of the aggregate demand and supply model, which will then be used in succeeding sections to analyse the effect of increases in the money supply, income and foreign prices on a floating exchange rate. In Section 5.2, we examine the implications of the same disturbances for the balance of payments under a fixed exchange rate regime. Section 5.2.4 analyses the effect of devaluation. Section 5.3 looks at the role played by interest rates. The final section provides a brief survey of the evidence for and (mostly) against the monetary model.

5.1 The simple monetary model of a floating exchange rate

We start by setting the scene. The model to be set out in this section is very much a simplification, but it will suffice nonetheless to generate the conclusions typical of international monetarism.

5.1.1 The setting

The monetary model rests essentially on three assumptions: a vertical aggregate supply curve, a stable demand for money, and purchasing power parity (PPP). We shall examine these assumptions in that order.

A1. The aggregate supply curve is vertical.

Two points should be remembered in this regard from Chapter 4. First, this does *not* imply that output is constant – simply that it can only vary as the result of a change in the productivity of the economy, in other words, broadly defined that is through technical progress, the accumulation of capital, growth in the labour force or its educational level and so on.

Second, a vertical supply curve presupposes perfect price flexibility in all markets.

A2. The demand for real money balances is a stable function of only a few domestic macroeconomic variables. In fact, for the moment and till further notice, we shall work with the Cambridge quantity equation (Equation 4.7) introduced in Chapter 4:

$$M^d = k\,Py \qquad k > 0$$

where y is real national income and k is a positive parameter.

This particular formulation simplifies matters considerably. Consider what it implies for the aggregate demand schedule. Given a money

Figure 5.1 Aggregate demand with the quantity equation.

stock, M_0^s, equilibrium means we have:

$$M_0^s = k\,Py = k\,Y \tag{5.1}$$

It follows that nominal income, Y, must be constant along the aggregate demand curve, since it is drawn for a given value of the money stock.

Look at Figure 5.1. The nominal national income $Y = Py$ associated with any point on the curve labelled $AD_0(M_0^s)$ is simply the area of the rectangle between it and the axes, for example OP_0Ay_0 at A and OP_2Dy_1 at D. If these areas are to be equal it must follow that, as we move from A to D, the fall in the price level is of the same proportion as the rise in income.[1]

More important for present purposes, consider the effect of an increase in the nominal money stock. As we saw in Chapter 4 this change shifts the aggregate demand curve upward and to the right. By how much, in the present case? Compare points A and B. Obviously, P_1 must be greater than P_0 by the same proportion as M_1^s is greater than M_0^s.

---

[1] In the language of microeconomics, the aggregate demand curve has unitary elasticity in this special case. It is in fact a rectangular hyperbola.

Note that in the present case, the LM curve is vertical, since the demand for money is unaffected by the interest rate. It follows that we are only concerned with the extent to which it shifts horizontally when the real money stock changes. We are also able to ignore the interest rate because the IS curve is implicitly flat, with saving and investment being equated by the interest rate alone, independently of income.

For example, if the change in question is a doubling of the money stock, the outcome has to be a doubling of nominal demand. At any given real income, y_0, that implies a doubling of the price level.

A3. Purchasing Power Parity (PPP) obtains at all times.

Remember from Chapter 2 that the PPP hypothesis stated that, given a domestic (UK) price level of P, and a foreign (US) price level of P^*, equilibrium would be obtained when the two price levels stood in the following relationship:

$$SP^* = P \qquad\qquad\qquad\qquad (2.4)$$
$$\text{repeated}$$

so that nothing could be gained by shipping goods from one country to the other. Remember also that this is equivalent to stating that the purchasing power of each country's currency must be the same whether spent on the domestic market or converted into foreign currency and spent abroad.

Now consider Figure 5.2(a), where the vertical axis plots the domestic price level, and the horizontal plots the sterling price of US dollars. The line drawn out from the origin is the locus of all combinations of S and P that satisfy Equation 2.4 – call it the PPP line. Plainly, it has a gradient equal to P^*. Points above and to the left of the line are ones where the UK economy is uncompetitive (the domestic price level is too high), so that it is worth importing goods from the USA in place of relatively expensive UK products. The opposite is true below the line.

In terms of the *real* exchange rate (look back at the definition in Section 2.4, if necessary), above the PPP line a real depreciation is required to restore equilibrium, and below it, the opposite is true.

5.1.2 Equilibrium

In Figure 5.2(b), the aggregate demand and supply curves are plotted for given values of the money stock and output capacity. With an initial money supply of M_0^s, P_0 is the 'closed economy' equilibrium price level, that is, the one consistent with conditions in the domestic economy.

In fact, P_0 is still the equilibrium price level, even in this open economy model. Furthermore, *its value is determined without any reference to conditions in the external sector of the economy.*

However, in the external sector, PPP requires that a price level of P_0 be associated with an exchange rate of S_0. A lower value of S would leave domestic output uncompetitive on world markets, and hence result in an excess supply of the home currency, and vice versa at a higher level of S.

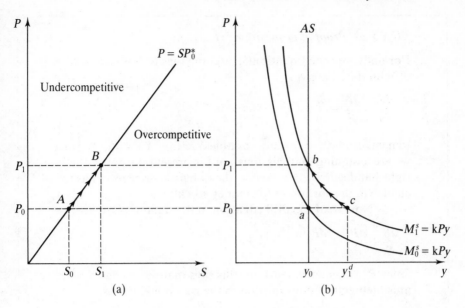

Figure 5.2   Money supply increase under floating rates.

We can see the nature of equilibrium formally by combining Equations 2.4 and 5.1 to give:

$$M_0^s = kPy = kSP^*y \tag{5.2}$$

so that we can solve for S as:

$$S = \frac{M_0^s}{kP^*y} \tag{5.3}$$

So the exchange rate in this ultra-simple model is the ratio of the money stock to the demand, measured at the foreign price level. Whatever serves to raise that ratio, in other words to increase the numerator or decrease the denominator, will cause the price of foreign exchange to rise (the domestic currency to depreciate).

Now consider the effect on this equilibrium of three types of disturbance: a monetary expansion and a rise in real income respectively in the domestic economy, and an increase in the world price level.

5.1.3 A money supply increase under floating exchange rates

Start with an expansion of the money stock to a new level, M_1^s. Assume the other exogenous variables (real income, y, and the foreign price level, P^*) are unchanged.

BOX 5.1   Proof of proposition 5.1.

Formally, rewrite Equation 5.1, taking logs of both sides, then differentiate, to give:

$$\frac{dM}{M} - \frac{dP}{P} = \frac{dy}{y}$$

remembering that, for any variable X, $d(\log X) = dX/X$. Since we are assuming that y is constant for present purposes, the right-hand side is zero. Hence, the domestic price level has to change in proportion to the money stock.

Now treat the PPP equation in the same way, to give:

$$\frac{dS}{S} + \frac{dP^*}{P^*} = \frac{dP}{P}$$

Since P^* is assumed constant, this says that the exchange rate must depreciate in proportion to the rise in UK prices.

At the old price level, P_0, there is clearly an excess supply of money, which will cause economic agents to increase spending so as to reduce their money balances. (Recall that the quantity theory is based on the assumption that the only way for agents to reduce their money balances is by buying goods and services.) The counterpart of the excess supply of money is therefore an excess demand for goods, as measured by the distance $(y_1^d - y_0)$ in Figure 5.2(b).

Given our assumption of a fixed real income and output, the extra spending must drive up prices (hence the arrows between points c and b, and points A and B). As the price of goods rises, the price of dollars must increase (the pound depreciate) in order to keep domestic output competitive, in other words, to prevent a flood of relatively cheap US output into the UK economy in response to the real exchange rate appreciation.

It is easy to see how great a depreciation is required to restore equilibrium. With domestic prices higher in proportion to the monetary expansion, and the US price level unchanged, preservation of PPP implies an increase of the same proportion in the price of dollars (see Box 5.1).

We have reached the first important conclusion in our analysis of the monetary model:

Proposition 5.1: In the monetary model, a given percentage increase in the domestic money supply leads, other things being equal, to a depreciation of the same proportion in the value of the domestic currency.

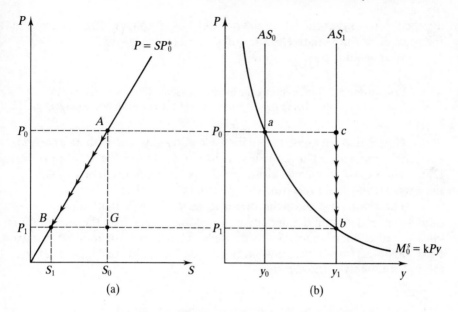

Figure 5.3 Income increase under floating rates.

5.1.4 An income increase under floating exchange rates

Now consider the effect of an increase in real income, from y_0 to y_1, with no change in the money stock (Figure 5.3).

At any price level, higher real income implies a greater demand for money. Put differently, with a given money supply we must have constant *nominal* income, Py. So, the higher is real income, the lower must the price level be.

Since nominal income has jumped to P_0y_1 (at point c in Figure 5.3(b)), the impact effect must be to create an excess demand for money and an excess supply of goods equal to the gap $(y_1 - y_0)$ at the original price level, P_0. As we have already seen, real balances can only be replenished by reducing spending.

The result must be deflation, bringing the price level down from P_0 to P_1. In the new equilibrium, at b, both money and goods markets clear, with the same demand and supply as before the income increase, and with the same nominal income.

In the open sector of the economy, however, the exchange rate must have fallen (that is, the pound appreciated) from S_0 to S_1. Otherwise, the fall in domestic prices (depreciation in the real exchange rate) would have made the UK overcompetitive, causing a massive excess demand for sterling (as would have been the case at G, for example). PPP is preserved by appreciation, so that the fall in the price of UK output is offset by a rise in the price of sterling relative to the dollar.

We conclude then as follows:

Proposition 5.2: In the monetary model, a rise in domestic real income leads, other things being equal, to an appreciation of the home currency.

Notice that we associate an increase in real income with an *appreciation* of the currency. This conclusion flatly contradicts the wisdom of the DIY model that, as income rises, the domestic economy tends to suck in imports, causing a depreciation in a floating exchange rate.

The reason we have the opposite result here is that the monetary model concentrates on the impact of an income increase on the demand for *money*, rather than goods. Since it swells the demand for money, it must cause a contraction in the demand for goods, which in turn must lead to a fall in the domestic price level.

5.1.5 A foreign price increase under floating exchange rates

An important feature of the model is its conclusion regarding the effect of a change in the remaining exogenous variable, P^*, the foreign price level.

Concentrate on the PPP line in Figure 5.4(a). How will it change when P^* increases? Since its gradient is $P/S = P^*$, it will become steeper, so that the original UK price level P_0 is associated with a lower price of US dollars, in other words a higher exchange rate for the pound.

The reason for this result should by now be obvious. With higher US prices, UK goods are overcompetitive at the old exchange rate. The demand for sterling by potential US importers of cheaper UK goods is overwhelming, and drives the pound's value up until US competitiveness is restored.

In the new equilibrium, the fact that US output is higher priced in dollar terms than previously is offset by the higher relative price of the UK currency. We conclude:

Proposition 5.3: In the monetary model, a rise in the foreign price level, other things being equal, is associated with an appreciation of the domestic currency (that is, a fall in the price of foreign exchange, S), and no other change in the domestic economy.

From the point of view of macroeconomic policy, this proposition is highly significant. It suggests that world inflation need have no impact on the domestic economy. The UK price level is determined in UK money markets in exactly the same way it would be if the rest of the world never

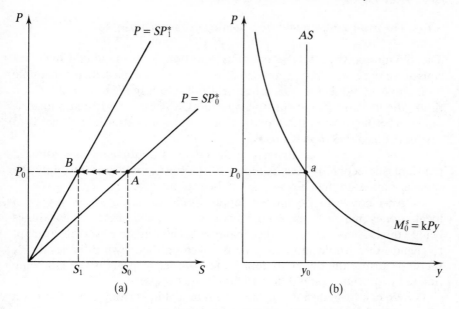

Figure 5.4   Foreign price increase under floating rates.

existed. The floating exchange rate acts like a valve, continually sliding up or down as required to preserve PPP in the face of disturbances originating in either or both countries' domestic money markets.

The implication is that the sovereignty of each country's macro-economic policy is preserved by exchange rate flexibility. Each can independently choose its inflation rate[2] without regard to the actions of the other. If independence is to be regarded as a desirable feature of an international monetary order, the floating exchange rate system appears highly attractive on the basis of the analysis in this section.

Notice that, in arriving at Proposition 5.3, we had no need to consult Figure 5.4(b). Does that mean the money markets are irrelevant to the outcome?

There are two reasons why the money markets are certainly not irrelevant. Firstly, it is the fact that money market equilibrium is unaffected by the change in US prices which keeps the domestic price level fixed at its initial level P_0, and forces the burden of adjustment on to the exchange rate.

Secondly, ask yourself the following question: *what can have caused the US price level to rise?*

---

[2] Of course, in this simple model the inflation rate is the only variable left for the government of either country to choose.

5.1.6   The two-country model of a floating exchange rate

The obvious answer to the previous question is: something which has caused an excess supply to appear in the US money market, for example an increase in the US money stock or a fall in US income. In fact, if you think about it for a moment, the way the US price level is determined is likely to be the same as the way the UK price level is determined, that is to say, in the local US money market.

Look back at our analysis of the effect of a monetary expansion in the domestic economy (see Section 5.1.3). Why should we not apply the same argument to the USA as was applied to the UK?

An increase in US money supply would cause an excess supply in local money markets, causing Americans to spend more, other things being equal, so as to reduce their balances. The outcome of their attempt to spend more would ultimately be to drive up their own price level, P^*, thereby causing the dollar to depreciate in order to prevent the US being flooded with what would otherwise be cheaper imports.

We can formalize this symmetrical model by writing the US version of our quantity equation (Equation 4.7) as follows:

$$M^{d*} = k^* P^* y^* \tag{5.4}$$

which simply says the US demand for money, M^{d*}, is proportional to US nominal income, $P^* y^*$. Notice the factor of proportionality is k^*, to allow for the possibility that the US demand for money may be *quantitatively* different from that of the UK, even though it is *qualitatively* similar (that is, of the same functional form).

Now assume that, just as UK money stock is initially M_0^s, US money supply starts off at M_0^{s*}. Divide the UK demand for money equation (Equation 4.7) by Equation 5.4, and set the respective demands for money equal to supply in each country, to give:

$$\frac{M_0^s}{M_0^{s*}} = \frac{kPy}{k^* P^* y^*} \tag{5.5}$$

Since, under PPP, we have $P/P^* = S$, it follows that we can rewrite Equation 5.5 as:

$$\frac{M_0^s}{M_0^{s*}} = \frac{kSy}{k^* y^*} \tag{5.6}$$

Now if we solve for S, we have:

$$S = \frac{M/M^*}{ky/k^* y^*} \tag{5.7}$$

This says the exchange rate equals the ratio of the numerator (relative money stocks) to the denominator (relative real demands). Therefore, anything which tends to increase the UK money stock relative to the US, or diminish UK demand for money relative to the US, will cause the pound to depreciate (*S* to rise).

To see how we must modify our previous conclusions, rewrite Equation 5.7 more simply, as follows:

$$S = \frac{\widetilde{M}}{\widetilde{k}\,\widetilde{y}} \tag{5.8}$$

where the convention has been introduced (and will be followed wherever necessary throughout the book) that a tilde over a variable denotes the ratio of its domestic to foreign value, so $\widetilde{M}$ means M/M^*, and so on.

Now remember that a 10% increase in the UK money supply relative to the US, $M/M^* = \widetilde{M}$, can come about *either* from a 10% rise in the UK money stock *or* from a 10% fall in the US money stock *or*, more likely, from some combination of both, say a 15% increase in UK money supply, with a 5% rise in US money.

It follows that, although we can stick to our original conclusion (Proposition 5.1) that an increase in UK money supply, other things being equal, leads to a depreciation in sterling (rise in *S*) of the same proportion, we now recognize that *the same is true of anything which changes relative money stocks*. Thus, for example, a 10% fall in US money while the UK money stock remained constant would cause a 10% depreciation in the pound's exchange rate, other things being equal.

Similarly, it is *relative* real income that counts in determining the demand for one country's money relative to another, so an increase in US income has the same impact as a fall in UK income, and we know from Proposition 5.2 that the latter causes a rise in the relative price of dollars.

> It follows, then, that we can generalize both Propositions 5.1 and 5.2 by substituting for the domestic variables their value relative to the same foreign variables.

5.2 The simple monetary model of a fixed exchange rate

Now consider a situation where the exchange rate is not allowed to move. The analysis here is slightly more complicated, so it will help if we start by clarifying which variables are being taken as exogenous and which endogenous.

Real income, *y*, is assumed to be given by factors outside the scope of our model, as before, and the foreign price level, P^*, is determined by foreign money supply, income and so on, and hence is also taken as given.

Recall the discussion of the money supply in Section 4.1.2. Under a fixed exchange rate regime, we concluded that the money supply was *not* an exogenous variable. Instead, the policy variable was domestic credit, *DC*, and we could write:

$$FX + DC \equiv M^s \tag{4.10}$$
$$\text{repeated}$$

so that the burden of adjustment to changes in the exogenous variables fell on the foreign currency reserves, *FX*.

The only remaining exogenous variable is the exchange rate itself, which is fixed by the decision of the authorities at some level, $\overline{S}$.[3]

5.2.1   A money supply increase under fixed exchange rates

Now look at Figure 5.5, which shows the effect of an expansionary monetary policy, in other words, an increase in domestic credit, from an initial level of DC_0 to a higher level, DC_1.

Start with Figure 5.5(c), which plots levels of the money stock (vertical axis) against levels of the foreign exchange reserves, *FX* (horizontally). Measure off the quantity DC_0 on the vertical axis, and from that point, extend a 45° line. That ray then shows how the money stock increases with additions to the reserves, given the initial quantity of domestic credit, DC_0. For example, if the reserves were nil, the whole money stock would be credit. As we move to the right, each additional pound of reserves increases the money stock by one pound exactly.

If we start with reserves of FX_0, the money stock must be:

$$M_0^s = FX_0 + DC_0 \tag{5.9}$$

so that the starting point in that diagram is at *H*.

Now let us set the initial value of the money supply and the price level at unity. In other words, assume we happen to have: $ky_0 = 1$. This device is for purposes of illustration only. It has the advantage that it allows us to translate the money stock value on the vertical axis of Figure 5.5(c) directly into the implied price level in Figures 5.5(a) and (b).

Exploiting this fact, the initial price level given a money stock of M_0^s must be P_0. Hence the economy starts off at point *a* in Figure 5.5(b). Notice that as far as aggregate demand and supply are concerned, the diagram is unchanged, since at this stage we have no reason to believe that the private sector's behaviour will be any different under fixed rather than under floating exchange rates.

---

[3] We ignore another complication here which is that, in practice, countries running so-called fixed exchange rates invariably allow some measure of freedom for the rate to move up or down from its central parity (see Section 1.2).

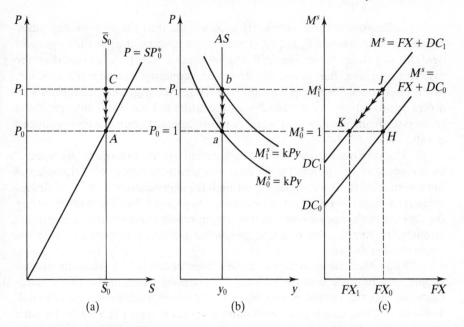

Figure 5.5 Domestic credit increase under fixed rates ($M_0^s = P_0 = 1$).

As with Figure 5.4, the left-hand diagram (Figure 5.5(a)) plots the PPP line. However, with the exchange rate pegged at $\overline{S}_0$, the economy must at all times be restricted to points that lie along the vertical line. Since, as before, equilibrium requires that the domestic price level be at purchasing power parity, it follows that the system must start off at A, at the intersection of the PPP line with the fixed exchange rate line. Put formally, we must have:

$$P = \overline{S}_0 \overline{P}^* \tag{5.10}$$

where the bars over the right-hand side variables remind us that both S and P^* are fixed exogenously.

The economy is in full equilibrium initially, because the PPP price level defined in Equation 5.10 is precisely the one consistent with the (endogenous) money stock, and hence with equality of aggregate supply and demand at the point a in Figure 5.5(b).

Now suppose the initial equilibrium illustrated by points A, a and H is disturbed by a monetary expansion.

With the expansion of domestic credit, the 45° line in the money supply diagram Figure 5.5(c) shifts upward by the amount of the expansion, so that, with the foreign exchange reserves still at their previous level (of FX_0), the money stock has now swelled to M_1^s, as we can see at the point J.

Following the line across from J, we see that the new money stock implies a price level of P_1 (at b), thanks to an upward shift in the aggregate demand schedule. From the PPP line in Figure 5.5(a), it is clear that the higher price level has made the domestic economy uncompetitive, since, given unchanged foreign prices and the fixed exchange rate, it amounts to a real appreciation. At C, there is an incentive for domestic entrepreneurs to import from abroad and none for foreigners to buy locally-produced goods.

The obvious outcome must be a deficit on the balance of payments[4] as the economy responds to the changed terms of trade. The situation is unsustainable. It would cause an immediate depreciation if the authorities permitted one. However, by assumption, they avoid that outcome by using the foreign exchange reserves to buy the domestic currency or, to put it differently, to finance the ongoing payments deficit. The result is that *the reserves start to fall.*

Each successive reduction in the reserves tends to reduce the money supply, pushing the economy along the arrowed paths in the three quadrants, so that the system moves from J to K, from b back to a, and from C down to A. The process ends with competitiveness restored and the balance of payments deficit reduced to zero, back at A on the PPP line, with the price level restored to its old level of P_0 (at the point a). The reinstatement of the original equilibrium is possible because the money supply has contracted, to the point where it is once more at its initial level, M_0^s.

To understand why we get this result, recall from Equation 4.7 that our demand for money, given PPP, must equal:

$$M^d = k\,Py = k(\overline{S}\,\overline{P}^*)\overline{y} \tag{5.11}$$

The final term is the demand for money. Notice that all its components are exogenously given variables. It follows that, under our assumptions, nothing the domestic monetary authority does can affect the demand for money. If the market is to clear, then it follows equally that the money supply must automatically find its way back to its pre-expansion level.

Equating demand and supply:

$$M^d = k\overline{S}\,\overline{P}^*\overline{y} = M^s = FX + DC \tag{5.12}$$

so that, solving for FX gives us:

$$FX = k\overline{S}\,\overline{P}^*\overline{y} - DC \tag{5.13}$$

---

[4] The monetary model is normally seen as dealing with the balance of payments rather than the balance of trade alone. In the present context, the distinction hardly matters.

Equation 5.13 tells us that the foreign currency reserves, *FX*, must be exactly equal to the gap between the given demand for domestic money and the supply generated by the local banking system, through the process of domestic credit expansion. It follows that the more sparing are the domestic authorities in their credit creation, the greater will be the shortfall which has to be made up by the reserves.

In terms of *changes*, we can state that:

Proposition 5.4: Under fixed exchange rates in the monetary model, starting from a position of equilibrium, domestic credit creation will be neutralized, other things being equal, by a fall in the reserves as a result of a temporary balance of payments deficit. Conversely, domestic credit contraction will cause a temporary balance of payments surplus and a consequent offsetting rise in the reserves.

Notice that, as always in the monetary model, the mechanism involved here could be expressed purely in terms of the excess demand for money.

The right-hand side of Equation 5.13 is the excess demand for money balances. It is this excess demand which is satisfied by the supply of international currency. An increase in domestic credit from an initial equilibrium generates an excess supply of money balances in the local market. As in the closed economy context (see Section 4.1.2), the effect is to cause domestic residents to run down their excess money balances by spending. With real income fixed, however, the consequent inflation makes foreign products relatively cheaper and the home country's exports more expensive. The external deficit is a by-product of the private sector's attempt to substitute goods for excess money balances. As reserves flow out, the foreign component of the money stock falls along with domestic prices until equilibrium is reinstated.

Notice that since it is *stocks* of money that count in this model, the *flow* of reserves in or out of a country can only be a temporary phenomenon, as the money stock adjusts over time to the demand. In other words, balance of payments deficits or surpluses are viewed as inherently transient by-products of the adjustment mechanism. Once that process is complete, and the money market is back in equilibrium, the deficit or surplus will have evaporated.

If the money supply, price level and balance of payments all return to their previous level, what has changed in the new equilibrium?

Compare the points *K* and *H* in Figure 5.5(c). Although the money supply is unchanged at *K*, its *composition* has altered as a result of the cumulative impact of the balance of payments deficit which persisted throughout the period of adjustment. The new money supply is made up as follows:

$$M_0^s = FX_1 + DC_1 \tag{5.14}$$

In other words, the net outcome is that the money stock now consists of more domestic credit and less foreign exchange than previously. What has occurred is a kind of debasement of the currency – a dilution of the international asset-backing of the domestic money supply. Obviously, the process has a well defined limit – at the point when the reserves have fallen to zero and the entire money stock is composed of domestic credit.

Sterilization of reserve changes

Notice that the process described here amounts to a type of automatic stabilization. In fact, this is broadly the mechanism relied on to guarantee the stability both of the pre-World War I Gold Standard and the Bretton Woods system (see Section 1.5.1). With a fixed exchange rate, flows of reserves act automatically to adjust the money stock so as to reinstate equilibrium. Government monetary policy is not only impossible, it is also unnecessary.

In particular, viewed from this standpoint, balance of payments deficits (or surpluses), far from requiring remedial macroeconomic policy, are actually the channels through which disequilibria are spontaneously rectified.

Nonetheless, a government which wishes for whatever reason to resist these stabilizing forces might in principle be able to do so, temporarily at least. To see how this can be achieved, go back to the situation facing domestic policymakers at the start of what has been called here 'the adjustment phase', in the aftermath of the initial destabilizing domestic credit expansion, when the economy is at points c, b and J respectively in Figures 5.5(a) to (c).

At that juncture, the UK is running a balance of payments deficit, and is therefore losing reserves. In other words, the UK money stock is falling because, in the identity:

$$\Delta FX + \Delta DC \equiv \Delta M^s \tag{4.11}$$

repeated

the first term is negative. Since the second term is constant (the once and for all increase is assumed to have already taken place), the money supply is falling. Hence, it is only a matter of time until the cumulative effect of the continuing deficits reduces the money supply to its pre-disturbance level.

Now suppose the authorities decided to try and prevent the money stock falling by further expanding domestic credit. It would appear that, in so doing, they could pre-empt the fall in the money supply. If they increased credit enough to offset the fall in the foreign currency reserves in each period, it looks as though they could neutralize the deficits completely.

The following piece of jargon is commonly used:

Sterilization is the process of neutralizing the effect of a balance of payments deficit (surplus) by creating (retiring) enough domestic credit to offset the fall in the foreign exchange reserves.

There has been a great deal of debate, among both researchers and policymakers, about how far sterilization is actually feasible. Even its most enthusiastic advocates would not claim it can work for very long. Whether it can work at all in today's currency markets is extremely dubious.[5]

To see why its usefulness is likely to be limited, we need to follow through the implication of the second-stage increase in domestic credit. Obviously, the effect of an increase in domestic credit starting from the situation at J in Figure 5.5(c) will be to move the money supply line even further up the vertical axis. The result will be to further dilute the foreign currency backing of the UK money stock.

Nor is that all. We have already established that, as long as the money stock is above its equilibrium level, the UK will be haemorrhaging reserves. Clearly, anything which prolongs that situation will reduce the reserves below what they otherwise would be in the absence of any attempt at sterilization.

It follows that sterilization is likely to prove a treadmill. Each expansion of domestic credit will prolong the reserve loss and hence generate the need for further credit creation. At each stage, the domestic credit component of the money stock gets larger and the reserve component smaller.

In theory, at least, there will come a stage when the reserves are exhausted, and the game will be over. In reality, the limit to this process is likely to come some time before the country's reserves are actually exhausted, simply because currency markets will anticipate the evil day and thereby hasten its arrival by rushing to sell pounds at the current exchange rate while they still can.[6]

5.2.2 An income increase under fixed exchange rates

As far as changes in real income and the world price level are concerned, the analysis involves a straightforward application of the results from the floating rate case.

---

[5] The issue is clouded by all kinds of other problems, for example the apparent instability of the demand for money in the UK and USA, interest differentials (see Section 5.1.3) and risk premiums (Chapter 13), and many others.

[6] The sterilization mechanism is also likely to prove self-defeating because of its impact on interest rates.

With the price level unchanged, an increase in real income amounts to a rise in the demand for real money balances, other things being equal. Starting from a position of equilibrium, then, the impact will cause domestic residents to spend less, so as to raise their balances to a level commensurate with their new, higher volume of transactions. In doing so, they force the price level down, which with a fixed exchange rate makes the home country's output overcompetitive on world markets, leading to a balance of payments surplus, and consequent rise in the reserves. This process will come to an end only when the domestic money stock has grown sufficiently to match the new, larger demand.

So, as the reader may confirm by redrawing Figure 5.5 and shifting the aggregate supply line to the right, we can state the following:

> **Proposition 5.5**: Under fixed exchange rates in the monetary model, starting from a position of equilibrium, the result of a rise in (the domestic country's) real income will be to cause an increase in the reserves as a result of a temporary balance of payments surplus, other things being equal. In the new equilibrium, the domestic money stock will have risen and the home price level will have returned to its PPP level.

Again, note the contrast with the DIY model (Section 1.4).

5.2.3   A foreign price increase under fixed exchange rates

As for a rise in the world price level, the effect under a fixed exchange rate is to directly increase the home country's competitiveness, causing a payments surplus and consequent rise in the reserves. (In terms of Figure 5.5, the impact effect is to cause the PPP line to become steeper.) This in turn brings about a rise in the money stock, pushing up the home country price level until it reaches parity with that of the outside world, at which point PPP and external balance are restored. So, for completeness:

> **Proposition 5.6**: Under fixed exchange rates in the monetary model, starting from a position of equilibrium, the result of a rise in the rest of the world's price level will be to cause an increase in the reserves as the result of a temporary balance of payments surplus, other things being equal. In the new equilibrium, the domestic money stock will be greater, and the home price level will have risen to its PPP level.

Note the implication: a country which pegs its exchange rate has ultimately to accept the world price level. In the common jargon of the 1960s and 1970s, it is forced to 'import inflation' from the rest of the world. The fact that it cannot control its own money supply means it cannot choose its price level or inflation rate independently of developments beyond its borders.

Hence, an important conclusion of the monetary model is that, subject to one qualification we shall deal with in a moment, *a country cannot follow an independent monetary policy under fixed exchange rates – nor, as a consequence, can it choose a price level or inflation rate different from that of the rest of the world.*

To see the qualification that needs to be added to this statement, ask yourself the following question: what determines the world price level, P^*? What causes world inflation – at any rate, in this simple model?

The answer must be that world prices rise when the world's money stock increases faster than world demand. Also, world money supply and demand are simply the sum of the supply and demand in all of the countries in the world. It follows that, when we analyse the effect of, say, an increase in the home country's money stock, *we can only treat the world price level as exogenous if the additional money creation is of negligible significance to the world as a whole.* In other words, we have to be able safely to ignore the impact of the money supply increase on the rest of the world's money markets, and hence on world prices. Obviously, this assumption only makes sense if the domestic country is 'small' enough in economic terms relative to the world economy for us to be able to ignore the repercussions of its policy measures on the world economy.[7]

5.2.4 Devaluation under fixed exchange rates

Before leaving the analysis of fixed exchange rates, there is one special case which merits attention, because it provides a particularly clear insight into the nature of the monetary model.

No fixed exchange rate is fixed forever. Sooner or later the authorities find themselves forced to move the rate to a new level, higher or lower. That is why a fixed exchange rate regime is sometimes referred to as an adjustable peg. What happens when the peg is adjusted?

---

[7] It is an awkward question, of course, to decide how small is small enough for present purposes. On the one hand, the USA or Japan are obviously far too large to be able to ignore the feedback effects of their policies from the world economy. On the other hand, the vast majority of countries in the world are clearly small relative to world money markets. But what about medium-sized economies such as the UK, France, Italy, Canada, for example? The answer is not obvious.

Those readers who are familiar with elementary price theory will recognize a similarity here with the simple model of the perfectly competitive firm. Remember the paradox there was that market price was unaffected by the typical small firm's output decisions. Although the perfectly competitive firm acting alone cannot influence market price, the small firms in aggregate determine the price by their independently-taken decisions. By the same token, we assume here the small country cannot on its own have an impact on the world economy, but the monetary policy of small countries in aggregate (together with the large countries) determines the world price level.

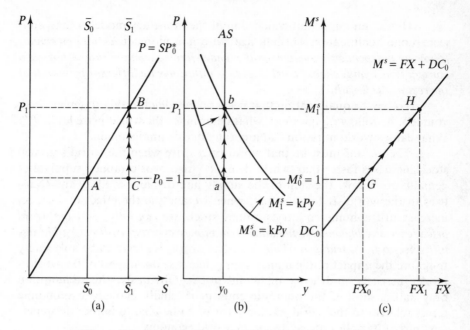

Figure 5.6 Devaluation under fixed rates ($M_0^s = P_0 = 1$).

Figure 5.6 shows the effect of a devaluation, an announced, once and for all rise in the price of foreign currency. It must be emphasized that the analysis is only applicable to a devaluation which is an isolated event, and perceived as such, not one that generates the expectation of further devaluation (or, for that matter, revaluation) to come.

Following the pedagogic convention in economics, we start the analysis from a position of equilibrium, which is somewhat unrealistic in this case because countries usually alter a fixed exchange rate only when absolutely necessary to correct an obvious disequilibrium. Nonetheless, it is easy to see how the conclusions could be modified to deal with an initial balance of payments deficit.

The economy starts off in equilibrium at points A, a and G in the three diagrams in Figure 5.6, with, as before, an exchange rate of $\overline{S}_0$, a price level under PPP of P_0, and a money supply of M_0^s, made up of domestic credit in the quantity DC_0 and reserves of FX_0.

The home country then devalues, raising the price of foreign currency to $\overline{S}_1$.

The overnight, impact effect is to move the economy instantaneously to a point like C. In other words, with a given foreign price level, and as yet with no time for domestic prices to change (suppose the devaluation took place over a weekend, as is the fashion nowadays in the European Monetary System) the home country is now *over*competitive. Had it started off from a position of being uncompetitive (that is, above the PPP line), the impact effect would have been to move it to the right, making it more competitive than previously, which would, presumably, have been the object of the whole exercise in the first place.

The interim verdict has to be: so far, so good. With both domestic and foreign prices unchanged, it is the *real* as well as the nominal exchange rate that has been devalued. Foreign goods now cost more, while domestic goods are unchanged in price. The result must be a tendency for home country consumers to buy more domestically-produced output than previously, and fewer imports. Conversely, foreigners find the home country's products more attractively priced, on average, than prior to the devaluation.

Starting from equilibrium, the outcome has to be a balance of payments surplus. If we had started, more realistically, from a position of deficit, we would only have been able to assert that the result would be a less unfavourable foreign balance.

The story of what happens during the next stage, as the economy adjusts to the devaluation, can be told in several different ways, each focusing on the adjustment process in a different sector, all leading inexorably to the same conclusion.

First, consider what is happening to the money supply when the economy is 'bounced' over to C.[8] With its balance of payments in surplus, the country must be accumulating reserves – hence the arrows on the path from G to H in the money supply diagram (Figure 5.6(c)). Since the volume of domestic credit is unchanged, the money supply must be growing, shifting the aggregate demand schedule upwards. In terms of the money market, with real income and output constant, and hence an unchanged demand, the price level must be bid up as agents attempt to reduce their excess real balances by buying additional goods. As the price level rises, of course, the competitive advantage and consequent external surplus is eroded, until the new equilibrium is reached at B in Figure 5.6(a).

In terms of the goods market, if output is pegged at y_0, the increased demand by domestic residents (for cheaper import substitutes) and by foreigners (for the home country's exports) cannot be satisfied. The excess demand must simply generate an inflation, which persists until enough of the additional demand has been priced out of the market in order to restore equilibrium.

The version of this process that gained wide acceptance in the early 1970s, particularly in the UK, emphasized the reaction of labour markets to devaluation. It was argued that a key role would be played by wage inflation, induced *either* by a cost-push process as workers reacted to the higher price of imports by demanding compensating wage rises *or* by a

---

[8] We ignore the second-order effect on the money stock of the rise in the sterling value of the UK reserves when the pound is devalued.

demand-pull mechanism, as employers bid up the wage rate in an attempt to satisfy the excess demand for goods by recruiting more labour.

Whichever of these processes is the dominant one, there can be no doubt about the conclusion. Ultimately, the economy ends up at *B*, with PPP restored, and the real exchange rate back where it was before, thanks to domestic inflation.

What has changed, if anything, compared to the pre-devaluation situation? Obviously, the higher price level is 'supported' or sustained by a larger money stock, M_1^s, made up of the same level of domestic credit plus a larger stock of foreign currency reserves – the accumulation of the intervening weeks, or months, or possibly years of balance of payments surplus. So:

> **Proposition 5.7**: Under fixed exchange rates in the monetary model the result of a once and for all devaluation will be a temporary improvement in the competitiveness of the home country and consequently a balance of payments surplus, leading in turn to a rise in its foreign currency reserves. However, the accompanying inflation will, as time passes, erode the country's price advantage, until the economy finds itself back where it started, with a higher price level, greater reserves and a larger *nominal* money stock, but the same *real* money supply.

From a policy point of view, the good news is that, if the monetary model's message is to be believed, devaluation works. It does indeed generate a balance of payments surplus, or at least reduce the deficit of a country which starts off in disequilibrium. Devaluation replenishes the reserves, or slows down the rate of reserve loss for a deficit country.

On the other hand, the bad news is that its beneficial effect is temporary. It cannot permanently affect competitiveness. It causes inflation, thereby ultimately neutralizing the benefits that it is supposed to confer. How long the adjustment takes is an empirical question, to which the answer would probably vary from country to country and case to case.

In any case, there may well be a delay before the balance of payments effect of a devaluation appears. It is often argued that the immediate impact of a devaluation is to worsen rather than improve the situation. The logic is as follows.

If trade flows are usually invoiced in the currency of the exporting nation, a devaluation of the pound will reduce the average dollar price of UK exports, but have no effect on the (dollar) price of our imports. Furthermore, if the very short-run elasticities of demand for exports and imports are negligible (because of inertia in consumer tastes, difficulty in switching production and so on), the immediate outcome will be unchanged trade volumes priced less favourably for the home country. Each unit of exports will now earn fewer dollars, while each import still costs the same. The result will be a deterioration in the UK balance of payments, which will only be rectified with the passage of time, as trade volumes react to the new relative price.

If this analyis is correct, devaluation will be followed by an initial increase in the current account deficit, reversing itself gradually, until it surpasses its former position and carries on improving the so-called **J-curve** effect.

While the *J*-curve is often regarded as a problem, it is obvious from what has just been said that it relates exclusively to the current account.[9] So, if the objective of devaluation is to improve the current account, the possibility of a *J*-curve effect may be a worry. Conceivably, the cost pressures generated in the domestic economy by the devaluation could be felt even before the supposed benefits appear. If, however, the aim of devaluation is to replenish the reserves, there is no obvious reason why the benefits should await an improvement in the current account.

5.3   Interest rates in the monetary model

Until now, we have made use of a particularly simple form of the demand for money, the Cambridge quantity equation. In Chapter 4 (Section 4.1.2), however, it was argued that a plausible view of the demand for money would include a role for interest rates, as a key determinant of the opportunity cost. We now proceed to examine the implications of incorporating interest rates into our simple model of exchange rates.

Our first approach will be naive, or rather myopic, because we shall temporarily ignore the important conclusions we reached in Chapter 3.

Look back at the formulation of the demand for money in Equation 4.9. As we have already seen, it implies that the demand for real balances will be lower, at any given level of income, the higher are interest rates. In other words, at any price level, the nominal demand will be smaller at a higher interest rate r_1 than at a lower interest rate, r_0.

It follows that, with an unchanged money stock, the effect of a rise in UK interest rates is to create a temporary excess supply of money and excess demand for goods. Hence, in Figure 5.7(b) the aggregate demand schedule shifts to the right[10] at the initial price level, P_0, generating immediate excess demand equal to $(y_1^d - y_0)$, and consequent inflation. As the price level rises, the economy moves up its new aggregate demand curve from c to b.

---

[9] In fact, it dates back to arguments about whether devaluation could improve the current account even in the long run. Thus, economists afflicted by 'elasticity pessimism' in the 1950s believed that the *J*-curve was all tail and no upswing.

[10] In *IS–LM* terms, the upward shift in the horizontal *IS* curve cuts the unchanged *LM* curve further to the north-east.

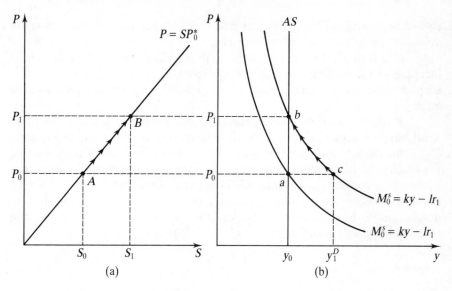

Figure 5.7   Interest rate increase under floating exchange rates.

Translating the argument into money market terms, at the point *c* the higher opportunity cost induces agents to economize on real balances by attempting to spend more. In the process, they drive up prices until the real money stock has been reduced sufficiently to reinstate equilibrium at the new, higher interest rate. When equilibrium is reached, at the new price level, P_1, nominal income has increased so as to generate a transactions demand great enough to offset the impact of the higher opportunity cost.

Switching attention to Figure 5.7(a), if the exchange rate is floating, the higher interest rate must be associated with a higher value of *S*, in other words a more expensive dollar and a cheaper pound. Furthermore, it is easy to see that a similar logic would apply to a change in the foreign interest rate. Hence, as before, since increased US interest rates mean a cheaper dollar, other things being equal, and higher UK interest rates imply a cheaper pound, the net effect on the exchange rate depends on *relative* interest rates.[11] We appear to have arrived at another general proposition:

> **Proposition 5.8**: According to the monetary model, with given nominal money stocks and real incomes, a rise in domestic interest rates relative to those in the foreign country will be associated with a depreciation in the domestic currency.

---

[11] A formal demonstration of this fact would be a little messier and more complicated than was the case in Section 5.6 with relative money stocks and incomes. The reason is to be found in our formulation of the demand for money which is linear in natural numbers. Fortunately, there is more or less universal support amongst researchers for a log linear formulation. In this case, it turns out that exchange rates depend on relative values of all variables, provided that income and interest elasticities are the same in each each country.

Again, note the contrast with the DIY model.

However, this proposition is not as simple as it seems. Look back, if necessary, at the conclusions we reached in Chapter 3. In particular, recall the discussion of what determines the interest differential between two countries: under interest rate parity, we came to the conclusion it would reflect the expected rate of currency depreciation.

What Proposition 5.8 says then, is that if something occurs which causes agents to expect the exchange rate to depreciate more rapidly, the domestic country's interest rates rise, and the exchange rate does indeed depreciate – *immediately*. In other words, in an international context, we can view the opportunity cost of holding a currency as the rate of change in its international value, that is to say its command over goods in world markets.

A caveat is in order, though. Consider for a moment the question of what determines the market's expectations with regard to currency movements. Answering this question fully will take up a large slice of the remainder of the book (see Chapters 11 and 12). For the moment, we will be content to sketch a vague outline of the kind of factors likely to play a part in influencing market perceptions.

It is highly likely, we assert, that currency speculators will base their predictions of future exchange rate movements on their forecasts of what is going to happen to those variables which they believe are the ultimate determinants of long-run exchange rates. In other words, they first forecast the 'fundamentals', then form their expectations as to the exchange rate accordingly.

What this implies, of course, is that interest rate changes are not exogenous events, they don't just *happen*, they are themselves very much the outcome of changes in expectations.

But now ask yourself another question: what kind of factors are these 'fundamentals' likely to be?

It is very probable that the fundamentals will turn out to include, among others, the very variables that figured in the simple monetary model we sketched in Section 5.1 – relative money stocks and income. Changes in the market's anticipations with regard to these fundamentals will trigger reassessments of the future outlook for exchange rates, and this in turn will cause instantaneous fluctuations in the demand for the different currencies and hence in their international values. So we may well have a situation where an event which is seen as foreshadowing a change in the domestic money stock for example, brings about an immediate adjustment in the interest rate and a simultaneous movement in the exchange rate.

This type of 'bootstrap' situation is one that will be familiar to anyone who has ever observed the behaviour of a typical financial market. The price of the asset in question, whether foreign currency, share or bond or commodity, is expected to rise at some point in the future. So the rise occurs *not in the future, but right now*. The very fact it is expected to rise pushes it up immediately.

This type of feedback mechanism will be examined at length later in the book (see Chapter 12). For the moment, all we can do is to note that the association between interest rates and exchange rates is complicated by the fact that, unlike money and income, interest rates cannot seriously be regarded as exogenous variables. Our conclusions in this case, therefore, ought to be viewed as provisional.

5.4   The monetary model as an explanation of the facts

Before going on to look at the question of how well the monetary model explains the facts, it is worth pausing for a moment to try and guess the answer, because we already have a clue from Section 2.5 of Chapter 2. Remember that we concluded then that, for all the plausibility of the PPP hypothesis, it came nowhere near to explaining the wide fluctuations in exchange rates in the last decade or so. Since the PPP hypothesis is one of the two central building-blocks of the simple monetary model, need we bother to go any further? Surely, if the foundations are rotten, there is no need to go on and look at the rest of the edifice?

This is certainly a persuasive argument. At the very least, it is hard to be anything other than extremely pessimistic about the prospects for using the monetary model to explain the facts. Nonetheless, it is worth pro-ceeding – just about. It is still possible (though unlikely) that the monetary model might work for the following reason.

Suppose the reason for the apparent failure of PPP to explain the facts is that the tests use the wrong price index. Suppose furthermore that the 'true' price index (the one that actually measures the prices that agents face) is unobservable. As long as that same unobservable price index fig-ures in the demand for money, we could end up finding that the monetary model fitted quite well in spite of the failure of PPP.[12]

If this seems a forlorn hope, the reader can comfort himself with the thought that sooner or later, in a book of this nature, we would have to take a look at the broad outline of what has happened to relative money stocks and incomes in recent years. Now is as good a time as any.

Figures 5.8 to 5.10 illustrate graphically the recent history of the UK, West Germany and Japan in this regard. In each case, the variables

---

[12] The possibility referred to here would also imply that demand for money studies using the standard price index were misspecified and should be expected to fit poorly. In fact, they fit reasonably well – certainly far better than PPP models (see the Reading Guide).

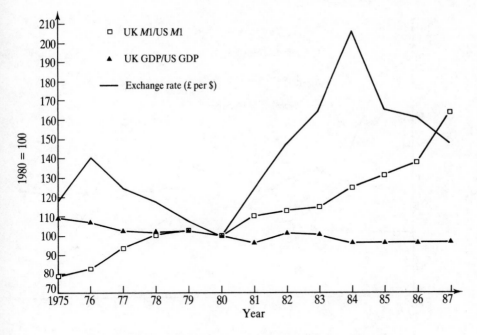

Figure 5.8   UK money, income and exchange rate 1975–87.

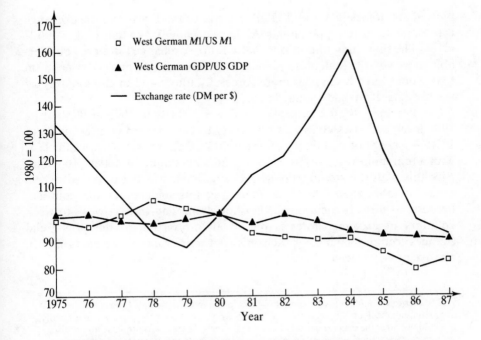

Figure 5.9   West German money, income and exchange rate 1975–87.

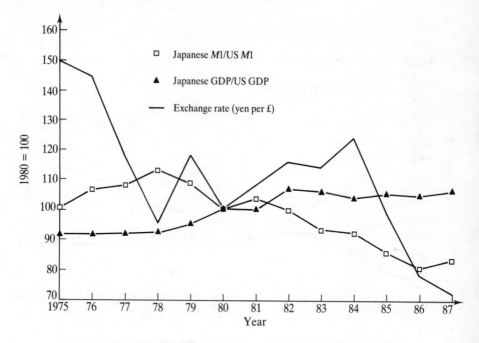

Figure 5.10 Japanese money, income and exchange rate 1975–87.

plotted are domestic $M1$ and GDP, relative to the USA, and the exchange rate, in home currency per dollar. All have been scaled so that 1980 = 100.[13]

The first thing to notice is that all three exchange rates are considerably more volatile than money stocks and incomes, and this is a conclusion that would have been even more forcefully illustrated in the monthly or weekly data, if we had included any.

For the UK, for example, relative $M1$ starts in 1975 at 80% of its 1980 level, and rises almost continuously to end the period at an index of 137.5 – a range of variability of under 60%. Relative GDP varies far less, with a minimum value of just over 96 and a maximum of under 110. Compare this with the sterling/dollar exchange rate, which has varied over a range of more than 100%. Furthermore, this understates the contrast, because, as already mentioned, the short term, day-to-day, week-to-week volatility of exchange rates is out of all proportion to the slow trend changes seen in incomes, or the somewhat more rapid movements seen in relative money stocks.

---

[13] The pictures would look very similar if we defined money as $M3$ ($M1$ plus time deposits) and, although recalculating on a different base year would change the pictures superficially, it would not alter the general nature of our conclusions. There are in any case no sound reasons for preferring one definition of money to another in the present context, nor any overwhelming arguments in favour of any particular base year.

Next, look at the trends in the data (where there are any). There has unquestionably been a rise in UK $M1$ relative to that of the USA over the data period, and a less marked fall in Britain's relative GDP. Both trends would be expected to cause the pound to depreciate steadily relative to the dollar, according to the monetary model, and, indeed, the sterling price of a dollar *was* higher in 1987 than in 1975. However, that bald fact conceals two protracted spells of sterling *appreciation* (1976 to 1980 and 1984 to 1987). The net outcome that the pound ends up in 1987 lower relative to the dollar than in 1975 is entirely due to the depreciation over the years 1980 to 1984.

This may seem bad enough news for the monetary approach, but there is worse to come when we turn to consider Figures 5.9 and 5.10.

The first point to notice is that the dollar rose relative to the Deutsche Mark in 1979 to 1984, albeit to a slightly lesser extent than it did compared to the pound. It even rose somewhat relative to the yen. In other words, we can in no way attribute the fall in the pound's exchange rate in the early 1980s to the trends in UK money and income. It was the dollar that was 'strong' throughout the world in these years, not the pound that was 'weak'.

That assessment of the situation is supported very clearly by Figure 5.9. In general, the movements in the DM/$ rate follow the same broad pattern as we saw in the case of the pound. Yet the trend in the relative West German money stock is downward for the most part, with little observable trend in relative income. As we know from Proposition 5.1, the net effect ought to be an *appreciation* of the DM, not a repetition of the pound's history.

In fact, the only support[14] for the monetary model is to be found in Figure 5.10. Although the dollar appears to have followed the same three phases of depreciation in the late 1970s, appreciation in the early 1980s and depreciation again since 1984, there is at least a clearly discernible upward trend in the value of the yen, and this is plainly warranted by the rise in Japan's relative GDP and fall in its relative money supply.

Nonetheless, the evidence presented here is not, on the whole, very encouraging. All that can be said in favour of the monetary model (and it is not something to be dismissed altogether) is that it does appear to explain the facts over the very long run, at least in broad outline. This is particularly true of fixed rate periods.

For example, ever since the early 1950s, the West German economy has consistently enjoyed more rapid growth than either the UK or USA. It has also stuck to a monetary policy that was markedly less expansionary than most other industrialized countries. As predicted by the models we have examined in this chapter, the outcome has been balance of payments surpluses and reserve accumulation, as well as long-term appreciation of

---

[14] Strictly speaking, evidence cannot be said to support a theory, but only to be consistent with it, that is, in failing to contradict it.

the Deutsche Mark, whether in forced realignments, when a fixed rate regime was in force, or more gradually, when floating.

Conversely, for most of the post-World War II period until the late 1970s, the UK has suffered from relatively slow economic growth, while its policymakers permitted a rapid expansion in the UK's money stock – or at least in its domestic credit component. Again, the result was as predicted – declining reserves and a depreciating currency.

At the same time, Japanese growth averaged several percentage points more than that of the UK or USA, while its money supply expanded at a moderate rate, causing mounting balance of payments surpluses and an appreciating international value for the yen.

Perhaps unsurprisingly, the more marked are the divergences between rates of monetary growth (and hence inflation), the better the monetary model fits the facts. If we were to examine a currency under conditions of hyperinflation (inflation at rates of, say, 100% per annum and above), we would find its rate of depreciation against any of the 'hard' currencies more or less equal to the difference in rates of monetary growth. However, as was noted at the end of Chapter 2, this is simply a reflection of the fact that in these pathological cases PPP has to be broadly maintained, at least to within limits that are narrow compared to the gap between inflation rates.

However, economists are not in the habit of drawing conclusions on the basis of this kind of cursory examination of a small amount of data. There is a wealth of additional evidence that could be used to cast light on the viability of the monetary model as an explanation of exchange rate changes, and there are sophisticated statistical and econometric techniques that could be brought to bear on the detailed data.

Researchers have in fact left no stone unturned in searching for evidence on the validity or otherwise of the monetary model. They have examined annual, quarterly and monthly data.[15] They have looked at trade-weighted as well as bilateral exchange rates. They have used narrow measures of money ($M0$ and $M1$) and broad measures ($M3$ and so on). They have extended and complicated the simple model to take account of adjustment delays ('lags') of all types and they have used state-of-the-art econometric techniques to test the theory.

By and large, their conclusions have been similar to ours. For example, in a series of influential publications, Meese and Rogoff found little support for the monetary model[16] in the period since 1973. Studies of

---

[15] Higher frequency data exist only for the US money stock, and for financial variables (exchange rates and interest rates). Even then, there is no monthly data on national income, so most researchers have used the index of industrial production as a proxy.

[16] Though they also reached similarly negative conclusions with respect to all the other models they tested. It should be repeated that researchers have usually tested versions of the monetary model that were a good deal more complicated than the one presented in this chapter.

individual exchange rates, particularly the pound/dollar and the Deutsche Mark/dollar, but also of a number of other 'hard' and 'soft' currencies lead to similar conclusions.

Even where a clear pattern associating monetary growth with depreciation can be found, the relationship is rarely anything like the strict proportionality predicted by Proposition 5.1. It is often even harder to find a link between a country's national income and the value of its currency (Proposition 5.2), though in some cases this may be the result of the use of inadequate proxy measures in place of GDP.

Worst of all, such relationships which do appear tend to be unstable, with apparently satisfactory results over one period either reversing themselves or disappearing altogether in the next period.

5.5 Conclusions

The monetary model combines the quantity theory of the demand for money with purchasing power parity to generate unambiguous conclusions about the effect of changes in exogenous variables on a floating exchange rate, or on the balance of payments, as the case may be. It remains an important benchmark with which to compare other models – not least because as we shall see in Chapters 6–9 its predictions accord in most cases with their long-run equilibrium results.

Unfortunately, as an explanation of the facts, the monetary model must be regarded as grossly inadequate in anything but the very long run, which is hardly surprising given the failure of PPP. If a model that assumes perfect flexibility of prices cannot explain the facts, we direct our attention in Chapter 6 to one that starts from the assertion that the price level is constant.

■ Summary

- The monetary model of a *floating exchange rate* predicts that the domestic currency will *depreciate* when any of the following occurs:

    - The domestic (foreign country) money stock increases (decreases).
    - Domestic (foreign) national income falls (rises).
    - The foreign price level falls.

    The depreciation will be proportionate to any increase in the relative money stock.

- The monetary model of a *fixed exchange rate* predicts that the balance of payments will *deteriorate* and the home country will lose reserves when any of the following occurs:

  - The home country's domestically-generated money stock (that is, domestic credit) increases.
  - Domestic (foreign) national income falls (rises).
  - The foreign price level falls.

- *Devaluation* of a fixed exchange rate results in a period of balance of payments surpluses, which comes to an end when the home country's reserves have risen sufficiently to restore the value of the *real* money stock to its pre-devaluation level. Once this has happened, the *real* exchange rate is back at its former level (that is, PPP is reinstated) and the temporary competitive advantage enjoyed by the home country as a result of the devaluation has been completely eliminated by inflation.

- Since higher interest rates mean a smaller demand for money, other things being equal, they also imply a higher price level and therefore a lower value for the home country's currency. However, this conclusion must be qualified by our finding in Chapter 3 that interest rates, far from being an exogenous variable, are likely to reflect the market's expected rate of currency depreciation or appreciation. A firmer conclusion must await the analysis of how market expectations are determined in Chapters 11 and 12 of this book.

- Since PPP does not fit the facts of the 1970s and 1980s very well it is not surprising that the monetary model turns out to be able to explain the facts only very weakly, and even then only over the long run. A cursory examination of annual data for the UK, West Germany and Japan since 1975 is not encouraging, and this is broadly the conclusion reached by most researchers in detailed scientific studies of the data.

READING GUIDE

On the monetary model, the starting point (well worth reading) is Hume (1741). The simplest modern statement of its basic propositions is in Johnson (1977). Other influential work was by Mussa (1976) and Bilson (1979). The analysis of devaluation is due to Dornbusch (1973).

Influential empirical work has been carried out by Frenkel (1976) and Frankel (1979), among others. The last (empirical) word on the monetary model appears to have been said by Meese and Rogoff (1983), which also contains a useful bibliography.

On exchange rates under hyperinflationary conditions, see Frenkel (1977).

6

Fixed Prices: The Mundell–Fleming Model

■ Introduction

In Chapter 5, we looked at the way that the exchange rate is determined when the price level is perfectly flexible. In this chapter, we look at the opposite extreme. What happens when the price level is completely fixed?

The Mundell–Fleming (M–F) model adheres to the Keynesian tradition that it is aggregate supply which takes the passive role of fixing the price level, while aggregate demand variations determine the level of economic activity.[1] It was highly influential in the 1960s, particularly in policymaking circles, not least because it focuses mainly on normative questions relating to the optimal combination of monetary and fiscal measures for demand management in an open economy.

---

[1] The reader would be well advised to acquire a firm grasp of the analysis in Chapter 4 before starting the present chapter.

At the time that the M–F model was developed the Bretton Woods system was still more or less unchallenged, in the currency markets at least (though it had never enjoyed universal support in academic circles). Not surprisingly under the circumstances, most attention was focused on its conclusions about fixed exchange rates. In this chapter, we look at the M–F analysis of both fixed and floating rates.

As we shall see, the distinguishing feature of the M–F approach is in the emphasis placed on the different conditions determining the current balance, on the one hand, and the net capital inflow, on the other. The outcome is an uneasy stock-flow equilibrium – not too implausible a description of the short-run response of a small open economy, but becoming less and less realistic the longer the time horizon involved.

In Section 6.1, the scene is set and the assumptions made explicit, and in the succeeding section, the initial equilibrium is described. The next four sections (6.3 to 6.6) analyse the results of the following policy experiments: a monetary and a fiscal expansion under floating rates, and the same exercises in a fixed rate regime. Section 6.7 compares and contrasts the M–F model with the monetary model in the last chapter.

6.1   The setting

The M–F model is set in the context of a macroeconomic model which is simply the special case referred to as Keynesian in Chapter 4. For that reason, we shall limit the exposition here to a brief recap.

6.1.1   The domestic economy

We start with the supply side of the economy, where it is assumed that:

A1. The aggregate supply curve is flat.

Remember that this implies that the burden of adjustment to aggregate demand fluctuations falls on the level of economic activity – y,[2] in the notation used here – rather than on the price level, P. In fact, with the latter fixed, we might as well simplify matters by setting $P = 1$, so that, for the duration of this chapter, M signifies both nominal and real money stocks.

---

[2]   Notice that the superscript d (for demand) used in Chapter 4 is unnecessary here, because aggregate demand is automatically identical to actual income and output.

What this means in terms of the analysis is that we can concentrate on the demand side of the economy. In fact, since output adjusts passively, we need only consider the *IS–LM* framework (see Section 4.1) within which aggregate demand is determined.

6.1.2 The balance of payments

The distinctive feature of the M–F model is in the specification of the external sector of the economy. In particular, the current balance is determined independently of the capital account, so that the achievement of overall balance requires adjustment in the domestic economy.

The current account

As far as the current account is concerned, the starting point is the following assumption:

> **A2**. PPP does not hold, even in the long run. Instead, the size of the current account surplus depends positively on the (real) exchange rate and negatively on (real) income.

This is essentially no more than was assumed when the *IS* curve was introduced in Section 4.1.1. It amounts to asserting that the current account surplus, *B*, is given by:

$$B = B(y, q) = B(y, S) \qquad B_y < 0 \; B_s > 0 \quad \text{[see Footnote 3]} \quad \textbf{(6.1)}$$

The second equality is possible because, given both domestic and foreign price levels, the real and nominal exchange rates are identical.

The part played by income is the familiar one: the higher is income, the greater is the demand for imports and hence the smaller the surplus or greater the deficit.

It would be possible at this stage to give a symmetrical role to foreign income, allowing for it to have a positive impact on the current balance, via the US propensity to import. For the sake of conciseness it is ignored here. It should be easy for the reader to deduce what effect an increase in US income would have on the value of the pound.

There are a number of other exogenous 'shift' factors which could be incorporated into Equation 6.1: shocks to international tastes, shocks to export demand, and so on.

---

[3] The notation F_x means the partial derivative of the function F with respect to the argument x, that is, the effect of a minute increase in the variable x on the value of the function, holding all the other arguments constant.

By convention, when there is only one argument in F the derivative is written F'.

The capital account

The role of interest rates is absolutely central to the M–F model. In the case of the balance of payments, the reason why this is so is to be found in the following two assumptions:

>   **A3**. Exchange rate expectations are static.
>
>   **A4**. Capital mobility is less than perfect.

In Chapter 3, we examined the implications of perfect capital mobility. The analysis there presupposed perfect capital mobility, in the sense that even the smallest deviation from interest rate parity was assumed to be pre-empted by a potential flood into or out of domestic money markets.

In the Mundell–Fleming context, perfect capital mobility is regarded as a special case. In general, international interest rate differentials are assumed to provoke *finite* flows into or out of a country.

As we saw in Chapter 3, one possible rationalization for imperfect capital mobility would take as a starting point the limited supply of arbitrage funds.[4] More plausibly, it could be argued that, given risk aversion, the flow of funds into the home country will be an increasing function of the risk premium offered on securities denominated in the domestic currency, and vice versa for outward flows.

In other words, if we define r^*, the exogenously given foreign interest rate, to include any expected depreciation of the domestic currency, then we have:

$$K = K(r - r^*) = K(r) \qquad K' > 0 \qquad\qquad (6.2)$$

This simply says the UK's net capital inflow, K, is an increasing function of the extent to which the domestic interest rate is greater than the one ruling in the US, inclusive of any depreciation expected in the value of the pound.

The balance of payments locus

Balance of Payments (BP) equilibrium obtains when the flow of capital across the exchanges is just sufficient to finance the current account deficit or absorb the surplus. Of course, by definition, under a pure floating

---

[4] In the 1960s this view of international capital markets seemed far more realistic than today. At the time, most countries other than the USA and Switzerland still imposed tight restrictions on movements of foreign exchange, the Eurocurrency markets were tiny compared to their present size and there were few large portfolios owned outside the industrial world, as is much of today's oil wealth. In addition, the large financial institutions which nowadays operate as arbitrageurs were at that time more closely regulated and far less competitive.

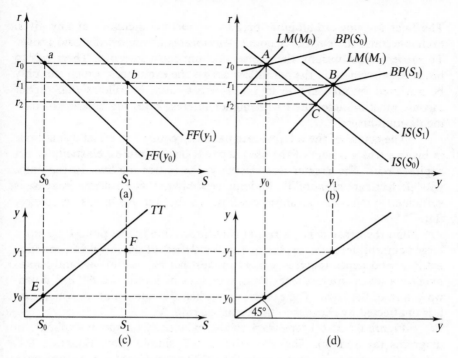

Figure 6.1 Monetary expansion under floating rates in the Mundell–Fleming model.

exchange rate regime, the *overall* balance of payments[5] must be in equilibrium at all times. This means that the sum of the surplus on capital and current account must be zero, in other words, a surplus on one account must be balanced by a deficit on the other.

If we add Equations 6.1 and 6.2 for the current and capital accounts respectively, a pure float requires the following condition to apply at all times:

$$B(y, S) + K(r) = 0 \tag{6.3}$$

or, more compactly when necessary:

$$F(y, S, r) = 0 \qquad F_y < 0 \; F_s > 0 F_r > 0 \tag{6.4}$$

This relationship is plotted twice in Figure 6.1.

In Figure 6.1(b), the *BP* lines plot the combinations of y and r consistent with balance of payments equilibrium for different values of S.

---

[5] That is, the balance for official financing or the net change in the foreign currency reserves (see Section 1.3, if necessary).

The lines are upward sloping, because as income increases at any given exchange rate, the current account deteriorates as import demand grows. To preserve equilibrium, the capital account must improve. There has to be an improvement in the net inflow across the exchanges, which can only be achieved by an increase in UK interest rates. It follows that higher income must be associated with higher interest rates for balance of payments equilibrium.

The extent of the interest rate increase required to offset a small rise in income (the gradient of the line) depends on the interest elasticity of net capital flows. The greater this elasticity, the flatter the line. In the limit, with perfect capital mobility, an imperceptibly tiny interest rate increase is sufficient to stimulate an infinite inflow, so that the *BP* line is completely flat.

On the other hand, a rise in *S* (depreciation of the pound) means a larger current account surplus or smaller deficit at any level of economic activity, and hence requires a more modest net capital inflow, and consequently a lower interest rate. Thus, increases in *S* shift the *BP* line downward and to the right. The exception is when the line is flat, in which case it is unaffected by changes in the exchange rate.

Figure 6.1 also keeps track of the balance of payments explicitly in diagrams (a) and (c). The line labelled *TT* simply plots Equation 6.1. Notice the superficial similarity to the PPP line of Chapter 5. However, in the present case the price level is constant. In the same way that, in the domestic economy, income carries the burden of adjustment previously borne by the price level, so in the external sector, it is income which, along with the exchange rate, now determines the current account balance. The higher it is, the greater must be the exchange rate (that is, the lower the value of the pound) for the current account to balance.

> Notice, that even in a pure float, the economy does not have to settle on the *TT* line, because we do not require the current account to balance – neither in short nor long-run equilibrium. We only insist that any current account deficit (surplus) be offset by a capital account surplus (deficit) of the same size.

Figure 6.1(a) simply plots Equation 6.4 in (r, S) space. Balance of payments equilibrium associates higher interest rates (a more favourable capital account) with a lower price of foreign currency (and hence a less competitive foreign sector). It follows that the *FF* line slopes downward for a given income level. As income increases, it shifts to the right, since equilibrium requires depreciation to compensate for the additional import demand.

Again, the *FF* line is flat if capital is perfectly mobile, and hence there is no horizontal shift when income increases.

6.2 Equilibrium

For the sake of convenience, we start off in equilibrium in Figure 6.1 at the points *A*, *a* and *E*.

At interest rate r_0 and exchange rate S_0 the balance of payments is in equilibrium, as can be seen from the fact that points *a* and *A* lie on the *FF* and *BP* lines respectively. Furthermore, at the associated real exchange rate, the product market clears along the curve marked $IS(S_0)$, so that the combination (r_0, y_0) is consistent with general equilibrium in the domestic economy.

Furthermore, tracking the level of income from y_0 down via the 45° line in Figure 6.1(d) over to the *TT* line, we see (at *E*) that there is a zero current account deficit at this exchange rate-income combination, with no net tendency for capital to leave or enter the country.

6.3 Monetary expansion with a floating exchange rate

Now consider the effect of expansionary monetary policy, for example a doubling of the money stock. The first point to note is that, since the price level is fixed by the flat aggregate supply curve, the increase in the *nominal* money stock is equivalent to a pro rata rise in the *real* money stock. Hence, referring to Figure 6.1(b) the *LM* curve moves permanently rightwards, so that the interest rate has to fall.

How far must it fall? At first glance, the answer appears to be: as far as r_2. But this cannot be correct for a number of reasons. *C* cannot be an equilibrium because, in the first place, with a lower interest rate the net capital inflow is smaller than it was prior to the money stock expansion. Furthermore, at the higher level of activity, the current account balance must have deteriorated. For both reasons, the combination at *C* must involve substantial balance of payments disequilibrium.

Obviously the exchange rate must depreciate. It is tempting to conclude that the pound's value needs to fall far enough to bring the current account into balance. This is not true, however. Remember, it was purely for analytical convenience that we chose to start from a zero current account balance – nothing requires this condition to apply in equilibrium.

Instead, as the (nominal and real) exchange rate depreciates, the competitiveness of domestic production improves and demand for UK output increases, shifting the *IS* curve outwards to $IS(S_1)$. The boost to demand has the effect of pushing interest rates part of the way back to their original level of r_0.

Ultimately, the economy settles at *B*, where the interest rate is at the level r_1, and the UK's external payments are back in balance, as evidenced by the line marked $BP(S_1)$. The external sector is returned to equilibrium by two mechanisms: the partial climb back by the interest rate has the effect of reducing the capital account deficit to a level where the current account surplus created by the depreciation in the currency is sufficient to cover it.

Notice that the current account surplus (at F) is the net outcome of a positive influence, the rise in S, and a negative influence, the increase in y. Thus, the former effect must be assumed the stronger of the two.

In the limiting case of perfect capital mobility, no fall in the interest rate is possible, so that the full burden of external adjustment falls on the exchange rate. The outcome is a greater increase both in income and in the price of dollars.

We conclude:

> **Proposition 6.1**: In the M–F model of a floating exchange rate, a money supply increase causes:
>
> (a) A depreciation in the exchange rate.
>
> (b) An increase in income.
>
> (c) A fall in the interest rate, provided capital is not completely mobile.
>
> (d) An improvement in the current account of the balance of payments.

Notice the first conclusion is *qualitatively* the same as in the monetary model, though there is no reason here to suppose that the depreciation will be in proportion to the money supply increase. Likewise, the income increase is unsurprising. It is simply the counterpart of the price rise that would take place with a classical aggregate supply curve.

As has already been mentioned, however, the focus of the Mundell–Fleming work, published as it was in the heyday of demand management, was mainly on policy implications. In this respect, it was regarded as highly significant that the net effect of expansionary monetary policy on the level of economic activity could be shown to be unambiguously positive – even allowing for the crowding out effect of the increase in demand induced by the fall in the exchange rate.

Furthermore, as we have seen, if the *BP* line were flat – in other words, if there were perfect capital mobility, the interest rate would be completely fixed, eliminating secondary crowding out altogether and resulting in the maximum expansionary impact on aggregate demand.

6.4 Fiscal expansion with a floating exchange rate

By contrast, Figure 6.2 illustrates the effect of a pure fiscal expansion, in other words, an increase in government expenditure (from G_0 to G_1) *with an unchanged money stock*.

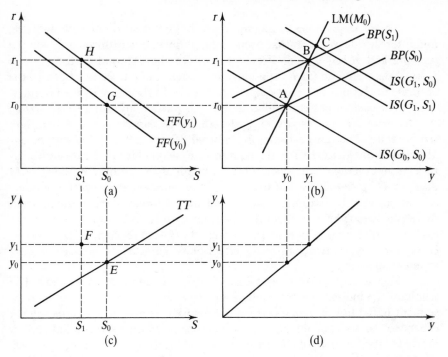

Figure 6.2 Fiscal expansion under floating rates in the Mundell–Fleming model.

In this case, with a fixed money stock and constant price level, the *LM* curve of Figure 6.2(b) is unmoved. On the other hand, as we have seen, fiscal expansion shifts the *IS* curve to the right, via a direct injection into the flow of expenditure. However, if printing money is ruled out, as we are assuming here, the government can only finance its extra spending by borrowing more. Since the money and credit markets were in equilibrium at the outset, significant additional borrowing is only possible at the cost of a higher interest rate. It follows that the impact effect of the policy is to increase income and the interest rate.

Point *C* of Figure 6.2(b), where $IS(G_1, S_0)$ cuts the original *LM* curve, is inconsistent with equilibrium in the external sector, however. A higher interest rate implies an influx of funds into London, which in turn means, starting from an initial balance on external payments, an emerging excess demand for pounds. Nor is the deterioration in the current account caused by the increase in income likely to be enough to offset it.

The pound must therefore appreciate, as Americans join the rush to lend to the British Government at the newly attractive interest rate, in the process converting dollars to sterling and bidding up the exchange rate. As the exchange rate rises, UK goods, as distinct from UK securities, become less attractive to foreigners, shifting the *IS* curve back down to the left, and pushing the interest rate some of the way back to its pre-expansion level.

The process comes to an end when the combination of exchange rate and interest rate are such that domestic equilibrium is restored at *B*, on the line marked $IS(G_1, S_1)$ of Figure 6.2(b). In the external sector (Figure 6.2(c)), the outcome (at *F*) is a current account deficit, thanks both to the increase in income and, particularly, to the rise in the value of the pound.

The case of perfect capital mobility is particularly interesting. When the *BP* and *FF* curves are flat, the *IS* curve cannot move other than temporarily. The reason is simply that, with both *BP* and *LM* curves unaffected by the disturbance, the equilibrium income–interest rate combination cannot change – the system must remain at the point *A* in the *IS–LM* diagram (Figure 6.2(b)). Put in terms of the money market, with the interest rate pegged by external factors, and the real money stock unchanged, there is a unique level of income consistent with equilibrium. It follows the exchange rate must move so as to keep the *IS* curve unchanged, that is, enough to offset the expansionary effect on demand of the increase in government spending.

Hence, with perfect capital mobility, crowding out is complete. The whole of the increase in government expenditure is neutralized by the consequent equal fall in demand from the external sector of the economy. In other words, with the interest rate pegged *de facto* by international capital markets, the burden of adjustment falls entirely on the exchange rate, which has to appreciate by enough to generate a current account deficit as great as the increase in fiscal spending that started the process off. In flow of funds terms, in this limiting case, the whole of the increase in government expenditure is funded by borrowing from overseas. Therefore, each pound spent by the government adds one pound to the capital account surplus, and equilibrium requires that it be offset by the same amount of net imports of goods and services. Demand is therefore pushed back to its original level, and the impact of fiscal spending on output is nil.

We conclude:

Proposition 6.2: In the M–F model of a floating exchange rate, fiscal expansion causes:

(a) An appreciation in the exchange rate.

(b) An increase in income, provided capital is not completely mobile.

(c) A rise in the interest rate, provided capital is not completely mobile.

(d) A deterioration in the current account of the balance of payments.

Notice that, as far as policy considerations are concerned, the result is that the ultimate expansion of demand (and hence activity) is smaller than would be predicted purely on the basis of a closed economy analysis. The reason is that the closed economy mechanism, whereby a rise in the interest rate crowds out some of the injection of autonomous spending, is supplemented in the present context by the rise in the value of the domestic exchange rate, which further crowds out spending – this time by foreigners on UK (net) exports.

For policy purposes, then, the conclusion drawn from the Mundell–Fleming model was that, in a floating exchange rate regime, monetary policy is more powerful than fiscal policy and furthermore that this was more true the more elastic was the net supply of capital.

6.5 Monetary expansion with a fixed exchange rate

We now switch our attention to fixed exchange rate regimes, to see how far our conclusions need to be changed.

In Figure 6.3(b), the initial equilibrium at A is the same as in the floating rate case. To remind ourselves of the difference, a vertical line has been drawn at the fixed exchange rate $\overline{S}$ in both Figures 6.3(a) and (c).

Now consider the effect of a once and for all monetary expansion or more precisely, of an expansion of domestic credit from DC_0 to DC_1.

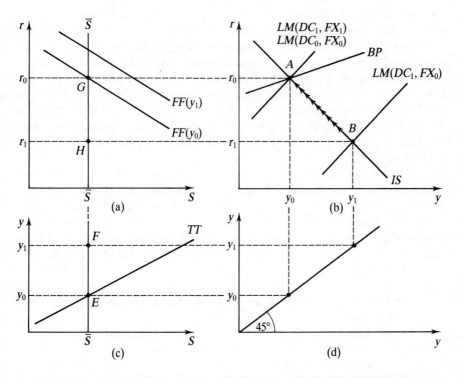

Figure 6.3 Monetary expansion under fixed rates in the Mundell–Fleming model.

The impact effect of the increase in the total money stock has to be the downward shift in the *LM* curve in Figure 6.3(b). Notice that the new curve has been labelled $LM(DC_1, FX_0)$. The new equilibrium at *B* is the outcome of an increase in the domestic component of the money supply with an as yet unchanged quantity of foreign currency reserves.

The sequence of events from this point onwards is clear. Starting from balance of payments equilibrium, as we did, the fall in the interest rate (from r_0 to r_1) must worsen the capital account balance. At the same time, the increase in income (from y_0 to y_1) with an unchanged exchange rate causes a deterioration in the current account, as we can see at the point *F* in Figure 6.3(c).

It follows that the new situation can only be a temporary resting point. The overall balance of payments deficit and associated excess supply of sterling means that the fixed exchange rate can only be preserved by running down the reserves. As we saw in Chapter 5, in the absence of further action by the authorities, the inevitable outcome is a gradual reduction in the foreign currency component of the monetary base. The process only ends when the money stock (and hence the *LM* curve) are back where they started.

In the new equilibrium, everything is as before: interest rate, income and the balance of payments all are back at their pre-disturbance level. The only difference is in the composition of the money stock, which is now made up of a lower quantity of foreign currency (FX_1, instead of FX_0) and a greater quantity of domestically-generated assets (DC_1, instead of DC_0).

In the limiting case, with perfect capital mobility it must be assumed that any fall in the interest rate is ruled out (even in the short term) since it would provoke an immediate run on the foreign currency reserves. So in this case the adjustment process would be more or less instantaneous, with the new money draining straight out of the country across the foreign exchanges.

As long as capital movements are not completely elastic, the possibility exists in principle at least, of sterilizing the induced outflows of reserves. However, as we saw in Chapter 5, it is hard to believe that the policy could work other than in the very short term, since it ultimately relies on the currency markets being completely myopic in their acceptance of an ever-falling stock of reserves, with no sign of an end to the deterioration in view.

The conclusion is:

Proposition 6.3: In the M–F model of a fixed exchange rate, a money supply increase causes:

(a) In the short term, and provided capital is not completely mobile: the interest rate to fall, income to increase and the balance of payments to deteriorate on both current and capital account.

(b) In the long term: a fall in the foreign currency reserves, but no change in income, the interest rate, or the balance of payments.

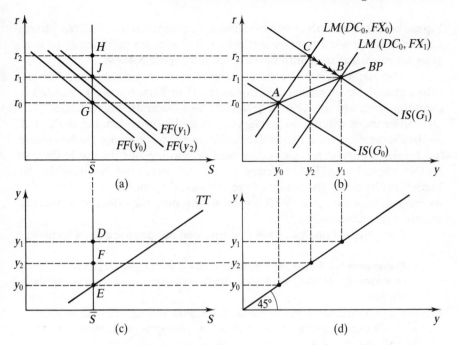

Figure 6.4 Fiscal expansion under fixed rates in the Mundell–Fleming model.

6.6 Fiscal expansion with a fixed exchange rate

Finally, consider the effect of government spending financed by borrowing in the context of a fixed exchange rate (Figure 6.4).

Starting from point A of Figure 6.4(b), the impact effect is to shift the IS curve upward. The interest rate must rise as the authorities try to expand their borrowing from financial markets which are already satisfied with their holdings of government paper. The new IS curve cuts the unchanged LM curve at C.

However, C is not a situation of long-run equilibrium, as evidenced by the fact that it lies above the BP line. The higher interest rate, r_2, improves the capital account by more than the deterioration in the current account brought about by the simultaneous increase in income (to y_2). In terms of the balance of payments diagram (Figure 6.4(a)), even after the upward shift in the FF schedule, the interest rate is still too high for long-run equilibrium, as we can see at the point H.

Again the solution lies in a change in the endogenous component of the money supply, which duly occurs through reserve accumulation, as foreigners take advantage of the high UK interest rate by buying pounds so as to hold British securities. In the process, the money stock swells, pushing the LM curve down to generate a long-run equilibrium at B in

Figure 6.4(b), where the further increase in income and fall in the interest rate have worsened both current and capital account sufficiently to bring external payments back into balance (at *J* in Figure 6.4(a)).

The net outcome, then, is a balance of payments that shows a substantial deficit on current account (at *D* in Figure 6.4(c)) financed by capital inflows attracted by the relatively high domestic interest rate.

The more willing are foreigners to increase their lending to the UK, the less is the need for a rise in British interest rates, because the less spending by the domestic private sector needs crowding out. In the limit, with perfect capital mobility, foreigners can be persuaded to shoulder the burden of financing the whole of the additional spending at no perceptible increase in interest rates. With no crowding out, the effect is to increase income very substantially.[6]

The general conclusions in this case can be summarized as follows:

> **Proposition 6.4**: In the M–F model of a fixed exchange rate, fiscal expansion causes the following changes, provided capital is not completely mobile:
>
> (a)   In the short run: a rise in the interest rate and income, and an overall surplus on the balance of payments (a net reserve gain).
>
> (b)   In the long run: a further increase in income while the interest rate falls somewhat, and the overall balance of payments surplus shrinks to zero, leaving a substantial current account deficit.

6.7   The monetary model and the Mundell–Fleming model compared

It is useful to compare the monetary model and the Mundell–Fleming model directly. The differences can be considered under the following three headings: the price level, income, expectations and interest rates.

6.7.1   The price level

In the monetary model, since the aggregate supply curve is vertical at all times, the price level moves with perfect flexibility to clear both money and goods markets. Then PPP ensures that the real exchange rate is preserved at its equilibrium level.

In the M–F model, the price level is simply an exogenously fixed index which can have no role to play in the domestic macroeconomy. Nor can it play any part in determining equilibrium in the open sector.

---

[6] In fact, by an amount equal to the increase in government expenditure times the Keynesian income-expenditure multiplier.

6.7.2 Income

The corollary of these contrasting assumptions about the supply side of the economy is two totally different views of the part played by income in the model.

In the monetary model, with full employment and perfectly functioning factor markets, changes in real income can only be exogenous events. Furthermore, consumption is implicitly taken to depend on interest rates rather than income. It follows that the only role left for income to play is in helping to determine the demand for real balances. As we saw, because exogenous increases in income swell the demand for money, they are associated with currency *appreciation*.

On the other hand, income is one of the three endogenous variables in the M–F system, the others being the domestic interest rate, and the exchange rate (if floating), otherwise the balance of payments. An (endogenous) increase in income is associated with three types of effect in this context. Firstly, in so far as it raises the demand for money, it leads to a rise in the interest rate, other things being equal. Secondly, by feeding back on to consumption (the Keynesian multiplier effect) it boosts demand for goods and services. Thirdly, and more particularly, it is associated with a worsening current account via the marginal propensity to import and, *ceteris paribus*, either reserve losses or currency *depreciation*.

6.7.3 Expectations and interest rates

Neither model provides an explicit role for expectations, though both have provided the framework for more complicated models that fully rectify this omission, as we shall see later on in the book.[7]

Nonetheless, the flavour of the monetary model is *either* that expectations are exogenously given *or* that they depend in some more complicated fashion on the other variables (see Chapter 12). Furthermore, in the spirit of the Classical tradition to which it belongs, the monetary approach assumes the real interest rate is determined purely in the savings market.[8] When combined with interest rate parity, these two facts imply that nominal interest rates cannot fluctuate freely to clear the money markets. That job is left to the price level. The domestic interest rate is effectively tied to (though usually not equal to) the foreign rate.

---

[7] In Chapter 7, we examine what amounts to an M–F model modified to incorporate expectations. The same is done for the monetary model in Chapter 12.

[8] In other words, the Classical model assumes an *IS* curve which is flat at the interest rate which equates savings to investment (plus any other injections in the economy). Remember that in this view savings are not a function of current income.

The Keynesian approach takes goods market equilibrium as dependent at least as much on income as on interest rates. The corollary is that, in a domestic context, the interest rate is free to help clear both money and goods markets. Viewed from the international perspective, the link with foreign interest rates is almost completely broken. In place of UIRP, we have something like:

$$r = r^* + \Delta s_t^e + \rho \qquad (6.5)$$

Now if the required risk premium (the last term) rises with the quantity of domestic-currency assets held, it follows that the scale of the capital inflow at any point will be an increasing function of the domestic interest rate, *for a given value of the expected rate of depreciation* (the second term on the right-hand side).

This is all very well, provided firstly, that the expected rate of depreciation can actually be taken as given in the face of significant macroeconomic policy shifts and, secondly, that the required risk premium is determined independently of the other variables. On this last point, we shall have more to say in Chapter 13.

As far as expectations are concerned, it seems highly unlikely that the policy measures considered in this chapter would leave expectations unchanged.[9] Once it is allowed that expectations are very likely to depend on the government's policy stance, the logic behind the M–F conclusions begins to unravel.

Stocks and flows

The differing treatments given to interest rate determination in the two models is very much related to their contrasting approaches to defining equilibrium.

Following the Classical tradition, equilibrium in the monetary model, in its floating rate version at least, is a steady state in the fullest sense: the stocks of both money and goods are willingly held, with no tendency for net flows in either direction. Once the economy has adjusted to a monetary expansion, for example, there is no reason why the new equilibrium should not persist forever, if left undisturbed.

Contrast this with the M–F analysis: the response to money supply expansion involves a depreciation-induced surplus on current account, which then finances the continuing net export of capital, in response to the new, lower level of domestic interest rates.

---

[9] Even if this were credible where a once and for all policy change is concerned, the same could certainly not be true of any change which provoked expectations of further changes to come, for example the issue of domestic money to sterilize a reserve loss under fixed exchange rates.

Now this cannot be an equilibrium in the full, static sense. A net capital flow into or out of a country is prima facie evidence that disequilibrium holdings are in the process of being adjusted, and it is quite plausible that adjustment may be protracted. In fact, the international capital markets are never at rest.[10] But, however long the process may take, at some point it will be complete. Stocks of assets will have fully adjusted to the disturbance, with no further tendency for capital to move into or out of the country – and *this is the situation one would expect to find in full equilibrium.*

Nor is this purely a theoretical nicety. If, for example, the capital inflow following on fiscal expansion under a floating exchange rate is only temporary, the current account deficit which it finances can only be temporary. As the influx of funds dries up, the exchange rate must depreciate, other things being equal, thereby reducing the current account deficit, pushing interest rates up even further and reducing income. In the limit, there would be no change in income or the interest rate. There would simply be an appreciation of sufficient scale to crowd out the additional spending.[11]

As has already been mentioned in the Introduction, the M–F analysis was highly influential precisely because of its conclusions about the relative efficacy of monetary and fiscal policy under fixed and floating rates. No comparable analysis is possible in the context of the monetary model, simply because it has nothing to say about the effect of changes in government spending. Why not?

One way of understanding this feature of the classical model is to go back to the goods market identity of flows of injections and leakages. Rewriting Equation 4.3, we have:

$$Savings \equiv I + G + B \qquad (6.6)$$

When net government spending expands, there is a *ceteris paribus* rise in the volume of injections on the right-hand side of this identity. How is the equality maintained?

In the Keynesian view, the equality is preserved by some combination of a rise in income, which increases savings, and an increase in interest rates, which also raises savings somewhat but which, more importantly,

---

[10] Though why this should be so is not always clear. For a bank to adjust its holdings of, say, US Treasury Bills should take no more than a few hours, or days at most. It is precisely these kinds of considerations that have led some researchers to look for explanations to the impact of 'news' on currency markets (see Chapter 12).

[11] In terms of Figures 6.1 to 6.4 this would amount to saying that the *BP* and *FF* lines are ultimately vertical, since the external balance depends only on income and the exchange rate. Fiscal expansion would then shift the *IS* curve temporarily to the right, as in Figure 6.2. In the long run, however, the *IS* curve would be pushed by exchange rate appreciation all the way back to its original position.

deters investment ('crowding out'). The M–F analysis follows through the open economy implications of this mechanism.

By contrast, the Classical view[12] is that an increase in the government's budget deficit will bring forth the requisite additional saving spontaneously. The reason is simply that economic agents realize the extra spending will have to be paid for by future taxation, even if it is financed by borrowing at the moment. They will therefore wish to step up their current saving *at any given interest rate* so as to be able to pay the taxes when they fall due.

In fact, it can be shown that, provided taxation does not actually distort the savings decision,[13] responsible, non-myopic agents will be happy to buy the additional government debt issued to finance its extra spending *at the same price as before the change took place*. They will do so because the return they earn on the debt, properly measured,[14] will be just sufficient to cover the additional tax burden.

If we can rely on this mechanism of Ricardian equivalence, as it is called, after the great Classical economist, David Ricardo, we need not distinguish between spending by the private and public sectors. The government is simply an agency created by a democratic state to act on behalf of its citizens – in borrowing as in everything else. The fact that a private citizen prefers to buy now and pay later does not automatically raise interest rates. Why should it do so when he or she channels the whole process (spending and borrowing) through the agency of the government?[15]

On these and similar grounds, one would expect an increase in *G* on the right-hand side of Equation 6.6 to be automatically associated with the increase in savings needed to finance it. In other words, the *IS* curve need not shift as a result of what is simply a change in the share of spending between public and private sectors.

In practice, there are certain to be a number of breaks in the circuit leading from the nation's budget to our household budgets.

In the first place, households may simply be myopically unconcerned about the future tax burden being imposed on them. The facts are not easily accessible: government spending changes are made public only in the opaque form of official statistics, nationalized industries' accounts, White Papers, and so on. In any case, it is one thing to absorb the fact that £1 of extra government spending today will have to be paid for at some point in

---

[12] Revived by Barro (see Reading Guide).

[13] For example, by taxing interest earned on savings.

[14] That is, discounting appropriately both the flow of payments to the debt holder and to the future taxation.

[15] In addition, in a democracy much of public sector spending ought in principle to be perceived as substituting directly, pound for pound, for private consumption (for example, government purchases of medicines, school meals, textbooks and so forth).

the future by additional taxes whose present value is £1.[16] It is quite another to accept that *I* or even my children, if I have any, will have to pay those taxes. By the time the chickens come home to roost, I may no longer be inside the tax net, I may be dead, retired, emigrated, or unemployed. Moreover, unless my coupon payments are exempt from income tax, buying government securities will yield less than I need to pay the tax bill, when it falls due.

For these reasons, the most likely outcome for an economy like that of the UK or USA would seem to be some degree of crowding-out greater than zero (as predicted by Ricardians) but smaller than is suggested in Keynesian models like the one analysed in this chapter.

The question is ultimately an empirical one and one that, in spite of its importance, has yet to be satisfactorily answered.

6.8 Evidence

It is not of very great interest to test the M–F model in the form presented here, at least as far as the floating rate era is concerned – it seems pointless to try and explain the facts by starting from the assumption that prices are fixed. On the other hand, introducing price flexibility in one way or another changes the model quite drastically, as we shall see in Chapter 7.

Nonetheless, certain episodes in recent years have prompted interpretation by some economists in terms of the M–F mechanism.

In particular, the simultaneous rise of both the dollar and US real interest rates to record levels in the first half of the 1980s, led many commentators to point to the growing Federal deficit as the likely culprit.

Unfortunately, whatever may be true in the criminal courts, in economics circumstantial evidence rarely points in a single direction. In the present case, real interest rates were (and still are) at or around their peak levels throughout the industrialized world, in spite of the conservative budgetary stance of some of the countries involved. Moreover, the dollar's subsequent fall took place well in advance of any tangible sign that the US deficit could even be stabilized, let alone reduced.

Of course, the dollar's fall, when it finally took place, was immediately rationalized by some commentators as a market reaction to ... the Federal deficit.

It is easy to be facetious about these *ad hoc* explanations. However, it should be realized they *could* both be correct, and attempting to

---

[16] It is the author's impression that the average member of the public is and always has been well aware of the truth that there is no such thing as a free lunch – and certainly less inclined to forget the fact than some members of the economics profession.

reconcile these two apparently contradictory positions takes us back to one of the central weaknesses of the M–F model.

The point has already been touched on in discussing the issue of capital mobility in the section on stocks and flows. Suppose that the US was able to fund additional Federal spending by borrowing from abroad (primarily Japan) in the early 1980s. In return, it offered a (very slightly) higher return. However, if the Japanese had fully adjusted their holdings of dollar securities by the mid 1980s, they would then stop exporting capital to the USA unless the risk premium rose still further, a development which failed to materialize, for some reason or other. Hence, the dollar had to fall. International money managers could hardly ignore the fact that where they had initially (in 1982) been lending to the world's largest creditor nation, by 1987, they were being asked to lend to the world's largest debtor – with no end in sight to the deterioration in the US's external finances.

This retrospective rationalization (it certainly does not merit being called an explanation) illustrates the shortcomings of the M–F concentration on flows rather than stocks of capital. Of course, it also illustrates the need to beware of the spurious power of *ex post* rationalizations![17]

6.9   Conclusions

A quarter of a century after it was developed, the analysis presented in this chapter looks naive, as well it might, in view of the upheavals that have taken place in currency markets in the intervening years. Nonetheless, the model focuses on mechanisms which are almost certainly still at work in one guise or another today, and in the process provides some useful insights.

Moreover, although this book is not primarily concerned with issues of policy design, it is worth noting that the questions raised by Mundell and Fleming with regard to the appropriate assignment of policy instruments are very much alive in the UK today. However, answering them satisfactorily involves analysing models that are vastly more complicated than the one given here.

Much of the more recent research derives directly or indirectly from the work of Mundell and Fleming, as we shall see. In Chapter 7, we shall examine a model which attempts to rectify two of the weaknesses of the M–F model: the constant price level and the static expectations. Chapter 8 extends the model further to provide an explicit specification of asset market equilibrium.

---

[17] For example, why should it have taken so long (two or three years) for Japanese investors to adjust their dollar holdings in the first place? And what stopped the relative return on dollar assets rising sufficiently to sustain the flow of funds into the USA in 1985 and beyond?

■ Summary

- The M–F model is set in the context of a flat aggregate supply curve (that is, a constant price level), the absence of PPP, less than perfect capital mobility and static expectations.

- With a floating exchange rate, equilibrium requires the domestic money and goods markets to clear, as in the *IS–LM* model, while in the open sector the sum of the deficits on current and capital accounts is zero. The latter condition ensures a balance of supply and demand in the currency market.

- With a floating exchange rate, expansionary monetary policy causes depreciation and a fall in interest rates, while fiscal expansion has the opposite effect.

- With a fixed exchange rate, expansionary monetary policy has the long-run effect of causing a fall in the reserves, while fiscal expansion produces a rise in income and the interest rate with a short-run reserve gain.

- The M–F model contrasts with the monetary model in a number of respects: its emphasis on the level of activity and interest rates rather than the price level, its concentration on flows of spending and capital movements rather than stocks of assets, and the central role it gives to the crowding-out mechanism.

READING GUIDE

Of the original work on which this chapter is based, the most accessible (technically and physically) is Mundell (1962) and Fleming (1962). If you can get hold of a copy, the book by Mundell (1968) is well worth reading, as it goes into some detail and provides proofs, generalizations and so on.

For an up-to-date assessment and further references, see Frenkel and Razin (1988).

On Ricardian equivalence, the most important modern reference is Barro (1974). For a textbook treatment, see Barro (1984), Chapter 15.

7

Sticky Prices: The Dornbusch Model

◼ Introduction

As we saw, the monetary model of the exchange rate is incapable of explaining the facts, not least because it relies on the assumption of purchasing power parity, but possibly also because it ignores the role played by expectations in determining international interest rate differentials. In particular, it appeared that exchange rate fluctuations were far more violent than could ever be explained by the comparatively sluggish movements we observe in relative money stocks and national incomes.

On the other hand, the Mundell–Fleming model not only takes no account of expectations, it also assumes a fixed price level, which limits its relevance to only the very shortest horizons.

The model to be outlined here, which was published by Professor Rudiger Dornbusch of the Massachusetts Institute of Technology in 1976, is a hybrid. In its short-run features, it fits into the established Keynesian tradition, with its emphasis on the stickiness of prices in product (and labour) markets. On the other hand, it displays the long-run characteristics of the monetary model.

The originality of Dornbusch's work lies in his exploration of the consequences of the following observation: while product markets adjust only slowly, financial markets appear to adjust far more rapidly – virtually instantaneously, in fact. The consequence of allowing for this feature of the real world turns out to be that financial markets have to *over* adjust to disturbances, in order to compensate for the stickiness of prices in goods markets. The reason is that, with goods prices initially fixed, a change in the *nominal* money stock, for example, amounts to a change in the *real* money stock. It follows that there has to be an instantaneous change in the demand for real balances if the money market is to clear, and the change can only be brought about by an upward or downward movement in interest rates – especially if output is assumed fixed. In the short term, therefore, monetary policy changes have what is nowadays known as a 'liquidity effect'.

However, the deviation of domestic interest rates from world levels can only be temporary. Ultimately, as product prices begin their delayed response, the change in the real money stock starts to reverse itself, and with it, the whole process goes into reverse, driving interest rates, aggregate demand and the real exchange rate back towards their original values. The process ends with all the real magnitudes back where they started, as in the monetary model, and the nominal exchange rate at a new long-term level which reflects the proportionate change in the money supply.

The overshooting phenomenon is also likely to characterize the response to a real (rather than monetary) disturbance, for example the UK's emergence as an oil exporter in the late 1970s. Again, the exchange rate is likely to overadjust to the disturbance, with potentially damaging consequences for UK industry and employment.

Since the material to be covered in this chapter is somewhat more complex, the approach will be in two stages. In Section 7.1, we shall set out the Dornbusch model in informal terms, relying for the analysis on an extension of the diagrammatic framework introduced in Chapter 6. In Section 7.2, we examine the aftermath of a monetary expansion in the same context.

The subsequent section, however, marks a change of pace. A formal, but highly simplified version of the model is set out and used to re-examine the response to monetary policy and, in Section 7.4, to outline the likely reaction to a disturbance like the discovery of North Sea oil.

7.1   Outline of the model

Two conventions will be followed.

(1)   We continue to focus on a single, 'small' economy, say the UK. By this, we mean that developments in Britain are assumed to have no

perceptible effect on the economy of the rest of the world. In particular, we may take as given the price level, P^*, and the interest rate, r^*, obtaining in the outside world ('the USA').

(2) The analysis will proceed from a 'standing start'. In other words, we assume there is initially no inflation and static exchange rates, and we consider the impact of an increase in the *level* of the money supply on the *level* of the exchange rate and of goods prices.

The model has a similar general structure to that of the Chapter 6. In fact, we can start with the following assumption:

> **A1**: Aggregate demand is determined by the standard open economy *IS–LM* mechanism.

Remember this means that the position of the *IS* curve is determined by the volume of injections into the flow of income (for example, government expenditure) and by the competitiveness of UK output, as measured by the real exchange rate, $Q = SP^*/P$.

We depart from the Mundell–Fleming model in making two special assumptions, one regarding the determination of interest rates, the other relating to aggregate supply.

7.1.1 Financial markets and expectations

We start by specifying the model of financial markets:

> **A2**: Financial markets adjust instantaneously. In particular, investors are risk neutral, so that uncovered interest rate parity (UIRP) holds at all times.

As we saw in Chapter 3, this means that perfect capital mobility preserves a situation such that expected depreciation or appreciation is just great enough to offset any interest rate differential between London and New York. In other words:

$$r = r^* + \Delta s^e \tag{7.1}$$

where r is the UK interest rate, r^* is the (exogenously given) US interest rate and Δs^e is the expected rate of depreciation in the value of the pound sterling relative to the dollar.

The question now arises: how are expectations actually determined? Dornbusch provides a simple, but elegant answer to this question.

Suppose there exists at any moment a (long-run) *equilibrium* exchange rate, $\overline{S}$, which is assumed to be determined at any moment by the level of the UK money stock, national income and interest rates, relative to those of the USA, in other words, by what we have so far called the monetary model. (As before, denote long-run equilibrium values of the variables by a bar.)

The difference is that here, in the Dornbusch model, the exchange rate is assumed to be at its equilibrium level only in the long run. In the short run, as we shall see, it will deviate from its equilibrium level, as a result of the sluggishness with which goods prices react to a disturbance.

> Now Dornbusch argues that when the exchange rate is below its long-run equilibrium level there will be a natural presumption that its future path will carry it upward in the direction of equilibrium, rather than downward and away from equilibrium and vice versa when it is above equilibrium. Moreover, the exchange rate will be expected to converge quicker on its long-run level the further away it is at any moment, that is, the greater the distance it has left to cover.

Formally, this expectations mechanism amounts to the following:

$$\Delta s^e = \theta(\bar{s} - s) \qquad \theta > 0 \tag{7.2}$$

The right-hand side is simply the gap between the (natural) logarithm of the current *actual* exchange rate, s, and the logarithm of its current equilibrium value, $\bar{s}$. (Note the lower case s, to denote the log of the exchange rate, S). Remember that the difference of the logs is equivalent to the log of the ratio (see Box 7.1). The parameter θ is a coefficient

---

BOX 7.1   *How the Dornbusch expectations mechanism is derived.*

Equation 7.2 could have been derived by starting from the following assumption:

$$\frac{S^e - S}{S} = \left(\frac{\bar{S} - S}{S}\right)^\Theta$$

The left-hand side is the expected depreciation, relative to the current level of the exchange rate. On the right, we have the gap between its equilibrium and actual levels, likewise in proportionate terms, raised to the power of Θ. So, when the rate is at its equilibrium level, the ratio on the right equals zero, and hence no change is expected – the left-hand side is also zero.

Now take natural logs of both sides, write: $\theta = ln\,\Theta$, and note that, for two numbers, X and Y, which are reasonably close together, the following approximation applies:

$$\frac{X - Y}{X} \approx ln\,X - ln\,Y = x - y$$

and Equation 7.2 follows.

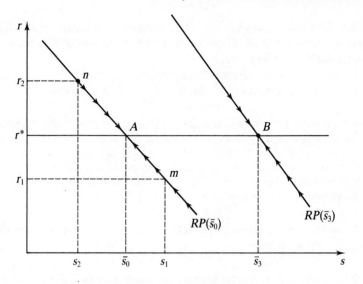

Figure 7.1 Short-run equilibrium in the securities market.

reflecting the sensitivity of market expectations to the (proportionate) over- or undervaluation of the currency relative to equilibrium. The greater it is, the more rapidly the exchange rate is expected to depreciate, for any given degree of overvaluation. This relationship is illustrated in Figure 7.1.

Suppose, initially, we are in equilibrium at the point A, with an exchange rate of $\bar{S}_0$, the UK interest rate equal to the US rate, r^* and hence with the exchange rate expected to remain unchanged.

Now, imagine for some reason the domestic interest rate were suddenly to fall to r_1. By the UIRP condition, we know that could only occur if market participants became convinced that the pound would appreciate against the dollar over the coming months, so as to compensate for the lower explicit interest paid on sterling securities. Given Dornbusch's special assumptions about how market forecasts are made, it follows that the pound's value will have to be *below* its long-run level (s be greater than its equilibrium level), so as to generate the expectation of a future sterling appreciation as it moves back towards equilibrium. Furthermore, the lower the UK interest rate relative to the US, the lower will the pound's value need to be in order to ensure that the future prospects are for it to appreciate sufficiently. We conclude that the system will need to settle in the short run at a point like m in the diagram, where the exchange rate is s_1.

Conversely, when the UK interest rate is relatively high, say r_2, the market must be anticipating a fall in the pound's external value, otherwise assets denominated in sterling will be irresistibly attractive relative to those in dollars. The short-run problem will be resolved at the point n, where the pound has appreciated (s fallen) to s_2, and the expectation is for a future fall to its equilibrium level, back at point A.

Clearly, the same argument applies to short-run divergences from any other long-run equilibrium, like the one at B, for example.

> We conclude that, for any equilibrium long-run exchange rate, like $\overline{S}_0$ or $\overline{S}_3$, there is a line (labelled RP in the diagram) sloping downward from left to right, which plots the feasible combinations of s and r consistent with short-run equilibrium. Along that line, the pound will either be appreciating (at points below the horizontal line through r^*), or depreciating, at points above r^*.

Note that the gradient of the RP lines is equal to (minus) the value of the expectation-adjustment parameter, θ.

> Notice also that uncovered interest rate parity holds at all points along the RP lines – the international financial markets are in (short-run) equilibrium at all times.

Summing up, the sub-model outlined in this section amounts simply to an implementation of uncovered interest rate parity, incorporating a specific expectations mechanism.

By contrast, the treatment of the goods market is very different, as we now see.

7.1.2 The goods market

Deviations from the equilibrium exchange rate result from the following assumption:

> A3: The price level is sticky. In other words, the aggregate supply curve is horizontal in the immediate impact phase, increasingly steep in the adjustment phase, and ultimately vertical in long-run equilibrium.

This scenario should be familiar from Section 4.2.3.

In the long run, the exchange rate is at its equilibrium level, in other words its market-clearing real value, given UK and US price levels.

However, *in the short run* the price level is fixed, due to the inherent rigidities that are so typical of markets for labour and goods: long-term contracts, lack of information in thousands of far-flung product markets, sluggishness in changing prices and wage rates, and so on. As a result, shocks which move the nominal exchange rate are associated with changes in the real exchange rate, and hence with current account deficits or

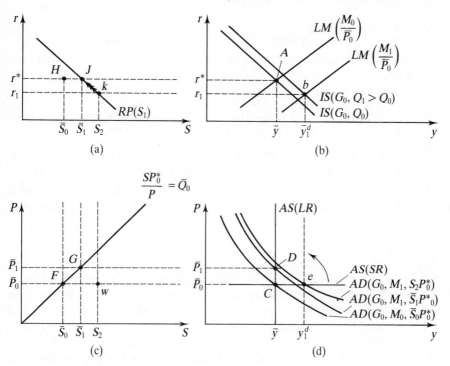

Figure 7.2 Money supply increase in the Dornbusch model.

surpluses. With the passage of time, unless there are further disturbances, the economy moves back to its long-run real exchange rate, as a result of movements in both the nominal exchange rate and the price level.

From this point on, all we need do is follow through the implications of these assumptions to understand how Dornbusch arrives at his conclusions. For this purpose, we shall make use of Figure 7.2.

Notice that Figure 7.2(a) illustrates the path taken by the exchange rate to satisfy UIRP, more or less repeating Figure 7.1. Figure 7.2(c) shows a version of the familiar PPP diagram, plotted for a given value of the US price index, P^*. It is assumed that the UK current account clears at the real exchange rate $Q_0 = SP_0^*/P$. At combinations of P and S above the line, the pound's real value is higher than Q_0, so that the UK is uncompetitive, and hence runs a current account deficit, and vice versa below the line. UK trade is only in balance when the exchange rate/price level combination is such as to place the domestic economy exactly on the line.

Figure 7.2(b) contains the *IS–LM* diagram, showing the determination of aggregate demand, for given real money balances, while the aggregate demand curve for each nominal money stock is plotted in Figure 7.2(d), along with the long and short-run aggregate supply curves.

7.1.3 Long-run equilibrium

By definition, long-run equilibrium is characterized by the following conditions:

(1) Aggregate demand is equal to aggregate supply. Hence, there is no upward or downward pressure on the price level.

(2) UK and US interest rates are equal, so that the exchange rate is static, with no expectation of either depreciation or appreciation.

(3) The real exchange rate is at its long-run level. It follows that there is neither a surplus nor a deficit in the current account of the balance of payments.

These conditions are satisfied at points A, C, F and H in Figure 7.2 (b), (d), (c) and (a) respectively. With the initial equilibrium domestic price level, P_0, and the nominal money suppply, M_0, the real money stock implies that the *LM* curve is the one that cuts the *IS* curve at the interest rate, r^*, and the aggregate demand, $\bar{y}$. This in turn implies a zero interest rate differential with the USA, and hence no expected depreciation or appreciation in the exchange rate (at H). It also means the goods market is in equilibrium, with national income and output at the long-run level of $\bar{y}$ (point C). Finally, as we can see from point F, the combination of a domestic price level of $\bar{P}_0$ and an exchange rate of $\bar{S}_0$ means that the UK current account is in balance.

We now consider the effect of a specific disturbance: an unanticipated money supply increase.

7.2 Monetary expansion

It will be recalled that monetary policy had no real effects in the monetary model. In the present case, this is no longer true, at least in the short run.

Suppose the UK economy's equilibrium is subjected to the following disturbance:

> The UK authorities increase the money supply from M_0 to M_1. For example, suppose they actually expand the money stock by a quarter. In other words, $M_1 = 1.25 M_0$.

What will be the effect of the disturbance, in the short and in the long run?

7.2.1 The long-run effect

Sometimes it is easier to understand the plot once we know the end of the story. At any rate, the way to handle the Dornbusch model is always to start by looking at the effect of a disturbance on its long-run properties, then go back and look for the route the variables must have taken to get there.

The consequences for long-run equilibrium are straightforward. Start in Figure 7.2(d) and (b). The new long-run equilibrium must lie somewhere along the original, unchanged vertical supply curve, which means that aggregate demand will have to equal $\bar{y}$. On the other hand, the interest rate will have to end up at r^*, since long-run equilibrium requires that no further change in the exchange rate be expected. It follows that *both the IS and LM curves will have to end up in the same position as before the money supply increase*.

As far as the *LM* curve is concerned, this can only be the case if the real money stock is back at its pre-disturbance level, which obviously requires a 25% rise in the price level, since:

$$\frac{M_1}{\overline{P}_1} = \frac{1.25 M_0}{1.25 \overline{P}_0} = \frac{M_0}{\overline{P}_0}$$

In the absence of any change in fiscal policy, the position of the *IS* curve depends only on the real exchange rate, $Q = SP^*/P$. For the *IS* curve to be unchanged in long-run equilibrium therefore, the real exchange rate will need to have returned to its initial, pre-disturbance level.

The rise in the price level means the aggregate demand curve will need to shift upward, in proportion to the increase in the money stock, so as to keep output unchanged at its long-run level, $\bar{y}$. The new equilibrium will therefore be at *D*.

Reading across from the new price level to Figure 7.2(c), it follows that we require the exchange rate to have depreciated (*S* to have risen) to $\overline{S}_1$, at point *G*, where there is again a zero balance on the UK current account.

Notice that, as in the simple monetary model, the new equilibrium involves a depreciation in strict proportion to the rise in the domestic price level and the money supply increase that brought it about. In other words, the sterling price of US dollars will have risen from $\overline{S}_0$ to $\overline{S}_1 = 1.25\overline{S}_0$, to offset the 25% inflation in the price of UK output, thereby keeping relative competitiveness constant.

As we have seen, with the *real* money stock back at its original level and the economy again in equilibrium at the point *A* in the *IS–LM* diagram (Figure 7.2(b)), the interest rate must also be at the US level, r^*. Thus, interest rate parity will obtain, as always, but with a zero expected change in the current exchange rate. In terms of Figure 7.2(a), the new equilibrium is at *J*, instead of *H*.

7.2.2 The impact effect

Now that we have established where the change in the money supply is ultimately going to land us, it will be easier to work out the impact effect.

Start in Figure 7.2(b), where it can be seen that the *LM* curve has shifted down because, with the nominal money stock increased and the price level unchanged, the real money supply is now one and a quarter times as great as before the disturbance. The result has to be an immediate fall in interest rates.

Why does the interest rate fall?

The reason is that, with national income unchanged and the real money stock greater by a quarter, there would be an excess supply of money at the old interest rate, r^*. But remember, we are assuming financial markets clear at all times. So any incipient excess supply of money will be instantaneously choked off by a fall in the interest rate, offsetting the increase in the supply of real balances by a compensating increase in the demand. Thus, the lower interest rate is necessary to bring about the absorption of the new, temporarily higher real money stock.

The impact on the interest rate, sometimes known as the *liquidity effect*, is the key to understanding the Dornbusch model. We can see its implications in Figure 7.2(a), where the fall in the interest rate creates a differential in favour of New York. To prevent a flood of money out of London, there needs to be some compensating attraction for holders of sterling securities. In fact, the compensation is provided by an instantaneous depreciation in the exchange rate to a point at which the market views the pound as being so undervalued, relative to its new equilibrium level of $\overline{S}_1$, as to offer the prospect of appreciation sufficient to offset the lower interest rate on UK securities.

However, the fall in the interest rate is mitigated somewhat by an induced shift in the *IS* curve. Since the nominal exchange rate has fallen while the domestic price level stayed fixed, the competitiveness of the UK economy has improved, stimulating demand for its output and pushing the *IS* curve to the right. The net effect is to leave the economy in short-run equilibrium at point *b*, where aggregate demand has been boosted by both these effects and the interest rate has fallen to r_1.

At the same time, aggregate demand has risen to y_1, and given our assumptions about supply conditions, this is also the real national income actually produced (at the point *e* in Figure 7.2(d)).

With an interest rate of r_1, temporary equilibrium is at the point *k* in Figure 7.2(a), on the *RP* line through the new, long-run equilibrium exchange rate, $\overline{S}_1$. (There was, of course, an *RP* line through the old equilibrium exchange rate, $\overline{S}_0$, but it has not been drawn, since it plays no part in the proceedings.) We assume that, as soon as the money supply is increased, the financial markets form their view as to where the exchange rate is going to end up, once the dust has settled. So it is with respect to this new long-run exchange rate that they judge what is going to happen to the rate over the near future. With the exchange rate at S_2, they reckon on balance that the pound is going to appreciate (S to fall) by just enough to compensate for the lower interest rate on sterling deposits, in other words, at the rate $(r^* - r_1)$.

> This is the key to the whole mechanism. The immediate effect of the monetary expansion has been to cause the exchange rate to rise from its initial position at $\overline{S}_0$ to the point, S_2, beyond what we know will be its long-run resting place, at the level $\overline{S}_1$. To get to its new long-run equilibrium position, at $\overline{S}_1$, it will need to fall. In other words, the impact effect is to make the pound overshoot its long-run devaluation, with a consequently exaggerated effect on UK competitiveness, driving the economy to a point like w in Figure 7.2(c).

In numerical terms, the 25% increase in the money stock leads *ultimately* to a 25% *rise* in the UK price level and 25% *fall* in the value of the pound, keeping the relative price of UK output on world markets constant. However, since the price level is fixed, the *instantaneous* effect on the value of the pound might be to cause it to fall by 40% say, giving a temporary boost to UK competitiveness of the same scale.

We can see from Figure 7.2(a) that the extent of the overshoot depends on two factors:

(1) The interest sensitivity of the demand for money, denoted by l in Equation 4.9.[1] The smaller it is, the steeper is the *LM* curve and the greater the fall in the interest rate resulting from any given increase in the real money stock.

(2) The slope of the *RP* line. The flatter it is the more the exchange rate must overshoot its long-run equilibrium, for any change in the interest rate. Since, as already pointed out, the gradient of the *RP* line is (minus) the expectation adjustment parameter, θ, it follows that the more sluggish are market anticipations, the greater the degree of overshooting.

The intuitive explanation is that, when θ is small, any given interest rate differential (and hence required rate of expected depreciation) must be balanced by a larger gap between the current and equilibrium levels of the exchange rate. In fact, if it were zero, no differential would ever be possible because, however large the gap between S and its equilibrium value, it would generate no expected depreciation.

---

[1] In fact, in Dornbusch's paper, and in most modern work of this type, the demand for money is set in a log linear formulation so that the parameters correspond to elasticities.

7.2.3 The adjustment process

So much for the impact effect of monetary expansion. What will happen in the weeks and months following the increase in the money supply?

Obviously, the excess demand for goods and services will tend to push up prices in the domestic economy, at a speed which will depend on the scale of the initial disequilibrium and on the rapidity with which the individual product (and labour) markets respond. In the process, we can think of the economy moving successively through a series of aggregate supply curves, each steeper than the last.

As prices rise, the excess demand is progressively eliminated in two ways. First, the UK's temporary competitive advantage is gradually eroded by the rise in domestic prices, so the demand for UK output is reduced, that is, the *IS* curve slips back towards its original position. Secondly, assuming no further monetary expansion, the real money supply is progressively reduced by the inflation, shifting the *LM* curve back to its pre-disturbance position. In the process, as the real money stock falls back, the interest rate rises to choke off the additional demand for money, at the same time helping to reduce the differential in favour of New York. As the domestic interest rate rises, the exchange rate appreciates up the $RP(\overline{S}_1)$ line, further eroding the UK's competitive advantage, and hastening the return to equilibrium.

Presumably, if the Dornbusch model is a true picture of the working of a floating exchange rate, most economies are to be observed most of the time in the adjustment phase.[2] It is important to note, then, that in this model the adjustment phase following a monetary expansion is characterized by:

(1)   A domestic currency whose value is *appreciating*, albeit at a diminishing rate.

(2)   A (decreasing) current account surplus.

(3)   (Decelerating) price inflation.

(4)   (Relatively) low, but rising interest rates.

At a first glance the association of an appreciating currency with rising interest rates corresponds with a pattern that is frequently observed. Exchange rate appreciation is often attributed to an accompanying rise in interest rates. However, it should be apparent that, in the Dornbusch model, rising UK interest rates cannot be said to *cause* the rise in the value

---

[2] Though, of course, they will often be in the process of adjusting to a number of earlier disturbances which, if not simultaneous, took place at intervals close enough for their adjustment phases to overlap. Of course, many of the disturbances will not have involved money supply increases, some may have been decreases. Still others may have been real rather than monetary disturbances.

of the pound. Rather, both phenomena result from the same cause: expansionary monetary policy, and the concomitant, temporary undervaluation of sterling.

By the same token, the current account surplus accompanies, but does not cause the appreciation. In fact, by the time the process of adjustment has worked itself out fully, the surplus has disappeared – but the value of the pound is at its highest level since the monetary expansion took place.

★ 7.3 A formal explanation

The analysis so far has been only heuristic. Unfortunately, there is a limit to how far one can go with diagrams backed up by nothing more than intuition. In this section, we give a more formal presentation of one (simplified) version of the Dornbusch model, and use it to derive some further results. In fact in Section 7.4, with only a slight modification to the same framework, we shall be able to draw some conclusions about the impact of oil on the UK economy.

First, we set down the equations, which should by now look broadly familiar – especially the first two, the UIRP condition and the exchange rate expectations mechanism introduced in Section 7.1, both of which are repeated here for convenience:

$$r = r^* + \Delta s^e \qquad\qquad \text{Uncovered interest} \qquad \textbf{(7.1)}$$
rate parity

$$\Delta s^e = \theta(\bar{s} - s) \qquad\qquad \text{Expectations} \qquad\qquad \textbf{(7.2)}$$

$$m - p = ky - lr \qquad\qquad \text{Demand for money} \qquad \textbf{(7.3)}$$

$$y^d = h(s - p) = h(q) \quad q \equiv s - p \qquad \text{Demand for UK} \qquad \textbf{(7.4)}$$
output

$$\dot{p} = \pi(y^d - \bar{y}) \qquad\qquad \bar{y} \text{ constant} \qquad \text{Demand adjustment} \qquad \textbf{(7.5)}$$

$$\dot{p} \equiv \frac{d \ln p}{dt}$$

With regard to the remaining equations, notice that we have stuck to the convention that m, p, s and y denote natural logarithms of the respective upper-case variables.[3] All the parameters are assumed positive.

---

[3] Unfortunately, the convention that y is real and Y nominal income clashes with this. At any rate, here y is the log of real income, and we shall simply avoid references to nominal income. Another caveat relates to the parameters in Equation 7.3, which obviously should not be the same in a log-linear demand function as they were in the natural number version. However, we persist with the letters originally used in Chapter 4 (k, l, h and so on) in order to economize on two scarce resources – symbols and memory (the reader's and the author's).

Notice that the interest rates, r and r^*, are most certainly not logs.

Equation 7.3 is simply a log-linear formulation of the demand for money. Since we are treating the money stock as given exogenously, the condition that $m^d = m^s$ is implicit: both demand and supply are written simply as m.

Equation 7.4 is a deliberately simplified aggregate demand schedule. To include a relationship between demand and other variables (income, the interest rate and so on, as in Section 4.1.1) would complicate matters without adding any significant insight into what follows. As it stands, the equation captures the essential link between aggregate demand for domestic output and the (log of) the real exchange rate, which is $q = s - p$, if we scale the (constant) foreign price level, P^*, to unity.[4] The higher the real exchange rate, the more competitive are UK products and hence the greater the demand.

Equation 7.5 is a price adjustment equation, which says that the wider the gap between demand and capacity output, $\bar{y}$, the higher the rate of inflation, $\dot{p}$. Again, in order to simplify matters, income is taken as fixed exogenously at the 'full-employment' level.[5] If demand deviates from that level, the outcome is a protracted change in the level of prices in the economy.

The system can be reduced to two equations. Substituting from Equation 7.1 and Equation 7.2 to eliminate the domestic interest rate from the demand for money equation (Equation 7.3), we derive:

$$p = L - l\,\theta(s - \bar{s}) \tag{7.6}$$

where:

$$L \equiv m - k\bar{y} + lr^*$$

and, using Equation 7.4 to replace y^d in Equation 7.5:

$$\dot{p} = \pi[h(s - p) - \bar{y}] \tag{7.7}$$

7.3.1 Long-run equilibrium

In long-run equilibrium, the following conditions apply:

(1)   The rate of inflation is zero. In other words, we have $y^d = \bar{y}$. That means, denoting steady state values of the variables by a bar, we must have:

$$\bar{s} - \bar{p} \equiv \bar{q} = \frac{\bar{y}}{h} \tag{7.8}$$

---

[4] Remember the log of one is zero. Alternatively, when $P^* = 1$, we have:
$$log\,(SP^*/P) = log\,(S/P) = s - p$$

[5] In other words it is determined along the lines described in Section 4.2.

from which we conclude that, in the long run, the only thing in the model which changes the real exchange rate is growth in capacity output. *Otherwise, any change in the nominal exchange rate is matched by a change in the price level.*

(2)   The expected rate of depreciation is zero. The exchange rate is static, and is not expected to change because it is at its equilibrium level. From Equation 7.6, this means we have:

$$\bar{p} = L \equiv m - k\bar{y} + lr^* \tag{7.9}$$

which simply says the equilibrium price level is the ratio of the money stock to the level of demand when it is at its long-run level, that is, when the UK and US interest rates are equal.

Using Equation 7.9 in Equation 7.8, it follows that the nominal exchange rate settles at the level:

$$\bar{s} = (h^{-1} - k)\bar{y} + m + lr^* \tag{7.10}$$

Our conclusions from the informal model of Section 7.2 are vindicated by Equations 7.9 and 7.10. Plainly, a given percentage rise in the money stock pushes up the long-run values of both the nominal exchange rate and the price level in the same proportion (see Box 7.2), and hence leaves the real exchange rate untouched. In this respect, the properties of the monetary model are preserved in long-run equilibrium.

On the other hand, it can also be observed from Equation 7.8 that a rise in output ultimately results in a real depreciation. The reason is that an increase in capacity requires an improvement in competitiveness to stimulate demand and thereby absorb the extra supply. Although it causes a fall in the price both of goods and foreign currency, as it does in the monetary model and for the same reason, the appreciation is proportionately smaller than the reduction in the price level.

BOX 7.2

Remember, m is the log of the money stock. Hence:

$$dm = d \ln M = \frac{dM}{M}$$

is the proportionate change or growth rate of M.

7.3.2 Disequilibrium

Now let us see how the model behaves out of equilibrium.

The standard practice is to rewrite the two basic equations (Equations 7.6 and 7.7), in terms of deviations from the steady state values. To accomplish this, all we need do is note that Equation 7.7 implies, in equilibrium, that:

$$0 = \pi[h(\bar{s} - \bar{p}) - \bar{y}] \tag{7.11}$$

Now subtract this from Equation 7.7 itself to give:

$$\dot{p} = \pi h(q - \bar{q}) \tag{7.12}$$

In other words, the rate of inflation is positive whenever the real exchange rate is above its equilibrium level, and vice versa below. So, for given values of the exogenous variables determining $\bar{q}$, the combinations of s and p consistent with zero inflation lie along a 45° line. See Figure 7.3, where the goods market equilibrium line has been drawn through the origin, on the harmless assumption that, by appropriate choice of units, we start with $s = p$.

Now apply the same treatment to the money market equation. Take Equation 7.9 from Equation 7.6 to give:

$$p - \bar{p} = -l\theta(s - \bar{s}) \tag{7.13}$$

which shows the conditions necessary for *short-run* equilibrium in the money market. Once the values of $\bar{p}$ and $\bar{q}$ have been set, or rather reset by a change in one of the exogenous variables, the system adjusts in such a way as to preserve this relationship at all times. It follows that, even in the adjustment phase, the economy lies somewhere along a downward-sloping line in (s, p) space, like the Money Market (MM) lines in Figure 7.3.

Notice that the *MM* lines have a gradient of (minus) $1/l\theta$. It follows that they are steeper the less sensitive the demand for money to changes in the exchange rate relative to its equilibrium level. This sensitivity is the product of the interest semi-elasticity and the expectations adjustment parameter.

At a position like A in Figure 7.3, the system is in short-run equilibrium, as always, because it is on the appropriate money market line, $MM(m_0)$. However, it is also in long-run equilibrium, because it is on the zero excess demand line ($\dot{p} = 0$).

7.3.3 Monetary expansion revisited

Now return to the example of an unanticipated money supply increase.

The ultimate outcome, we know, will be to raise both the exchange rate (from $\bar{s}_0$ to $\bar{s}_1$) and the price level (from $\bar{p}_0$ to $\bar{p}_1$). However, the stickiness of the price level precludes an immediate move from A to B.

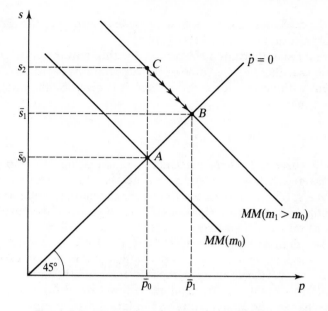

Figure 7.3 Dynamics of a money supply increase.

To see what happens initially, notice first that the zero inflation line is unaffected by the disturbance, because goods market equilibrium depends only on the real exchange rate, and that is going to remain unchanged. On the other hand, the money market clearing conditions certainly are affected. With a larger money stock, any given exchange rate is consistent with a proportionately higher price level, so that the MM schedule must shift outward to $MM(m_1)$. (As can be confirmed by differentiating Equation 7.13 and setting $d\bar{s} = d\bar{p}$.)

Now from the fact that the economy must be on the relevant (that is, new) MM line at all times, but that the price level is initially fixed at its old level, $\bar{p}_0$, we conclude the exchange rate must jump to s_2, carrying the system to point C on the downward-sloping arrowed path.

This confirms that, in this simple case, the nominal (and real) exchange rate overshoots in response to a monetary shock. The scale of the overshooting is dependent on the gradient of the money market line: the steeper the line, the greater the overshoot. Now it has been shown that the gradient of the MM line is inversely proportional to the product of the interest rate semi-elasticity of the demand for money and the expectation-adjustment parameter. It follows that overshooting is greater when the overall expectation-sensitivity of money demand is smaller. The reason is simple: the less sensitive is the demand for real balances to depreciation, the more the exchange rate needs to depreciate in order to raise the demand to equality with the supply (see Box 7.3).

Given the important role played by this parameter it should be pointed out that there is one value of the expectations coefficient, θ, which is consistent with perfect foresight; in fact, it is given by the positive solution of the equation:

$$\theta = -\pi h[1 + (l\theta)^{-1}]$$

While there is nothing particularly illuminating in computing this value, it is nonetheless interesting to note that the model as presented includes as a special case the situation where the market's rule of thumb is self-fulfilling, so that its anticipations always turn out to be correct in the short run, as well as the long run.

Notice that, with the price level fixed, the depreciation at C in Figure 7.3 is real as well as nominal. The impact effect of a monetary expansion is a temporary improvement in the competitiveness of UK output.

From this point on, the economy adjusts by moving from C to B, with the exchange rate appreciating and inflation decelerating.

7.4   Oil and the UK economy

More complicated versions of the Dornbusch model have been used quite extensively to provide insights into the effect of North Sea oil on the UK economy (see the Reading Guide). None of the models are able to take account of all the possible channels through which a disturbance of this

---

BOX 7.3   Proof that the exchange rate overshoots in the Dornbusch model.

The interested reader may confirm this result by differentiating Equation 7.6, noting that $dp = 0$ at the moment of impact, and that $dm = d\bar{s}$, as we have seen, from which it follows that:

$$ds \,|_{dp=0} = [1 + (l\theta)^{-1}]dm$$

The term in the square bracket is obviously greater than unity.

nature could affect the international value of the pound. However, if we make a number of simplifying assumptions, we can arrive at some useful conclusions with only two slight modifications to the model set out in the last section.

In the first place, no attempt will be made to distinguish between the effects of the oil price increase of 1979 and the build-up of production in the British sector of the North Sea which took place throughout the 1970s. Instead, we shall treat the total disturbance as though it were a sudden oil discovery. (Of course, it makes no difference from a macroeconomic point of view whether an increase in oil revenues is due to a rise in the number of barrels extracted or a rise in the price per barrel. For macroeconomic purposes the 1979 oil price shock affected the UK in exactly the same way as a sudden discovery – provided that we ignore the impact on other countries, which ultimately must impinge on the British economy.)

Specifically, we make the following assumptions:

(1) The oil discovery is unexpected in advance. Revenues are untaxed.

(2) The extraction costs of oil are zero.

(3) The oil produced in the UK is sold at a price determined exogenously (on world markets). For simplicity, assume this price is constant.

(4) Oil carries negligible weight in both UK and world consumption baskets, and hence its contribution to the price index can be ignored. Likewise, its importance as an input to production is ignored.

(5) The UK authorities change neither fiscal nor monetary policy in response to the oil shock.

To see how we need to modify the basic equations, consider first the impact on aggregate demand for non-oil goods. What counts for consumption is the underlying change in the wealth of the UK household sector, as measured by the permanent income value of oil revenues.[6] We can therefore rewrite Equation 7.4 as follows:

$$y^d = h(s - p) + c\overline{V} \qquad h, c > 0 \qquad \text{Demand for UK} \qquad \textbf{(7.4a)}$$
$$\text{non-oil output}$$

where the parameter c is the average propensity to consume, V is the value of oil revenues at any given moment, and the bar denotes, in this case, a permanent income value.

---

[6] For readers unfamiliar with the concept, permanent income can be visualized simply as the average over time of a variable flow, after appropriate discounting. Alternatively, it is the annuity which could be bought with the present value of the stream of oil revenues.

On the other hand, the *current* value of oil revenue seems more consistent with our transactions motive interpretation of the income term in the demand for money. That being so, we replace Equation 7.3 with:

$$m - p = k(y + V) - lr \qquad k, l > 0 \qquad \text{Demand for money} \qquad \textbf{(7.3a)}$$

which makes the demand for money at any moment dependent on national income at the time, inclusive of current revenue from oil, V.

These two modifications turn out to have somewhat different effects. To highlight the difference, we take them one at at time.

7.4.1   The wealth effect in the goods market

Undeterred by the artificiality of the assumption, let us temporarily set V to zero. In other words, suppose the oil discovery has no effect on transactions requirements.

If we now follow the same procedure as before in solving the system with Equation 7.4a in place of Equation 7.4, but with the other equations unchanged, we find that as far as equilibrium is concerned:

(1)   With the volume of non-oil production fixed, the real exchange rate must ultimately fall, so as to reduce the relative competitiveness of UK non-oil production. The appreciation crowds out enough foreign demand to make room for additional consumption by the newly-enriched UK residents.

In terms of Figure 7.4, this means the goods market equilibrium line ($\dot{p} = 0$) shifts outward, associating a higher price level with any given nominal exchange rate.[7]

(2)   On the other hand, the equilibrium price level is unchanged. The reason is obvious from the long-run demand for money (Equation 7.9). Nothing has occurred to affect the money market, so the price level cannot move.

There are two immediate corollaries of this result. Firstly, in the long run, the system must settle at B in Figure 7.4, and hence the new money market line must go through this point. Secondly, if no change is required in the price level in the long run, there can never be any disequilibrium. The initial disturbance never opens up any gap between the short and long-run price levels. With only the nominal exchange rate needing to change so as to effect the reduction in competitiveness, there is nothing to prevent the entire adjustment taking place at once. We conclude the price of foreign

---

[7]   While it is still a 45° line, the new goods market equilibrium locus is obviously associated with a lower value of $s - p$.

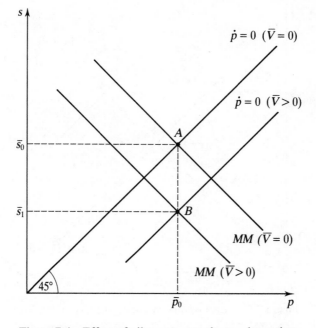

Figure 7.4 Effect of oil revenue on the goods market.

currency falls from s_0 to s_1 immediately, and the economy moves smoothly and instantly to its new steady state.

7.4.2 Transactions effect in the money market

By contrast, we now switch to a scenario where the oil revenue has no permanent income value whatsoever, and therefore has no effect on demand for output, but is simply a transient addition to the level of economic activity. In this case, we replace Equation 7.3 by Equation 7.3a, but stick to the remaining original equations, in particular Equation 7.4.

If we do so, we find:

(1) Because the product market is not affected by the original shock, the real exchange rate must remain unchanged, since it is the sole determinant of demand. The product market line ($\dot{p} = 0$) is therefore unmoved (Figure 7.5).

(2) On the other hand, the addition to the demand for real balances must result in a lower equilibrium price level.

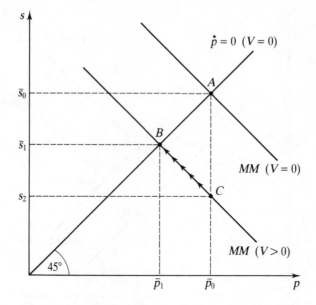

Figure 7.5   Effect of oil revenue on the money market.

At the same time, a lower price level can only be consistent with a constant real exchange rate if it is accompanied by appreciation. Thus, the new equilibrium is at *B*, where the real exchange rate is preserved by deflation and appreciation of equal proportions, keeping $s - p$ constant. This effect ought to be familiar: it is identical to a rise in income in the monetary model (Section 5.1.4).

In the short run, however, we again find overshooting. This is simply the reverse of the process we saw with a monetary expansion. In the present case, increased demand for money with an unchanged supply means interest rates have to rise, rather than fall. Higher interest rates are only possible if depreciation is anticipated, a condition that would only apply when the exchange rate is perceived by the currency market as overvalued – as it is when it has overshot as far as *C* in the diagram.

7.4.3 The general case

What the special cases confirm is that overshooting is inherently a money market response to the sticky price level. Changes which do not affect the money market cause no overshooting.

Putting the two effects together, Figure 7.6 shows the outome when oil revenue takes the form of a constant stream, so that $\overline{V} = V$. Not

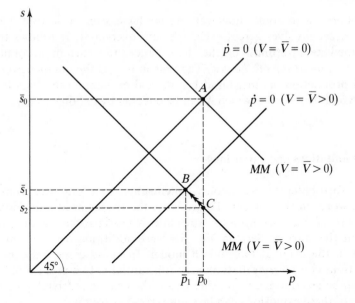

Figure 7.6   Effect of oil revenue on both money and goods market.

surprisingly, we have overshooting in the short run and real appreciation in the long run.

The impact effect is, as we saw, to raise interest rates so as to choke off the additional demand for money. Adjustment is then characterized by a depreciating currency and falling price level.

In summary, the depressing conclusion seems to be that the discovery and exploitation of oil is bad news in both the short and the long run. In particular, consider the implications for the current account. As always, assume the domestic country starts from a position of a zero deficit.

First, the long-run real appreciation must cause a fall in net exports of non-oil products, an example of the phenomenon sometimes called the Dutch disease.[8] This conclusion has an obvious interpretation.

Ultimately, the proposition involved is simply that, since in long-run equilibrium the current account must balance, an addition to net exports must be offset by an equal increase in net imports. In the present case, the large surplus on oil trade must have as its counterpart an equal deficit on non-oil items so as to keep the overall current account in balance. In that sense, *the oil surplus crowds out (net) exports of non-oil products, and the real appreciation is the mechanism whereby the crowding out takes place.*

---

[8] After the syndrome that is supposed to have afflicted the Netherlands, following the discovery of large reserves of natural gas.

Worse is to come, however. As we have seen in Section 7.4.2 the impact effect involves a real exchange rate overshoot. It follows that, in the immediate aftermath of the disturbance, the current account is in deficit, *in spite of the oil 'bonus'*. The reason is that the competitiveness of non-oil production, as measured by the real exchange rate, has deteriorated beyond the point at which it can be covered by net oil exports.

7.4.4 Limitations and extensions

Perhaps fortunately, these gloomy conclusions are a long way from being the last word on the subject. To see why, the reader need only look back at the list of the assumptions we made when introducing oil into the model at the start of Section 7.4. All were additional to the limitations implicit in the original Dornbusch model. In many cases, relaxing these assumptions complicates matters very substantially, to a point well beyond what can be covered here. In other cases, the change is trivial. The results of some of these extensions can be summarized as follows:

(1)   The formal analysis in Sections 7.4.2 and 7.4.3 involved a simplification of the original Dornbusch model in so far as we ignored the dependence of aggregate demand on the interest rate. Allowing for this relationship makes no qualitative difference to the results.[9]

(2)   The conclusions are substantially mitigated if we allow for the fact that, in an open economy, the appropriate deflator relevant to money balances is a price index including an import component. This modification means that the exchange rate plays a part in equilibrating the money market even in the long run. It also means that undershooting rather than overshooting is a possible reaction to oil revenue, depending on whether the dominant impact of the disturbance is felt in the goods or money market.[10]

(3)   Incorporating a 'core' rate of inflation by adding a constant to the right-hand side of Equation 7.5 makes the model more realistic, especially when applied to the UK, but otherwise changes little. All it does is introduce a long-run equilibrium rate of depreciation, and consequently a steady state interest rate differential of the same scale.

---

[9] The reader may easily verify that its main result is to make the goods market equilibrium line ($\dot{p} = 0$) steeper than the 45° line.

[10] It should be pointed out that whether or not a model of the Dornbusch type exhibits under- or overshooting depends only on its structure. If it overshoots in reaction to one disturbance, it does so to exactly the same extent in response to another disturbance.

(4) Another possibility would be to replace the price adjustment equation with something like:

$$\dot{p} = \pi(y - \bar{y})$$

a relationship which will be familiar to many readers as a version of the famous Phillips Curve. When output is at its long-run level,[11] the inflation rate is zero. Otherwise, if it is above (below) its capacity level, the price level is rising (falling). This change can have no effect on the long-run outcome, of course, but it too can be shown to open up the possibility of short-run undershooting.

(5) In each of the cases analysed, the disturbance was assumed to arrive like 'a bolt from the blue': the money supply increase, for example, unleashed by the authorities on a completely unsuspecting market. It is easy to see if this were not the case, we would get different results, because currency speculators would buy or sell the currency (as they do, in reality) on the strength of their guesses as to future money supply changes.

In an important extension of the Dornbusch model, it was demonstrated that if a money supply increase is anticipated (for example, if it is announced in advance), the effect on the exchange rate is somewhat moderated, with less overshooting and a longer adjustment period. Intuitively, the reason is that, from the moment the market becomes aware that the money supply is going to increase, it will change its judgement as to the long-run equilibrium. The result will be to start the whole process of adjustment immediately, thereby smoothing somewhat the impact of the money supply increase when it actually takes place. Of course, this presupposes that the market is correct in anticipating a money stock increase – in practice it may often anticipate monetary expansion that fails to materialize, causing exchange rate movements that cannot be rationalized retrospectively.[12]

In the oil discovery case, the situation is even more complicated, because in reality what happened was that the true nature and scale of the shock only emerged gradually over a number of years during the 1970s. First came encouraging geological reports, then an enthusiastic response to the auction of drilling permits, then the first discoveries and finally, assessment of the rate of flow from a

---

[11] Usually known in the labour market literature as the 'natural' level, nowadays given the more long-winded title: non-accelerating-inflation-rate output.

[12] More generally, what counts is not the absolute value of the change in an exogenous variable, but rather the extent to which the change comes as 'news' to the market, that is, the extent to which it had not already been discounted in the market prior to announcement or implementation. The implication (that we should be looking only at disturbances viewed as 'surprises' or 'innovations', given pre-existing expectations) will be followed up in Chapter 12.

succession of wells. Even then, after the major discoveries had been made, a number of questions remained open (and still do today): the technological feasibility of exploiting some of the finds, the life expectancy of existing wells, the likely rate at which exhausted resources would be replaced by new discoveries in the area, and most of all the future (relative) price at which the oil could be sold.

Viewed from this angle, what actually took place was a process of slow resolution of uncertainty. Each new item of information will have caused the financial markets to react (in the Dornbusch world, to over-react) by buying or selling sterling securities, depending on whether the information involved an up- or downgrading of future North Sea production prospects. Furthermore, at each stage the exchange rate will have reflected probability assessments, rather than established certainties.

(6) The analysis in this chapter takes the world economic environment as completely static. While this may be acceptable for many purposes, it is very unrealistic if the objective is to find the cause of the pound's appreciation in the early 1980s, at a time when the world economy was subjected to so many different types of shock, the effects of which, even taken individually, are often impossible to gauge. For example, if the owners of the new oil wealth (that is, OPEC governments and their citizens) had smaller relative demands for sterling than did the old wealth owners (the oil consumers), this fact might on its own reduce the value of the pound, other things being equal.

★ 7.5 Empirical Tests: The Frankel model

As it stands, the Dornbusch model is difficult to test. This is particularly true of its predictions about the dynamics of exchange rates. Most researchers have used an extension of the Dornbusch model developed by Jeffrey Frankel: the so-called real interest differential model.

The starting point is a small addition to the Dornbusch expectations mechanism. Instead of Equation 7.2, we have:

$$\Delta s^e = \theta(\bar{s} - s) + \Delta \widetilde{p}^e \qquad \theta > 0 \tag{7.14}$$

which asserts that when the exchange rate is at its equilibrium level, instead of being constant, it is expected to depreciate by the difference between the expected domestic and foreign inflation rates. (Remember, the tilde signifies the ratio of the domestic to the foreign variable.) This amounts to no more than a generalization of Equation 7.2 to accommodate long-run inflation: the deviation from equilibrium determines whether the currency's depreciation is thought likely to accelerate or decelerate.[13]

Exploiting UIRP to eliminate the expected depreciation from Equation 7.14, and solving for $\bar{s}$, we have:

$$\bar{s} = s + \frac{1}{\theta}(\tilde{r} - \Delta \tilde{p}^e) \tag{7.15}$$

Finally, follow Dornbusch in assuming the monetary model only determines the *equilibrium*, not the *actual* exchange rate. Specifically, suppose we have:

$$\bar{s} = \tilde{m} - k\tilde{y} + l\Delta \tilde{p}^e \tag{7.16}$$

where, for simplicity, we take domestic and foreign demand for money parameters as equal. This formulation is familiar, apart from the last term. Frankel notes that, in the absence of PPP, real interest rates must diverge. It follows, therefore, that the inflation rate (differential) is reflected in long interest rate (differentials), but not necessarily in short rates.[14]

The equation most often tested by researchers comes simply from combining Equations 7.15 and Equations 7.16 to give:

$$s = \tilde{m} - k\tilde{y} - \theta^{-1}\tilde{r} + (\theta^{-1} + l)\Delta \tilde{p}^e \tag{7.17}$$

or, alternatively:

$$s = \tilde{m} - k\tilde{y} - \theta^{-1}(\tilde{r} - \Delta \tilde{p}^e) + l\Delta \tilde{p}^e \tag{7.18}$$

which shows more clearly the role played by the real interest rate differential.

Provided one can find a way of measuring inflation expectations then Equations 7.17 or 7.18 are testable. Indeed, as an added bonus, they include the basic monetary model as a special case: if the exchange rate expectations elasticity, θ, is infinite, the coefficient of real interest rates will be zero.

Frankel himself, proxying inflation expectations by long-run interest rates, found this hypothesis appeared to fit the facts for the DM/$ rate in the mid 1970s – explaining some 80 or 90 per cent of the exchange rate variation over the period. However, virtually all work since then suggests equations like these fail to track the major exchange rates, particularly in the 1980s (see Reading Guide). Furthermore, this remains the case even when alternative measures of inflation expectations are used.

---

[13] Frankel justifies this mechanism by demonstrating that, under certain circumstances, it is consistent with perfect foresight.

[14] A view which has a long Keynesian pedigree is that short rates reflect monetary tightness (via the liquidity effect), while long rates are determined by trends in the (relatively sluggish) core inflation rate. According to this view monetary policy acts on the short end of the yield curve rather than on the general level of interest rates.

7.6   Conclusions

The Dornbusch model appears at first glance to offer a potentially power-ful explanation for the observed volatility of floating exchange rates, in particular the tendency for currencies to swing erratically from positions of apparent overvaluation to massive undervaluation, and back again. The assumption that price levels are sticky is extremely credible, and Dorn-busch successfuly demonstrates that a consequence could well be over-reaction by the exchange rate to a disturbance. Furthermore, in the light of the evidence discussed in Chapter 2 that PPP does not hold in the short run, but possibly in the long run, the analysis here looks superficially plausible, since it generates the same conclusions as the monetary model in the long run, but allows for real effects in the short run.

The limitations discussed in Section 7.4.4 are real enough, however. On the other hand, as was indicated there, the strength of the model is as a prototype for more complicated examples of the genre. Furthermore, the mechanism at its core can be shown to have wide applicability: similar dynamics are displayed whenever two related prices adjust at different speeds.

Nevertheless, the poor performance of the model and its derivatives in explaining the facts is undeniable, and has acted as a spur to the develop-ment of other approaches to exchange rate modelling.

■   Summary

- Financial markets are assumed to clear instantaneously, with perfect capital mobility ensuring uncovered interest rate parity (UIRP) is maintained at all times.

- Market expectations are for the exchange rate to depreciate at a rate proportional to the gap between its current level and its long-run equilibrium value.

- In the goods market, the price level is sticky, adjusting over time at a rate proportional to the excess demand.

- The conclusions of the monetary model are preserved in long-run equilibrium.

- In the immediate term, since the price level is fixed, shocks which create excess supply (demand) in the money market have liquidity effects, requiring a fall (rise) in the interest rate to clear the domestic money market. The change can only be reconciled with UIRP if there is a simultaneous expectation of exchange rate appreciation (depreciation). Given the assumption about the way market expectations are formed, this in turn is only possible if the exchange rate jumps to a level beyond (in other words, overshooting) its long-run equilibrium.

- An extension of the Dornbusch model suggests the discovery and exploitation of North Sea oil may have been associated with long-run real appreciation and short-run overshooting in the sterling exchange rate.

- The original Dornbusch model can be extended in a number of different directions to make it more realistic. However, these modifications result in models which sometimes exhibit under- rather than overshooting.

- One derivative of the Dornbusch model, developed by Frankel, has been extensively tested, with results that are generally disappointing. Apart from a short period in the 1970s, it fails either to track or forecast the exchange rate adequately.

READING GUIDE

Readers are strongly recommended to progress from reading this stripped-down version of Dornbusch's model to tackling the original journal article in Dornbusch (1976a) or, for a slightly different presentation, Dornbusch (1976b). An excellent textbook discussion is to be found in Begg (1982).

The original article is only moderately technical, the extensions are much more so. Subject to this caveat, the important landmarks in extending the model are Wilson (1979) on pre-announced policy changes and Buiter and Miller (1981).

On oil shocks, see Eastwood and Venables (1982) and Buiter and Purvis (1983). Copeland (1983) extends the Dornbusch analytical methods, so as to calculate the impact on the UK economy of a shock to public sector prices.

The model in Section 7.5 is from Frankel (1979). More recently, see the influential work by Meese and Rogoff (1983). Macdonald (1988) gives a summary of the tests and results achieved.

8

Portfolio Balance and the Current Account

■ Introduction

In Chapter 7, we modified the monetary model to allow for the possibility that adjustment in the real sector may well take longer than in financial markets. The models to be analysed in this chapter rely on the same assumption. They differ from the Dornbusch model, however, in a number of important respects.

The point at which the divergence starts is the uncovered interest rate parity assumption. Portfolio balance theorists argue instead that risk aversion is the predominant motive in investors' choice between domestic and foreign currency securities and that financial markets will therefore be characterized by risk premiums large and pervasive enough to make UIRP inoperative.

Now the detailed implications of allowing for risk aversion involve the analysis of utility maximization under conditions of uncertainty, and for that reason coverage of the whole subject has to be deferred to much later in the book (Chapter 13). However, it turns out for once that the economics profession's misfortune is good news for the textbook writer (and reader). In fact, portfolio balance models of the exchange rate make use only of the ultimate conclusions of risk premium

239

analysis. No attempt has yet been made to integrate the two literatures, so that it is quite convenient to treat them separately in this way.

The only insight from the risk premium literature that is relevant here is that *investors will tend to diversify their holdings of risky assets, with portfolio shares that increase as the return on them rises relative to competing assets*. To put the matter differently, assets are no longer perfect substitutes, particularly if they are denominated in different currencies. Instead, they are, at least in part, complements within a diversified portfolio, so that the interest rate elasticity of the demand for securities will be far less than infinite.

Portfolio balance theorists therefore specify the model of the financial sector in much greater detail than the models considered so far. In doing so, they also integrate the process of wealth accumulation (saving) into the model, as the vital link between short-run equilibrium in the financial sector and long-run equilibrium in the rest of the economy. Now private sector saving can only take the form of accumulation of foreign currency assets via the capital account of the balance of payments, and under a floating exchange rate the balance on capital account has to be the reflection of the current account surplus or deficit. It follows that a role has been found for the balance of payments – or at least a link between events in that sector and the exchange rate.

The outcome is a model which is very general indeed – to such an extent that it can be formulated to include all the other models in this book as special cases. As we shall see, it is perhaps best regarded as an integration of the Mundell–Fleming and Dornbusch models, sharing with the former the assumption of imperfect capital mobility, and with the latter, the assertion that product prices adjust slowly. It is also richer in its insights and in some respects more plausible than the models covered in the book so far. In particular, many economists and commentators (and possibly market participants) would find it difficult to accept a view of the exchange rate that did not allow some role for the balance of payments, even if only in the long run.

Unfortunately, however, the portfolio balance approach is also far more complex. The price of the complications is not only analytic difficulty. The result is also the introduction of variables which are almost impossible to measure (for example, wealth), a fact which makes the whole approach difficult to apply in practice and of little use for forecasting purposes.[1]

We start in Section 8.1 by describing in some detail the model of the financial sector. In Section 8.2, we analyse the short-run impact of

---

[1] In general, the models share most of the advantages and disadvantages of the closed economy macroeconomic models of Tobin and others, from which they largely derive (see the Reading Guide).

three different types of disturbance, before going on to cover long-run equilibrium and the significance of the current account. The chapter closes with a brief consideration of the evidence and some conclusions.

8.1 The specification of asset markets

The portfolio balance model takes as its setting a small country, which in the present context means one whose assets are not held by foreign residents (unlike the UK, in reality). The opposite is certainly not taken to be the case. In other words, UK residents *are* assumed to hold foreign currency assets. In fact, the residents of the domestic country – we shall continue to call it the UK – hold three types of asset: the sterling money supply, M, the total stock of bonds issued by the British Government, B, and a quantity, F, of dollar-denominated assets[2] issued by the Federal Government in Washington. The latter is taken as fixed in the short run (but not in the long run) at the level $\$F$, which is equivalent to £FS. We assume that other forms of wealth can safely be ignored.[3]

Given this framework, UK nominal wealth (in pounds) at any moment will consist of:

$$W = \overline{M} + \overline{B} + SF \tag{8.1}$$

where the bars denote the variables that are taken as exogenous.[4]

Consider the demand for each of the assets. What factors will determine the level of demand for the three assets?

To understand the answer given by portfolio balance theorists, it is necessary to place the demand for money, domestic and foreign bonds in the appropriate setting.

In the first place, the demand for each of the assets is taken as interdependent. In other words, rather than considering the demand for any single asset in isolation, we need to think of a decision process whereby an individual's stock of wealth is distributed between the available list of

---

[2] Either short-term securities (for example US Treasury Bills) or Federal bonds near maturity. Both domestic securities, B, and foreign securities, F, have to be assets of maturity short enough for us to be able to ignore holders' capital gains or losses when the interest rate changes.

[3] This simplification will be justified if other, mainly non-financial assets are poor substitutes for financial assets, at least in the short run. If this is the case, it means wealth owners (or, more likely, the institutions which act on their behalf) will select their portfolios of financial assets without paying any attention to their holdings of non-financial assets – surely not a grossly implausible assumption to make.

[4] Note that the portfolio balance model cannot be formulated in terms of logs, because of the adding-up condition defining wealth, hence the reversion to upper case S and so on in this chapter.

assets.[5] The problem for investors then is how to choose what *proportion* of their wealth (or net worth) they should hold in each possible form: money, domestic bonds or foreign bonds. Moreover, their objective in selecting a particular portfolio is taken to be the maximization of their future welfare, as measured by their utility.[6]

Notice the change in emphasis compared with the models examined hitherto, where individuals were viewed as preoccupied with financing a flow of transactions in goods and services.

Now the problem of how investors can maximize their utility in this type of context is complicated, because the return on some of the competing assets is uncertain, so that the investor's decision will typically involve trading off prospective returns against potential risk. The problem will be analysed in some detail in Chapter 13. For the moment, we rely on an intuitive justification of the model.

Consider an individual faced with a choice between (for the moment) only two assets, one riskless, *A*, and one risky, *B*. *A* offers a guaranteed return of r^A over the holding period. On the other hand, the return on *B* is highly uncertain, but the most likely outcome is for it to turn out at r^B.

Now we know that if in general people are risk averse, as we assume in this chapter they are, they will require compensation for the uncertainty associated with asset *B*. They will not simply plunge all their wealth into asset *B* whenever the likely return r^B is greater than r^A. Instead, they will compare the two returns to see if the gap between them is great enough to offer what they regard as adequate compensation for the risk associated with *B*.

But if the excess return $r^B - r^A$ *is* great enough to persuade an individual to take a chance on B, how great a proportion of his wealth should he risk? The answer is not obvious. What is clear, however, is that it would be foolhardy to respond to a tiny increase in r^B by suddenly plunging 100% for *B*. Common observation shows that people usually follow the old maxim: 'don't put all your eggs in one basket'. In other words, they *diversify*. So the most likely response, and one that can be shown to be consistent with rational behaviour, is for the individual to respond to each small increase in r^B by increasing his holding of *B*. There will be some level so low that he will choose to hold none at all. There will equally be some level so high that he will choose to convert his total portfolio to holding *B*. But as long as r^B remains within these bounds, he will hold a mix, that is, a *diversified portfolio* of both *A* and *B*.

---

[5] The portfolio selection process has to be thought of as taking place after (in the logical rather than chronological sense) the vital decisions about how much to spend and how much to save have already been made. In the accepted jargon, we assume that the separation theorem can be applied here.

[6] Those with a background in microeconomics will recognize the concept of utility as the economist's (largely invisible) index of satisfaction. Note that, in the context of uncertainty, as here, it is only the *expected* value of utility that can be maximized, as we shall see in Chapter 13.

Moreover, *the individual will usually hold a greater proportion of any asset the higher is the return it offers and the lower is the return on competing assets, other things being equal.* This will be the case because the higher the return, the greater the compensation for risk (if any).

The next point to notice is that, if the demand for one of the assets, say B, depends on *both* rates of return, r^A and r^B, so must the demand for the other asset, A. This must be true for two reasons. Firstly, because the statement in italics obviously implies that the demands are symmetrical. Secondly, with the amount available for investment fixed, whatever proportion is invested in B – call it b – it follows that the proportion $1 - b$ must be held in the asset A.

Bearing these points in mind, and applying the same logic to our three-asset case mentioned at the beginning of this section, it follows that equilibrium in each market will be defined by these equations:

$$\overline{M}/W = m(r, \bar{r}^* + \Delta s^e) \qquad\qquad m_1 < 0 \quad m_2 < 0 \qquad \textbf{(8.2)}$$

$$\overline{B}/W = b(r, \bar{r}^* + \Delta s^e) \qquad\qquad b_1 < 0 \quad b_2 < 0 \qquad \textbf{(8.3)}$$

$$SF/W = f(r, \bar{r}^* + \Delta s^e) \qquad\qquad f_1 < 0 \quad f_2 < 0 \qquad \textbf{(8.4)}$$

In each case, the left-hand side represents the supply (relative to wealth) and the right-hand side the demand as a function of the two rates of return: the interest rate on domestic bonds, r, and the sterling value of the return on foreign securities, which is equal to the sum of the (exogenously given) foreign interest rate, r^*, and the rate of depreciation of the pound, Δs^e (see Box 8.1). Notice that in previous chapters, it was assumed

---

BOX 8.1 *Why we can ignore the price level in the asset demand function.*

Some readers may feel uneasy about the absence of any reference to the price level in these equations, particularly in view of the necessity, stressed in Chapter 4, of treating the demand for money as the demand for a stock of purchasing power.

In fact, the problem does not arise here for two reasons. First, we assume the price level is constant in the short run. Second, even if we explicitly included the price index, P, it would cancel out on the left-hand side in each equation, because both numerator and denominator are nominal quantities. So we would have:

$$\frac{\overline{M}/P}{W/P} = \overline{M}/W$$

and so forth.

these two rates of return were driven to equality by risk-neutral arbitrageurs. Here, of course, the risk premium drives a wedge between domestic and foreign interest rates, as it implicitly does in the Mundell–Fleming model.

This argument is summarized in the signs given to the partial derivatives on the right-hand side of the equations, where we follow the standard notation for a function $g(x, y)$:

$$g_1 \equiv \frac{\partial g}{\partial x} \quad \text{and} \quad g_2 \equiv \frac{\partial g}{\partial y}$$

Thus, the demand for money decreases when either rate of return falls, while the demand for each type of bond is affected positively by increases in its 'own return'[7] and negatively by increases in the return on the other asset.

To understand the remainder of this section, it is essential to bear in mind that the variables in the portfolio balance model are of three types:

(1) Endogenous, even in the short run: the (spot) exchange rate, S, and the interest rate, r. Both react instantaneously, so that financial markets clear at all times.

(2) Exogenous in the short run, endogenous in the long run: total wealth, W, the stock of foreign securities, F, the UK price level, P, and the expected rate of depreciation, Δs^e, all are assumed 'sticky', that is, slow to react to disturbances.

(3) Exogenous in both short and long run: the US variables (interest rate, r^* and price level, P^*), and the (UK) government policy variables: the stocks of money, M, and gilt-edged securities (bonds), B – all marked with a bar.

These equations are very general indeed, and moreover it is easy to see how the model can be generalized further in order to incorporate additional assets. However, the complications can easily get out of hand, since each additional asset involves not only one more equation, but an extra rate of return argument in each equation! Therein lies both the strength and the weakness of the model.

The first point to notice is that nothing is specified with regard to the form of the demand functions m, b and f, other than a number of restrictions on the partial derivatives. In each case, as can be seen in

---

[7] We assume money balances pay neither an explicit nor an 'own' return.

Equations 8.2 to 8.4, it is assumed that demand responds positively to changes in its *own* rate of return and negatively to returns on competing assets. Furthermore, the own-return effect is usually assumed greater, in absolute terms, than the cross-return effect:

$$b_1 + b_2 > 0 \quad \text{and} \quad f_1 + f_2 > 0$$

In the jargon, assets are 'gross substitutes'.

Finally in this regard, it should be noted that the definition of wealth in Equation 8.1 means that for a change in either rate of return, the sum of the impact effects on all three assets must be zero. In other words, we must have:

$$m_1 + b_1 + f_1 = 0 \quad \text{and} \quad m_2 + b_2 + f_2 = 0$$

In a world with a zero-risk premium, all four of the partial derivatives of the functions b and f would be infinite, reflecting the fact that since investors view domestic and foreign bonds as perfect substitutes, the slightest deviation from the (common) world rate of return would result in massive flight to or from the asset in question. This was why, in Chapter 7, we were able effectively to replace asset demand equations with a simple, (uncovered) interest rate parity condition.

In the present case, by contrast, a rise in the return on, say, UK bonds causes (British) investors to reallocate their portfolios instantaneously in favour of UK securities and at the expense of both the other assets. However, the shift in portfolio composition is marginal – which is not to say small necessarily, but certainly not infinite. In other words, instead of converting their total wealth into domestically-issued bonds, as they would if they were risk neutral, they switch to holding a greater proportion in bonds and less in money and foreign assets. In other words, they remain appropriately diversified after the change.[8]

8.2 Short-run equilibrium

The standard way of analysing the model's short-run properties is with the aid of portfolio balance lines: *MM*, *BB* and *FF* for the money, bond and foreign asset markets respectively (Figure 8.1). The curves show equilibrium combinations of S and r, given the initial level of the return on

---

[8] The question of what is meant by an appropriate level of diversification will be dealt with in Chapter 13.

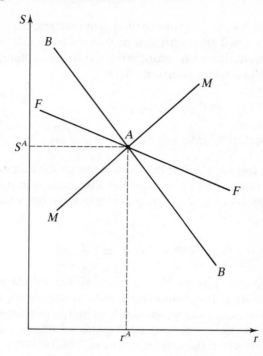

Figure 8.1   Short-run equilibrium in the portfolio balance model.

foreign assets, the value of total UK wealth, and the stocks of money and bonds.[9]

To understand the diagram, consider the effect of an increase in the price of foreign exchange, S. The key here is that the fall in the value of the pound has two effects. By raising the sterling value of the given stock of dollar assets (with F given, the value of SF increases), it brings about an increase in the value of wealth, hence raising the demand for all assets, *other things being equal*.

As far as the money market is concerned, the increased wealth would lead to a rise in the demand for money. With the supply unchanged, equilibrium can only be preserved by a rise in one of the rates of return – and

---

[9]   The interested reader may prove any of the propositions in this section (the slopes of the schedules, the effect of changes in the exogenous variables and so on) by the standard methods of comparative static analysis. In other words, simply differentiate each equation totally, holding appropriate variables constant, and make use of the restrictions on the partial derivatives of the three functions.

   Notice that one way of looking at the three portfolio balance schedules is as an open economy generalization of the *LM* curve (see Chapter 4).

the return on dollar assets is assumed constant in the short run. Hence, a *rise* in UK interest rates is required to preserve equilibrium, and the *MM* schedule slopes upward, associating higher values of *S* and *r*.

In the market for UK gilt-edged, the opposite is true: excess demand needs to be offset by *lower* interest rates, in other words, higher bond prices. It follows that the *BB* line slopes downward.

Finally, the impact on the market for foreign assets of the increase in *S* takes two forms. The effect of the rise in total wealth, which tends to increase the demand, is more than offset by the increased sterling value of the supply. The *net* impact is to create incipient excess supply. This can be prevented by reducing the attractiveness of competing assets, which means given our assumptions, a *lower* domestic interest rate. Hence, the *FF* schedule is also downward sloping.

Since we have assumed the impact of a lower UK interest rate is likely to be greatest in the domestic bond market, the *BB* line will be steeper than the *FF* line, as can be seen in Figure 8.1.

The intersection of any two of the lines generates the equilibrium exchange rate-interest rate combination, (S^A, r^A). The third line must pass through the same point, A, by virtue of the adding-up condition: given fixed wealth, equilibrium in any two of the markets implies equilibrium in the third. This is obvious as soon as it is realized that total asset demand as well as supply must add up to wealth, simply because the only way to demand any asset is by offering another in exchange. So we could choose to ignore the bond market for example, since equilibrium in the other two markets would mean that Equations 8.2 and 8.4 were satisfied at the current exchange rate and interest rate, which would in turn mean that:

$$b \equiv 1 - m - f$$

$$= 1 - \overline{M}/W - SF/W = \overline{B}/W$$

The model as it stands allows us to ask a number of questions about the impact of changes in policy variables (the stocks of money and/or bonds), in the short-run exogenous variables (the quantity of domestic wealth or of foreign assets) or even in the behavioural relationships summarized by the functions m, b and f.[10] The answers are often complicated and not always unambiguous. For illustrative purposes, we shall confine our attention to the examples of an increase in the money supply and in the stock of foreign assets. There turns out to be an immediate complication to be sorted out before we can proceed.

---

[10] The model is probably most useful for analysing the impact of monetary policy.

So far, whenever expansionary monetary policy was considered in previous chapters, the question of *how* the money stock actually increased could safely be ignored. In the present context, however, this is no longer the case, since money supply changes have differing effects depending on whether they involve changes in the stock of bonds or foreign exchange. In other words, we have two alternative types of open-market operation. The possibility of money creation as a result of deficit spending is ruled out at this point, because money created in this way would have to be treated as asset accumulation, that is, an increase in (nominal) wealth. Although this case is not explicitly analysed in this chapter, the reader ought to be able to work out the implications with the help of the three cases which are covered here. We shall take each possibility separately.

8.2.1   Case 1: Money supply increase, domestic asset decrease

Suppose that the UK authorities buy up their own gilt-edged with newly-printed money, an *open market purchase* in the jargon of central banking. In this way, the government engineers an equal and opposite change in the stocks of money and bonds.

Consider the impact effect in domestic financial markets. Other things being equal, and assuming we start from a position of equilibrium where investors are content with their portfolio allocation, there has to be an immediate excess supply of money and excess demand for bonds.

The outcome must be that a large proportion of the new money goes to swell the demand for bonds, driving the interest rate down (and the price of bonds up). It can be shown that the net effect is to cause both money and bond market lines to shift to the left, as in Figure 8.2. The *MM* line moves further than the *BB* line. The reason is that the direct effect in the money market is greater than the impact on the bond market, because the latter is in part dissipated by a spillover effect on to the demand for foreign assets, which become more attractive when domestic interest rates fall. The increased demand for dollar-denominated securities explains the rise in the price of foreign exchange at the new equilibrium (point *B* in Figure 8.2).

We conclude that the money supply increase results in a short-run fall in the interest rate and a rise in the price of foreign currency. But notice: there is no reason to suppose that the depreciation will be anywhere near in proportion to the change in the money stock.

8.2.2   Case 2: Money supply increase, foreign currency asset decrease

Alternatively, the UK authorities could buy dollar-denominated securities from British holders. (In practice, of course, it might be difficult to distinguish the nationality of the sellers. For our purposes it is essential

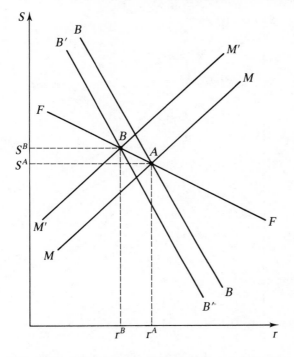

Figure 8.2   Open market purchase of domestic bonds.

they are UK residents, otherwise the whole framework of asset market equations, wealth constraint and so on breaks down.)

Obviously, the impact on the MM schedule would be the same as in the previous case. On the other hand, the decrease in F (the dollar value of the stock of foreign currency assets) creates an excess demand which can only be offset by an increase in the price, S, at which those securities translate into sterling. Hence, the equilibrium moves up the BB schedule, with a fall in r and rise in S, as before (Figure 8.3).

The difference between this case and the previous one is quantitative rather than qualitative. Given the assumptions made here, it can be shown that open-market operations in domestic securities have a greater effect on the UK interest rate and a smaller effect on the exchange rate than do purchases of dollar assets.

8.2.3   Wealth effects: an increase in the stock of foreign currency assets

Now consider a very different type of disturbance. Suppose there is an increase in the (dollar value of the) supply of foreign securities. This case differs in two important respects from those analysed so far.

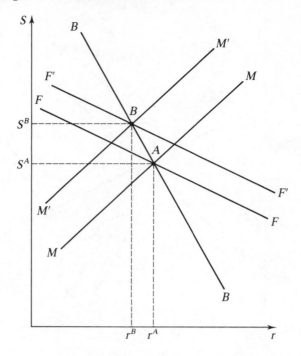

Figure 8.3 Open market purchase of foreign bonds.

Firstly, we are concerned here with a net increase in wealth, rather than the exchange of one type of asset for another, as before. In other words, what is involved is *private sector asset accumulation (that is, saving) rather than public sector policy changes.*

Secondly, not only is an increase in foreign currency assets equivalent to saving, it is also the *only* form saving can really take, given the structure of the model. Thus, saving is to be understood in the present context as a flow accumulation of dollar assets via a current account surplus.

In terms of the balance of payments (see Chapter 1), as long as the pound is floating freely, a UK capital account deficit (that is, the accumulation of claims on the USA) must be the counterpart of an equal surplus on the current account of Britain's balance of payments. Conversely, a UK current account deficit must be associated with the net import of capital, in other words dissaving in the form of a reduction in UK net dollar claims on the USA.

This is in fact the central feature of portfolio balance models. As in the Dornbusch model examined in Chapter 7, prices (and output) are assumed fixed in the short term, as a result of the relative sluggishness of goods and labour markets. Hence, short-run adjustment is confined to the

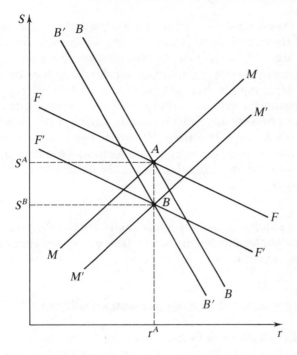

Figure 8.4 Increase in the stock of foreign bonds.

financial markets, which may well settle on an exchange rate-interest rate combination incompatible with equilibrium in the goods market (that is, a zero current account balance), given the initial price index and level of national income. The result will be a continuing flow of capital across the exchanges, adding to or subtracting from the stock of claims on the rest of the world, and causing a perpetual shift in the financial markets.

It is a shift of this nature which is illustrated in Figure 8.4.

Take the *FF* schedule first. It must shift downward, because the increased supply of dollar assets can only be absorbed if sterling appreciates (*S* falls), thereby neutralizing the rise in the value of *F* through a fall in the price of dollars and keeping the product, *SF*, constant.

Furthermore, since there is no possibility of a change in the interest rate (there has been no change in the quantities of either of the domestic currency assets), the other two schedules must shift vertically downwards. The mechanism whereby this occurs will be as follows.

As UK residents accumulate dollar securities, they attempt to exchange them for domestic assets, in the process generating an excess supply of dollars and driving down their price, *S*. The induced excess demand for money would, in other circumstances, require a rise in the UK interest rate, while the excess demand for gilt-edged would require the very opposite. In the event neither can occur, and the system remains in disequilibrium until the change in the exchange rate has been sufficient to reduce the sterling value of foreign currency assets to their previous value.

The size of the required appreciation should by now be clear. If the interest rate is to remain constant, wealth must be unchanged once the short-run adjustment process is complete. Since the quantities of domestic securities are constant, that must mean the sterling value of dollar securities ends up back where it started. We must therefore have an appreciation in proportion to the increase in the quantity of dollar claims which initiated the whole process. In other words, the outcome has to be:

$$\frac{\Delta S}{S} = \frac{\Delta F}{F}$$

This conclusion about the short run is critical, because it provides the key to the whole adjustment process, as we now see when we move on to describe the long run.

8.3   The long-run and current account equilibrium

The model of equilibrium in financial markets takes a number of variables as given, as we have seen. The background against which the financial markets adjust is a real economy, where the values of the two key long-run variables, the price level, P,[11] and the volume of foreign currency assets, F are determined. We shall continue to assume that expectations are unchanged.[12] The model of the real sector, of which there are are a number of possible variations, will only be given in broad outline here.

The specification of the real sector can be thought of as simply an extension of the goods market model analysed in Chapter 7. Again, excess demand for goods is mainly a function of the real exchange rate, Q, which is simply the ratio S/P, given that the foreign price index is fixed. Other factors which impinge directly or indirectly on aggregate demand or supply are taken as exogenous 'shift factors'. Excess demand (supply) in domestic goods[13] markets results in net imports (exports), in order to maintain short-run equilibrium.

---

[11] The foreign price level, taken as given and constant, can be set equal to 1.0 and ignored from now on.

[12] Note that as far as the dynamics of adjustment are concerned, the assumption that expectations are either fixed or at least backward-looking is vital. As can be seen from several of the references at the end of the chapter, imposing rational expectations makes the adjustment process far more complicated to analyse, and in any case is less compatible with the essentially Keynesian tone of the rest of the model.

Of course, the expectations mechanism makes no difference to our conclusions about long-run equilibrium.

[13] We assume that all goods are traded, though the model can accommodate a non-traded goods sector – at the cost of increased complexity, as always.

The volume of net exports is not quite the same thing as the current account surplus, however. Some portfolio balance theorists stress the importance to the current account of the balance of payments of investment income accruing to the domestic economy from UK holdings of dollar assets. A short-run increase (decrease) in the value of these holdings, if not reversed in the long run, will be associated with a rise (fall) in UK dollar interest income, r^*F, and a consequent decrease (increase) in the surplus required on other current account items consistent with a zero balance. It follows that, in the long run, the higher F is, the less competitive the UK needs to be for the current account to balance, and vice versa.

Any particular current account surplus (or deficit) will determine a rate of accumulation (or depletion) of the UK's dollar assets. It is this interaction between the real sector and the financial markets which ultimately returns the economy to long-run equilibrium.

As far as the price level is concerned, inflation is assumed to take place as a result of the gap between the current real money stock and the level consistent with equilibrium in the goods market, that is, with the long-run level of the real exchange rate.

Long-run equilibrium occurs when both the UK price level and the quantity of foreign securities in the domestic economy are such as to generate a zero balance on current (and therefore capital) account. When this position is reached there is no further disequilibrium in UK product markets, so that the price level is constant, and there is no net tendency to accumulate or decumulate wealth in the form of dollar securities.

8.3.1 A money supply increase in the long run

We shall consider the long-run impact of only one type of disturbance: a once and for all permanent increase (of say, 10%) in the UK money stock, accomplished by a central bank purchase of domestic bonds at time 0.

One might expect that the outcome would ultimately be the same as in the benchmark monetary model (Chapter 5): a 10% increase in the price level and in the price of foreign exchange, with all real variables back at their pre-disturbance equilibrium levels.

Now, in this context, the rise in the UK money stock, from whatever cause, raises the long-run equilibrium price level in proportion (that is, by 10%), so that the real money stock is unchanged. However, the pound depreciates by less than 10%, so that the *real* exchange rate, $Q = S/P$, ends up lower. In other words, the net effect is to reduce the competitiveness of UK production.

The reason is to be found in the adjustment process following the money supply increase.

Recall our conclusion in Section 8.2.1: the impact effect of an open market purchase would be to increase the price of foreign currency. Now, as in the Dornbusch model, with the price level still at its pre-disturbance level, the pound's depreciation must be real as well as nominal: the numerator of the ratio S/P increases at time 0, before the denominator can react.

Assuming that the UK was in long-run equilibrium prior to 0, the result has to be an incipient current account surplus, as the improved competitiveness shows up in increased net exports, and hence *in a build-up of dollar claims on the USA*. Now we have seen in Section 8.2.3 that a rising stock of foreign currency assets implies exchange rate appreciation. It follows that adjustment to the shock must be characterized by sterling appreciation, tending to reverse the impact of the real devaluation.

Moreover, as time passes, prices begin to rise in the domestic economy, further eroding the competitive advantage provided by the devaluation. At some point, say at time t, the UK price index has risen by 10%, so that the real exchange rate is back where it started, and the relative competitiveness of UK and US production is restored. At this point net exports from the UK are zero and the volume of dollar assets is constant.

Even though the stock of dollar claims on the USA has stopped growing at time t, it is still positive and therefore still generating a flow of investment income to the UK private sector. The fact that the UK's real exchange rate is back where it started no longer implies a zero current account balance. Instead, with zero net exports from the UK, it implies a current account surplus equal to the investment income on the net asset accumulation which took place over the period between 0 and t.

We conclude that the exchange rate needs to continue appreciating so as to carry the real exchange rate to a level higher than prior to the disturbance. The system will only be back in full long-run equilibrium when (at some time, T) the real appreciation relative to time 0 is sufficient to generate an excess of UK imports over exports equal to the value of the income accruing on the dollar assets accumulated over the period from 0 to t.

In other words, by the time the economy is back in long-run equilibrium at time T, its competitive position will have been eroded (compared to before the monetary shock), and it will be paying for net imports with capital service.

Furthermore, the *nominal* exchange rate will have undergone a sudden depreciation, at time 0, followed by a protracted appreciation until long-run equilibrium is restored at T. The appreciation will have taken the exchange rate part of the way back in the direction of its original, pre-disturbance value, though it will of course still ultimately be devalued. Thus, as in the Dornbusch model, *the slow adjustment of goods markets leads to the conclusion that the nominal exchange rate will overshoot its long-run equilibrium value in the immediate aftermath of a disturbance.*[14]

---

[14] The conclusions about the adjustment process are sensitive to the expectations mechanism assumed. However, overshooting seems likely in most cases.

8.4 The evidence on portfolio balance models

The portfolio balance model generates a number of qualitative predictions which one might expect to see reflected in the data. Apart from overshooting and the appearance of PPP only as a long-run phenomenon, if at all (both of which were discussed in the last chapter) perhaps the most obvious implication concerns the role of the balance of payments.

If the portfolio balance model is correct, current account surpluses will be associated with appreciating and deficits with depreciating currencies. Notice that this is not a genuine relationship of cause and effect. The current account imbalance is itself a consequence of a disturbance, the adjustment process to which requires a long-run change in the volume of foreign currency assets in the economy.

Figures 8.5 to 8.10 show effective exchange rates and current account balances for six industrialized countries: UK, USA, West Germany, Japan, France and Switzerland. If there is any underlying relationship between the two variables, it is far from obvious. The USA is perhaps the extreme case, with the value of the dollar appreciating more or less

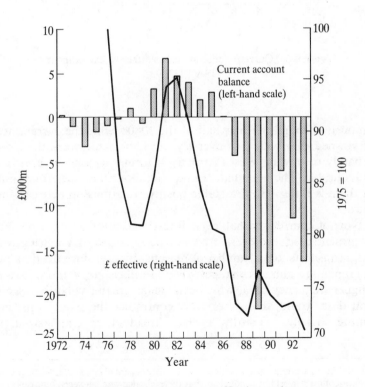

Figure 8.5 Current account versus effective exchange rate: UK 1972–93.

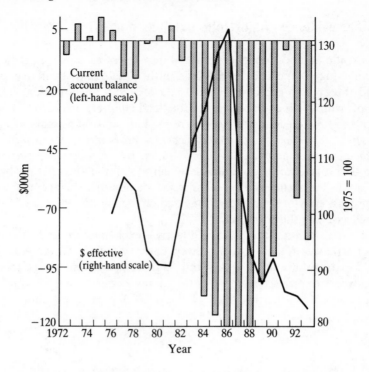

Figure 8.6   Current account versus effective exchange rate:
USA 1972–93.

continuously through the first half of the 1980s while the current account deficit yawned ever wider. Conversely, over the same years the Deutsche Mark barely rose while West Germany's current account became increasingly favourable. The best that can be said about the other four countries is that there is little sign of a stable positive relationship between the two variables.

Now of course a casual 'eyeball test' like this can never be decisive. In the present case, however, it cannot be regarded as auguring well for more rigorous tests, for a number of reasons. Firstly, since the data plotted in the graphs are annual averages, they are likely to be more favourable than higher frequency data, which exhibit far greater volatility. Secondly, bilateral data would almost certainly contradict the model's predictions even more sharply.[15] Thirdly, as has already been emphasized, if the

---

[15] Bilateral current account data is difficult to obtain and probably unreliable. In any case, in the real (*n*-country) world, it is not clear that the exchange rate between countries A and B ought even in theory to be unaffected by the current account balance between countries A and C – particularly in a world of increasingly well-defined currency blocs.

Figure 8.7 Current account versus effective exchange rate:
West Germany 1972–93.

portfolio balance model is to be believed, the link between current account
and exchange rate is not causal: the former is simply a by-product of
changes in the latter. The natural interpretation is, then, that *the relationship ought to be more or less contemporaneous.* It follows that the apparently weak link cannot be explained away by delays in the chain from
cause to effect.

As far as rigorous tests of the portfolio balance model are concerned, the published results are of two kinds. Some writers test the model
directly, while others use portfolio balance equations in an attempt to
answer the question of whether or not there is a risk premium, and if so,
what determines it. The latter will be considered in Chapter 13.

The first problem that confronts researchers in this field is finding
data. It is virtually impossible to find reliable data on holdings of assets
denominated in the different currencies – at least at a frequency high
enough to be of any use for research purposes. In some cases, writers have
taken an initial estimate, and added each period's current account surplus
adjusted for central bank purchases so as to arrive at an approximate
series for domestic holdings of foreign assets. This method has a number

Figure 8.8   Current account versus effective exchange rate:
Japan 1972–93.

of disadvantages: it ignores capital gains or losses, it effectively assumes
all domestic assets are domestically owned, and it also builds into the
estimates the widely-acknowledged inaccuracy of current account
statistics.

The second problem is more fundamental. As has already been made
clear, the portfolio balance approach relies on an analysis of the determination of the risk premium. As we shall see, this analysis implies stable asset
demand functions only under fairly restrictive conditions, which are probably inconsistent, even in principle, with the context to which they are
being applied here.[16] Nonetheless, most researchers have attempted to fit
equations that simply have the exchange rate on the left-hand side and the
financial variables on the right.[17]

In addition, remember that in order to explain a *bilateral* exchange
rate in what is in practice a *multilateral* world, we need to make use of six

---

[16] For those familiar with time-series jargon, we require stationarity of expected returns, a
condition which is difficult to reconcile with a world of fluctuating interest rates.

[17] Note that the rates of return are usually excluded, on the grounds that they can be
substituted out, since they in turn depend on the asset stocks.

Figure 8.9   Current account versus effective exchange rate:
France 1972–92.

financial stock variables, even if we maintain the fiction that the UK's bonds are not held in the USA, and vice versa.

In view of these problems, it is perhaps not surprising that research results have been largely disappointing, and certainly do not represent a significant improvement over simpler models. In the first place, it has proved largely impossible to fit equations in which all six financial stock variables (UK and US money stocks, UK and US holdings of domestic bonds, UK and US holdings of foreign currency bonds) make a significant contribution. The problem often necessitates eliminating more or less arbitrarily one or two of the variables at the cost of potentially distorting the estimates of the remaining variables. Even then, the typical shortcomings of fitted exchange rate equations were still present: poor fit, evidence of persistent autocorrelation (possibly indicating omitted variables), poor forecasting ability, and so forth.

Furthermore, this failure applies even to tests on data from the 1970s, a period when simpler exchange rate equations appeared to fit reasonably well.

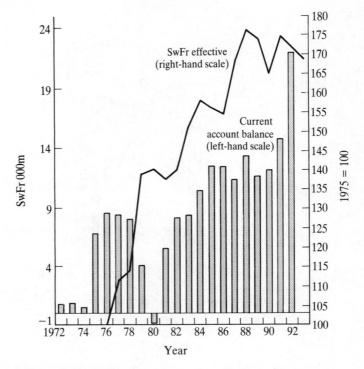

Figure 8.10 Current account versus effective exchange rate:
Switzerland 1972–92.

8.5 Conclusions

To travel hopefully, it is said, is better than to arrive. In this chapter, we have presented a model with a relatively sophisticated financial sector. Its analytic properties provide insights that are both interesting and plausible, not least with regard to the linkage between the balance of payments and the exchange rate.

Unfortunately, if the ultimate test of a theory's acceptability is its ability to explain the facts, the portfolio balance model fails on at least two counts. Firstly, because of lack of data, it is well-nigh impossible to test in its full-blown form. Secondly, in truncated form, it fails to fit the data – even for the early part of the floating rate era. It seems that successful implementation of the model must await the collection of more accurate data, and probably also a tighter specification of the demand functions.

Nonetheless, the portfolio balance model has been influential in shaping thinking about asset markets, not least because it is the most general model of exchange rates – by comparison, most other models can be regarded as special cases.

■ Summary

- Portfolio balance models concentrate not simply on the demand for money, but on the demand for a menu of assets.

- The demand for each type of asset is seen in the context of a general portfolio allocation problem and, since it is the proportion of total wealth to be held in a particular form which is to be decided, the determining variables are rates of return on the whole spectrum of available assets. So the demand for any asset as a proportion of wealth will tend to rise when its own return rises, and fall when the return on competing assets increases.

- We assume domestic residents hold only three types of asset: domestically issued money and bonds, and foreign currency bonds issued by a foreign government or central bank. As in the Dornbusch model, (goods) prices are taken as fixed in the short run.

- Under these conditions and assuming financial markets clear at all times, short-run equilibrium will be obtained when the exchange rate and (domestic) interest rate are at a level such that demand is equal to supply for any two of the three assets.

- Open market purchases of either domestic or foreign bonds will cause depreciation and a fall in the interest rate in the short run, the repercussion on the exchange rate being greater and on the interest rate smaller, in the case of operations in the market for foreign securities.

- Increases in the stock of foreign bonds can only come about as a result of current account surpluses. The short-run impact on financial markets is an appreciation, keeping the domestic currency value of foreign bonds constant.

- Long-run equilibrium is characterized by a zero balance on current account, as well as static prices, interest rates and exchange rate.

- The production sector adjusts to a disturbance as a result of changes in the real exchange rate. As the price level moves during the adjustment phase, it interacts with the (nominal) exchange rate to change the balance of aggregate demand and supply, hence generating a current account surplus or deficit which persists until the stock of foreign currency assets has reached a level consistent with long-run equilibrium.

- In practice, the portfolio balance model is difficult to apply and the approximations tested have not been very successful in explaining the facts.

READING GUIDE

The antecedent of the portfolio balance model is to be found in the general equilibrium monetary theory of Tobin (1969), which itself harks back to Metzler (1951).

The most prominent exponent of the portfolio balance approach is Branson – see particularly Branson (1983), Branson and Halttunen (1979) and Branson, Halttunen and Masson (1979). Frankel (1983) is also worth reading for a taste of the problems involved in implementing this approach.

Branson and Henderson (1985) is a survey which will be of help to those readers who can cope with the analysis of wealth dynamics – the first half deals with the subject of this chapter, the second half covers the material of Chapter 13.

9

Currency Substitution

■ Introduction

In Chapter 8, we allowed for the possibility that the demand for nominal assets may not be perfectly elastic with respect to expected depreciation, as the result of a non-zero risk premium. At the same time, we persisted with the assumption first introduced in Chapter 7 that financial markets adjust more rapidly than goods markets.

In this chapter, both of these assumptions will be maintained while we investigate the implications of what is known as *currency substitution*.

Now it should be said at the outset that the name is something of a misnomer, because in one respect what is involved hardly amounts to currency: we are concerned here exclusively with money as a store of value. In other words, we ignore the means of payment function of money and treat it instead as simply an asset which happens to carry a fixed, zero rate of interest.[1]

---

[1] In fact, none of the conclusions in this chapter would be changed if we allowed for a non-zero rate of interest on money balances, as long as the rate was constant.

Notice that this is one of the weaknesses of the model. If (domestic or foreign) money is not used for transactions purposes, there is no reason to hold it – it is dominated by riskless (domestic or foreign) bonds, which pay an explicit rate of interest. So the true alternative to sterling nominal assets is dollar nominal interest-bearing securities.

Nonetheless, even defined in this restricted sense, the question of how currency substitution might affect exchange rates is potentially of considerable interest, not least because of its practical relevance. Among the factors which seem likely to make currency substitution more and more prevalent in the next few years are: widespread deregulation of financial markets and further reduction of exchange controls in a number of countries, the continuing trend to international financial and commercial integration, and increasing sophistication in attitudes to money management. Nowhere is the trend likely to be more pronounced than in the European Common Market, where currency substitution seems likely to proceed rapidly, perhaps further emasculating domestic monetary policy and possibly adding to pressure for a common currency. The motivation for considering the issues covered in this chapter is therefore not so much a matter of explaining the past as of predicting what the future might hold.

The starting point for the analysis is to consider the situation of a (reasonably sophisticated) inhabitant of a country where holding foreign as well as domestic currency is both feasible and legal.[2] What will determine the proportions of the two currencies in the agent's portfolio of non-interest bearing assets?

The answer depends in general on what other assets are available. Here, and in most of the literature, we assume there are only two assets involved in the choice: domestic and foreign money (pounds and dollars). It follows that the proportions in which the two currencies are held will depend exclusively on the rate of currency depreciation. The risk-averse wealth owner will respond to a higher rate of depreciation by raising the proportion of foreign money in his portfolio.[3]

It can be seen that what is involved is only a small modification to the portfolio balance model. Instead of domestic and foreign bonds as alternatives to money, the menu of assets is restricted here to the two currencies.

Now consider how the (dollar value of the) stock of foreign currency can change. If we continue to suppose the home currency is *not* held by agents outside the domestic economy, as in the last chapter, and

---

[2] Conditions which narrow the field down considerably, more or less to the industrialized world in fact. Moreover, prior to 1979 neither the UK nor most of the European countries would have been included, at least as far as the household sector is concerned. Currency substitution was believed to be rife in the UK corporate sector during the fixed exchange rate era – disguised as what were known at the time as 'leads' and 'lags', that is, delayed payments for exports and pre-payments for imports whenever sterling devaluation seemed imminent.

Currency substitution is probably most prevalent in hyperinflating countries where it is illegal and involves black market trading, over-invoicing of imports and under-invoicing of exports and possibly even non-economic crime, like drug trading.

[3] Notice, we have to insist on risk aversion. Otherwise, all exchange rates would have to remain fixed. At the slightest sign of possible weakness, a currency's value would collapse as investors attempted to dump their entire holdings.

given that neither borrowing nor lending is allowed,[4] it follows there is only one way the stock of foreign exchange can increase, and that is *via a current account surplus*. Once more we have the same broad structure as in the portfolio balance model, with instantaneous equilibrium in the financial sector, and a flow excess demand or supply in the real sector changing the stock of foreign currency during the adjustment phase.

At the same time, we introduce a richer specification of the real sector, with two products: a traded good whose price is determined in world markets and a non-traded good whose price depends only on conditions in the local economy.[5] The result is that changes in the real exchange rate affect the value of wealth both through a real balance effect and over the longer term, through the impact of a change in the terms of trade on the current account of the balance of payments.

As the complete model is relatively complicated to analyse, even diagrammatically, the analysis in this chapter is in outline form only. More detailed analysis is available in a number of the references given in the Reading Guide at the end of the chapter.

The model generates a number of conclusions about the short and long-run impact of changes in macroeconomic policy, only one of which is covered here. It is shown that the effect of accelerated monetary growth is to cause instantaneous exchange rate overshooting, with a consequent temporary boost to the competitiveness of the domestic economy, as in the Dornbusch model of Chapter 7.

The chapter starts with a description of the model, which is then used to examine the impact of a change in the rate of monetary growth. Section 9.2 gives a brief overview of the evidence on currency substitution.

9.1 The model

We start by listing the assumptions underlying the model, before going on to describe the working of the production and financial sectors. Finally, we look at the properties of the model in long-run and short-run equilibrium with the help of Figures 9.1 and 9.2.

9.1.1 Assumptions

(1) Two goods are produced in the domestic economy: a tradeable and a non-tradeable.

---

[4] That is, as we have said, there are no bonds in existence – or at least if there are, the stock is constant.

[5] The distinction between traded and non-traded goods (or tradeables and non-tradeables) was discussed in Chapter 2, Section 2.2.

(2) The price of the non-tradeable, P_N, is determined in the domestic economy by the condition that *the market for non-traded goods clears at all times.*

(3) The (dollar) price of the tradeable is determined exogenously in the international economy. For simplicity, assume it is fixed at 1.0.[6] It follows that the sterling price of tradeables is simply S, the price of a dollar.

(4) Portfolio choice is restricted to only two assets: non-interest bearing currency issued either by the domestic monetary authority ('pounds') or by a foreign government ('dollars').

(5) The value of financial assets held ('wealth' for short) is measured with respect to the *traded* good.[7] So, we have:

$$W = \frac{M}{S} + F \tag{9.1}$$
$$= m + F$$

where, for convenience:[8]

$$m \equiv M/S$$

(6) Economic agents enjoy the benefit of perfect foresight which means that their expected rate of exchange rate depreciation is equal to the actually occurring rate.[9]

9.1.2 The production sector

What will determine the volume of production in the two sectors of the domestic economy?

Under competitive conditions, productive resources will be attracted into a sector the higher the relative price of its output, other things being

---

[6] It is easy to reconstruct the model putting the foreign price level back in, if we want to analyse the effect of international inflation on the domestic economy.

[7] It appears the same results would apply if we defined wealth in terms of the non-traded good, as do Calvo and Rodriguez (see the Reading Guide), or even in terms of a price index.
Note that in either case we are concerned with real wealth, rather than nominal wealth as in the portfolio balance model.

[8] And at the expense of consistency with the convention used in earlier chapters that lower-case letters represent logarithms. The variables in this chapter are all in natural numbers.

[9] The assumption of perfect foresight is the analogue under conditions of certainty of rational expectations (see Chapter 11). In the present context, it serves the purpose of allowing us to reach definite conclusions about how the system behaves out of equilibrium. Our conclusions would not be very different if we allowed expectations to be determined by the same mechanism as in Chapter 7.

equal.[10] In the present case, with only two sectors, the relative price in question is obviously the ratio of the price of traded goods, S, to the price of non-traded goods, which we shall call P_N. In fact, the ratio S/P_N is almost the same thing as the real exchange rate, so we shall ignore the slight difference and denote it by Q, as we did when it was first introduced in Chapter 2.

It follows therefore that when the real exchange rate, Q, is high the supply of traded goods will be *greater* and the supply of non-traded goods *lower*.

Now consider the demand by consumers in the domestic economy. The relative price will have the opposite effect on demand: when the price of traded goods is relatively high, demand will be relatively low, while consumption of non-traded goods will be comparatively strong, and vice versa.

Putting the two halves of the story together, when the real exchange rate is high, the supply of traded goods will be high and the demand low, so the *excess supply* (the difference between supply and demand) will be large. The opposite will be true of non-traded goods.

There is only one point to be added to this characterization of the way that the economy works. While we can sweep away all other influences in the catch-all expression 'other things being equal', we have to recognize explicitly the role played by wealth. Plainly, the greater is wealth, the higher we would expect would be the demand for *both* products.

We can summarize the discussion so far in two equations, one for each sector. As far as non-traded goods are concerned, remembering that this market is assumed to be in equilibrium at all times, we have:

$$X_N^S = H(Q, W) = 0 \qquad H_1 < 0, H_2 < 0 \tag{9.2}$$

where X^S means the excess supply, and the subscript, N, refers to the non-traded goods sector. The two inequalities on the right simply capture our convictions about the effect of the relative price of traded goods and wealth respectively on excess supply, H.

This relationship is plotted as the upward-sloping line labelled NT on the left-hand side of Figure 9.1, where, note, the vertical axis measures wealth and the horizontal plots the real exchange rate, Q. The slope of the line is easily explained in the light of what has already been said. At high levels of wealth, the demand for non-traded goods is relatively buoyant.

---

[10] This proposition is familiar from microeconomics: given production costs, the higher the price (and therefore marginal revenue), the greater the profit-maximizing output of the competitive firm and industry.

For those unfamiliar with microeconomics, it amounts simply to stating that the higher relative prices are in an industry, the higher the real wage it will offer (thereby attracting labour from industries with low relative prices and hence low real wages), and the greater the profitability it will offer to investment (to the detriment of investment in low-price industries).

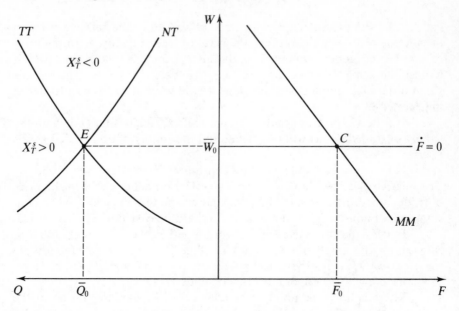

Figure 9.1   Long-run equilibrium in the currency substitution model.

Hence, equilibrium requires a large supply and therefore a high relative price, or low real exchange rate. Conversely, when wealth is low, so is consumption. Therefore, excess supply can only be prevented by having a high relative price in the other sector, that is, a high value of Q.

> Notice that, since the market for non-traded goods is assumed to clear at all times, the economy must always be somewhere on the NT line.

As far as traded goods are concerned, we assume equilibrium is only obtained in the long run. In the short run, an excess supply amounts to a current account surplus whose counterpart must be the accumulation of foreign currency, written $\dot{F}$.[11] So, if we use the subscript 'T' for traded goods, we have:

$$X_T^S = J(Q, W) = \dot{F} \qquad J_1 > 0,\ J_2 < 0 \qquad \textbf{(9.3)}$$

Again, we can plot all the combinations consistent with market equilibrium. They will lie along a line like the one labelled TT in Figure 9.1. As before, high levels of wealth are associated with strong consumption, other things being equal, and must therefore be offset by a high relative price, Q, to damp down demand and stimulate supply, and vice versa at low levels of wealth.

---

[11] The notation $\dot{F}$ means dF/dt: the change in X over a very small interval of time.

Since the traded goods market is not always in equilibrium, the economy is not always to be found on the *TT* line. Points on that line are associated with a zero balance on current account and therefore with static foreign currency balances – conditions which are only satisfied in long-run equilibrium.

What will happen when the economy is *not* on the *TT* line? Suppose for argument's sake that the economy were at a point above and to the right of the line. This would imply a level of wealth too great to be consistent with equilibrium, given the real exchange rate at the time. Clearly, this in turn must mean demand for traded goods in excess of supply, and hence a current account deficit, with consequently declining balances of foreign currency. Conversely, below and to the left of the *TT* line, the current account is in surplus, with rising stocks of foreign money.

Where the two curves cross, at *E*, the combination of the value of wealth and the level of the real exchange rate, $(\overline{Q}_0, \overline{W}_0)$ is the unique pair compatible with equilibrium in *both* product markets.

On the right-hand side of Figure 9.1, the horizontal line marked $\dot{F} = 0$ is at a height $\overline{W}_0$. It divides the space into two halves. Above the line, wealth is greater than its equilibrium level: hence there is a current account deficit and a consequent outflow of foreign exchange. Below it, the country is adding to its stock of foreign currency. Notice the line is flat because the volume of foreign currency balances at any point in time has no direct bearing on equilibrium in the market for traded goods.

9.1.3 The money markets

The specification of the relative demand for money – the currency substitution function – is the crux of the model. It can be expressed as follows: the ratio of real domestic balances to foreign currency, m/F, depends on the rate of change of the nominal exchange rate, $\dot{s}$:

$$m/F = L(\dot{s}) \qquad L' < 0 \tag{9.4}$$

Note the critical importance of our assumption that economic agents' expectations about the future rate of depreciation can be identified with the actual rate, $\dot{s}$. In reality, the future is never known with certainty. However, this simplification allows us to use the actual rate in place of its expected value.

It will help in what is to come if we transform the relative demand for money relationship into its inverse. If the ratio m/F is a function, L, of $\dot{s}$, the reverse must equally be true: $\dot{s}$ must depend on m/F. So we can write:

$$\dot{s} = l(m/F) \qquad l' < 0 \tag{9.5}$$

where the function on the right-hand side is simply the inverse of the one in Equation 9.4. Notice the inequality at the end: market clearing requires a lower ratio of domestic money to foreign currency when the rate of depreciation rises. It follows that higher rates of depreciation are associated with lower values of m/F, and vice versa.

Another helpful change is to use the definition of wealth in Equation 9.1 to eliminate m on the right-hand side of Equation 9.5, giving:

$$\dot{s} = l\left(\frac{W - F}{F}\right) \tag{9.6}$$

$$= l\left(\frac{W}{F} - 1\right)$$

Now consider the conditions necessary for wealth to be static. Plainly, since the change in wealth will be the sum of the change in its two components, it will only be zero if we have:

$$\dot{F} = -\dot{m} \tag{9.7}$$

that is, if the change in the volume of foreign and domestic currency balances offset one another. To see what this implies, remember that the variable m is the *nominal* quantity of domestic currency, M, deflated by the price of traded goods (alias the exchange rate), S.

Now the change in any ratio can always be written in terms of the difference between the growth rates of the numerator and of the denominator (see Box 9.1). In other words, the increase in real domestic currency balances is given by:

$$\dot{m} \equiv \frac{d}{dt}\left[\frac{M}{S}\right] = \frac{M}{S}(\mu - \dot{s}) \tag{9.8}$$

This simply says the real value of the domestic money supply increases by a multiple equal to the difference between the growth rate of the nominal money stock, μ, and the rate of currency depreciation, $\dot{s}$.

It remains only to substitute Equation 9.6 in Equation 9.8 to eliminate $\dot{s}$, and then use the resulting expression for $\dot{m}$ in Equation 9.7 to end up with:

$$\dot{F} = \frac{M}{S}\left[l\left(\frac{W}{F} - 1\right) - \mu\right] \tag{9.9}$$

---

[12] The reason for the ambiguity about the slope of the MM line is as follows:

As we move down the graph in the direction of decreasing W, the current account deficit is decreasing or the surplus is increasing, so that the left-hand side of the equation becomes greater.

The ratio of wealth to foreign currency, W/F, has two kinds of effect on the right-hand side of Equation 9.9. First, since M/S outside the bracket is equivalent to $(W - F)$, a decrease in W and increase in F diminishes the right-hand side. This on its own would suggest we need an upward-sloping line, associating increases in W with increases in F. On the other hand, the contents of the bracket on the right-hand side will only increase if $l(W/F)$ rises (that is, if the ratio W/F falls) which suggests a downward-sloping line.

which is the desired relationship between $\dot{F}$, W and F consistent with a constant level of wealth.

For illustrative purposes, this relationship has been plotted as the downward-sloping line MM on the right-hand side of Figure 9.1, though it could possibly be upward sloping.[12] It crosses the horizontal line at the point C, where long-run equilibrium is obtained with static wealth, that is, a balanced current account and a foreign currency money stock of $\overline{F}_0$.

9.1.4 A change in monetary policy

In this context, the effect of a change in the domestically-printed money stock, M, is as in the benchmark monetary model: as long as it has no effect on expectations, a once and for all increase in M causes a rise of the same proportion in the price of both goods, leaving the real money stock, wealth and foreign currency balances unchanged.

BOX 9.1   The meaning of log differentiation.

For those readers uncomfortable with log differentiation, consider as an example the change in a country's per capita income. Suppose it starts the year at £10,000 per annum. If national income grows by 10% during the year, while the population rises by 3%, the country's per capita income will change during the year by:

$$£10,000 \times (10\% - 3\%) = £700$$

that is, the change in the ratio of income to population = the ratio itself times the difference between the growth rate of income and the growth rate of population.

For those able to take the fast track:

$$log\,(M/S) = log\,M - log\,S$$

so that:

$$d\,log\,(M/S) = \frac{d\,(M/S)}{M/S} = d\,log\,M - d\,log\,S = \frac{dM}{M} - \frac{dS}{S}$$

which gives Equation 9.8 once we multiply both sides by M/S, and substitute:

$$m \equiv M/S \qquad \frac{dM}{M} \equiv \mu \qquad \frac{dS}{S} \equiv \dot{s}$$

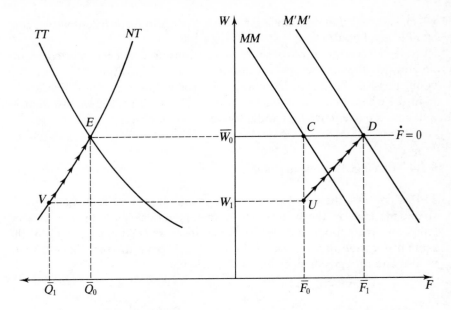

Figure 9.2 Monetary acceleration in the currency substitution model.

The question which this model is meant to answer is rather the effect of a *rise in the rate of monetary growth*, μ. It is easy to see that starting from a position of long-run equilibrium at C, the change in monetary policy will have the effect of pushing the MM curve out to the right.[13] Since μ does not occur in either Equations 9.2 or 9.3, the change has no direct effect on either of the product markets, so that the TT and NT schedules remain where they were.

The new long-run equilibrium position is at D in Figure 9.2. At this point, wealth is constant and back at its pre-disturbance level, $\overline{W}_0$. Similarly, the real exchange rate is back where it started – if that combination of relative price and wealth cleared the product markets *before* the change, it ought to do so *after* it as well. The only change, once the dust has settled, is that the proportion of wealth accounted for by foreign currency increases at the expense of domestic money. The reason is obvious. In the steady state, the rate of monetary expansion equals the rate of currency depreciation. Hence, the monetary acceleration leads in long-run equilibrium to a higher opportunity cost of holding domestic money, and therefore to a rise in the share of foreign relative to domestic currency in the total asset portfolio.

---

[13] Starting at C with the current acount balance at zero (hence the right-hand side of Equation 9.7 is zero) a higher value of μ means the value of the function $l(W/F)$ needs to increase, which requires a lower value of W/F – therefore an increase in F at the current level of $W = \overline{W}_0$.

Figure 9.2 also illustrates the mechanism by which the increase in foreign currency holdings (from $\overline{F}_0$ to $\overline{F}_1$) takes place. The moment the acceleration is announced, the opportunity cost of holding domestic money is perceived to rise, with a consequent fall in the desired proportion m/F. However, the quantity of foreign currency balances cannot be changed in an instant. For the moment it must be regarded as fixed. It follows that the only immediate way the desired reduction in the ratio m/F can be achieved is via a fall in the numerator, $m = M/S$. Since the nominal stock is momentarily constant, S has to rise: the exchange rate must depreciate.

The outcome is not only a fall in the real value of domestic money but a fall in wealth, too, from $\overline{W}_0$ to a temporarily lower level, W_1 at the point U. With lower wealth, consumption falls. The fall in demand for non-traded goods must be offset by a lower relative price for the industry's output, so as to reduce the supply (remember that this sector clears at all times). Hence the higher real exchange rate, Q_1, at the point V on the left-hand side of the diagram.

The instantaneous rise in the real exchange rate, $Q = S/P_N$, implies the rise in the numerator, S, is greater than the rise in the denominator, P_N. This means that, judged by a crude price index made up of some type of weighted average of S and P_N, the nominal exchange rate changes by *more* than the price level – in that sense, it *overshoots*.

The transition to the new long-run equilibrium (along a path like the one marked with arrows in the diagram) is characterized by a falling real exchange rate, so that the overshooting pattern is reversed, with the rate of depreciation less than the rate of inflation in the non-traded goods sector. Notice that, at V, the combination of a relatively high price of traded goods, Q_1, with low wealth, W_1, leads to a current account surplus. It follows that in the aftermath of the monetary acceleration and consequent depreciation, the domestic economy gains foreign exchange, and consequently the level of wealth begins to recover from its initial fall.

It is now clear what we should expect to see in an economy passing through this adjustment phase (the phase in which economies are presumably to be found most of the time). In the wake of monetary acceleration, the economy will be characterized by:

(1) Currency depreciation at a slower rate than domestic inflation, hence an appreciating real exchange rate.

(2) A current account surplus, on a decreasing scale as adjustment proceeds.

(3) A consequent rise in foreign currency balances and wealth.

Notice, we observe the combination of *nominal* depreciation (albeit at a diminishing rate) with a current account surplus, in contrast with the predictions of the portfolio balance model. The basic reason is the currency substitution process itself: higher domestic inflation implies a long-run shift in desired asset proportions in favour of foreign currency, which can only be satisfied by a short-run payments surplus.

The central mechanism of the currency substitution model can be viewed as a hedging process. Given the constant, or at least exogenous, dollar price of traded goods, it follows that foreign currency represents a direct and riskless claim on a fixed consumption basket. In fact, one can go further and identify foreign currency with an (undated) forward purchase of traded goods. From this standpoint, economic agents respond to a rise in the rate of monetary expansion by increasing the inflation-hedge proportion of their portfolios, in the process 'locking in' the price of their future imports. Of course, since the quantity of foreign currency in the country is fixed at the moment of the change, they cannot *in aggregate* achieve any increase in their dollar holdings. The only possible outcome is a rise in the price of foreign currency.[14]

9.2   Evidence on currency substitution

There are really two questions one would like to see answered with regard to currency substitution: is it significant in practice and, if so, is its effect captured by theoretical models like the one analysed in this chapter?

There is one very serious problem that arises in trying to get to grips with the first question, and it is obvious as soon as we consider how a researcher might go about testing the hypothesis of currency substitution. In reality, all such tests are bound to involve fitting some form of open economy demand for money, with interest rates measuring the opportunity cost of holding money – more or less as in the monetary or portfolio balance models. So, in that sense, tests of these models were, indirectly, tests of currency substitution too.

As such, we encounter all the problems already mentioned with this approach, particularly as regards the correct way to deal with expectations. In addition, however, we face the specific difficulty that it is never clear whether interest elasticities estimated in this fashion measure the degree of substitutability between domestic and foreign money, or between money and bonds, or even between one or other currency and goods.

Subject to these very serious reservations, it has to be said that surprisingly little evidence to support direct currency substitution has been reported so far, even for economies which are obviously linked very closely

---

[14] Readers familiar with the Cagan (closed economy) hyperinflation model and its derivatives may notice a similarity. In that model, monetary expansion leads people to substitute in favour of the inflation hedge: either consumer goods, in the original Cagan model, or capital goods, in the Mundell–Tobin–Johnson money-in-growth literature. In either case, the outcome is a long-run fall in holdings of real money balances relative to the inflation hedge, as a result of the more rapid fall in the value of money.

(for example Canada and the USA).[15] By and large, such evidence as has been produced seems to suggest the cross elasticities are small relative to the coefficients on the 'own rates', and very often insignificantly different from zero.

As far as the second of the two questions listed at the beginning of this section is concerned, no answer has yet been attempted. In part, this reflects the nature of the currency substitution model. The literature should be viewed more as an investigation into the implications of a particular mechanism than as an attempt to actually build a complete model of exchange rate determination. As such, assumptions like the absence of a bond market are made more for simplicity than realism – and, of course, reintroducing them takes us straight back to the portfolio balance model. Similarly, the specification of the product market in terms of traded and non-traded goods has theoretical attractions as well as, more debatably, some measure of plausibility. Unfortunately, however, it is extremely difficult to apply operationally.

In a sense, then, answers to the empirical questions can really be found, by default, in tests of other more or less general models of the exchange rate, since they amount to asking: can currency substitution be ignored? So far, the answer seems to be: yes, at least for the industrialized countries.

9.3 Conclusions

In this chapter we have examined a model with, at its core, a demand for money mechanism which is *potentially* very important in any truly open economy. Furthermore, it is a mechanism which may well become more important if there is a continuation of current trends towards increased convertibility, deregulation, a greater degree of economic integration and so forth.

However, the extent to which currency substitution actually affects exchange rates remains an empirical question.

Empirical issues apart, however, there are a number of theoretical drawbacks to the currency substitution analysis. Perhaps the most obvious is the absence of a transactions role for money. In one sense, this makes little difference. Simply introducing a means of payment function for domestic money explicitly seems unlikely to change the conclusions to any great extent.[16]

---

[15] Furthermore, much of the published work looks increasingly out of date, because it relates either to the fixed exchange rate era or to the early or mid 1970s.

[16] In fact, if foreign currency is not used as a means of payment domestically, it can never find a place in portfolios held by UK residents, since they would always prefer interest-bearing dollar assets.

Nonetheless, it would be of interest to know what happens if this function is in part usurped by foreign currency, as is likely to happen precisely in those circumstances where currency substitution becomes most prevalent, for example under hyperinflationary conditions or where economies are exceptionally open. This development has two possible aspects: first, a reduction in the demand for domestic money at a given level of economic activity, and second, the spread of foreign currency accounting.[17]

A related issue is the exclusion of foreign holdings of domestic currency. This restriction is not introduced merely for simplicity. It serves among other things to rule out the possibility of UK and US wealth owners exchanging pounds for dollars *directly*, independently of any immediate transactions requirements. If this were permitted – and it seems a plausible enough scenario for a country the size of the UK – it would sever the link between the stock of foreign currency and the current account, with consequences for the model that are far from obvious, though almost certainly critical.

■ **Summary**

- If economic agents in an open economy are free to hold foreign as well as domestic money, they will hold a mix of currencies – at the margin, substituting one that seems likely to depreciate rapidly for one which looks set to appreciate (the currency substitution mechanism).

- In an economy with a non-traded goods sector which clears at all times, long-run equilibrium obtains when the value of wealth and the real exchange rate are such as to clear the traded goods sector, thereby bringing the current account into balance and keeping the stock of foreign assets constant. Short-run equilibrium requires only that wealth and the real exchange rate clear the non-traded goods and monetary sectors, with a current account surplus or deficit changing the foreign money stock as the economy adjusts.

- Expansionary monetary policy in this context causes the real exchange rate to depreciate, raising domestic competitiveness and causing a short-run surplus in the current account. Over the adjustment phase, however, the stock of foreign currency rises, increasing wealth and replacing domestic money in portfolios.

---

[17] Thus, prices were often quoted in foreign currency in the high inflation economies of the 1980s (for example, Israel, Argentina) especially for 'big ticket' items and, at the time of writing, both Deutsche Marks and US dollars are widely used throughout the former Soviet bloc. The same is true of prices in Canada due to the proximity of the USA.

We conclude that rapid monetary growth leads to accumulation of foreign currency.

● The model is very difficult to test for a number of reasons – theoretical, technical and practical. Such results as have appeared in published work are inconclusive, but by and large not very supportive of the currency substitution hypothesis.

READING GUIDE

There are a number of published papers incorporating a currency substitution mechanism, though not always as the centrepiece of the analysis.

The best known and most influential work has been the single-sector analysis of Kouri (1976) and (1983) and, particularly, Calvo and Rodriguez (1977).

Perhaps the most worthwhile reading of all is the paper by Frenkel and Rodriguez (1982) since, in addition to the currency substitution model on which this chapter is based, it also sets out the conditions required for over- and undershooting. In particular, it shows the importance of the choice of inflation hedge. It turns out that, if the alternative to domestic money is non-traded rather than traded goods, the exchange rate would *under*shoot its long-run equilibrium.

Further investigation of the dynamics of this type of model is to be found in Dornbusch and Fischer (1980).

McKinnon (1982) is of interest not only for the data presented but also for the useful discussion of the relationship between capital mobility and currency substitution.

None of these include any empirical work. For the results of some single-equation tests, see Hamburger (1977). Also of interest is Chrystal (1977), which takes the portfolio balance approach. Both, inevitably, look out of date, so that the relevance of their results to the present day is in some doubt.

10

Optimum Currency Areas and Monetary Union

■ Introduction

For most of the time in this book, we have been taking for granted that each currency was unambiguously and irrevocably identified with one particular country, in spite of the fact that, as has been pointed out before, there are many examples of countries in which foreign currencies are widely used, officially or unofficially. Chapter 9 focused explicitly on the issue of currency substitution, that is, a situation in which the association between currencies and countries becomes blurred. In this chapter, we move on to address the question of whether there is such a thing as an *optimal* currency area.

The question has to be answered in two stages. First, we need to deal with a set of preliminary questions of a positive nature.[1] What economic difference does it make whether countries or regions share a common currency? What, if any, are the real effects?

---

[1] Positive analysis attempts to explain why the economy is the way it is, whereas normative analysis seeks to prescribe how government or corporate policies, laws, institutional arrangements and so on ought to be framed for the economy to operate in a desirable fashion.

To what extent do countries entering a currency union sacrifice their economic independence? Then we can attempt to provide an answer to the normative question: what is the optimal scope of a single currency?

Fortunately, we have already answered most of the positive questions in earlier chapters, so that much of the analysis will be simply an application of previous models.

In what follows, it will help if we have some examples of currency union in mind. For this purpose, we shall focus for the most part on the case of the proposed European Monetary Union (EMU), which has the virtue of being topical, already widely researched and involving issues which are largely familiar. But it should be clear that we could have picked any region as a potential candidate for currency union.

More importantly, the reader should be aware that the arguments for and against monetary integration can always be turned on their head, and related instead to the question of monetary *dis*integration. In that sense, this chapter is equally concerned with the question: what are the implications for a region or country of starting to issue its own money?[2] Would Scotland or Wales or California be better off issuing their own currency? Or London or New York? Would the UK or USA be left any worse off if those regions opted for independent currencies?

As it happens, California does issue its own money. Dollar bills printed there carry the inscription *'Issued by the Federal Reserve Bank of California, San Francisco'*, and the same is true of all the Fed's twelve regional branches across the USA. Scottish banknotes too carry the name of the private commercial banks which have issued them.

Nonetheless, neither Scotland nor California[3] can be said to have its own currency at present. The reason is not simply that, in both cases, the notes issued are printed under licence to the respective central banks. Rather, it is that, having subcontracted the job of printing banknotes to its agents, each central bank then treats the currency issued as indistinguishable from those it prints itself. In particular, it stands ready to exchange any or all regionally printed notes for those

---

[2] Monetary disintegration is actually far more topical than monetary integration. After all, EMU is the only formal example of monetary union to be taken seriously since World War II, whereas almost every ex-colony has issued a new currency on gaining its independence, and the components of the old Soviet Empire are doing the same. In general, monetary disintegration has been far more common than monetary integration.

[3] Examples like these are not frivolous. On grounds of size alone, California is a very serious candidate for monetary independence. After all, its economy is larger than that of Canada, or indeed any European country except Germany. Even Scotland has a slightly larger population than Denmark, whose monetary independence is usually taken for granted.

issued centrally. It follows that an individual who feels inclined can exchange any number of Californian dollar bills for the same number of dollars issued by the New York (or Philadelphia or St Louis) Federal Reserve, and Scottish and English banknotes are similarly interchangeable.

At this point, it should be clear that what we are talking about is simply a special case of a fixed exchange rate. These are examples of currencies which are physically distinguishable, but which are governed by an exchange rate regime with two essential features which can be regarded as being the defining characteristics of a single currency system:

> *A Single Currency Zone (or Monetary Union) is one where the accepted means of payment consists either of a single, homogeneous currency, or of two or more currencies linked by an exchange rate which is fixed (at one-for-one) irrevocably.*

It is worth noting the properties which have *not* been included. There is no reason, at least in principle, why a monetary union cannot embrace a proliferation of currency issuers, printing notes or coins as different from one another as are today the banknotes of any two members of the United Nations.[4] Nor is there any mention of political or geographic requirements. There are plenty of cases of currencies being used and even officially accepted over areas that are non-contiguous, politically diverse or even currently at war with each other. Panama, for example, has used the US dollar in place of a national currency for many years.

However, the most important feature of the definition given here is in the final word. What really distinguishes a monetary union from a fixed exchange rate regime is more than just the fact that the exchange rate is fixed at one-for-one. That is merely an arithmetic convenience. Rather it is the fact that the exchange rate is fixed irrevocably and irreversibly, and moreover is universally *believed* to be so. It is easy to see why this feature is so critical. Suppose it were thought possible that at some future date the Californian dollar was going to be revalued against, say, the New York dollar. Plainly, the result would be an immediate deviation from the current one-for-one exchange rate, as holders of New York dollars rushed to swap their money for Californian

---

[4] Not only do Scottish banknotes differ from each other, depending on the particular commercial bank issuing them, they even include one-pound notes, in spite of the fact that in England the one-pound note has long since been phased out in favour of a small nickel coin. In some situations, this feature limits substitutability. For example, there are few if any machines that will accept both notes and coins of the same denomination.

| Pure float | Managed ('dirty') float | Crawling peg (regular adjustments to fixed rate) | Fixed rate | Monetary union |

Figure 10.1   Exchange rate regimes (more fixed →).

dollars. Moreover, lenders and borrowers would soon start to specify in their contracts the currency in which repayment was to be made. In short, the situation would be unstable, and the New York dollar would cease to exist, as the whole stock found its way back to the vaults of the Federal Reserve. In this respect, it helps if a currency is homogeneous. Because there is no way of distinguishing between one hundred franc note and the next, there is no way they could ever differ in value. Where the fiction of a separate currency is maintained, the mechanism for creating a separate currency is already in place, and therefore the threat or promise may still be felt to exist.[5]

Monetary union can be viewed as the extension of a fixed exchange rate regime to a point where the possibility of parity changes is ruled out completely (Figure 10.1). The distinction is an important one, as EMS members have discovered to their cost. As long as countries or regions preserve separately issued currencies, the market will always take the view that they have preserved the potential escape route of exchange rate changes in order to make use of it when fixity proves too painful.

Before proceeding to the analysis, there is one other aspect of the question which ought to be acknowledged. Obviously, there is a sense in which a country's currency is widely perceived as a vital part of its national sovereignty. Like its postage stamps or its national airline or even its own armed forces, a country's currency is felt to be a vital part of its identity, one of the essential insignia of statehood. Why this should be the case is not entirely obvious, except as a particular example of the general rule that from the moment any activity becomes state sponsored rather than private, it is liable to become the focus of a

---

[5] This is more or less what happened with the Irish Punt, which had been unofficially interchangeable with the UK pound for many years, prior to being floated as an independent currency on 13 March 1979. On the other hand, the very fact that Scottish and Californian banknotes are universally accepted throughout the UK and USA respectively can be taken as evidence that virtually nobody takes seriously the possibility that they might one day be independent currencies.

degree of nationalistic fervour. What is true of sport is certainly true of currencies. Anyone who doubts the fact need only consider the haste with which most of the new states of Eastern Europe have declared their intention to issue their own national money.[6]

However, these issues are appropriate to textbooks on economic psychology and politics, not economics. The question of sovereignty will be viewed here exclusively from the economic angle.

Nonetheless, it should be said that the subject matter of this chapter is more closely linked to political value judgements than the material in the rest of the book. At a number of points, we will find the train of the economic argument running into the buffers of political issues. In order to avoid trespassing into these areas, therefore, we shall have to come to an abrupt halt at several points in the discussion as we reach the boundaries of economics. The reader should not feel frustrated by this coyness. In dealing with a topic of this nature, the job of the economist can never be any more than to follow through the implications of the policy options under consideration. Perhaps the most important outcome of the analysis will be to delineate clearly the points at which the economic arguments end and political concerns take over.[7]

In Section 10.1, we shall consider the benefits of monetary union, in terms of reduced transaction costs and the elimination of exchange rate uncertainty. In Section 10.2, we turn to a consideration of the factors determining the costs of integration: the degree of labour mobility and the openness of the economy. Section 10.3 addresses an assortment of other issues: the impact of currency union on government monetary and fiscal policy choices, the transition costs of integration, and the relationship (or lack of it) between common markets for goods and common currencies. Conclusions are in Section 10.4.

---

[6] Their flight from the rouble is understandable in the light of the near-hyperinflation in Russia. But since dollars and DM are already widely circulating throughout the old Soviet Empire, the 'temporary' solution of relying on foreign money would appear perfectly reasonable. Issuing their own currency is hardly something which ought to figure very highly among the priorities of governments facing the kind of problems seen today in that part of the world.

[7] The author has tried to remain neutral in this chapter as elsewhere in the book, though his views may well be apparent if only because, alongside the most frequently-aired arguments, we also give space to aspects of the question which are only rarely discussed by British economists.

10.1 The benefits of monetary union

The benefits of monetary union are all microeconomic in nature.[8]

In a sense, the case for monetary union is a negative one, since the supposed benefits stem from eliminating the costs of maintaining multiple currencies. Essentially, the argument is that the existence of multiple currencies imposes costs on individual economic agents or on society as a whole. These costs, which reduce overall welfare both directly and indirectly, via their inhibiting effect on trade and investment, can be grouped under two broad headings, depending on whether they arise out of the conditions of economic life under certainty (mainly transaction costs of one type or another) or out of the intrinsic uncertainty of floating or potentially variable fixed exchange rates.

It is straightforward to enumerate the costs imposed by the existence of multiple currencies. However, in evaluating the potential savings from their elimination by a monetary union, it is important to bear the following points in mind:

(1)   Not all the costs of foreign currency transactions could be saved by the use of a common currency. For example, some foreign currency loans are simply hedging exchange rate risk. On the other hand, firms often borrow in foreign markets because they find it the cheapest source of finance. Only in the former case is there a potential saving from monetary union. In the latter case, there would only be scope for saving if the reason for the difference in borrowing costs was attributable to exchange rate risk. Very often, however, the reasons have little to do with exchange rates. For example, a multinational company may find it cheapest to raise funds on its 'home' capital market, simply because it is better known there and therefore attracts a higher credit rating.

---

[8] This is not to deny that a variety of supposed macroeconomic advantages have been adduced to support the case for currency union. For example, it could be argued that, under fixed exchange rates, currencies perceived as depreciation-prone may need to be protected by high interest rates for long periods, presumably until the national monetary authority in question has 'earned' enough credibility. In this respect, a national currency could be viewed as a liability, imposing higher interest rates than would otherwise be necessary on the domestic economy.

Even if one takes this argument at face value, however, it has the drawback of being symmetrical: if low-credibility countries (like the UK, Italy and France in the ERM) carry the burden of excessively high interest rates, high-credibility countries (Germany and Holland) enjoy the benefit of relatively low interest rates.

More to the point, the argument appears to rest on the assumption that currencies are divided into devaluation or revaluation candidates on a more or less arbitrary basis, or at the very least that there is no close connection between a country's monetary policy and its credibility. If there is any rationality in the way the market assesses the reputation of the respective national monetary authorities, the credibility of a supranational currency (and hence the accompanying level of interest rates) will depend on the respective national shares in the post-union monetary decision-making process (see Section 10.3.2).

(2) Some of the apparent costs of foreign trade are simply rents extracted by banks, currency dealers and other intermediaries, exploiting the economies of scale open to them from the volume of transactions they handle on a regular basis. To some extent, there are genuine resource costs which could be avoided by monetary union. But the rents in excess of true marginal (social) cost would only be redistributed to other sectors of the economy, a change which may or may not be considered desirable depending on one's outlook. In other cases, costs may be not so much illusory as zero-sum, so that one country's cost is another's benefit. Again, monetary union results in no overall benefit, but simply a reallocation of income from pre-union winners to losers.

(3) Even where monetary union seems likely to yield cost savings, there may often be other, less radical ways to achieve the same results, as we shall see.

10.1.1 Foreign exchange transaction costs

We are all familiar with some of the costs of converting from one currency to another. As we saw in Section 1.1.3, large-scale currency conversions involve a bid-ask spread. On the one hand, this spread is probably quite small relative to the size of the individual transaction, and hence of negligible importance in terms of its impact on behaviour. However, given the staggering volume of foreign currency transactions compared even to the world economy as a whole, the aggregate resource cost could be quite substantial. For example, if total currency transactions in the London market add up to around $300bn on an average business day, and the typical spread is about 0.05%, the implied cost is $150m, or well over $30bn per year – a very large amount by any standards.

However, from the point of view of a single country, for example the UK, the potential resource saving from EMU is probably far smaller than this. For one thing, as the City of London's public relations machine cheerfully reminds us at every opportunity, a large proportion of the currency traded there is on behalf of foreign principals and hence, far from a resource cost to the UK, represents service exports by the British financial sector. Moreover, even where the costs are borne by UK residents, the potential savings from EMU are not applicable to the considerable proportion of transactions with countries outside Europe.

Of the remaining trade volume, the bulk almost certainly involves little or no true transaction cost to the economy. In the first place, the $300bn figure is gross, that is, counting offsetting trades. Many trades are netted out and hence, are either not charged the spread, or at any rate involve a genuine marginal cost which is only a tiny fraction of the quoted spread. Moreover, even where costs apply, economies of scale are likely to mean the spread is far greater than the marginal cost which could be saved by a common currency.

The 'bottom line' is that savings in transaction costs are likely to be somewhere between one quarter and one half of one per cent of EU income.[9] Although this may not seem a very large sum, it would be enough to justify the change to a single currency – if we could be sure the sacrifices were negligible.

10.1.2 The costs of uncertainty

The argument most often used to justify monetary union is that exchange rate uncertainty is inherently damaging to the volume of real flows of trade and investment. The proposition is superficially persuasive. There can be little doubt that businessmen prefer certainty to uncertainty, other things being equal. This means that, faced with investment or trade opportunities, entrepreneurs are likely to be less enthusiastic where the decision involves the risk of currency fluctuations.

However, on closer examination, the issue is nowhere near as clear cut as might appear at first glance. Consider an example. Suppose a British multinational is considering building an aircraft assembly plant in Germany. At the time of writing the £/DM exchange rate is apparently floating freely. Therefore, in so far as the costs of the project are primarily denominated in DM, and moreover spread out over a number of years, the sterling cost is uncertain, as is the exchange rate at which the cashflows from operating the plant will be converted into pounds.

But clearly the contribution of currency volatility to the risk of the project is likely to be very much overstated by, say, the variance or standard deviation of the exchange rate. In the first place, the UK company if it is truly multinational may well have DM-denominated assets with which it can finance the project. Failing that, it has the alternative of funding the investment by borrowing in Germany, a policy which amounts to hedging its prospective DM asset by a liability in the same currency. As we saw in Section 3.3, this is equivalent to a forward purchase of DM, with the useful difference that it offers more flexibility over both contract size and maturity dates. Similarly, the cashflows from the sale of the product (aircraft) can be hedged by forward sales of DM against pounds.

Moreover, the ultimate risk to the company associated with the investment and the ensuing cashflows is measured by their impact on its

---

[9] The estimates, which may well be over optimistic, are those published by the EU itself. They assess potential savings as being somewhat greater for the smaller countries and those with less sophisticated financial markets.

net position (sometimes called *net exposure*) in DM in any period, not by their gross foreign currency value. Most cross-border transactions of this type will be netted out in the balance sheets of large multinational companies. Thus, if the company in our example has previously been a seller of aircraft to Germany, the DM-denominated proceeds of the sale, though risky taken in isolation, obviously help to offset the foreign currency risk of the company's investment.[10]

This is far from being the end of the story, however. To make matters simple, suppose the British firm in our example has no other business in DM, so that we can consider the proposed investment project in isolation. Under these circumstances, it is obviously true that if the DM falls by, say, 10% after the investment is made, the sterling value of the company's German asset will also fall by 10%, *other things being equal*. But, as is so often the case in economics, other things are unlikely to remain equal because, in so far as the exchange rate is not expected to change any further in the interim, the competitiveness of production at the new assembly plant has been enhanced. The increase in prospective cashflows will to some degree offset the fall in asset values resulting directly from the DM depreciation, and might even reverse it.

In general, then, it is easy to overstate the true costs of exchange rate uncertainty, at least as far as the typical multinational corporation is concerned.[11] Smaller companies have to rely on the ability of financial intermediaries to match positions in different countries, charging fees

---

[10] Readers familiar with modern portfolio theory will recognize the fundamental proposition involved here. In general, the riskiness of an investment can never be judged in isolation. What determines an investment's contribution to the total risk borne by a company is the covariance of its return with the return on the rest of the company's activities. In so far as the two returns are dependent on a single common factor (for example, the pound/DM exchange rate), there will be some covariance between them. The covariance will be positive if both returns tend to rise when the pound strengthens, negative if one return rises in situations where the other falls. Unless the covariance is so great as to create 100% correlation between the new risk and the pre-existing risks, the investment still increases the degree of diversification of the company's activities, reducing the overall risk. Indeed, if the covariance is actually negative, it is a case of swings and roundabouts, with good news on one front offset to some extent by bad news on the other. Under these circumstances, the new investment provides a degree of hedging for the rest of the company's business.

[11] These are some of the reasons why, in practice, it is often a very complicated exercise indeed to estimate the impact of exchange rate fluctuations on a company. The situation is further complicated by the fact that the answer very much depends on the currency in which the multinational chooses to do its accounting. Shareholders of US-based multinationals, for example, are normally assumed to prefer to see the accounts in dollars, so management is preoccupied with currency exposure relative to the dollar. Whether this presumption is correct in a world with increasingly integrated equity markets is dubious. It is probably even less relevant in Europe, where the major Dutch-based multinationals have millions of shareholders outside the Netherlands. In any case, if they are concerned at the impact of currency fluctuations on their balance sheets, they can always draw up their accounts in ECUs.

which are reduced to the level of the transaction costs referred to in the last section. What is left is the residual risk that has to be carried either by the individual company or by the forward market.[12]

As far as the latter option is concerned, it is often said that covering foreign exchange transactions is costly. The statement is somewhat misleading. As we saw in Chapter 3, forward cover is likely to involve a cost in the form of a risk premium. However, most of the published research suggests the premium is probably quite small (Chapter 13). Nonetheless, the situation involves a number of subtleties which have been a source of confusion in some commentaries. Take an example.

Suppose at some point the situation with regard to the £/DM exchange rate is as follows:

Spot rate: DM1 = £0.40
30 day forward rate: DM1 = £0.404
Expected 30 day ahead spot rate: DM1 = £0.403

Comparing the spot and forward rates, it is plain that the DM stands at a forward premium to the pound of $(0.404/0.40) - 1 = 0.01$ or 1%. However, there is no reason to regard this figure as giving an indication of the potential saving from uniting the UK and German currencies. For one thing, the pound's discount is the DM's premium. When, as here, sterling holders have to pay more than the spot rate for 30-day German currency, DM holders pay less than the spot rate.

Moreover, most of the forward premium has nothing at all to do with risk as such. In the example given above, three-quarters of the forward premium (that is, 0.75%) reflects the market's (albeit unobservable) expectations. This component of the premium is hardly to be regarded as a cost, because if the market's expectations are fulfilled, it will be just sufficient to compensate DM borrowers and sterling lenders for movements in the exchange rate during the month.[13] It is only the residual 0.25% that is a genuine cost of insuring against exchange rate fluctuations, and therefore potentially a saving through currency union.

---

[12] In reality, there is nowadays a whole range of different so-called derivative instruments which can be used for hedging currency risk, for example, futures, options, swaps and such like. For an explanation of how they work, see the relevant chapter of any up-to-date textbook on Finance.

[13] In terms of domestic macroeconomics, there is no reason to suppose real (that is, inflation-corrected) interest rates will diverge between UK and Germany. The reason is that, under CIRP, nominal interest rates will differ only by the forward premium, which in turn is mostly accounted for by the expected depreciation of the currency, and if PPP holds the latter reflects relative inflation rates.

10.1.3 The international unit of account

Economists view money as having a number of important functions, of which one of the most important is as a *unit of account*. In this respect, it fulfills an essential information-bearing role, shortcutting what would otherwise be the cumbersome mechanism of barter. Without a stable unit of account, the drafting of long-term contracts would be impossibly complex. However, when this analysis is applied to cases like EMU, there turns out to be somewhat less to the argument than meets the eye, as we shall see.

To understand the point, suppose I am looking through a mail order catalogue in the UK. Now in the absence of anything qualifying as money (that is, in a world of barter), the catalogue would have to be very thick indeed if it were to serve the purpose of telling me the true price of anything more than a handful of goods. The reason is that the price of each good would have to be quoted in terms of all other goods. So for example, instead of a money-price of £10 for a compact disc, the catalogue would have to quote a long series of *relative prices*: 20 large white loaves of bread, two tickets for the cinema (specifiying the cinema and the film), 0.75 days of tuition on a first degree arts course (specifying the university etc.), and so on.

Put like this, it should be clear why it is absolutely essential to agree on a substance – commodity, paper, metal or whatever – to nominate as a unit of account.[14] Having done so, the information problem becomes manageable. Once I get used to pounds sterling, I know immediately what is meant by a cost of £10 in terms of all the goods and services I buy regularly and, equally important, I have a fairly precise idea of its cost in terms of leisure, that is, how many hours I have to work in order to pay for it.[15]

Obviously, the advantage of any form of money resides in its very uniqueness as a common standard of account. Hence, some proponents of currency union go on to argue that a common currency for Europe, for example, would be a substantial informational improvement on the 12 national currencies it replaces.

The argument is possibly correct, up to a point. But in the first place, its force really relates to the advantages of fixed compared to floating exchange rates. After all, the 12 currencies add a mere 11 prices – the 11

---

[14] It should also be clear why people organized in barter rings in the UK and the USA are deluding themselves if they think they are somehow behaving more efficiently than those of us in the monetary economy. Even allowing for high transaction charges in banks, they are unlikely to be saving anywhere near enough to cover the inconvenience of barter. However, if barter enables them to avoid or evade direct or indirect tax, it could be worthwhile for the individuals involved, though not of course for society as a whole.

[15] Suppose there are N goods in the economy. It turns out that, with barter, $N(N-1)/2$ (relative) prices need to be given in the catalogue, whereas nominating one of the N goods as money reduces the number of (money) prices required to only $N-1$. So even if the number of different goods and services traded in the UK is only 10,000 (an extremely conservative estimate), monetary exchange is more efficient by a factor of 5000!

exchange rates against the pound – to the thousands of sterling prices with which a UK resident must live. This is hardly a significant burden. Second, the argument relies for its superficial attraction on a number of conditions which are not really satisfied. Perhaps most importantly, it is not obvious that a single currency is optimal when relative prices differ between regions, as they do in Europe.

To be explicit, ask yourself how much better off the average European would be, informationally speaking, if all prices were quoted in, say, ECU. Would a Londoner really benefit if supermarket prices were quoted in the same currency in Madrid? Very little, one suspects. Indeed, the most likely reaction to a changeover would be total apathy. The reason Spanish prices are of little interest to UK residents has nothing to do with the fact they are currently quoted in pesetas, but most obviously because there are very few practical ways for a Londoner to take advantage of any bargains in Madrid, and vice versa. Moreover, that is true even though many of the goods in question are eminently tradeable. But, as we have seen, the problem for traders who may or may not arbitrage away any price differentials is one that is straightforwardly handled by forward covering.

Take a more controversial example. It is well known that, when converted at current exchange rates, prices of many motor vehicles appear to be as much as 25% more expensive in the UK than in Belgium. Anyone seeking to establish whether the price differential is real or only apparent must examine carefully the makers' claim that the specification of UK vehicles is higher than in continental Europe, as well as the additional cost of shipping cars across the English Channel, where necessary. Having estimated the costs of converting the vehicles to a common specification and added the charges for transportation, insurance and so on, those costs have then to be translated into a common currency.

It should be clear that, in all these tiresome computations, the role played by uncertainty about the number of Belgian francs per pound is negligible. The complications all arise from the failure of the European single market, which has nothing whatever to do with the existence of multiple currencies, as we shall see (Section 10.3.5). In general, the reader may look back at the discussion in Chapter 2 to see that few of the reasons given there for the failure of PPP have anything to do with exchange rate uncertainty.

Of course, it is just about conceivable that at some future date products may have become standardized across the European market to such a degree that currency considerations really do stand out as the most serious remaining obstacle to integration. Other than in this unlikely (and unattractive) scenario,[16] however, the benefits from a shared unit of account seem likely to be extremely slim.

---

[16] Standardization is unlikely to be successful beyond a certain point simply because pressure from the authorities is in large part offset by the continuing market tendency towards product differentiation. Moreover, it is hard to see why product diversity should be any less attractive to economists, politicians and civil servants than it is to consumers.

10.2 The costs of monetary union

Two points need to be clear at the outset regarding the costs of monetary union.

First, they are largely *macroeconomic* in nature. There are no obvious microeconomic disadvantages.

Second, they are not primarily concerned with the nature of the macroeconomic equilibrium under currency union and disunion, but with differences in the patterns of *adjustment to disequilibrium* following a disturbance in the foreign sector. In other words, while there is little reason to suppose the ultimate outcome of a disturbance is affected by whether countries share a common currency, there is every reason to expect the adjustment mechanism to vary considerably, with important consequences for output and employment over what could be a very protracted period. The reason why the equilibrium outcome is unchanged by currency union is easily stated. As has already been pointed out, currency union is to all intents and purposes the same as a permanently fixed exchange rate as regards its comparative static properties. It is only when we come to examine the implications for adjustment that the differences become apparent.

To understand what is involved, take the monetary model as the starting point. As usual, we take as our benchmark a pure float with perfectly flexible prices, and we contrast the effect of a disturbance in this simple case (Section 5.1) with the effect in the fixed exchange rate case (Section 5.2).

The type of disturbance to consider for our purposes is a shock to the domestic country's price level relative to the foreign price level. Suppose, for example, the foreign price level falls suddenly by 10%, while the domestic price level is initially unchanged. We saw in Chapter 5 that the final result is the same in both cases: competitiveness is restored, with real income, output and the real exchange rate back where they started. The difference is that, whereas under a floating exchange rate regime the domestic currency depreciates so as to restore competitiveness (Section 5.1.5), with a fixed exchange rate the process involves a fall in the domestic money stock and price level.

Take the fixed exchange rate case first. As we saw in Section 5.2.3, in the aftermath of a relative price shock, equilibrium is restored through reserve changes impacting on the domestic money market. In this case, the home country loses reserves as a result of the deterioration in its competitive position, until the fall in its money stock reduces its price level to match the 10% fall in foreign prices.

Now it is a sad fact of macroeconomic life that falling price levels tend to be accompanied by considerable economic pain, in the form of unemployment, bankruptcies and misery. The critical question is this: *is the process more painful when the option of devaluation is ruled out because the home country and the foreign country are bound up in a currency union?* If it is, then it would obviously be desirable from the macroeconomc point of view to preserve that option (if not actually to allow the exchange rate to float freely). If however the adjustment mechanism is no more sluggish when the exchange rate is fixed irrevocably, then the microeconomic benefits of union are available at little or no macroeconomc cost.

10.2.1 The labour market

The consensus among economists is that the labour market is the critical factor in determining how smoothly adjustment proceeds.

Consider the impact of the initial disturbance on wage levels in the domestic economy. The fall in foreign prices means that, at pre-existing money wages, domestic production has become uncompetitive because real wages are now higher than before by an amount of up to 10%. Roughly speaking, if internationally traded goods prices account for, say, 40% of the cost of living, real wages will have risen by 4% (that is, 40% of 10%), with a consequent loss of competitiveness, other things being equal. As long as this situation persists, there will be downward pressure on the level of economic activity, with accompanying increases in unemployment, the level of bankruptcies and so forth.

The question is: to what extent, if any, would devaluation make the return to equilibrium speedier and less painful?

With the exchange rate fixed, as the domestic economy loses reserves, the excess demand for money exerts downward pressure on product prices and may also push up interest rates (Chapter 6). If prices fall faster than money wages, it follows that real wages increase, resulting in unemployment. In fact, if the price level falls by the full 10% while money wages are unchanged, real wages increase by 10%, and the level of employment bears the brunt of adjustment to the disturbance. Unless both money wages and prices fall at the same rate, and more or less immediately, there must be temporary unemployment.

By contrast, if the domestic currency depreciates, whether under a free float or a once-and-for-all devaluation, the domestic price of traded goods rises by 10%, reducing real wages pro rata and preserving labour market equilibrium – provided money wages remain unchanged in the face of the fall in their purchasing power, a point to which we shall return later.

The importance of labour mobility (Mundell)

At this point, it would appear that floating exchange rates are unambiguously superior to fixity, because they allow a near-painless reduction in real wages, through a devaluation-induced inflation of the domestic price level. Does that mean every country should have its own currency with a freely floating exchange rate? Why stop there? After all, everyone agrees that unemployment is undesirable. Why not have currency zones smaller than countries? Then California could reduce or even eliminate its unemployment by devaluing its currency, reducing real wages in the state relative to the rest of the USA, as well as the rest of the world. Or go further: in US cities where unemployment is high as a result of the post-Cold War cuts in defence spending, a devaluation would provide a useful boost to the local economy, and the same applies to the small towns in Northern England currently suffering from the impact of pit closures. It looks as though there are arguments in favour of ever-smaller currency zones.

There is in fact an obvious limit, however, as is clear from the last example. As Mundell pointed out over 30 years ago, the argument for flexible exchange rates presented here presupposes that labour is immobile.

By contrast, suppose labour is mobile internationally or interregionally. Then it is easy to see that, even with a fixed exchange rate, equilibrium can be restored without transitional unemployment. Instead, workers who cannot find jobs in the domestic economy will move abroad (or to the next town or region), where they will be absorbed into employment because at the lower prices and wages, production is relatively profitable. As the domestic economy loses labour, its marginal product rises, until higher real wages are validated. Thus labour mobility obviates the need for exchange rate flexibility, by making it possible to preserve full employment, more or less, without devaluation.

Now international labour mobility is unusual in anything but the very long run. By and large, people only leave their own country to emigrate, drawn by what they see as vastly better prospects stretching into the indefinite future. But within a small country or group of countries (for example, Benelux) or a single region, they may well be ready to move in response to temporary differences in labour market conditions.

For these reasons, Mundell concluded that the optimal zone for a single currency was determined by the area within which labour was willing and able to move freely. In practical terms, this would appear to mean very small currency zones indeed, far smaller than most (though not all) of the countries in the industrialized world. For example, it probably means a separate currency for California, or better still for the South-West USA. Likewise, on these grounds Scotland needs an independent currency,[17] as

---

[17] Notice that the presence of hundreds of thousands of Scots or people of Scottish descent in England, North America, Australia and so on is evidence, not of labour mobility, but rather of the exact opposite. For the most part, Scots in London have not moved south in reponse to temporary employment opportunities resulting from the sluggish response of wages to random demand shocks, any more than have the Scots now living in Australia. Instead, insofar as they have been drawn by economic factors, they relate to very long term growth prospects that have little or nothing to do with exchange rate regimes or indeed with macroeconomics altogether.

do the other regions of the UK. On the other hand, West and East Germany are probably better off having a common currency, and it may be that the Benelux countries could also be integrated.

In general, considerations of labour mobility militate in favour of smaller currency zones. Moreover, on these grounds there ought to be more currencies in Europe than in the USA if, as is normally assumed, the degree of population mobility is lower in Europe. It is also worth noting that anything which serves to reduce labour mobility (for example, language differences, generous unemployment benefits) will also tend to make the optimal currency area smaller.[18]

In fact, recently published evidence suggests that wages fall very little in the states of the USA in response to unfavourable demand shocks. Virtually the whole burden of adjustment falls on labour migration between states, so that it is estimated to take about six years for regional unemployment rates to return to the national average in the aftermath of a disturbance. From this point of view, it would appear that the USA is a candidate for monetary disintegration.

The importance of openness (McKinnon)

We appear to have arrived at the conclusion that, in terms of macroeconomics at any rate, the optimum currency area is very small, at least relative to present-day nation states. It turns out however that the requirements of labour market adjustment can equally be taken as justification for a movement in the opposite direction altogether.

The issue turns on the mechanism whereby devaluation serves to reduce real wages. Recall that, in the aftermath of a devaluation, it was assumed that money wages remained unchanged, in spite of the rise in prices, allowing the real wage to fall – hence, the desirability of a flexible exchange rate in the absence of labour mobility.

Notice that what is involved is a kind of sleight of hand, a monetary confidence trick whereby devaluation and the consequent rise in prices bring about a fall in real wages, *because labour suppliers fail to notice or respond to the inflation by raising* their money wage *demands*. To the extent that wage earners *do* respond, no reduction in real wages takes place and

---

[18] Unemployment benefits should of course be interpreted broadly to include all the benefits available to those not working, including other welfare provisions, benefits in kind and such like. Experience in the USA shows that where labour mobility exists, the unemployed have a tendency, not surprisingly, to gravitate to wherever the benefits are most generous.

hence depreciation is ineffective. The Mundell case for flexibility therefore requires an inert labour force.[19]

How likely is such passivity on the part of the labour force? Obviously, it very much depends on the circumstances: how competitive the labour market, how far wages are fixed by long-term contract, and so forth. But, as McKinnon argued in reply to Mundell, other things being equal (that is, given the other features of the labour market), there will be one overriding factor determining how far workers passively accept a fall in their real wage as a result of devaluation: the degree of openness of the economy.

To see the force of the argument, consider the following question: how far do real wages fall when the exchange rate depreciates, say, by 10%? The answer obviously depends on the impact of the devaluation on the cost of living.

At one extreme, in a very small economy, almost all consumption is likely to consist of imports or import-competing goods, that is, tradeables. The effect of a 10% devaluation is therefore likely to be a near-10% rise in the cost-of-living index. The probability of workers accepting this without attempting to claw back some of the drop in their standard of living by pressing for higher money wages seems small.

On the other hand, in a large economy, where imports may well be only a negligible proportion of the typical consumption basket, the impact of even a 10% devaluation will be small. For example, if imports carry only a 5% weight in the consumption price index, the direct effect will be only ½% (that is, 10% of 5%). Hence, McKinnon argues, in large economies, devaluation is unlikely to provoke a significant response on the part of wage-earners.

In general, therefore, McKinnon puts forward the case for very large currency areas. The larger the zone, the more closed the economy of the region it covers. Hence, the smaller the weight of traded goods in the consumption baskets of its workforce, and the easier it will be to sneak a reduction in the real wage without workers realizing or bothering to respond.

It looks as though labour market considerations suggest a trade-off between labour mobility, which suggests smaller currency areas, and openness, which indicates choosing larger areas.

---

[19] Notice it cannot be argued that workers are simply unable to retrieve the situation. After all, unless labour market participants suffer from some form of what economists call money illusion, one would expect agreements between employers and the labour force to relate implicitly or explicitly to real rather than nominal wages. Hence, what was an equilibrium real wage prior to devaluation will still be the equilibrium afterwards, unless there has been some other change affecting the relative bargaining strengths of the two sides of the labour market.

10.3 Other considerations

10.3.1 Government behaviour: common currency versus fixed exchange rate

The macroeconomic arguments about the efficacy of devaluation as a tool for preventing unemployment really relate to the debate over the relative attractions of floating versus fixed exchange rates, rather than to the pros and cons of currency union. The reader may well wonder whether there are likely to be any macroeconomic implications specific to currency union. According to Mundell, one difference is to be found in the probable response of governments under the two types of arrangement, which he argues is likely to be different under a common currency than under a multiple currency system with fixed exchange rates.

His argument is as follows. Suppose there is a sudden decrease in the demand for the output of country (or region) A, to the advantage of country or region B. If the two zones are linked by a fixed exchange rate, the natural reaction will be for A's monetary authority to tighten credit so as to reduce the money stock, thereby raising interest rates and strengthening the balance of payments. These measures will inevitably have the effect of reducing demand even further in B, leading to multiple deflation.

Notice the problem arises out of a basic asymmetry of fixed exchange rate systems. The burden of adjustment falls mainly on the country or region whose currency is in excess supply, which is forced to deflate, while there is no comparable pressure to reflate on members of the system whose currencies are in excess demand.

By contrast, Mundell argues, if A and B form part of a common currency area, the authorities will be preoccupied with preventing unemployment in A. Hence they will tend, in response to the same initial demand shift, to loosen monetary conditions, in the process giving a boost to inflation in both A and B.

Mundell concluded, therefore, that while fixed exchange rate systems suffer from an inherent deflationary bias, common currency zones have a built-in inflationary bias.

A similar argument has often been put in balance of payments terms. Fixed exchange rate systems, whatever their written rules, invariably impose an unofficial burden of adjustment on deficit rather than surplus countries. On the other hand, within any single country there is pressure to equalize levels of employment and output at the level of the most fortunate region, in other words to increase demand in the deficit regions.

The argument is not entirely convincing, however. Take, for example, the Bretton Woods system (Section 1.5.1). In most cases, it did appear to throw the burden of adjustment on to the deficit country, while surplus countries felt immune to pressure to reflate their economies. However, the one glaring exception to this *de facto* rule was the USA itself, which was able to run unlimited deficits, thereby swamping any possible deflationary bias in a tide of newly printed dollars. In a sense, the Bretton Woods system involved enforced transfers to the USA from each member country in proportion to its dollar reserves, by a mechanism which is the international analogue of what is called *seigniorage* in the context of the domestic economy.

By contrast, the ERM fulfilled Mundell's prophecy. In the early 1990s, Germany generated domestic inflation within the new currency union so as to sustain the level of demand in its Eastern provinces. At the same time, it attempted to preserve the external purchasing power of the DM by a tight credit policy, thereby imposing deflation on its ERM partners.[20]

Unfortunately, as the last example makes clear, Mundell's argument is difficult to verify, because the issue is inseparable in practice from questions of sovereignty, as currencies have so far invariably been associated with independent countries. Putting the matter crudely, the government of a surplus country in a fixed exchange rate system usually feels free to pressure deficit countries to deflate, secure in the knowledge that it will not have to face voters embittered by higher levels of unemployment, interest rates, bankruptcies and recession. On the other hand, the pressure on a government to inflate so as to reduce unemployment within one of its own regions obviously arises out of political necessity, rather than from the fact that the regions share a common currency. Whether the same pressure would be felt within a system like the proposed EMU is doubtful.[21]

In any case, since neither an inflationary nor a deflationary bias can be considered desirable outcomes, it is hard to see how this factor can decisively affect the choice between the two systems. If anything, it would be preferable to have a system which was neutral rather than one with an inherent bias.

In practice, the inflationary bias within individual countries tends to be mitigated somewhat by the existence of so-called fiscal stabilizers. For example, suppose the demand for Scotland's output declines, its unemployment rises, its income falls and its balance of payments with the rest of the UK deteriorates. The result is that tax revenues from Scotland fall, as Scots

---

[20] Notice that the scope for Bundesbank seigniorage under the ERM was presumably much smaller than was available to the USA under Bretton Woods, simply because ERM members had a more or less free choice as to which reserve currencies to hold. On the other hand, at the time of writing at least, it is impossible to know how much of the increase in the Deutschmark money stock during the late 1980s and early 1990s is actually circulating as currency in the ex-Soviet bloc countries.

[21] One example to illustrate the point is the Republic of Ireland, which until 13 March 1979 was in a *de facto* currency union with the UK, since it kept the exchange rate of the Irish pound fixed at par with the pound sterling. Yet, of course, no British Government felt under any compulsion to reflate in the UK so as to eliminate unemployment in Ireland.

As far as EMU is concerned, it very much depends, of course, on whether any significant degree of democratic accountability is introduced into the formulation of European macroeconomic policy.

earn lower incomes and spend less, in the process reducing both their direct and indirect tax bills.[22] In addition, there will usually be an immediate inflow of Government transfer payments, in a variety of forms: more unemployment benefits, higher means-tested welfare payments, and so forth. The net effect amounts to an automatic (that is, unlegislated) fiscal stimulus to offset, at least partially, the deflationary effect of the original demand fall. Under these circumstances, the perceived need for Government intervention to boost demand in the stricken region is reduced, as indeed is the urgency of a real devaluation, at least in the short run.

It follows that, from this point of view, a common currency is likely to be tolerable where significant fiscal stabilizers are in place, as in the UK and, in particular, in federal systems like the USA or Germany. The same is certainly *not* true of the EU, where fiscal transfers are negligible in scale, and virtually never automatic. Europeans still pay taxes to their national governments, not to Brussels. Hence, there is no spontaneous fiscal subsidy to the UK when its balance of payments with the rest of the EU deteriorates,[23] though in the long term poorer countries do enjoy some slight (and politically contentious) subsidies through the EU Regional Fund and a number of other programmes.

10.3.2 Fiscal sovereignty and the Treasury

The need for fiscal stabilization is only one of the arguments which have motivated the demands from a number of sources for the imposition of constraints on national fiscal policy and its ultimate subordination to a centralized European budgetary process.[24] Whether or not surrendering national fiscal autonomy in this way is judged to be desirable depends on one's political perspective, and is therefore not our concern here. All that can be said is that the desirability or otherwise of a common currency cannot nowadays be considered independently of the issue of fiscal sovereignty.

Apart from the question of fiscal stabilizers, it might appear that fiscal policy independence and currency union are unrelated issues, and

---

[22] Direct taxes are those paid on personal and corporate incomes, while indirect taxes are imposed on expenditures, which in the UK means mainly Value Added Tax and Customs and Excise duties.

[23] At the risk of labouring the point, it must be emphasized that, just because the UK's balance of payments would be more or less unobservable within a currency union, it certainly does not follow it would be unimportant. Going back to the example of Scotland, a regional balance of payments deficit indicates a net outflow of wealth to the rest of the world. The fact that the region is not faced with the immediate problem of how to preserve the external purchasing power of its currency is of little comfort if it faces instead a loss of output and employment.

[24] In principle, at least, this type of concern is completely independent of arguments about the desirability or otherwise of 'coordinating' (that is, unifying) the detail of fiscal policies, as it affects tax rates, subsidies, payments to and receipts from social security, and so forth, though of course the two arguments are likely to be mutually reinforcing in practice.

indeed *in principle* there is no connection between the two. Nonetheless, in the European case at least, fiscal policy has been fully drawn into the sphere of supranational political economy.

Again, the reason has little or nothing to do with macro- or micro-economics. To understand what is at stake, consider the analogy with local government budgeting within a country like the UK. Broadly speaking, local authorities face a budget constraint which is almost the same as that facing the central government, with one exception (see Section 4.1.2). Both levels of government can finance their expenditure either by raising tax revenues or by borrowing. The only difference is that *de facto* the central government is able not only to borrow in the normal way (that is, by issuing short- or long-term debt), but can also fund its activity by printing IOUs which are treated as money by the rest of the economy.

We have already mentioned in the last section the fact that this power generates revenue for the central government from seigniorage. What has not so far been pointed out is that this power to print money has another dimension. Take the case of the UK. As long as the British government restricts itself to borrowing in sterling denominated forms, it need never, indeed can never default on its debt. For example, its gilt-edged stock promises to pay the holder nothing more than a certain number of pounds every six months (the 'coupon') and one hundred pounds at maturity. Her Majesty's government will never run out of pounds as long as it controls the Bank of England's printing presses. In other words, its obligations to repay its sterling debts can always be covered by printing pounds, and its only obligation to holders of pounds is to redeem banknotes with more banknotes.

Notice that the same is certainly not true of the British government's borrowing in foreign currency. The Treasury cannot repay debts denominated in DM or Yen by printing those currencies. That right belongs exclusively to the Bundesbank and Bank of Japan respectively.[25]

By contrast, a local authority in Britain could well default, if allowed to do so by central government. If it is either unable or unwilling to pay for its spending by local taxation, it must borrow, and it makes no difference whether it borrows sterling or foreign currency. In either case, it incurs debts which are not denominated in terms of its own IOUs, and therefore cannot be repaid from its own printing presses. In this sense, *all local authority borrowing is denominated in a foreign currency*, that is, a currency which is 'foreign' or externally printed from the point of view of the local government in question.

---

[25] This is precisely why a number of countries, mainly in Latin America and Africa, were forced to default on their debts in the 1980s, in spite of the insistence of one confused commercial banker in the previous decade that 'National governments don't go bankrupt'.

The reader may well wonder what would be the case in a country with an independent central bank. It all depends what one means by independence. One might think an independent central bank could refuse to print money to redeem a government's (domestic currency) debts. However, this scenario is hard to imagine in practice, at least in any Western country.

The dilemma is obvious. Again, *in principle* this simply puts the local authority on a par with private institutions like firms, households, and so forth. But this presupposes the central government would be willing ultimately to allow the local authority to default or even be driven into bankruptcy, if ever it were unable to pay its debts. By and large, central government is very unhappy indeed about this possibility, and tries to avoid it at all cost. In order to do so, it is forced to place direct or indirect constraints on the spending decisions of local government,[26] so as to preempt as far as possible a situation where it is forced to choose between being compelled to finance a local authority's borrowing on the one hand and allowing it to default on its debts on the other. This unenviable choice would of course be made more difficult by the fact that it would almost certainly involve conflict between local and central governments of different political complexions.[27]

Now since EMU will reduce national governments to the status of local authorities, with no power to issue money, either they must be permitted to default on their debts or they must be constrained. The new integrated monetary authority, the European central bank, cannot be forced to monetize any and every budget deficit a national government is unable or unwilling to fund by borrowing, at least if it is to have any control over the supply of the common currency. On the other hand, the prospect of a member country becoming insolvent is presumably too awful to contemplate, at least for governments that are less than wholeheartedly committed to market disciplines in other, less sensitive areas of economic life. The only remaining alternative is the imposition of permanent constraints on the fiscal policies of national governments, which become essentially instruments of the central government, restricted to determining the allocation of expenditures and the tax burden (that is, the microeconomics of fiscal policy), with no direct control over the key macroeconomic variable, the budget balance.[28]

Ultimately, the dilemma will have to be resolved before currency union can proceed. All that can be said here is that its resolution is likely

---

[26] The way these limits actually operate is extremely complicated, and not relevant to the issues involved here. Note that half or more of local authority spending in the UK is in any case funded directly or indirectly by central government. The bulk of the subsidy is in the form of a grant computed according to a formula which is both complicated and little publicized, a fact which if anything makes it even harder for the central government to simply turn its back on an insolvent local authority.

Whether the EU will draw any lessons from this sort of situation (and similar problems in other European countries) remains to be seen.

[27] As in the case of the City of Liverpool's insolvency in the early 1980s. A similar scenario when New York City was in financial difficulties prompted the notorious headline in one local newspaper 'RON (Reagan) TO CITY: DROP DEAD'.

[28] Notice that even the microeconomic control may ultimately be reduced to near zero (see footnote (24)).

to be considerably more painful than it has so far proved in the context of any single country, since the local and central governments will be divided not only by political persuasion, but also by nationality.

It is not possible to assess the costs and benefits of this abrogation of fiscal policy by national governments. What can be said is that there are at least two aspects to be considered. In the first place, countries face a cost in so far as they may be forced to relinquish the right to operate a counter-cyclical fiscal policy. The cost in this respect could be higher unemployment and lower output.

As far as the benefits are concerned, if the constraints are binding, the imposition of fiscal rectitude from above may well reduce the borrowing costs for previously profligate member governments, especially if the European central bank is a guarantor of their debts. On the other hand, governments which have a long-established record of conservative budgeting will have little to gain, and may well lose. Indeed, an anomalous situation may well arise whereby the conservative countries end up being forced into less responsible fiscal policies.

To see why, consider the situation of a country like Switzerland, which is expected to join the new union at some stage. Suppose the rules of the currency union permit budget deficits which are higher than Switzerland is running prior to entry, by whatever measure is adopted (probably in relation to GNP). Under the circumstances, it appears Switzerland would have little to gain by keeping its borrowing below the maximum permitted. As long as its common currency debt is credibly guaranteed by the European central bank which issues it, Swiss government debt would carry no default risk (but then neither would the debt of any other member country), and hence it would pay the same interest rate on its borrowings whether its deficit was bumping up against the ceiling level or only one quarter as high. Moreover, the less it borrowed, the more it would be subsidizing the more profligate governments. There would be no rewards to persuade any country to borrow less than the maximum permissible level. On the contrary, the fact that a thrifty government (especially for a large country) was directly reducing the borrowing costs for less conservative neighbours would act as a strong disincentive to saving.

We conclude that the fiscal constraints will need to be set at a lower level than otherwise (that is, than the pre-entry average or maximum of the member countries) in recognition of the fact that the maximum levels are likely in practice to become the norm. This in turn implies a greater degree of stringency for the majority of member countries.

10.3.3 Monetary sovereignty and the central bank

In practice, the type of monetary policy found in a currency union is likely to depend far more on the character and political complexion of the central bank than anything else. Thus, the current hyperinflation in Russia has far more to do with the internal politics of its government sector than with the fact that the rouble is used over so many regions with such diverse and divergent economies.

Let us return to the example of Europe. We saw in Chapter 5 that a fixed exchange rate regime is consistent with an independent monetary policy only in the very short run. In practice, this meant that ERM member countries found themselves forced to accept Bundesbank monetary discipline as the cost of remaining in the system.[29]

Now there are two ways of interpreting this fact.

On the one hand, ERM members by and large had far less convincing records of monetary discipline than Germany. By making a public commitment to accept the monetary discipline imposed by the Bundesbank, they hoped to be able to achieve relatively rapid credibility as low-inflation countries. They tried, as it were, to hitch a ride to their desired destination of credibility as low inflation countries on the Bundesbank's coattails. Without ERM membership, they would have been forced to tolerate far higher interest rates to compensate for the risk indicated by their pre-ERM history of relative laxity in monetary policy. Moreover, they would have had to sustain these high interest rates for as long as it took to convince markets that they really had changed their priorities and were now truly committed to permanently lower inflation. According to this view of events, while it survived the ERM allowed the UK, France and Italy to reduce their inflation at lower cost (in terms of lost output, high interest rates, unemployment and so on) than would have been possible outside the system. Of course, with the demise of the ERM this interpretation looks somewhat implausible.

On the other hand, the freedom to purchase short-term benefit at whatever cost in inflation might be regarded by some people as worth preserving. In so far as a country's inflation is the freely-chosen outcome of democratic choice, it is hard to see how it can be renounced without some meaningful loss of freedom.[30]

---

[29] That is to say, their interest rates followed German rates up or down, while in most cases (especially UK, France and Italy) remaining above German levels.

[30] Anyone who doubts this is the case ought to ask themselves the following question: why are Germany or Switzerland so zealous in their pursuit of low inflation, while the UK and, to a lesser extent the USA, are so much laxer? The answer surely relates ultimately to the priorities of voters in the different countries, embodied not only in their directly expressed preferences regarding inflation rates, but also in the institutional framework they erect. Thus, apart from obvious differences in the extent to which governments exert political control over monetary policy, one notable distinction is in the fact that both the USA and the UK have tax regimes that encourage people to invest in inflation. In the USA, tax relief is granted on consumer borrowing, but interest income on lending is for the most part taxable. In the UK, tax and other incentives have been used over the years to persuade Britons to invest in real estate, thereby giving them a significant stake in inflation.

The issue only becomes acute if there is actually a divergence between member countries' preferences in this regard. Of course, the very fact that Germany had so different an inflation history from the other major economies is prima facie evidence of just such a divergence in tastes prior to entry into the system. Was ERM entry ever likely *on its own* to trigger a change in tastes? Or was it expected somehow to make the transition from high to low-inflation country less painful than otherwise by signalling unambiguously to financial markets a change that had already taken place?

Alas, we shall never know whether ERM entry was actually accompanied by the requisite convergence of tastes, because the system was undermined by an unforeseen calamity rather similar to the one which destroyed Bretton Woods. It will be recalled that a sudden increase in spending by the USA on fighting its wars against communism in Vietnam and poverty at home ultimately proved fatal to the world's fixed exchange rate system in the early 1970s (Section 1.5.2). In a bizarre parallel, the effort to raise East German living standards to West German levels dealt a mortal blow to the ERM. This has been the outcome in spite of the fact that the reaction of the monetary authority in the centre countries was completely different in the two cases. While the Federal Reserve accommodated US Government spending in the late 1960s by printing dollars and generating worldwide inflation, the Bundesbank has so far preserved its independence in the 1990s by refusing to accommodate an avalanche of fiscal spending it had never endorsed in the first place.

The resulting high real interest rates effectively forced the other ERM members to devote their savings to funding the rebuilding of East Germany. Thus, whereas US overspending in the 1960s was paid for by an inflation tax on Bretton Woods member countries, the ERM meant that German overspending in the 1990s was financed by forced loans from its satellite countries. If given the choice, the other European countries might have preferred the inflation tax to the forced lending, or possibly neither. As it was, the UK and Italy eventually found the price too high and left the ERM, followed soon afterwards by a crisis which finally put an end to the fixed exchange rate system in all but name.

How will matters change when (or perhaps if) European monetary unification takes place?

Obviously, that will depend critically on the nature of the new supranational monetary authority. What the example of German unification ought to teach us is that the outcome will depend not only on which country's tastes predominate with regard to inflation, but also on the domestic preoccupations of the dominant nation at the time. Thus, the German aversion to inflation and consequent support for a tight money policy was reinforced by its own domestic problems in the 1990s.

Subject to this proviso, however, the outcome is bound to be some form of compromise involving inflation higher than would ideally be preferred by the low-inflation countries (Germany, Holland) and lower than would be chosen by the others. Indeed, it is at the moment so difficult to imagine a compromise between the monetary conservatism of the Bundesbank and the relative liberality of the Mediterranean countries that the prospect of monetary union appears remote, though the situation could change, especially if Germany itself becomes more inflation-prone.

As we shall see when we turn to a consideration of the transitional arrangements for EMU membership, it is anyway difficult to visualize the Mediterranean countries meeting the convergence criteria. At the time of writing, Germany itself has a budget deficit which is too high to satisfy the conditions, and is still rising rapidly.

10.3.4 The costs of transition

For the most part, this chapter has concentrated on the advantages and disadvantages of two possible scenarios: a number of regions with and without a common currency respectively. Little has been said about the transitional costs of moving from one scenario to the other. To some extent, this was because the costs of arriving at a common currency are difficult to assess, and would seem to depend on the specific circumstances in the region or regions involved.

At the macroeconomic level, there are *in principle* no transition costs. In practice, however, just as some people might think a happy marriage requires the engaged couple to start the process of compromise while they are still courting, in the same way the proponents of EMU have laid great emphasis on the need for a timetable of economic convergence to precede the currency union. This compromise process is embodied in the so-called **convergence criteria** set out in Table 10.1, which lay down the conditions member countries must satisfy if they are to be admitted to the currency union now due to start in 1999. The criteria are intended to guarantee the convergence of inflation rates and the imposition of a measure of fiscal rectitude prior to monetary unification. As such, they are not prerequisites for currency union, only of a currency union that works in the way those who specified the conditions hope it will.[31]

It is impossible to quantify the costs these convergence criteria impose on the member countries. In so far as they require governments to renounce to a large extent their discretion in setting both monetary and fiscal policy, they actually impose very tight constraints on national

---

[31] Many people appear to be under the impression that fiscal conditions are included in the convergence criteria simply as a temporary transitional measure. They remain blissfully unaware of the need for some considerable degree of permanent fiscal constraint on member governments, for the reasons given in the previous section. This author believes that many of them will find the reality rather unattractive, so that the prospects for monetary integration depend in this respect (and a number of others) on how soon the public at large is allowed to appreciate the full implications of the union they are entering.

Table 10.1   EMU convergence criteria.

Fiscal policy	
1. Budget deficit	< 3% of GDP
2. Government debt	< 60% of GDP
Monetary policy	
3. Inflation (RPI)	< 1.5% above 3 best-performing countries
4. Long-term inflation rates	< 2% above 3 best-performing countries

macroeconomic management.[32] It is worth noting that only two EU member countries satisfied the convergence criteria by 1993: France and Luxembourg. In fact, at the time of writing, it is difficult to imagine the Southern European countries meeting these conditions before the end of the decade at the earliest.

As far as microeconomic costs are concerned, there is an important (if obvious) point to be made, one which serves to emphasize the extent to which the contentious aspects of monetary union are inevitably political rather than economic. The point relates to the cost of changing over to a new currency.[33]

Consider the options facing an economic agent when a new currency is introduced. Where the individual has a choice between using a national currency and adopting a new common currency, the relative attractiveness of the two alternatives will depend on how many other people have already made the switch. Everybody waits for everybody else. Nobody wants to be a pioneer, the lone user of a new standard which is incompatible with everyone else, with no guarantee, moreover, that the others will ever make the switch. Equally, nobody wants to be left stranded on the old standard. It is a dilemma which is familiar to all of us from many similar situations where new standards are being introduced.[34]

---

[32] Compare, for example, the monetarist programme propounded by Milton Friedman in the 1960s and 1970s, which set limits on monetary policy alone. By contrast, the EU convergence criteria are more like the stabilization programmes imposed by the IMF on insolvent Third World countries.

For examples of how the criteria have actually impinged on countries' economic policy to date, one need only speculate on how different might have been the responses of national governments to the recession of the early 1990s and the collapse of the ERM in 1993 if they had not been committed to convergence. In particular, it is difficult to imagine Italian fiscal policy being as stringent as it actually was without the pretext of the need to meet the convergence criteria.

[33] See the reference to Dowd and Greenaway in the Reading Guide.

[34] Among instructive examples of this type of situation are the changeover to unleaded petrol (or catalytic converters in the USA), the conversion of PC users to MS-DOS and more recently to Windows (and the attempts to wean them off those standards), the struggle to persuade people to communicate through e-mail, and so on. The *ne plus ultra* of standardization projects must be the Esperanto language, which has made little headway after over a century of efforts by its enthusiasts, in spite of the fact that the balance of argument must be vastly more favourable to the notion of a common language than to a common currency. Of course, while the notion of a government imposing a common language is regarded as undemocratic, coercion is for some reason viewed as acceptable in the case of money.

There is no easy solution to this problem, which is precisely why, under the arrangements for EMU, it is not proposed to allow economic agents any such choice. The new currency will simply be imposed, while national currencies are simultaneously abolished.

Now there will undeniably be costs involved in actually switching over from the old to the new common currency: resetting millions of prices and relabelling millions of goods, recomputing wages, presumably rewriting many contracts, and so on and so forth. These costs are unavoidable, with one obvious and important exception. *They can be reduced to a minimum by adopting as a common currency a national money already in circulation.* The reason is simply that, in this way, the switching costs are nil for at least one nation in the new union.

For example, if the Deutsche Mark is chosen as the common currency for Europe, at least the Germans will be saved the costs of switching over to a new money, while the costs of the other member countries will be no greater than if the ECU had been adopted.[35] The fact that this solution is not actually being proposed is testimony to the predominance of politics over economics, which is characteristic of most aspects of the plans for EMU.[36]

10.3.5 Common currency and common market

Before leaving this topic, there is one important confusion which needs to be clarified. The confusion arises because many of the arguments used to support the idea of currency union in Europe have in reality little to do with the subject. In some cases, the supposed benefits are actually the outcome of integrating markets for goods and services, and sometimes also of allowing free movements of capital across national borders.

Now there are some situations where it is natural to think of currency union in the context of a single market. There is, however, no *necessary* connexion. A single market without currency union is quite possible to visualize, and indeed is perfectly feasible, and though the reverse seems improbable, it is not inconceivable either.

---

[35] It should be clear that the argument about the choice of currency to minimize transition costs has nothing to do with the question of who ultimately controls the money supply. Thus, although the DM would be optimal in terms of switching costs, it does not follow that post-unification monetary policy ought to be any different from what is desirable for a new currency.

[36] The analogy of a common language for Europe is instructive (see footnote (34)). Thus, it would be wasteful to adopt Esperanto, for the same reason a new European currency would be wasteful. The obvious, most economical choice of a *lingua franca* would be English, which is precisely why nobody is contemplating a common language for Europe.

Take the case of the USA. On the one hand, the USA is a more or less completely integrated market[37] with a single currency. On the other hand, in the recently founded North American Free Trade Association, it shows no sign of wanting currency unification with Canada and Mexico. Moreover, the fact that wages and prices still vary somewhat between the different US states would appear to suggest that inter regional price differentials usually stem from transport and other transaction costs, geographic and climatic variation and, most importantly for Europe, cultural heterogeneity. If this is the case, there would appear to be little prospect of any immediate narrowing of intra-European prices, whether currency union goes ahead or not.

In fact, it has been pointed out by Krugman (see the Reading Guide) that in one important respect currency union is actually less attractive in the context of an established single market. Remember McKinnon's argument that a currency union is justified where the individual economies are very open, and hence where exchange rate changes would have a large impact on consumption baskets and, consequently, on wages. On this view, if economies are very open, the option of being able to respond to disturbances by devaluing is not very useful.

However, thanks to the single market, European economies are likely to become progressively more specialized, as production concentrates in the lowest-cost locations. Inevitably, the result will be a greater vulnerability to shocks. For example, when (if ever) a truly free market in coal is established, whichever country ends up with the lion's share of European production will have an economy which is highly sensitive to fluctuations in world energy markets. Thus, while it may be true that currency union involves few sacrifices in coping with a *given* level of shocks, future disturbances are likely to be increasingly severe for individual European countries as they become more and more specialized and hence more and more dependent on a small number of industries. In these circumstances, they may well regret the sacrifice of their own currencies.

One further comment should be made regarding the political economy of international trade. Few economists would doubt that there is at the moment a serious danger of trade war in the industrialized world. To a great extent, the battle lines are already drawn up, in three groupings that have been gradually coalescing over a number of years: Europe, North

---

[37] Notice it is not a completely unified market in terms of goods and services. For example, the export of banking services between the States of the Union is limited by the Glass–Steagall Act, which restricts the extent to which banks can set up branches outside their home territory. Moreover, if harmonization of indirect tax rates (as envisaged in the Delors Plan for Europe) and of social security benefits (as in the Social Chapter of the Maastricht Treaty) are to be regarded as essential for a single market, then the USA is a highly fragmented market, with little or no apparent tendency toward integration. Of course, by any sensible criteria, for example, the degree of convergence of prices and wages across the country, the percentage of interstate relative to international trade, and so on, the USA is undeniably a single market, far more so than Europe.

America and the Far East. The almost interminable skirmishing over the Uruguay Round of the GATT agreement exposed the divisions very clearly. The fact that the negotiations ended reasonably successfully is not entirely reassuring in this regard.

Now the construction of the EU has undoubtedly played a major part in splitting the industrialized world into three blocs. While there is no *economic* reason why currency union should hasten the slide towards a trade war, there is every reason to fear that it may well do so in terms of the political economy of international trade.

10.4 Conclusions

The reader may feel that what has been presented here represents a some-what jaundiced view of the costs and benefits of monetary union. However, this is not necessarily the correct interpretation of the arguments presented in this chapter.

Instead, the position taken here has been that, at least as far as Europe is concerned, the *economic* arguments deployed in support of monetary union are in most cases overstated, in some cases misguided and in others unconfirmed by the evidence produced to date. That broad conclusion should not detract from any purely *political* arguments for or against currency unions, though this is not a subject on which judgement can be passed here.

■ Summary

- A monetary union is simply a special case of a fixed exchange rate system, where the exchange rate is fixed irrevocably at one-for-one. It follows that the advantages and disadvantages of currency unions are for the most part those of fixed exchange rate systems.

- A monetary union holds out the prospect of lower transaction costs in international trade and investment, but the scope for savings seems likely to be small.

- Firms involved in international trade and investment would gain from the elimination of exchange rate uncertainty. But it is in any case only their *net* exposure which is relevant, and this will often be relatively small for multinational corporations. Moreover, there are a number different ways in which currency exposure can be hedged at low or in some cases negligible cost.

- In principle, the larger the area covered by a common currency, the lower the cost of gathering price information. The theoretical benefits, however, are likely to be rather limited in practice, at least in the European context.

- The costs of currency union depend on the behaviour of national labour markets, but two contradictory arguments need to be considered.

- Extending currency zones over areas within which labour is mobile is costless. However, where labour markets are separate for reasons of distance, immigration controls, travel costs and so on, exchange rate flexibility is helpful in returning real wages to their equilibrium level in the aftermath of a shock. It follows that common currencies should apply only over areas *small* enough to be characterized by labour mobility.

- On the other hand, devaluation can only reduce real wages as a result of a form of money illusion, and the illusion is likely to be preserved most easily where the cost-of-living increase following devaluation is smallest, in other words in relatively closed economies. Hence, on these grounds, currency zones ought ideally to be *large* enough to behave like closed economies.

- One of the few meaningful differences between common currencies and fixed exchange rates is in terms of the political economy of international policymaking. Because fixed exchange rate systems tend to impose the burden of adjustment on deficit countries, they probably suffer an inbuilt deflationary bias, while common currency zones may well suffer from an inflationary bias.

- It is hard to see how a currency union between a number of countries can avoid imposing constraints on the fiscal policies of the different ('local') authorities unless it is willing to contemplate a national government becoming insolvent.

- The question of sovereignty cannot be avoided in determining the complexion of monetary policy within a currency union. If national monetary policy reflects national tastes, it remains an open question how these tastes can or should be aggregated to determine a supranational monetary policy.

- There is no necessary connection between currency union and a common ('single') market. Currency union would be possible without integration of commodity markets, and the opposite is not only theoretically possible, but a commonplace occurrence.

READING GUIDE

The seminal contributions are Mundell (1961) and McKinnon (1963), though see also their very important precursors in Meade (1955) and Friedman (1953).

For a useful collection of readings on the topics covered in this chapter, see the Greek Economic Review, 1993, and in particular the contributions by Krugman, Frenkel and Goldstein and Christou and Dellas. This volume also contains the paper by Dowd and Greenaway mentioned in Section 10.3.3. The evidence on labour mobility within the USA mentioned in Section 10.2.1 was collected by Blanchard and Katz (1992) and quoted in Krugman (1993).

Feldstein (1993) covers many of the points raised here.

Part III

A World of Uncertainty

So far, we have only acknowledged the existence of uncertainty so as to sweep it aside and avoid having to deal with it explicitly. In this part, we confront the issues it raises, starting in Chapter 11 with the introduction of the concepts of rational expectations, market efficiency and unbiasedness. In this context, it is shown that the spot exchange rate can be thought of as containing three components: (1) the forward rate, reflecting market anticipations, (2) other, unobservable random components, resulting from 'news' about the fundamentals and (3) a risk premium. Chapters 11–13 deal with components (1) to (3) respectively. While the subject matter of the first two chapters overlaps somewhat, Chapter 13 is very different, since it analyses the determination of the equilibrium risk premium using the microeconomics of choice under uncertainty. Chapter 14 examines the mathematics of non-linear systems so as to explain another possible cause of exchange rate volatility, one which is only now being investigated by researchers.

11

Market Efficiency and Rational Expectations

■ Introduction

The idea of market efficiency is one we have already encountered in Chapter 3. Recall that an efficient market was defined there as one in which prices fully reflect all available information. In this chapter, we go into the subject in greater depth, and in particular see how market efficiency relates to the concepts of rational expectations and unbiasedness.

   Although market efficiency made its first appearance in the finance literature some two decades ago, the basic idea should be familiar. At some time or other, we have all been given a 'hot tip' on a horse, or a share, or nowadays perhaps even on a 'collectable' antique, *objet d'art* or painting. In order to profit from the tipster's information, it has to be true that the quoted odds on the horse, for example, fail to reflect its true prospects ('it can't lose', 'it's a dead cert' and so on). In

313

the case of the share tipster, if we are to make money, we need to know more than simply that company X is going to make large profits. We also need to be sure that those profits are underestimated by the stock market, and hence not fully reflected ('undiscounted') in its current price. Similarly, before investing in a painting, we need to be convinced not simply that it is good, but that its true worth has yet to be fully appreciated by the rest of the art world.[1]

The obvious question to ask before acting on a tip is: can we really believe the market has failed to take account of the true prospects for the horse, share, or painting, as the case may be? If our tipster has access to information which is not publicly available, we may be inclined to believe him, on the grounds that the horse's odds or the price of the share is unlikely to reflect 'inside' information, almost by definition.[2] However, if our tipster has no privileged access to information, we are unlikely to be impressed, unless there is some obvious reason why the rest of the market should be so sluggish in the first place.

In a sense, market efficiency is simply a special case of a fundamental principle of economics, one we have already encountered a number of times in this book. In essence, it is the application of the 'no free lunch' argument to the field of information, because in so far as the market price fails to incorporate publicly available information, there must exist unexploited profit opportunities.

Our concern in this chapter is with the consequences of market efficiency for the relationship between spot and forward exchange rates. In the first section, as an essential preliminary to the material in this part of the book, we explain what is meant by an expected value. (Readers who are familiar with elementary statistics can safely skip the section.) This concept is central both to the rational expectations hypothesis, which is the subject of Section 11.2, and to the idea of market efficiency, covered in the next section. We go on to look at two special cases of market efficiency: unbiasedness and the random walk model, in Sections 11.4 and 11.5 respectively.

When we turn to look at the facts, we find that there are some very severe difficulties to be overcome in arriving at any kind of test of

---

[1] We are, of course, considering the painting purely as an investment, abstracting from any non-pecuniary value that it may give to its owner.

[2] It is, however, not completely impossible for the market price to incorporate inside information. For example, in the equity market, once it becomes clear to market participants, or at least to a sufficient number of them, that a particular individual habitually trades on the basis of inside information, they can benefit from a 'free ride' by mimicking his trading pattern. In the process, they may cause the market price to behave exactly as though the inside information were publicly available. Arguments like these have led some people to argue that insider trading ought to be legalized.

the theories outlined in this chapter. These problems are described in Section 11.6. Some of them are apparent simply from an 'eyeball' scan of the data, as is shown in the next section. However, more rigorous methods have been applied by the many researchers in this field and their work is briefly surveyed in Section 11.8. The chapter ends, as usual, with some conclusions, a Summary and a Reading Guide.

11.1 Mathematical expected value

As a preliminary to the exposition in this section, we introduce a concept taken directly from the theory of statistics.[3]

> The (mathematical)[4] **expectation** or **expected value** of a (random) variable, X, written $E(X)$, is the weighted average of all possible outcomes, where the weight on any outcome is equal to its probability.

Since this concept is an important building-block for what follows in this and succeeding chapters, it is worth looking at a very simple example. Imagine a lottery, in which 300 tickets are sold, half of which (that is, 150) will win no prize at all. Of the remaining 150 tickets, half will win a prize of £1 and half the top prize of £5. To demonstrate what is meant by a mathematical expectation, the expected value of a ticket in the lottery has been calculated (see Table 11.1).

Now consider the value of a lottery ticket to a potential purchaser. In the first column, we have listed all three of the possible outcomes resulting from the purchase of a single ticket, and in the second column the probability of each outcome actually occurring. In Column 3, we put the product of the value of the outcome to the ticket-holder (that is, the prize) and the probability of it occurring. In Column 3, therefore, we have a zero whenever we are dealing with an outcome valued at zero, as in the first row of the figure, or whenever we are dealing with an outcome which has zero probability. Of course, there are an infinite number of outcomes with a zero probability weighting (that is, impossible events), all of which can safely be ignored since they contribute nothing to the total at the bottom of Column 3. On the other hand, we must include all outcomes which are associated both with a positive probability and a non-zero prize value.

---

[3] For more details, see any textbook in mathematical statistics or probability.

[4] Where there is no possibility of confusion, it is normal to refer simply to 'the expectation' or 'expected value' of a variable, with the *mathematical* expectation understood.

Table 11.1   How to calculate an expected value.

	2	3	4	5
Outcome of Ticket Purchase: Prize Value	Probability of Outcome	Product (1) × (2)	Error (1) − E(X)	Product (4) × (2)
£0	0.50	£0.00	−£1.50	−£0.750
£1	0.25	£0.25	−£0.50	−£0.125
£5	0.25	£1.25	+£3.50	+£0.875
Expected value of ticket: E(X)		£1.50	Expected value of error: E[X − E(X)]	£0.000

Notice that the probability weights in Column 2 add up to one, since we have taken account of all possible outcomes of the lottery. In that sense, the expected value of £1.50, calculated by totalling Column 3, is a weighted average.[5]

Since we could in principle compute the expected value for any prospect, however complicated, it should be clear that the expected value has considerable superficial attractiveness as the best single number to use in comparing alternative risky propositions. More importantly, it corresponds to what we might intuitively feel to be the best guess of a person's likely winnings, in the sense that, if we took a random sample of 10 ticket holders, the chances are they would win an average prize of £1.50 each.

Notice the paradoxical situation: the average prize is 'the most likely outcome' for the average taken over a random sample, or for an individual's average winnings if the lottery is repeated a number of times. Yet, at the same time, we can be absolutely certain that not a single ticket will actually end up winning £1.50.[6] A more intelligent guess for a single individual would be to take the most-frequently occurring outcome, or modal value, as it is called, which in this case is a zero prize.

---

[5] The reader may check for himself that if the probabilities of the three outcomes had been equal (that is, one third each), the expected value calculated in Column 3 would have turned out to be exactly the same as the (unweighted) average, or arithmetic mean, in other words (£0+£1+£5)/3 equals £2. We could, in this special case, safely ignore the probability weighting.

   Some readers might find it helpful to think of the mathematical expectation as analogous to a centre of gravity for the distribution of the outcomes.

[6] Of course, most of us have encountered this paradox before in the case of social statistics, for example, the average number of children per household or the average number of cars per person.

There is another sense in which the expected value provides the best forecast. In Column 4, we see the errors that would be made by someone using the expected value of £1.50 as a forecast of the pay-off to holding a ticket. Thus, if the outcome turned out to be a zero prize, the error made would be −£1.50, if it turned out to be £1.00, the error would be only −£0.50, and in the event that the ticket won the big prize the error would be +£3.50. Column 5 weights these errors by the probability of their occurrence, 0.5, 0.25 and 0.25 respectively, to arrive at their weighted average, in other words the expected value of the error. As can be seen, the expected error is zero, with overestimates exactly offsetting underestimates.

This calculation illustrates a very important property of expected values. What we have found is that, even in cases where the outcome is never equal to (or anywhere near equal to) the expected value, *a forecast based on it will still be correct on average.* Even though I know a lottery ticket picked at random will not win £1.50, that remains my best guess. Since, by definition of a mathematical expectation, the best forecast of the error is that it will be zero, there are no grounds for adjusting it either up or down.

Unfortunately, most decisions involving uncertainty are a lot more complicated than our hypothetical lottery. This is the case not only because we typically have to deal with far more complicated prospects, with a greater number of possible outcomes and consequently more difficult computations. Most important of all, it is really only in games of chance that we can be sure of the probabilities that are attached to the outcomes – which is precisely why examples like these figure so largely in textbook expositions of probability theory. In real-world situations, for example when we are forced to take a view about the future value of the exchange rate, there is no equivalent of the rulebook to tell us how many tickets have been sold and how many prizes are on offer. In this respect, we have to deal with a genuine forecasting problem, rather than a purely arithmetic exercise like the one in this worked example.

In practice, what we have to do is to make use of whatever relevant information is available, so as to arrive at an assessment of the probability of each possible outcome for the future exchange rate. From that point onward, the computation of the expected value is straightforward, as we have seen. What information will be used in arriving at an estimate of the probabilities? That will depend on the circumstances, but in principle any information which is relevant could be of use. We shall have much more to say on this question later. For the moment, we introduce an important extension of the concept of expected value:

The conditional (mathematical) expectation of a variable, X_t, written $E(X_t | I_{t-j})$ is the expected value computed with the aid of a particular set of facts, I_{t-j}, known as the **conditioning information set**.

The definition might appear to the reader too vague to be of practical application. After all what does it mean to say 'computed *with the aid of information*'? In fact, provided the conditioning set contains only quantifiable information, the problem is more apparent than real, since statistics and econometrics have established well-researched techniques for deriving an estimate of the expected value of a variable from the observed values of a set of conditioning variables.

11.2 Rational expectations[7]

We are now in a position to introduce the concept of rationality in expectations.

Consider a hypothetical agent in the foreign currency market.[8] Until now, we have taken for granted that all such individuals hold to some view or other of what is likely to be the value of the spot exchange rate in the future, and we have called that view 'the representative investor's expectation' or 'the market expectation'. From now on, since there is a possibility of confusion, let us refer to this as the investor's *subjective expectation*. It is subjective in the sense that it is 'inside the investor's head', unobservable and unquantifiable, other than by asking the agents directly.[9]

In particular, a subjective expectation need bear no specific, clearly defined relationship to the facts – which is not to say that it is formed without any reference whatever to the facts, simply that the relationship between a *subjective* expectation and the *objective* data is purely arbitrary. That is precisely why, so far, nothing has been said about how the investor arrives at his subjective forecast. It might be by pure intuition, by a more visceral 'gut reaction', or by consulting charts showing past movements in exchange rates or other variables. It might be with the aid of astrology, or it could be by frequenting the same places as the foreign currency traders and listening to their gossip. A subjective expectation is simply one held by

---

[7] The reader would be well advised to look back at Section 3.4 before proceeding.

Note that, for the most part, we ignore transaction costs throughout this and succeeding chapters. In practice, they are a negligible factor in currency markets, and in any case, allowing for them would change our conclusions only minimally and in straightforward ways.

It should be understood, however, that these remarks refer exclusively to the cost of actually dealing (brokerage commissions and so on). They certainly do *not* apply to the costs of collecting and processing information, which may well be very substantial, and whose existence may well have very important effects, some of which are considered in the text.

[8] We restrict attention to the currency markets at this point. In fact, the rational expectations hypothesis was developed in the context of (closed economy) macroeconomics, and has been applied to markets as diverse as those for financial instruments, labour, capital goods, consumer goods, shares, insurance and no doubt many others.

[9] For example, by survey methods. For some years, a number of economists in the USA have gone 'straight to the horse's mouth' in researching market expectations.

the individual in question, in other words *one which is not necessarily the same as the conditional expected value of the variable in question.*

Now suppose it happened to be the case that the two *were* the same. Suppose that an investor did hold a subjective expectation which happened to be the same as the (objective) conditional mathematical expectation. Furthermore, suppose the same state of affairs applied to the market as a whole, or at least to a majority of market participants. As we shall see, a number of important conclusions would follow from that fact with regard to the relationship between spot and forward exchange rates. For the moment, we introduce the following definition to refer to situations like this:

> An economic agent is said to hold a **(fully) rational expectation** with respect to a variable if his subjective expectation is the same as the variable's (mathematical) expected value, conditional on an information set containing all publicly available information. The **Rational Expectations (RE) hypothesis** states that the market's (subjective) expectations are in fact the same as the expected value, conditional on the set of all available information.

Put more loosely, an investor whose expectations are rational does the best that he (or anyone else) could do in forecasting the future exchange rate. A point worth noting, however, is that, for an expectation to be rational, it does not need to have actually been derived by performing any particular set of calculations, neither of the kind in the lottery example considered earlier on, nor of any other kind. It might have been calculated in a way we feel is completely subjective, or even by methods viewed as downright irrational, such as astrology, chartism, or whatever. As long as the outcome is a number that coincides with the objective conditional expectation, it is rational in the economist's sense of the term. Putting the matter differently, we could say that experienced traders, whose livelihoods depend on their ability to keep ahead of the market, behave *as if* they computed expected values.[10]

---

[10] Those familiar with elementary microeconomics will recognize the force of the 'as if' caveat. Consumers, for example, are assumed to maximize satisfaction without even knowing the meaning of the term 'marginal rate of substitution', let alone computing it and consciously equating it to the price ratio. Likewise, firms are supposed to maximize profits without, in most cases, consciously setting marginal cost equal to marginal revenue. The assumption is that, whatever considerations guide their decision making, they behave, on average, as if they follow the operating principles necessary to result in a profit-maximizing output choice.

If all this seems far-fetched, given the enormous difficulties in actually calculating the RE value of the future exchange rate, consider the following analogies from outside economics. If we wished to model the behaviour of a car driver, calculating whether or not he has time to overtake in traffic, we would have to build a horrendously complicated mathematical model of speeds of convergence, rates of acceleration and so on. We would then assume that the driver behaved as if he solved the problem instantaneously when deciding whether or not to overtake. Similarly, programming a snooker-playing robot to apply the correct force to the cue, so as to play even the simplest shot would involve some very involved mathematics indeed.

In each case, what we call a person's judgement, intuition or experience results in a short cut to the solution of an apparently complex mathematical problem.

Now, if we recall the properties of the mathematical expectation, we can see what is implied by the RE assumption. If investors are rational in forming their expectations they will often be wrong, in fact they may be wrong all the time (as in the lottery example), but however large their errors, *on average* they will be correct. In this respect, their behaviour is consistent with the traditional view of rational economic man. The rewards to being correct are large, potentially unlimited (at least in principle). It would therefore be irrational to employ any forecasting method that could be improved. Any forecasting process that generates systematic errors – that is, errors that exhibit a non-random pattern, however complicated – can be improved by a method that exploits the pattern in the errors. It would therefore be irrational of agents not to squeeze this remaining element of forecastability out of the data.

Consider the implications for an observer, an economist, say, watching the behaviour of rational investors. If he can build a model, however complicated, which forecasts more accurately than the subjective expectations of the agents in the market, then by definition their expectations cannot be rational. If, on the other hand, their expectations are truly rational, they will be identical with those emerging from the best model that the economist can build, putting all the available information to the best possible use. In this respect, RE can be viewed as a consistency requirement: if the economist believes in a particular model of the economy (or of a part of it), he must believe that agents form expectations consistent with its prediction.[11]

Before going any further, it would be as well to write the RE hypothesis formally. Up to this point, we have used S^e to denote the spot exchange rate that agents expect to see prevailing one period hence (say, at time $t + 1$, assuming that the current period is time t). Under RE, that subjective market expectation will be the same as the mathematical expectation of the next period's spot rate, conditional on a particular information set, the one containing all publicly available information. In terms of the notation introduced along with the definition in the last section, this conditional expectation is $E(S_{t+1} | I_t)$, where I_t is the set of all data in the public domain at time t. Since we will often have cause to refer to expectations conditional on this broad set of publicly available information at some period or other, we shall use the abbreviation, E_t. So $E_t S_{t+1}$ means the expected value of the period $t + 1$ spot rate, conditional on information

---

[11] For this reason, it might have been better if the theory had been called the consistent expectations hypothesis.

Note the paradox. The applied economist expends vast amounts of time, computer power and such brainpower as he can muster in an effort to arrive at the true model, while laymen operating in the market know the model and its predictions all along, or at least, behave as if they do. In this respect, the RE hyphothesis turns traditional approaches to economic modelling on their heads. Instead of models that assume an omniscient economist observing blinkered agents, we now have (almost) omniscient agents being observed by ignorant economists. Surely, such humility is unparalleled in any other profession?

available to the market at t. Similarly, $E_{t-j}S_{t+k}$ means the expectation of the period $t+k$ exchange rates, based on information dated $t-j$ or earlier.[12]

Using this notation, RE implies that market expectations can be written:

$$s_t^e = E(s_{t+1} \mid I_t) \equiv E_t s_{t+1} \qquad\qquad (11.1)$$

where the lower case s means the natural logarithm of the exchange rate.

It is normal to specify the RE hypothesis in terms of logarithms so as to avoid a problem in translating from pounds per dollar to dollars per pound. Obviously, it would be desirable to have a situation where, if the market anticipated an exchange rate of £1 = \$2.00 at some point in the future, it also expected to see at the same date that \$1 = £0.50. Since the sterling price of dollars, S, is the reciprocal of the dollar price of sterling, $1/S$, this amounts to requiring that the market's (subjective) expectation of S is the reciprocal of its (subjective) expectation of $1/S$, in other words that:

$$S^e = 1/\left(\frac{1}{S}\right)^e$$

or, alternatively that:

$$\frac{1}{S^e} = \left(\frac{1}{S}\right)^e$$

Unfortunately, however, it is a feature of the mathematical expected value that it does *not*, in general, satisfy this criterion. In other words by and large:[13]

$$\frac{1}{E(X)} \neq E\left(\frac{1}{X}\right)$$

The advantage of specifying Equation 11.1 in log terms is that, since the log of S is simply the negative of the log of $(1/S)$, we have $-E(\log S) = E(-\log S)$ or, in the shorthand introduced earlier in the book: $-E(s) = E(-s)$, and the problem is solved.

---

[12] We assume that information is never lost. In other words, the market's knowledge never decreases as time passes. New information arrives and is added to the information set, without anything ever being forgotten – at least, not if it is relevant to the expectation. It follows that the information set at any time includes all previously available information, plus whatever 'latest news' arrives during the period. So comparing $E_{t-5}S_{t+1}$ and $E_{t-4}S_{t+1}$ for example, if the two differ at all, the latter will be the more accurate forecast, as a result of new information arriving during the period $t-5$. If no new information that bears on the exchange rate for $t+1$ arrives during that period, then the two forecasts will be identical, since $I_{t-4} = I_{t-5}$. What can never arise is a situation where the later expectation is less accurate than an earlier one.

[13] This characteristic of expected values is known as Jensen's inequality.

Note that Equation 11.1 formalizes the RE assumption about the market's (period t) expectation of the period $t + 1$ exchange rate. Ask yourself the question: under RE, what will have determined the exchange rate the market expected at $t - 1$ for the current period, t? Plainly, at $t - 1$, the information set available consisted only of I_{t-1}, hence:

$$s_{t-1}^e = E(s_t | I_{t-1}) \equiv E_{t-1} s_t \tag{11.1'}$$

and so on.

Before going on to consider the implications for market efficiency, it will be helpful to introduce one more definition. Since the cost of collecting and processing information (measured in terms of effort, time or money) can be prohibitive, even when the information is in principle accessible, there may well be circumstances where rational individuals base their expectations on only a subset of the available data. In a sense, this is what we mean by 'a rule of thumb': trading a measure of accuracy, which may not always be needed, for convenience and speed, which certainly are needed, particularly in guiding day-to-day, hour-to-hour trading decisions.

One possible simplification would be for agents to limit themselves to looking at the past history of the series being forecast. For example, they might form their forecasts of the future exchange rate by deriving the best possible prediction, based solely on the history of the exchange rate over the more or less recent past. In other words, faced at time t with the problem of predicting the future exchange rate, S_{t+1}, they might simplify the task by limiting the conditioning information set to the series of past exchange rates: S_t, S_{t-1}, S_{t-2}, S_{t-3}...[14] We introduce the following definition:[15]

> An economic agent will be said to hold **weakly rational expectations** with respect to a variable if his subjective expectation is the same as the variable's (mathematical) expected value conditional on an information set containing only the past history of the variable being forecast. Formally, weak rationality implies subjective expectations of the variable, X_t, are given by:
>
> $$X_t^e = E(X_t | X_{t-1}, X_{t-2}, X_{t-3}, X_{t-4}, \ldots)$$

Notice that a weakly rational expectation can never be a better forecast than a fully rational one, and will usually be a poorer one. From now on, rational expectations will always be assumed to be *fully rational* – that is, conditioned on all publicly available information – unless we explicitly state otherwise.

---

[14] We assume here and throughout the book that the values of all variables subscripted t are actually known at time t.

[15] This definition is not in standard usage. It is introduced largely for consistency with the widely-used concept of weak form efficiency, which will be introduced in Section 11.3.

11.3 Market efficiency

Having dealt with market expectations, we now refocus attention on the way the currency market operates. Suppose the forward and spot markets are characterized by the following conditions:

(1) The presence of a number of investors with ample funds available for arbitrage operations when opportunities present themselves.

(2) The absence of barriers to movement of funds (no exchange controls).

(3) Negligible transaction costs.

Now consider the following scenario. Imagine a British investor who thinks that the spot price of dollars in terms of sterling is going to be 10% higher in twelve months than it is today. Will he be able to profit from his hunch?

Plainly, if he is willing to back his judgement, and transaction costs are negligible, he may be able to profit by buying dollars (selling pounds) forward, then selling the dollars spot at the end of 12 months. If he proves right, his profit will be 10%, less any transaction costs, *less the premium paid for forward dollars.*

However, if the same view is shared by the rest of the market, or at least by investors with access to sufficient funds, the situation cannot persist. In the absence of any impediment, the forward dollar will be bid up until the premium is high enough to deter any further speculation.

At what point will the forward premium be sufficiently high to deter speculators? It is tempting to argue that speculation will continue until the forward exchange rate has reached a point at which it is just equal to the consensus view of the future spot rate at the relevant horizon. That would be going too far, however. At some point, investors will feel that, although they can still see the likelihood of a profit from speculation, *the probable reward is no longer great enough to compensate for the risk of being wrong.* In other words, speculation will cease (equilibrium will be reached) at the point where the gap between the forward rate and the market's expectation of the future spot rate is just equal to the required risk premium.

Now if we assume the market's expectations are rational, we can write this equilibrium as follows:

$$f_t^{t+1} = E_t s_{t+1} + \rho_t \tag{11.2}$$

where the left-hand side is the (log of the) forward price of dollars at time t for delivery one period later (at $t + 1$), and ρ_t is the market's risk premium.

Equation 11.2 represents an efficient market equilibrium[16] because the forward rate reflects both the publicly available information summarized in the rational expectation, $E_t s_{t+1}$, and the market's attitude to risk, as embodied in the risk premium.

To see the implications, rewrite Equation 11.2 by subtracting s_{t+1} from both sides, to give:

$$f_t^{t+1} - s_{t+1} = [E_t s_{t+1} - s_{t+1}] + \rho_t \qquad (11.3)$$

$$= u_{t+1} + \rho_t$$

The crucial term is u_{t+1}. It has been substituted for the expression in the square brackets on the right-hand side, which is simply the percentage gap between what the market expected the exchange rate to be at $t + 1$ and the actual outcome. Now since, by assumption, the market's expectation is rational, that error will have very special properties, as we have seen. Specifically, it will be strictly random, showing no discernible pattern – with a mean value of zero and correlated neither with contemporaneous nor past spot or forward rates. In particular, u_{t+1} viewed in isolation will show no systematic pattern of variation over time.[17] The reason for this is that under RE, as we have seen, the expectational error must itself be unpredictable, otherwise potentially profitable information remains unexploited.

Equation 11.3 summarizes the efficient market hypothesis as stating that the gap between the forward rate and the spot rate actually ruling when the forward contract matures (the left-hand side) is the sum of two components: a completely random expectational error and a risk premium. The latter could be positive or negative, constant or variable, large or small relative to the expectation error – in the absence of any knowledge about investors' attitudes to risk, we are in no position to judge.

Finally, notice that Equation 11.3 implies:

$$s_{t+1} = -\rho_t + f_t^{t+1} - u_{t+1} \qquad (11.4)$$

or alternatively, shifting the process back one period:

$$s_t = -\rho_{t-1} + f_{t-1}^t - u_t \qquad (11.4')$$

which implies that the spot rate can be viewed as the sum of three components: the previous period's forward rate, plus the risk premium ruling in the market at the time, plus an unpredictable, expectational error. This

---

[16] Strictly speaking, the interpretation of efficiency given here corresponds to what Fama (1970) calls semi-strong form efficiency. Strong form efficiency applies when the market price reflects *all* information, whether publicly available or not. Since inside information is not usually regarded as important in currency markets, we ignore this distinction here.

[17] In the jargon of statistics, the time series u_t will be pure white noise, that is with a (theoretical) zero autocorrelation function and zero cross correlations with, in other words, other variables whose values are known at time t.

general relationship is the subject of the remainder of the present chapter. The next two chapters will focus on the factors determining the unpredicted component, u_t, and the risk premium, ρ_t.

In terms of estimation, which we shall consider at greater length in Section 11.4, notice that unless we are willing to make some assumptions about how the risk premium is determined, Equation 11.4 does not allow us to relate the spot rate time series to the series of forward rates observed one period earlier. However, if we are happy to impose some kind of tractable structure on the risk premium (for example, that it is constant over time, or that it fluctuates randomly about its mean value, or whatever), then we can proceed to test whether the spot rate and forward rate are related in the way predicted by the efficient market hypothesis.

Finally, notice it is quite possible to imagine a situation where the market price reflects only the restricted information set used in forming weakly rational expectations. In this case, the expected values in Equations 11.2 and 11.3 would be conditioned only on the past history of the exchange rate, rather than on the universe of publicly available information.

> **A weakly efficient market** is one where the market price reflects the information in its own past history. There are therefore no unexploited opportunities to profit by making use of the price series alone.

Notice that, in a weakly efficient market, there will normally remain opportunities to make a profit by exploiting information *additional* to the past history of the market price.

11.4 Unbiasedness

In Section 11.2 we saw what was involved in assuming that expectations were formed rationally. In the next section, we made additional assumptions about the way the currency market functions so as to allow us to follow through the implications of the efficient market hypothesis. In the present section, we take the process one stage further. In addition to the assumptions embodied in forward market efficiency, let us make the simplest possible assumption about investors' attitudes to risk: *suppose they are risk neutral*.

We saw in Section 3.1.3 that risk neutrality meant, by definition, that market agents required no risk premium to persuade them to undertake risky transactions. In the present instance, that means they are willing to speculate on their judgement as to the future spot rate for no reward – or at least, up to the point where the reward is negligible. In other words, they will push the forward rate to the point where it is equal to the rationally expected future spot rate, so that ρ_{t-1} in Equation 11.4' is reduced to zero.

At that point, we will have:

$$s_t = f^t_{t-1} - u_t \tag{11.5}$$

that is, the spot rate is simply the forward rate that was set in the previous period, plus or minus a random error. We shall refer to this restricted form of forward market efficiency as the unbiasedness hypothesis.[18] Formally:

> **Unbiasedness** will be said to obtain when the forward market is efficient and investors are risk neutral, so that the forward rate is equal to the (mathematical) expectation of the spot rate at the time the contract matures.

Notice that Equation 11.5 can be rewritten in terms of the rate of depreciation, by taking s_{t-1} from both sides to give:

$$s_t - s_{t-1} = (f^t_{t-1} - s_{t-1}) - u_t \tag{11.5'}$$

which says that the actual rate of change in the exchange rate is equal to the one anticipated in advance, as reflected in the previous period's forward premium or discount (in parentheses on the right-hand side), plus or minus a random error.

Consider the implication for exchange rate forecasting. If Equation 11.5 is a true description of the way that currency markets operate, the forward rate we actually observe at any time is actually an optimal forecast of the next period's spot rate, in the sense that it will be proved wrong only to the extent of a random error. As we have seen, that means it cannot be improved upon by any other forecast using publicly available data. In fact, since there is little in the way of inside information[19] in currency markets, we can say categorically that unbiasedness implies that the forward rate cannot be bettered as a forecast.

11.5 The random walk model

As already noted, the concept of an efficient market was developed in the finance literature, where it was applied for the most part to the operation of stock markets. The theory was developed to explain an apparent regularity in share prices observed by statisticians examining time-series patterns in stock markets. What the statisticians found was that stock prices seemed to follow a pattern known as a random walk. Ever since then the

---

[18] Though this usage is by no means universal. A number of writers identify Equation 11.5 with efficiency, which seems over-restrictive, while Bilson (1981) calls this condition speculative efficiency.

[19] It could be argued that knowledge of day-to-day central bank intervention policy constitutes inside information. Even so, it is hard to imagine this knowledge actually giving central banks a forecasting edge over the market.

notion of a random walk and an efficient market have been associated in many people's minds, though there is in fact no necessary connection, as will be demonstrated later.

First, the definition:

A time series, X_t, is said to follow a (pure) **random walk** if the change in X_t from one period to the next is purely random, that is, if we have:

$$X_t = X_{t-1} + u_t \qquad (11.6)$$

or alternatively:

$$X_t - X_{t-1} = \Delta X_t = u_t \qquad (11.6')$$

where u_t is *completely random*, displaying no pattern over time.

Slightly more generally:

A time series, X_t, is said to follow a **random walk with drift**, d, if the change in X_t from one period to the next is equal to the drift factor, d, plus a purely random component, that is, if we have:

$$X_t = X_{t-1} + d + u_t \qquad (11.7)$$

or alternatively:

$$X_t - X_{t-1} = \Delta X_t = d + u_t \qquad (11.7')$$

where u_t is completely random, displaying no pattern over time.

Now, as far as exchange rates are concerned, it is easy to show that:

(1) The random walk model is perfectly compatible with RE, efficiency and unbiasedness.

but that, on the other hand:

(2) There is nothing in RE, efficiency or unbiasedness that *requires* the spot rate to follow a random walk.

Take RE first. If the spot rate follows a random walk with drift:

$$s_t = s_{t-1} + d + u_t \qquad (11.8)$$

then, taking expectations in Equation 11.8 conditional on the information set at $t - 1$, we have:

$$E_{t-1} s_t = E_{t-1} s_{t-1} + E_{t-1} d + E_{t-1} u_t \qquad (11.9)$$
$$= s_{t-1} + d$$

because s_{t-1} is presumed known at time $t - 1$, so is the (constant) drift factor, d, and because the expected value of the next period's random error, u_t, is always zero. Hence, with a random walk, the RE forecast of the next period's spot rate is simply the currently observed rate plus or minus the drift factor, if any. In the absence of drift, an agent's best guess is that the next period's rate will be the same as the current rate. In fact, the reader will find it is quite straightforward to demonstrate[20] that, at time $t-1$, s_{t-1} is the RE forecast of the spot rate in *all* future periods, in the absence of any drift.

In terms of the *change* in the spot rate, the pure random walk model implies that agents with rational expectations forecast neither depreciation nor appreciation over the next period.

On the other hand, suppose that the spot rate does *not* follow a random walk. Take, for example, the following process:

$$s_t = \alpha s_{t-1} + \beta s_{t-2} + \gamma Z_t + \delta Z_{t-1} + u_t \tag{11.10}$$

where Z is some other variable (for example, the relative money stock). Since past values of both s and Z are assumed known at $t-1$, we have as the RE forecast of the next period's spot rate:

$$E_{t-1}s_t = \alpha s_{t-1} + \beta s_{t-2} + \gamma E_{t-1}Z_t + \delta Z_{t-1} \tag{11.11}$$

which, although more complicated than a random walk, is no less acceptable.

It is now easy to see that both efficiency and unbiasedness of the forward market are potentially consistent with *any* of these processes: the random walk (Equation 11.8), or the example of a more general process, (Equation 11.10), or indeed any other process. Looking back at our formal definition of forward market efficiency in Equation 11.2 it is obvious that, for a random walk, we will have simply:

$$f_t^{t+1} = s_t + \rho_t \tag{11.12}$$

in other words, the forward rate ruling at t for delivery at $t+1$ will be equal to the spot rate in the market at t plus the risk premium. Under unbiasedness (in other words, with risk neutrality) the forward rate fixed at any period will be simply that period's spot rate, so that the forward premium will always be zero.

On the other hand, with the spot rate generated by Equation 11.10 efficiency implies that the forward rate is given by Equation 11.11 plus any risk premium.

It has been demonstrated that a random walk is neither necessary nor sufficient for forward market efficiency. Nonetheless, it is worth giving an intuitive explanation of why a random walk is not a necessary implication of the 'no free lunch' condition. It might seem, at first glance, that any process other than a random walk leaves open the opportunity for profit. Certainly, it is true that the expected return from holding the currency over a single period, which is the same as the change in the (log of the)

---

[20] By repeated substitution, writing each future period's spot rate as the previous period's rate plus a random error.

spot rate, will only be zero if the spot rate follows a random walk. In virtually all other cases, the return will be predictably non-zero. How can this fact be reconciled with efficiency?

The crucial point to understand is that as long as any predictable component in the spot rate depreciation is fully embodied in the forward rate, as it will be in an efficient market, the opportunity for profit is illusory. Suppose that the spot rate is actually generated as in Equation 11.10, so that the expected spot is given by Equation 11.11. Subtract the latter from the former to give:

$$s_t - E_{t-1}s_t = \gamma(Z_t - E_{t-1}Z_t) + u_t \qquad \textbf{(11.13)}$$

as the profit made by a speculator paying the rationally expected spot rate at $t-1$ and selling on the spot in the next period. Now although this profit is likely to be non-zero in any particular instance, it is *on average* zero, as can be seen by taking expectations conditional on $t-1$ information in Equation 11.13, and remembering that, under RE, the error made in forecasting Z_t will itself be random.

Alternatively, if for simplicity we assume risk neutrality, the left-hand side of Equation 11.13 is the return to signing a forward contract at $t-1$ to buy foreign currency in the next period at the RE rate (that is, $E_{t-1}s_t$), and, on delivery at t, selling the currency spot.

A numerical example will show that the point amounts simply to a generalization of our conclusions in Chapter 3 regarding interest rate parity to take account of uncertainty.

Suppose that rational economic agents expect the exchange rate of the pound to depreciate by 5% over the next month, on the basis of their knowledge of the past history of the pound (if at all relevant), the past history of other relevant variables, if any (for example Z, in Equation 11.11) and, if necessary, their (equally rational) forecasts of future values of Z. If the forward rate is an unbiased index of the expected future spot rate, the pound will stand at a 5% discount so that a speculator will, on average, gain nothing by buying dollars forward in order to sell spot next period. Nor will speculating on the spot be profitable. Recall the conditions of interest rate parity: with the pound expected to depreciate by 5%, the interest rate on dollars must be 5% lower than on sterling. Hence, the gross 5% return from holding dollars for one month will be just equal to the opportunity cost in interest foregone. So much will be true whatever the underlying process driving the spot rate.

11.6 Testing for efficiency: some basic problems

We now move on to the problem of assessing the evidence on efficiency and the related concepts introduced in this chapter. In view of what has already been said the reader should not be surprised to learn that, in practice, there are a number of very serious obstacles to be overcome before we can arrive at satisfactory answers to questions like: are the currency markets actually efficient? is the forward rate an unbiased forecast of the future spot rate? are expectations rational? and so on.

Notice first that RE *on its own* is not a testable hypothesis. Looking back to the formulation in Equation 11.1 it is obvious that even if we had access to data on subjective expectations, from surveys of market sentiment for example, we would still need to specify a model of the exchange rate itself, from which to derive the objective, conditional expectation. We would then face the problem that, in so far as market expectations differed from the predictions of the model, the divergence could be attributed *either* to irrationality *or* to a misspecified 'objective' model. In other words, since we have no way of knowing the true model of the exchange rate, it is impossible to say whether the market's expectations are derived from the right model, while ours are from the wrong one, or vice versa. This dilemma should be familiar from Section 3.4, where it was referred to as the joint hypothesis problem.

Fortunately however, there is a way round the problem, provided that we have direct evidence on subjective market expectations, and it involves a stratagem which is frequently of use in applying RE models empirically. Consider the implication of writing s_{t+1} in place of $E_t s_{t+1}$ on the right-hand side of Equation 11.1. In view of what we know to be the property of the mathematical expected value this substitution would introduce a random error into the equation. In fact, we can always follow this strategy since, by definition, for *any* variable, X:

$$E_t X_{t+1} \equiv X_{t+1} + w_{t+1} \tag{11.14}$$

where w_t has a mean of zero and is serially uncorrelated. For convenience, we shall henceforth refer to this device as an **RE substitution**.

We shall defer consideration of the results of testing RE directly by this method until Section 11.8.

As far as efficiency is concerned, there are also very serious difficulties encountered when testing an equation as general as Equation 11.4. Intuitively, the problem can be seen from the fact that as long as we place no restrictions on the risk premium (which is, of course, not directly observable), there will always be some path or other which it might have been presumed, after the fact, to have taken in order to preserve the relationship – that is, to be consistent with a random error term, u_t. A practical test of efficiency, then, requires that some additional assumption be made about the behaviour of the risk premium, the obvious one being that it is constant, though more complicated time-series models have been tried.[21]

---

[21] Ideally, the assumptions would themselves be derived from a model of the determination of the risk premium (see Chapter 13).

Figure 11.1 The spot rate and the lagged forward rate.

11.7 Spot and forward rates: background facts

In looking at the background to efficiency studies, we shall concentrate on the exchange rate between the pound and dollar since January 1971. The reader may rest assured that the salient features of the relationship between the spot and forward rates are shared by all the major currencies.

Start with Figure 11.1, which plots the spot rate against the lagged one month[22] forward rate. Unbiasedness requires, as we have seen, that the spot rate on, say, 15 February 1984 is *on average* equal to the one month forward rate that ruled in the market on 15 January 1984. The graph superimposes those two observations (spot for February, forward for January and so on) so as to provide an 'eyeball test' of unbiasedness.

At first glance, Figure 11.1 may look encouraging. Certainly, the forward rate does appear to track the spot rate very closely. However, the match is more apparent than real. Look first at the turning points of the two graphs. In virtually every case, it is the spot rate that leads the change of direction, up or down. Only at the next observation does the (*lagged*) forward rate follow. In other words, February's change of direction was completely missed by January's forward rate, and is only reflected

---

[22] Strictly, the 30-day forward rate. We shall ignore this complication in the text, though the graphs plot properly synchronized series.

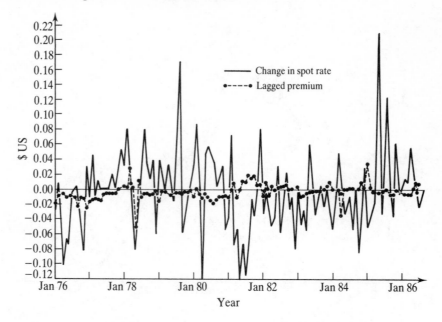

Figure 11.2   The spot rate change and the lagged premium.

in February's forward rate. The interpretation has to be that when market sentiment changes it results in a change of direction in both spot and forward rates simultaneously. For example, a sudden wave of bullishness about the pound pushes up both the spot price of sterling and its price for 30-day delivery, so that *the predominant influences on the forward rate are exactly the same set of factors that determine the spot rate.*

This suggests that spot rates may be more closely linked to contemporaneous rather than to lagged forward rates. In fact, this conjecture turns out to be absolutely correct – to such an extent that a graph of the spot exchange rate against the contemporaneous forward rate would show the two lines so close together as to be completely indistinguishable. In statistical terms, the correlation coefficient between the spot and unlagged forward rate is 0.9995,[23] compared with 0.9871 for the lagged forward rate.

Figure 11.2, which plots the relationship between the change in the spot rate and the previous period's forward premium, confirms the impression that forward rates simply mimic spot rates after the fact, with little or no predictive content. Notice first how small the premium or discount is compared to the amplitude of the subsequent changes in the spot rate. Furthermore, the premium is not only invariably smaller in absolute terms, it is also far less volatile. Not surprisingly, it seems that the volatility

---

[23] Meaning that over 99% of the variation in the spot rate was associated with a move in the forward rate.

of spot exchange rates, which has been mentioned so many times already in this book, has for the most part been unanticipated. Statistically, the forward premium has a standard deviation less than one fifth that of the actual outcome it ought to predict. Moreover, the correlation between the two series is virtually nil.[24]

At this point the reader might well pause and consider the following question: under what type of circumstances would it be *rational* for the market to set the forward rate equal to the concurrent spot rate? For what type of (spot rate) process is the observed value at *t* the best forecast one can make of the future rate?

The answer, as we have already seen in Section 11.5, is the random walk model. Now, it is probably not true that spot rates follow a pure random walk. But the approximation is close enough for a forecast based on a random walk to be quite hard to beat.[25] For the data period in the graphs, the forward rate forecasts better than the previous period's spot, in other words, the forward premium or discount is a better prediction than no change at all – but the improvement is tiny.[26]

11.8 Results

To summarize the facts, it appears that the forward rate contains little of use in the way of a *forecast* of the future spot rate, but instead is dominated by the trend in the spot rate at the time it is set. Does this finding in itself contradict the unbiasedness hypothesis?

Looking back at Section 11.3 it plainly does not. Nothing in Equation 11.5 or Equation 11.5′ requires the forward rate to be a *good* predictor of the future spot rate. All that is required for unbiasedness is that the forward rate be an *unbiased* predictor, in other words, one that is not systematically wrong.[27] In terms of Equation 11.5′ we have established, as background information, that u_t is both large and highly volatile relative to the lagged premium. But the question that is relevant to unbiasedness is whether u_t is random (that is, unpredictable) or not.

This question was the starting point for most of the early research and the results are now well established. While the first studies seemed broadly to support unbiasedness, most recent work has pointed to the

---

[24] In fact the correlation coefficient is negative, though not statistically significant.

[25] In fact, in two well-known papers, Meese and Rogoff (1983a, 1983b) showed that this naive model outperformed all other models on a number of different criteria.

[26] In terms of one of the standard criteria for assessing forecast accuracy, mean squared error (the square root of the mean of the squared prediction errors), the forward premium improves on the random walk model by less than one half of one per cent.

[27] To paraphrase Churchill on democracy, all we require is for the forward rate to be the worst predictor of the future spot rate ... apart from all the others.

opposite conclusion. This may be partly due to the more sophisticated and powerful tests applied by later researchers.[28] However, it may also indicate that currency markets have become more inefficient in the last decade or so, contrary to what one might reasonably have expected in view of the continued removal of controls on international capital movements, the enormous improvements in the technology of money transfer, and the consequent fall in the cost of transactions.

Specifically, most of the early work involved fitting equations of the following form:

$$s_t = a + bf_{t-1}^t + v_t \qquad\qquad (11.15)$$

by ordinary least squares regression.[29] Looking back at Equation 11.5 it is clear that unbiasedness implies that the fitted equation ought to have the following properties:

(1)   The estimate of the intercept, a, insignificantly different from zero.

(2)   The estimate of the slope coefficient, b, insignificantly different from unity.

(3) v_t serially uncorrelated.[30]

Tests on data from the 1920s seem broadly supportive. Results for the post–1972 floating rate era seem much less so, particularly when more powerful testing methods are deployed, with some currencies appearing not to satisfy properties 1 and 2,[31] and others not satisfying property 3.[32]

Notice that the evidence from fitting equations like Equation 11.15 is not only relevant to the question of unbiasedness. As noted in Section 11.2 efficiency implies an equation like Equation 11.15, *if the risk premium is constant*. Under these circumstances, we should only expect to find properties 2 and 3 satisfied. In fact, the evidence reported by recent research provides little or no support even for this hypothesis.

Among the other approaches to empirical testing have been:

(1)   A battery of tests on the properties of the forecasting errors (u_t in Equation 11.5).

---

[28]   Early work used single-equation regression, for the most part, while a majority of the studies appearing in recent years have involved estimating multivariate time-series models of one kind or another.

[29]   For an explanation of regression techniques, see any textbook of statistics or econometrics.

[30]   That is, uncorrelated with its own past, and hence containing no further information. In any case, the hypothesis tests on the coefficients a and b are invalid unless v_t satisfies this condition.

[31]   For technical reasons most researchers test the joint hypothesis: $a = 0$ and $b = 1$.

[32]   Interestingly, the currencies which tend to 'fail' the tests seem to vary from researcher to researcher, a fact which may indicate data inconsistencies.

(2) Similar tests on the errors from Equation 11.5'.

(3) Tests of Equation 11.15, allowing for a non-constant intercept, in other words allowing for a varying risk premium.

(4) Tests on the interest rate differential. Recall that under uncovered interest rate parity, the interest rate differential is equal to the expected rate of depreciation. If we can assume RE, then we have:

$$E_t s_{t+1} - s_t = r_t - r_t^* \tag{11.16}$$

Now an RE substitution in Equation 11.16, replacing the expected exchange rate by the *actual* exchange rate, should introduce only a random error, so we can write:

$$s_{t+1} - s_t = r_t - r_t^* + u_t \tag{11.17}$$

The question then is whether or not, in regressions of the change in the exchange rate on the interest rate differential, we find firstly a regression coefficient not significantly different from unity and secondly a truly random error term.

The enormous volume of published (and unpublished) research is in many cases highly technical, since it often involves the solution of some very awkward statistical problems.[33] Nonetheless, at this stage a consensus view seems to have emerged – and it is clearly *against* unbiasedness and, by and large, against the constant risk premium version of efficiency. In other words, in terms of Equation 11.15, even allowing for a non-zero intercept is insufficient to rescue the model.

This conclusion is reinforced by the results of direct tests of the no-unexploited-profit condition. If the foreign exchange market is efficient, then it should be impossible to find a trading rule to 'beat the market'. The best strategy ought to be simply: buy-and-hold, since this involves the minimum of transaction costs. A typical 'system' of the kind traditionally used by some traders can be defined as follows:

> **An x% filter rule** allows the would-be speculator to profit from a trend by buying a currency whenever the exchange rate rises by x% from a trough and selling it short[34] whenever it falls by x% from a peak.

---

[33] The literature concentrates, for the most part, on refining tests of different versions of the basic equation. Among the refinements are: multivariate tests (that is, taking account of possible linkages between the spot rate for currency A and the forward rate for B and so forth), tests with overlapping contract periods, spectral analysis, a number of non-linear tests and so on.

[34] An investor is said to be 'long', or have a long position in a currency (or other asset) when he has more assets than liabilities denominated in the currency (or asset). Conversely, he is short when his assets in the currency are less than his liabilities. 'Going short' or simply 'shorting' a currency, then, means borrowing in the currency so as to incur debts which will be devalued if the currency subsequently depreciates. A short position is therefore one which generates a profit if the currency's value falls, and vice versa if it rises.

This definition of a filter rule, while broadly accepted, is somewhat incomplete. Firstly, it needs to be modified in order to take account of transaction costs, since they are likely to be sizeable, at least in comparison with the naive, buy-and-hold alternative. Secondly, the returns to the filter rule need to be adjusted for interest costs in order to preserve comparability with the naive strategy.

Even allowing for these costs, however, the results for the most part show that a number of filter rules turned out profitable over the floating rate period. More surprising still is the fact that these trading rules appear to make money even in an *ex ante* sense: filter rules that were found to have been profitable in one period seem to have remained profitable for years after the original results were published![35]

However, looking beyond this more or less unanimous negative conclusion, the consensus evaporates.

There are, as we have seen in Section 11.6, two possible explanations of the failure of the efficiency hypothesis: *either* the market is efficient, but with a non-constant risk premium, *or* expectations are irrational, or both. This particular issue is at the moment still unsettled. A number of studies have been published purporting to show that, once allowance is made for fluctuations in the risk premium, efficiency is preserved, at least for some of the major currencies.

On the other hand, consider attempting to test RE directly, using survey data. To see how that could be achieved, introduce an RE substitution on the right-hand side of Equation 11.1 to give the following:

$$s_t^e = s_{t+1} + v_{t+1} \tag{11.18}$$

that is, under RE, market expectations will be fulfilled, plus or minus a random error. In other words, if we carry out a survey of market participants' forecasts of the future exchange rate they should turn out to be correct *on average*.

It might seem a simple matter to carry out the exercise of sampling the market participants' views and to compare them to the actual outcome. In practice it has proved difficult to accomplish until quite recently. In the first place, for a number of reasons (probably including cost) the requirements of research had to await those of the practitioners, who have only in the last few years organized an ongoing survey of market sentiment in London and New York. There is therefore relatively little data at the moment, though this problem will become progressively less important as the survey data accumulates.

---

[35] At least, according to Dooley and Shafer (1983), who used 1%, 3% and 5% filter rules. On the one hand, this could be taken as evidence that foreign exchange traders are missing out on the profits they could make by reading the academic literature. On the other hand, of course, it could be that traders are busy actually applying more successful trading rules than those found by academics – and are unwilling to share their secrets with the rest of us. Notice that, even if this is the case, it still begs the question of why the opportunities unearthed by Dooley and Shafer and others are left unexploited.

More intractable are the problems of actually interpreting survey findings so as to derive a single number that measures, on a particular date, the market's expectation of the exchange rate expected for a future date. For example, what is to be done about the fact that, while we have assumed that the market is unanimous in its view of the future, surveys tend in reality to find a wide divergence of expectations? The usual solution has been to take the median response as the 'market expectation', but this is obviously far from satisfactory, particularly if the degree of unanimity varies over the sample period. Furthermore, since in a postal survey there is no way of pinpointing with complete accuracy the date at which the expectation is formed, it is difficult to be sure that any apparent bias is not due to misdating.

In spite of these and a host of other problems a number of attempts have been made to extract information about market expectations from survey data, with mixed results. Again, early work seemed consistent with rationality. However, the most thorough study to date, by Frankel and Froot (1987),[36] concluded that:

(1)   Apparent irrationality was indicated by the persistent bias found in respondents' expectations, particularly in the mid 1980s.

(2)   Since expectations bias tended to be associated with forward premium bias it could not be explained by a risk premium. In any case, the gap tended to be far too large (an average of 7%) to be explained away in this fashion.

(3)   The nature of the bias appears to have varied over different episodes in the recent history of the currency markets.

However, note that the same authors, notwithstanding their own findings conclude that:

> 'There is nothing in our results to suggest that it is easy to make money speculating in the foreign exchange markets.'

11.9 Conclusions

What can we conclude about the forward market? Are the facts consistent with RE and/or efficiency and/or unbiasedness? It should be clear from Section 11.8 that unbiasedness looks, at least at this point in time, a completely untenable proposition. As far as rationality and efficiency are concerned, the jury may still be out, but the case for the prosecution certainly looks very strong, and it seems more and more likely that the verdict will ultimately go against either or both of the hypotheses.

---

[36] For the US dollar against the pound, Deutsche Mark, Swiss and French francs, and yen.

The theoretical implication is clear: there is money to be made in the forward market. However, the reader would be well advised to sit tight and finish the book rather than rush out to make his fortune as an amateur currency trader.

The recurring problem in financial markets is that opportunities always seem to open up *ex post* – with the benefit of hindsight – never *ex ante*. It is possible to identify discernible patterns in time series of exchange rate movements but, once isolated, the patterns seem not to be repeated. If the future cannot be reliably assumed to follow the patterns established in the past, any forecast will be built on shifting sand.

Nonetheless, this writer cannot help but finish an assessment of the research results with a sense of bewilderment at the apparent inefficiencies uncovered: the trading rules that seem to deliver clear profit, the expectational bias, and most amazing of all, the increasing evidence of irrational expectations.[37] To uncover such anomalies in labour or goods markets would hardly be surprising. But, as has been mentioned several times before, currency markets are dominated by the large-scale traders: commercial banks, investment banks, treasury departments of multinational corporations. They have instant access to massive databanks, and they have at their fingertips the technology with which to analyse the information. The rewards for being right are enormous, the penalties for being wrong are as great.[38] Can it really be the case that this type of market is *systematically, predictably* wrong – time after time? It is difficult to credit, and even more difficult to imagine why this should be so.

■ Summary

- The (mathematical) expectation or expected value is a type of average result, and it is computed by taking the probability-weighted sum of all the possible outcomes of an uncertain event. The expected value, conditional on a particular information set, is the mathematical expectation calculated using that information. The expected value of deviations from the mathematical expectation is itself zero.

---

[37] Evidence of irrationality has been reported by Taylor (1988), in survey data on forecasts made by professional investment managers with respect to inflation and stock market indices.

[38] For example, according to *The Economist* of 28 May 1988, one US bank made profits of $338m from foreign exchange trading in the final quarter of 1987 alone. It lost $19m in the same department over the next three months.

Of course, on the one hand the profit-switchback is an indication of the rewards to good forecasting. On the other hand, the profits earned are also prima facie evidence of *ex ante* market inefficiency.

- The rational expectations hypothesis is the theory that the market consensus forecast of the future value of a variable is identical to its (mathematical) expectation, conditional on all publicly-available information. If expectations are formed rationally the market will still make wrong forecasts, but its errors will be random.

- The forward market can be said to be efficient if the forward rate ruling at any time is equal to the rational expectation of the future spot rate when the contract matures, plus the risk premium that speculators require in order to compensate them for the additional risk they bear.

- If investors are risk neutral the risk premium will be zero. In this special case it follows that efficiency requires the forward rate be an unbiased forecast of the future spot rate – the so-called unbiasedness hypothesis.

- The so-called random walk model of the spot rate is not inconsistent with RE and efficiency. On the other hand, it is not required by either RE or efficiency.

- Even a casual examination of the facts reveals that the forward rate is without doubt a very poor forecast of the future spot rate. In general, the forward premium drastically underestimates the amplitude of subsequent spot rate fluctuations. Furthermore, it appears to be dragged along with the concurrent spot rate, showing no tendency whatever to foreshadow future changes of direction.

- Published research results indicate fairly conclusively – at least for the moment – that the forward rate is not an unbiased predictor of the future spot rate. Furthermore, the results are not encouraging for the more general hypothesis of market efficiency. There is substantial, though not overwhelming, evidence of unexploited profit opportunities in the currency markets. Moreover, the deviations from efficiency that have been uncovered seem difficult to square with any simple pattern of risk premium variation. Recent research using survey data appears to indicate the explanation may lie in irrational expectations.

READING GUIDE

See Begg (1982) or Sheffrin (1983) for a textbook treatment of RE in general. The classic reference on RE is Muth (1961) and on efficiency, Fama (1970).

Surveys of empirical work on forward market efficiency date very rapidly indeed. The most up to date is Levich (1985).

Among the most influential articles in the literature have been: Frenkel (1976), Frankel (1980), Hansen and Hodrick (1980) and Baillie, Lippens and MacMahon (1983), the latter two focusing on the technical issues and Frankel and Froot (1987), which uses survey data.

12

The 'News' Model and Exchange Rate Volatility

■ Introduction

Chapter 11 focused on the relationship between the spot exchange rate and the previous period's forward rate. In this chapter and the next attention is switched to the factors which account for the gap between the two. Look back at Equation 11.4': in words it says that the spot rate at time t can be written as the sum of the forward rate and risk premium set in the previous period, *plus a random error*.[1] We will be concerned in this chapter with the latter. As will be seen, the error arises from the mistakes made by economic agents in forecasting the future spot rate errors which, if we can assume rationality, must be attributable to newly-arrived information – 'news',[2] for short.

Now at a superficial level, identifying news might appear simple, in conceptual terms at least, if not in practice. We can all conceive of

---

[1] The fact that u_t in Equation 8.4' appears with a negative sign can be ignored, of course, since the positive sign it was given in Equation 8.3 was purely arbitrary in any case.

[2] Also often called 'surprises' or 'innovations'.

news items that are bound to be relevant to the exchange rate: announcements of economic statistics, political changes, new international monetary arrangements, and so on. But, apart from the (often insurmountable) problem of how to quantify the news, there remains the difficulty of actually isolating the element of surprise. This is critical because, taking a simple example, it is not the *gross* estimate of the UK trade deficit that has an impact on the pound's exchange rate. Rather, it is the extent to which the announced trade balance is greater or less than anticipated by the market before the fact. This, in turn, means that in order to arrive at a measure of the underlying *net* 'news' component in any 'gross' information, we need first to have an estimate of the market's *ex ante* expectations with regard to the variable in question.

The outline of this chapter is as follows. We introduce the concept of 'news' in Section 12.1 by analysing an ultra-simple model. The next section examines a more complicated example: the monetary model with interest rate parity imposed, an unresolved issue from Chapter 5. In Section 12.3, we look at some of the problems involved in making the 'news' approach operational, and Section 12.4 gives a brief summary of the main findings of empirical research in this field. The final section focuses in more detail on some of the possible explanations offered for the volatility of exchange rates, which is so difficult to reconcile with the 'news' approach – or, indeed, with any of the other models we have examined in this book.

Before going any further, it is worth drawing the reader's attention to one point about the material in the present chapter. As will become clear, the 'news' model is, by its very nature, less of a self-contained theory of exchange rate determination than an approach to estimating a variety of (possibly competing) theories. Because this is the case it is almost impossible to separate the analysis of the underlying model from the implications for empirical testing, so that the present chapter inevitably involves somewhat more detailed discussion of the technical (and especially econometric) issues than the other chapters in this book.

12.1 The 'news' model: a simple example

We start by examining an ultra-simple model in order to illustrate the 'news' approach, as well as some of the problems associated with it. The simplest and most general example of a news model would take the following form. Suppose the (log of the) spot exchange rate is given by the relationship:

$$s_t = \gamma z_t \tag{12.1}$$

where γ is a slope coefficient and z_t is the variable or variables[3] determining the exchange rate. We shall call z_t the 'fundamentals' or 'fundamental variables'.[4]

Now, assuming RE, agents will form their expectations of next period's spot rate using Equation 12.1. Specifically, at time $t - 1$ they will use the available information in the set I_{t-1} so as to form the conditional expectation of s_t, which, given Equation 12.1, means:

$$E_{t-1}s_t = \gamma E_{t-1}z_t \tag{12.2}$$

In other words, *forming a (rational) expectation of the exchange rate involves, as a prerequisite, forecasting the fundamentals.* In terms of the forecast errors we obviously have, subtracting Equation 12.2 from Equation 12.1:

$$s_t - E_{t-1}s_t = \gamma (z_t - E_{t-1}z_t) \tag{12.3}$$

The left-hand side of this equation is the unexpected component of the spot exchange rate. The term in the brackets on the right is the 'news': the surprise component of the fundamental variables in z_t. So Equation 12.3 tells us that the relationship between the unexpected exchange rate and the 'news' about the fundamental variables that drive it is identical to the one between the *level* of the exchange rate and the *level* of the fundamentals.

Notice that the RE assumption is critical in two respects. Firstly, because it amounts to assuming that economic agents know the true structural model linking the endogenous variable, s_t to the fundamentals, it allows us to conclude that the same structure will link expectations of those variables. So if, as in the case considered here, the spot rate is simply a multiple, γ, of the fundamental variable or variables in z_t, the *expected* spot rate will likewise be the same multiple of z_t.

Secondly, RE allows us to deduce that the 'news' will be that part of the fundamental variable which is not only unforeseen, but *unforeseeable* – at least using the data set I_{t-1}. This is a very important point. The term in brackets in Equation 12.3 is the deviation of the actual outcome of the fundamental variable (or variables) from its (or their) mathematical expected value. As we saw in Chapter 6 these deviations are random, in the sense that they have an average value of zero and display no systematic pattern over time. Any non-random component that remained would represent a potentially predictable element unexploited by market agents using the information available at the time.

Note that under *pure* RE (as distinct from weak rationality) the information set, I_{t-1}, includes all publicly-available information. Under

---

[3] Realistically, z_t will be a vector of values of the fundamental variables at t, possibly with a 1 as the first element, and γ a coefficient vector, so that Equation 12.1 relates the exchange rate to a constant plus a linear combination of a number of fundamentals.

[4] The expression comes from stock exchange jargon, where it has a long pedigree.

weak rationality it is simply the past history of each of the fundamental variables. We shall return to this point later.

In addition to demonstrating the philosophy of the 'news' approach, and in particular the central role of RE, this ultra-simple model illustrates two further points.

First, as already mentioned, Equation 12.3 bears a straightforward relationship to the efficient market model of the previous chapter, as can be seen by using Equation 11.2 to rewrite it as:

$$s_t = E_{t-1}s_t + \gamma(z_t - E_{t-1}z_t) \tag{12.4}$$
$$= f^t_{t-1} - \rho_{t-1} + \gamma(z_t - E_{t-1}z_t)$$

where, it will be recalled, the first two terms on the right-hand side are the forward rate set at time $t-1$ for currency to be delivered at t and the risk premium respectively. Now, Equation 12.4 is simply the general version of the efficiency model with the expectational error (u_t in Equation 11.4′ for example) written out explicitly in terms of 'news' regarding the fundamentals. In fact, it is in this setting that most researchers have preferred to deal with the 'news' model, for purposes of empirical testing at least. However, it should be emphasized that it is quite possible to formulate a 'news' model without any reference to forward market efficiency, as indeed has been done most simply at the start of this section. The only really essential building-block is RE, and it is by this assumption that the 'news' approach stands or falls.

On the other hand, the simple model illustrates the sense in which the 'news' approach is just that and no more – hardly a model at all, more a methodology or an approach to modelling. To see that this is the case, notice that nothing has so far been said about the contents of z_t. Nor is this accidental. The 'news' approach is essentially agnostic about the fundamentals of exchange rate determination, with the choice being based on the particular researcher's theoretical predilections or on purely *ad hoc* criteria, occasionally on market lore or sometimes simply on practical considerations of data availability.

Whatever kind of considerations guide the choice of fundamental variables, there is one inescapable feature of real-world foreign exchange markets which is ignored in this ultra-simple model: the central importance of the prospective capital gain or loss from holding a currency. It is now time to rectify this omission and, in the process, tie up a loose end from one of the earlier chapters of this book.

★ 12.2 The monetary model revisited

The reader may recall that one issue left unresolved in the analysis of the monetary model in Section 5.3 concerned the impact of interest rates. The problem arose because, while there could be no doubt about the sign of their effect on the exchange rate, it seemed implausible to treat interest rates as exogenous in view of what had already been said about Uncovered Interest Rate Parity (UIRP) in Chapter 3. We now return to the model so as to deal with this question.

Let us reformulate the problem. Recall that, in the monetary model, the exchange rate depends on three variables: relative money stocks, income and interest rates. If we again write the relationship in logs, we have:

$$s_t = \tilde{m}_t - c\tilde{y}_t + b\tilde{r}_t \tag{12.5}$$

where c and b are positive parameters, $\tilde{m}$ and $\tilde{y}$ refer to (the logs of) relative money stocks and income respectively (that is, the difference between the logs), and $\tilde{r}$ is the interest differential.

Now UIRP will not hold in the form we encountered it in Chapter 3 unless we persist in assuming risk neutrality, as we did there. Allowing for risk aversion, however, means replacing UIRP (as in Equation 3.4) by:

$$\tilde{r}_t \equiv r_t - r_t^* = \Delta s_t^e + \rho_t \tag{12.6}$$

where ρ_t is the premium required by speculators who switch from one currency to another in order to profit by expected, but uncertain, exchange rate fluctuations. The reader may verify by using the CIRP condition (in which there is, of course, no risk premium) that Equation 12.6 is consistent with the formulation of forward market efficiency in Equation 11.2 – the risk premium is one and the same, ρ_t, for both transactions.

Now if we use Equation 12.6 to eliminate the interest differential from Equation 12.5, we have:

$$s_t = \tilde{m}_t - c\tilde{y}_t + b\Delta s_t^e + b\rho_t \tag{12.7}$$
$$= \gamma z_t + b\Delta s_t^e$$

where z_t has been written as a shorthand to summarize the impact of fundamentals other than the interest rate (see Box 12.1).

Although our starting point in this section was the monetary model, this exchange rate equation is a very general example of the genre. Its only specific assumption (apart from linearity in the fundamentals) is that expectations are rational and that anticipated capital gains or losses influence the current spot rate – hardly a controversial proposition one would imagine. While the obvious candidates for inclusion as fundamentals are the variables figuring in the monetary model, there is no reason to insist on this. Simply by respecifying the list of fundamentals in z_t, the same framework could accommodate any other exogenous variables.

What Equation 12.7 says is that the spot rate at any time depends not only on the current level of a number of fundamental variables, *but also on the expected capital gain or loss from holding the currency* – which is simply (the negative of) its own rate of increase. The greater is Δs^e_t, in other words the more the pound is expected to depreciate against the dollar, the greater the capital loss to sterling holders, and hence the lower will be the pound's international value (that is, the higher the sterling price of dollars), other things being equal.

The mathematical complexities of the model (most of which will be bypassed here) all stem from this 'bootstrap' feature: *the more the exchange rate is expected to appreciate over the coming period, the higher will be its level today*. Its current level depends on its (expected) rate of change. This is a familiar feature of asset markets: other things being equal (that is, for given values of the fundamentals), asset prices are high when they are expected to go even higher and thereby yield capital gains to current holders.

It will now be demonstrated that, under RE, Equation 12.7 implies that the current level of the exchange rate depends on the market's view of the whole pattern of future movements in the fundamentals.

Start by noting the following:

$$\Delta s^e_t \equiv s^e_{t+1} - s_t \qquad\qquad (12.8)$$

which serves simply to define the expected depreciation as the (log of the) spot rate anticipated for next period, $t + 1$, less the rate actually observed at the present moment (period t).

Assuming RE, we can write Equation 12.8 as:

$$\Delta s^e_t = E_t s_{t+1} - s_t \qquad\qquad (12.9)$$

where the exchange rate level anticipated for $t + 1$ is conditioned on the information available at t.

BOX 12.1   The fundamentals in a 'news' model.

In other words:

$$\gamma z_t \equiv \tilde{m}_t - c\tilde{y}_t + b\rho_t$$

or more precisely, for readers who are familiar with vector notation:

$$\gamma z_t \equiv \begin{bmatrix} 1 & -c & b \end{bmatrix} \begin{bmatrix} \tilde{m}_t \\ \tilde{y}_t \\ \rho_t \end{bmatrix}$$

If we now substitute Equation 12.9 in Equation 12.7, we have:

$$s_t = \gamma z_t + b(E_t s_{t+1} - s_t) \tag{12.10}$$

which can be simplified by collecting terms involving s_t to give:

$$s_t = \gamma(1+b)^{-1} z_t + b(1+b)^{-1} E_t s_{t+1} \tag{12.11}$$

$$= \gamma(1+b)^{-1} z_t + \beta E_t s_{t+1}$$

where for convenience we have introduced the definition:

$$\beta \equiv b(1+b)^{-1}$$

This parameter, β, plays an important part in what follows. Notice that, since the coefficient b must be presumed positive – the value of a currency must be *higher* the greater the prospective capital gain – it follows that β must lie between zero and plus one.

Now, if Equation 12.11 tells us how s_t is determined as a function of z_t and $E_t s_{t+1}$, ask yourself the question: what will determine next period's exchange rate, s_{t+1}? The answer is, plainly:

$$s_{t+1} = \gamma(1+b)^{-1} z_{t+1} + \beta E_{t+1} s_{t+2} \tag{12.12}$$

Notice the capital gain term at the end: the exchange rate next period (that is, at time $t+1$) will depend on the level that it is expected to reach at $t+2$, on the basis of the information available *then*, at $t+1$.

However, what cropped up in Equation 12.11 was not s_{t+1} but its expected value at t, $E_t s_{t+1}$, so in order to make progress, take the expectation in Equation 12.12 conditional on the information set, I_t, to give:

$$E_t s_{t+1} = \gamma(1+b)^{-1} E_t z_{t+1} + \beta E_t(E_{t+1} s_{t+2}) \tag{12.12'}$$

$$= \gamma(1+b)^{-1} E_t z_{t+1} + \beta E_t s_{t+2}$$

The last line requires explanation. First, note that the information set, I_t, must contain less data than the next period's information set, I_{t+1} (see Footnote 12 of Chapter 11), the difference being 'news' about the fundamentals. It follows that the last term on the first line of Equation 12.12' is: the level of s_t the market expects now (at t) will be a rational expectation of s_{t+2} when the new information emerging at $t+1$ has become available. But, at time t, the market cannot know what will appear a rational expectation of s_{t+2} at time $t+1$, because that depends, as has been said, on information not yet available. It follows that the best guess the market can make about the level expected for $t+2$ on the basis of $t+1$

data is precisely the level that currently appears rational, as of t (see Box 12.2).

Now if we use the second line of Equation 12.12′ to replace $E_t s_{t+1}$ in Equation 12.11, we have:

$$s_t = \gamma (1 + b)^{-1} (z_t + \beta E_t z_{t+1}) + \beta^2 E_t s_{t+2} \tag{12.13}$$

which expresses the current exchange rate in terms of the current fundamentals, the expected value of next period's fundamentals and the expected exchange rate two periods hence.

The obvious next step is to repeat the process, in order to eliminate $E_t s_{t+2}$: write out the expression for s_{t+2} in terms of z_{t+2} and $E_{t+2} s_{t+3}$, take expectations conditional on the information set I_t, and use the result in Equation 12.13, to give s_t as a function of z_t, $E_t z_{t+1}$, $E_t z_{t+2}$ and $E_t s_{t+3}$. Then repeat the process to eliminate $E_t s_{t+3}$ ... and so on.

The result, as can be verified with a little patience and some rough paper, is that we can write the exchange rate after N substitutions as follows:

$$s_t = \gamma (1 + b)^{-1} (z_t + \beta E_t z_{t+1} + \beta^2 E_t z_{t+2} + \beta^3 E_t z_{t+3} + \dots$$
$$+ \beta^N E_t z_{t+N}) + \beta^{N+1} E_t s_{t+N+1} \tag{12.14}$$

This looks awfully messy at first glance. However, it can be simplified by noting, first, that since β is a fraction between zero and one, it will get smaller and smaller as it is raised to a higher and higher power. For a large number of substitutions (that is, large N), it follows that β^{N+1} will be so small as to be negligible, so that we can safely ignore the final term of the equation. Next, remembering that $\beta^0 = 1$, we can rewrite Equation 12.14 as follows:

$$s_t = \gamma (1 + b)^{-1} \left(z_t + \sum_{k=1}^{N} \beta^k E_t z_{t+k} \right) \tag{12.15}$$

$$= \gamma (1 + b)^{-1} \sum_{k=0}^{N} \beta^k E_t z_{t+k}$$

Consider the interpretation of the equations. At the outset, Equation 12.10 told us that the level of the exchange rate at time t was determined by

---

BOX 12.2   The law of iterated expectation.

More formally, since:

$$I_t \subseteq I_{t+1} \subseteq I_{t+2} \subseteq \dots$$

and so on, it follows that:

$$E\{E(s_{t+2} | I_{t+1}) | I_t\} = E(s_{t+2} | I_t) = E_t s_{t+2}$$

two factors: the level of the fundamentals at t and the expected capital gain or loss accruing to an investor who held the currency over the period from t to $t + 1$. The latter will be equal to the difference between the exchange rate expected for next period, $E_t s_{t+1}$, and its known current level. The question is then: what determines the exchange rate expected for $t + 1$? Under RE, the answer is clear. It is the value that the fundamentals are expected to take next period and the prospective capital gain from $t + 1$ to $t + 2$, which is equal to $(E_t s_{t+2} - E_t s_{t+1})$. The latter depends on the expected level of the fundamentals at $t + 2$ and the capital gain over $t + 2$ to $t + 3 \ldots$ and so on.

The conclusion is Equation 12.15. It tells us that *the value of the exchange rate at any point is determined by market perceptions of the entire future path of the fundamentals*, starting with z_t and up to z_{t+N}.

In principle, N should be infinite, because we could go on substituting for the expected future spot rate forever more. However, if we look more closely at Equation 12.15 (comparing it, if necessary, with Equation 12.14), we see that the summation term is in fact a weighted total of future expected fundamentals, where the weights on successive periods take the following pattern:

t	$t + 1$	$t + 2$	$t + 3$	$\ldots$	$t + N$
β^0	β^1	β^2	β^3	$\ldots$	β^N

This series of weights diminishes as we go further and further into the future. In fact, it is a geometric series, with each term equal to β times the preceding one. So the weights will diminish faster the smaller β is.

The practical implication of this weighting scheme is that the importance of expected future values beyond three or four periods is very small. For example, if the capital gains elasticity, b, were 0.9 (remember it is in any case smaller than one), the series of weights would go:

t	$t + 1$	$t + 2$	$t + 3$	$t + 4$	$t + 5$	$t + 6$	$\ldots$
1.000	0.474	0.224	0.106	0.050	0.024	0.011	$\ldots$

so that only 6 periods out, the weighting has fallen to barely 1%. For a smaller value of b the weights diminish even more rapidly, falling below 1% after only 3 periods when b is 0.25, and after 2 periods when b is 0.1.

We can sum up our conclusions so far as follows. If the current level of the exchange rate depends on the prospective capital gain or loss then it follows, assuming RE, that its level can be viewed as depending on the whole of the future path that the fundamentals are expected to take, with the weight attached to succeeding future periods diminishing as the period becomes more distant.

In mathematical terms, what we have accomplished, in this laborious fashion, is to solve a *difference equation*. Viewed from this standpoint, Equation 12.15 sets out conditions relating s_t and the future expected path of z_t, such that the difference equation (Equation 12.11) is satisfied at all times. The interested (or incredulous) reader can satisfy himself that this is the case by rewriting Equation 12.15 for $E_t s_{t+1}$ and using the result in Equation 12.11, to give Equation 12.15 again.[5]

For our purposes, it is convenient to write the model in a different form from Equation 12.15. To see how this can be achieved, look back at Equation 12.14 and ask yourself: what will be the value of $E_{t-1} s_t$? The answer is obviously:[6]

$$E_{t-1} s_t = \gamma (1 + b)^{-1} (E_{t-1} z_t + \beta E_{t-1} z_{t+1} + \beta^2 E_{t-1} z_{t+2}$$
$$+ \beta^3 E_{t-1} z_{t+3} + \ldots + \beta^N E_{t-1} z_{t+N}) + \beta^{N+1} E_t s_{t+N+1} \quad \textbf{(12.16)}$$

$$= \gamma (1 + b)^{-1} \sum_{k=0}^{N} \beta^k E_{t-1} z_{t+k}$$

Now simply subtract Equation 12.16 from Equation 12.15 to give:

$$s_t - E_{t-1} s_t = \gamma (1 + b)^{-1} \sum_{k=0}^{N} \beta^k (E_t z_{t+k} - E_{t-1} z_{t+k}) \quad \textbf{(12.17)}$$

This serves to emphasize the sense in which the 'news' model is really only a way of rewriting a generalized asset model, with RE imposed. The left-hand side of Equation 12.17 is that part of the current (time t) exchange rate that was unanticipated in the previous period (at $t - 1$), in other words, the exchange rate 'news' or surprise. The right-hand side is $\gamma (1 + b)^{-1}$ times the weighted sum of the 'news' about future fundamentals. The surprise for period $t + k$ is the difference between the value of z_{t+k} that is expected at t and the value that was anticipated last period, at $t - 1$. The summation therefore represents a weighted total of the extent to which expectations about the future are revised in the current period in the light of new information made public between $t - 1$ and t. If, having heard the 'news', the market has no reason to revise its forecast of z_{t+k}, then $E_t z_{t+k} - E_{t-1} z_{t+k}$ will be zero and will have no impact on the exchange rate.

It must be stressed that, however large or small the surprises are in any period, each term $E_t z_{t+k} - E_{t-1} z_{t+k}$ is purely random – for each and every period, $t + k$, and *for any or all fundamentals*. The reason is that a systematic pattern in the 'news' would imply, by that very fact, it was not a complete surprise. Expectation revisions that display a pattern over time could be predicted in advance.

It is worth dwelling for a moment on this point, because it illustrates both the empirical content of the 'news' approach and another important aspect of RE.

---

[5] As we shall see in Section 12.5, this solution is not unique.

[6] Making use of the fact that $E_{t-1}(E_t z_t) = E_{t-1} z_t$ (see Box 12.2).

To put matters in a personal context, suppose I hold a particular expectation with regard to a variable of importance to me, for example, my earnings in the year 2000. For simplicity, assume that I update my expectation with regard to that year each 31 December, so as to incorporate the new information that I have received in the twelve months since the last update. Now suppose I notice, as the years pass, that for every 1% I *up*grade my expectation of 2000 earnings by in one year, I end up *down*grading my forecast by 5% the next year. What would be a rational response to this discovery?

Clearly I cannot let matters rest if I am to preserve a reputation for rationality. Suppose, that on 31 December 1995, I decide that in the light of the good news received during the year I ought to raise my forecast of 2000 earnings by 7%. As things stand, I do so in the confident expectation that next year, on 31 December 1996, my 1995 forecast for 2000 will seem to have been outrageously overoptimistic – and will therefore be downgraded again by 35%. This plainly contradicts rationality. If I *know* I will hold a different expectation in the next period, I must adopt it *now* – or forego any claim to being a rational agent.

There may well be a simple explanation of why I find a repeated pattern in the way that I revise my earnings forecasts. Every time my employer grants a pay rise of 1%, it is reversed in the next year by a 5% fall, both of which I am naively extrapolating to arrive at my forecast for 2000. Obviously, I can improve my forecasting technique by taking this pattern into account, so as to replace my naive extrapolation process with a forecasting model that embodies the predictable component in my employer's behaviour.

In this simple example, an outside observer seeing the stable, systematic pattern to my expectation revisions would conclude (*correctly*) that I was irrational, because I was failing to make full use of all the information available to me. In the same way, as observers of the currency markets, we likewise would expect to find no consistent pattern to the revisions in traders' forecasts.

To see the relationship between Equation 12.17 and the forward rate models examined in Chapter 11, take $E_{t-1}s_t$ over to the right-hand side to give:

$$s_t = E_{t-1}s_t + \gamma(1+b)^{-1} \sum_{k=0}^{N} \beta^k (E_t z_{t+k} - E_{t-1}z_{t+k}) \tag{12.18}$$

At this point it is worth glancing back at Section 11.2 on the forward market efficiency condition. It is clear from looking at Equation 11.3, for example, that the 'news' term in Equation 12.18 can be identified with the random error, u_t, which was included but left unexplained throughout the last chapter. In fact, if we assume that the forward market is efficient we can rewrite Equation 11.4' as:

$$s_t = -\rho_{t-1} + f^t_{t-1} + \gamma(1+b)^{-1} \sum_{k=0}^{N} \beta^k (E t z_{t+k} - E_{t-1}z_{t+k}) \tag{12.19}$$

which says that the spot rate can be thought of as made up of three components: the previous period's forward rate plus the risk premium set when currently maturing forward contracts were signed, plus the impact of 'news' about current and all future values of the fundamental variables, the importance of the latter being less the further into the future they are dated.

Recall the background facts presented in Section 11.7. They indicated that, whatever else might be true, one thing could be said with absolute confidence: the forward rate is a very poor forecast of the future spot rate. If we set aside for the moment the possibility that the risk premium is highly variable, the conclusions we have reached in this section suggest that the explanation for the poor forecasting performance of the forward rate is to be found in the predominance of 'news'. If, month after month, major items of 'news' arrive, forcing agents in the market to make substantial revisions in their assessment of future fundamentals, the result will be that movements in the spot rate will overwhelmingly reflect these surprises. Any movements in the spot rate which are predictable in advance, as reflected in the forward premium, will be completely swamped by the impact of new information arriving like a bolt from the blue.

This explanation of the facts looks, at first sight, convincing. How well does it stand up to more rigorous testing? It is to this question that we now turn.

12.3 Testing the 'news'

Consider the simple model (Equation 12.3). In order to test how well it fits the facts we need to be able to answer three questions: first, how do we measure market expectations of the exchange rate itself? second, which are the fundamental variables? and third, how do we measure market expectations of their level?

As far as the first question is concerned most researchers have taken the line of least resistance and used the forward rate as a proxy for the expected spot rate. Looking back at Equation 12.4 it is obvious that this solution is far from ideal since it simply involves replacing one unobservable variable with an observable, the forward rate, and another unobservable, the risk premium. Now if we can safely assume that the risk premium is zero, or constant at least, this substitution will not bias the results. If the risk premium is variable however, it will almost certainly distort the conclusions.

On the second question, researchers have picked candidate variables on a more or less atheoretical basis. Most have recognized the claim of the basic monetary variables and a number of others have been tried, notably current account balances. There are many 'news' variables, or at least strong candidates, which have never been employed, usually because they are inherently difficult to quantify: for example, information bearing on the likelihood of a change of government (opinion polls and so on), 'news' affecting a possible future move to a fixed exchange rate regime (for example, the UK joining the European Monetary System) and so on.

The issue which has received most attention has been the measurement of expectations with respect to the fundamentals. A number of different approaches have been taken:

1. Univariate time series

Much of the early work involved modelling each fundamental variable as a univariate time series. This obviously amounts to assuming weak RE: market expectations are conditioned only on the past history of the variable in question, so that the innovations in each of the fundamentals is simply that part which could not be predicted by looking at the pattern of fluctuations in the variable in question, taken in isolation. So, for example, this approach would involve extracting an estimate of the future money stock, $E_t m_{t+1}$, from a linear[7] combination of m_t, m_{t-1}, m_{t-2} and so on, that is:[8]

$$m_t = a_0 + a_1 m_{t-1} + a_2 m_{t-2} + \ldots + a_p m_{t-p} + v_t$$

Then the 'news' is simply the residual from the estimating equation, v_t. Unless one believes that market expectations are only weakly rational this approach is unsatisfactory, though it has the attraction of simplicity.

2. Multivariate time series and vector autoregression

From a theoretical point of view, conditioning each 'news' variable on a broader information set is obviously preferable. Whether market agents are supposed to arrive at their RE predictions by formal forecasting procedures, crude rules of thumb or more likely by intuitive 'gut feelings', there is certainly no reason to suppose that they close their eyes to *all* information other than the past history of the variable in question.

To take this point a little further, consider a market forecast of the future money stock in the context of the RE version of the monetary model covered in Section 12.2. One approach would be to estimate $E_{t-1} m_t$ using a special array of variables selected by the researcher as relevant: say,

---

[7] Almost all published work has involved linear time series, though non-linear models would appear a promising avenue for future exploration.

[8] The example given here is known as p^{th}-order autoregressive. Along the same lines it is possible to include among the regressors on the right-hand side lagged values of the residual: v_{t-1}, $v_{t-2} \ldots v_{t-q}$, making the model autoregressive (of order p)-moving average (of order q), or ARMA(p, q) for short. Though the statistical properties are changed somewhat by this extension, its implications for RE are identical.

the government's budget deficit past and present, the rate of inflation, the growth rate of the economy and so forth. In fact, this arbitrary approach to the specification of the sub-model was the one taken in some of the early work on 'news' models.

Remember it is not only the money stock surprise that figures in the basic model: we also have to deal with an income variable. Now there is nothing to prevent us from following the same arbitrary approach to forecasting income. But, at the very least, it would make sense to include the money stock among the conditioning variables, on the grounds that orthodox closed economy macroeconomic theory suggests that it plays a central role in determining the level of activity, and the evidence by and large supports this view. Furthermore, it would be grossly inconsistent to exclude the money stock on the grounds that it is absent from the market's information set, or that agents pay no attention to it, *since it appears as one of the other fundamentals*. In that sense, its inclusion is not completely arbitrary.

In fact, taking this approach to its logical conclusion would suggest the following procedure. Suppose we have m variables in the set of fundamentals. Call the first z^1, the second z^2 and so on, so that z^4_{t-3}, for example, denotes the value of the fourth fundamental variable three periods ago. Then generate a forecast of z^1_t by using past values of z^1, in combination with past values of all the other fundamentals, z^2 to z^m. Similarly, condition a prediction of z^2_t on past values of z^2 itself as well as on the history of the other fundamentals. In general, the jth fundamental is modelled as:

$$z^j_t = f(z^1_{t-1}, z^1_{t-2} \cdots z^1_{t-L}, z^2_{t-1}, z^2_{t-2} \cdots$$
$$z^2_{t-L} \cdots z^m_{t-1} \cdots z^m_{t-L})$$

where L is the maximum lag (the 'memory length') judged relevant on the basis of the standard tests used in time-series statistics.[9] Again, the 'news' about z^j is simply the residual error from this equation.

---

[9] It should be noted that, in principle at least, this modelling procedure needs to be repeated for each exchange rate observation in the data set. In other words, if we are trying to explain monthly exchange rate movements starting, say, in January 1980, our 'news' variables for the first month will need to have been conditioned on data from the 1970s. For obvious reasons, market anticipations cannot have been predicated on information dated later than January 1980. On the other hand, by February more information will have arrived and there is no reason why market agents could not have updated their forecasting model. Hence, a new VAR with newly estimated parameters ought to be fitted, and so on, throughout the data period.

While this updating approach is undoubtedly correct, it is not only tedious, even with the latest computer technology, it appears to yield results that are little if any improvement on a VAR estimated once over the entire period. A cynic might say this is because the relationships between the variables are in any case so weak. More positively, if there really is a stable relationship between the (current) fundamentals and their past values – if they are 'stationary', in the jargon of time-series analysis – the distinction will not matter.

This type of very general, unstructured model is known as a Vector Autoregression or VAR. The VAR has the theoretical advantage that it is neither arbitrary in the selection of variables for the information set nor does it impose an arbitrary structure on the sub-model. In addition, it has two practical advantages: firstly, it obviates the need to build a sophisticated (and possibly incorrect) sub-model of the fundamentals and secondly, it can also be shown to have some desirable econometric properties.[10]

3. Survey data

As we saw in Chapter 11 a number of researchers have made use of data taken from direct surveys of market participants, or of the economists who advise them. In the present context, survey data has two advantages to offset against the shortcomings discussed in Section 11.8. Firstly, if we have survey data on market expectations of the fundamentals we can avoid having to build a sub-model altogether. Secondly, if our data allows us to measure market forecasts of the exchange rate directly, we have no need to use the forward rate in our main model – a very considerable advantage, given the problems we have already mentioned in using the forward rate.

4. Announcement/event studies

To be useful, survey data needs to be easily translatable into a statement about forecasts for a specific horizon. In the case of discontinuous variables – like the money stock or national income, which only have observable, measurable values on announcement dates – survey expectations can only be directly compared to outcomes if they are viewed as relating to a specific announcement.

A number of studies have been published attempting to relate movements in the exchange rate to the 'news' content of money supply announcements.[11] The work has the characteristics of an event study: data is examined over a very short time-scale surrounding announcements, often hourly.

Notice that, while this work can provide potentially important evidence on the impact of individual 'packages' of 'news', it is not really a test of the standard 'news' model. Firstly, this is true because announcements tend to wrap up several 'news' items in the same 'package'. For example, the figure for the UK narrow money supply is released at the same time as that for broad money, as is the data on the volume of bank advances.

---

[10] See the Reading Guide for references.

[11] This approach was actually pioneered by researchers looking at the relationship between interest rates and the money stock in the context of domestic macroeconomic policy.

Likewise, a number of different price index announcements are made simultaneously. It therefore becomes impossible to isolate the effect of any single element in the package. Secondly, the other approaches all relate to the impact of 'news' aggregated over the whole of the time period involved, whereas the announcement approach attempts to disaggregate the impact of 'news' by concentrating on very short periods of at most a few hours, so as to be sure of isolating the impact of a single 'news' package. Thirdly, and most importantly, using directly observed expectations involves no assumption of RE. It is quite possible to imagine a scenario where money supply announcements are consistently and closely associated with exchange rate fluctuations, but where the 'news' content of the announcements is the residual from a non-rational forecasting process. In other words, the results could be consistent with a non-rational 'news' model.

5. Financial variables

One possible way to sidestep some of the problems involved in modelling the fundamentals would be to look at other financial variables which may embody the same information as the spot exchange rate, albeit within a different structure. The only work along these lines published so far uses a share price index as a proxy for expected future national income.

On the one hand, there are some considerable potential advantages in using financial variables. Firstly, they share with the major currencies the intrinsically forward-looking characteristics of continuously traded assets: prices are continuous, instantaneously reflecting (or so one might hope) daily or hourly changes in market perceptions about the level of all the relevant variables, whether they are immeasurable (like political factors or market 'confidence'), or more straightforward macroeconomic variables. Secondly, since the same agents are often active in both markets, there seems reason to suppose what is true of perceptions in one will equally hold good in the other market.[12]

On the other hand, a major difficulty with this approach is that, if it is to avoid being completely arbitrary, it requires a model relating the stock price index or other financial variable to the fundamentals. Share prices *ought* in principle to be discounted (probably risk-adjusted) sums of expected future cash flows. If the latter are directly related to expectations with regard to levels of economic activity, then stock market indices embody useful 'news'.

---

[12] Though market commentary often produces, at first sight, convincing evidence of inconsistent behaviour in the two markets, for example, the episodes in spring 1988 when the pound's international value rose on the perception in currency markets that UK fiscal, and presumably monetary policy, was tight, while share prices fell in London, apparently on fears that monetary policy was far too permissive.

Before going on to a very brief survey of the type of results that have been published in the 'news' literature, return for a moment to the general model analysed in Section 12.2. Recall that the 'bottom line' of the analysis was an equation relating the exchange rate not simply to news about the immediate prospects for the fundamentals, but to the extent to which new information led agents to revise their expectations for *all* future periods. How should this complication affect our estimation methods?

In the event, the answer is: not a great deal. It turns out that for any *linear* time-series model of the fundamentals, whether multivariate or univariate (in other words, whether we opt for the methodology in items 1 or 2 of this section) future revisions will simply be multiples of the news for the most recent period, albeit somewhat complicated multiples in most cases. Given that the revision for period $t + k$ will in any case appear with a weight of β^k, it will be virtually impossible to unscramble the time-series weights from the values of β and γ in the coefficients of future 'news'. It is hardly surprising then, that researchers have regarded the problem as of second-order importance, and have only concentrated on looking for a relationship between the exchange rate and concurrent surprises.

12.4 Results

The objective of the 'news' approach is to explain the unexpected component of exchange rate movements. In view of the volatility of this variable this is a very tall order indeed, as can be seen from a glance at Figure 11.1 – a point which must be borne in mind in assessing the results of testing the 'news' approach.

Although the work of modelling 'news' is still in its infancy, the first published results only having appeared in 1981, the verdict so far seems to be that the approach is a qualified success. On the one hand, most researchers have found some 'news' variables contribute significantly to explaining (unanticipated) exchange rate movements. On the other hand, not only is it proving difficult to identify the fundamentals and thence to isolate their surprise components, it is also becoming apparent that the 'news' approach does little to answer the question it was originally advanced to resolve: why are exchange rates so volatile?

The conclusions emerging from the published literature so far can be summarized as follows:

(1) By and large, 'news' variables make a significant contribution to explaining exchange rate fluctuations. The percentage of exchange rate variation explained by surprises in the fundamentals depends on whether we look at weekly, monthly or quarterly data, on our choice of currency and of data period and on other factors, for example how the 'news' is extracted from the fundamentals. However, a fair

assessment of the evidence so far, in this author's opinion at least, would be to say that 'news' variables explain somewhere between 5% and 20% of monthly variation in the main currencies over the last decade or so.

(2)   The conclusions do not seem to be very sensitive to the way the 'news' is extracted from the fundamentals. In spite of the theoretical advantages of multivariate (and especially VAR) methods over univariate modelling, the increased sophistication has yet to yield any noticeable improvement in the results.

(3)   The variable which most consistently yields significant results is certainly the interest rate differential, though there is some doubt as to the direction of the effect, with possibly a positive coefficient in the 1970s (reflecting unexpected inflation?) and negative in the 1980s. Money supply variables give more erratic results, often appearing insignificant and frequently wrongly signed – at least for consistency with the monetary model.[13] Income variables are problematic in the extreme, almost invariably fitting very poorly. Nor does the problem appear to be relieved by the use of stock market price indices as a proxy for expected future levels of economic activity.

(4)   Some researchers quote results suggesting that lagged 'news' terms have a significant part to play. If this is not simply due to lack of synchronization between the date attached to the 'news' variables in question and their true publication date it could be an indication of irrationality or, less plausibly, slow portfolio adjustment by currency traders. In some cases, it could result from exchange controls.

(5)   Some of the most robust results emerge from studies of announcement effects. For example, a near-unanimous finding (at least for the USA and UK) is that unexpectedly rapid monetary expansion is associated with exchange rate *appreciation*. Furthermore, this result has in some cases been supported by proper 'news' studies (that is, using explicit models of the fundamentals). The explanation seems to be that where the authorities are seen as firmly committed to non-accommodating money supply policies, unexpectedly high monetary growth generates anticipation of policy countermeasures, the effect of which will be to cause an appreciation of the domestic currency. This view, known as the **policy anticipation hypothesis**, is consistent with evidence from a large number of studies of the

---

[13] It has already been noted that the 'news' approach is consistent with many possible models of the exchange rate. The monetary model was selected in Section 12.2 as a convenient example only. If, instead of tying ourselves down to a particular model relating the exchange rate to the fundamentals we take a more agnostic view we have no reason, a priori, to expect the signs on the 'news' variables to be positive or negative.

announcement effect in a closed economy context, most of which looked at exchange rate effects only in passing, if at all.

(6)   The unsatisfactory results, particularly the residual autocorrelation reported in some econometric studies, may possibly be due to some extent to the fact that most researchers use the lagged forward rate as their proxy for the expected spot rate. As already noted, this will make little difference to their results as long as the forward market is efficient and the risk premium is more or less constant. However, this procedure will almost certainly distort the results if, as the evidence would appear to suggest (see Section 11.8), either the forward market is inefficient or the risk premium is highly volatile.

As an alternative to the lagged forward rate, this author has used s_{t-1}, the lagged spot rate itself. The justification is simple. If the spot rate follows a path which is close to a random walk, as we saw in Section 11.7, then the best possible forecast (the rational expectation) of s_t is just s_{t-1}. And, indeed, this device does improve the 'fit' of the equation quite noticeably.

(7)   All of the published work suffers from one shortcoming. No combination of 'news' variables has yet come anywhere near explaining the *volatility* of exchange rates. Now this particular failing is not unique to work with 'news'. As we have already seen in previous chapters, it characterizes *all* attempts at exchange rate modelling so far. Nonetheless, the fact is a little more disappointing in the present case, precisely because the 'news' approach was originally advocated as an explanation (and rationalization) of the turbulence of currency markets.

Striking evidence that new information cannot be 'the whole story' comes from comparisons of volatility when currency markets are closed with volatility when they are open.[14] One researcher found the variance of the return on yen (per dollar) was three times as great when the exchange was open as when it was shut. Now, if 'news' arrives in a more or less steady stream over the week, this ratio cannot be rationalized as a reaction to perceived changes in the fundamentals.

If informational surprises cannot explain volatility, we now turn to the question of what alternatives remain.

---

[14] The contrast is between the extent to which rates vary over the business day and the variance overnight, that is, between closing rates in the evening and the opening rate on the following day (or the next Monday, for a weekend). Thus, if 'news' arrives evenly over 24 hours and the exchange is open, say, for 12 hours, one would expect to find the variance of the overnight change equal to that of the opening-to-closing change.

★ 12.5 Volatility tests, bubbles and the peso problem

One explanation for volatility that has received a considerable amount of attention in recent years is the possibility that currency markets may be characterized by temporary, *rational bubbles*.[15]

At an intuitive level bubbles are easy to understand, reflecting the familiar phenomenon of a self-reinforcing movement in the price away from its equilibrium level. Since time immemorial, laymen have observed that in this type of situation 'everyone thinks that the price is too high but no one expects it to fall yet'. And, indeed, it is hard to find any other explanation for some of the most spectacular price surges (or collapses) – even long after the event.

Viewed with the benefit of hindsight, it has usually been taken for granted that the most notorious price bubbles in history resulted from investor irrationality: 'market psychology', 'mass hysteria' and so forth. While this type of explanation certainly cannot be ruled out, recent work has shown that bubbles can be reconciled with rational market behaviour. Remember that, once a bubble has started, it becomes the reality with which the investor has to live. However loudly the economist may appeal to exchange rate fundamentals and the notional equilibrium they imply – it will all be irrelevant to the trader actually in the market as long as the bubble persists, *even if the trader is perfectly rational*.

Take an example. Many people (including the majority of economists, traders, bankers and politicians) believed that the US dollar was vastly overvalued on any reasonable criterion during the mid 1980s.[16] Yet, in the face of this consensus, the high exchange rate was maintained for two years or more. Why? It is difficult to say with any confidence, but what is certainly true is that it was *not* obviously rational at the time to sell dollars, even if one shared the view that the dollar was overvalued. On the contrary, it made sense to hold dollars – as long as one believed the bubble would last, and as long as one was adequately compensated for the perceived risk that the bubble might burst.

Now consider for a moment the implication of this. How can I be adequately compensated for the risk of holding a currency which, as a rational agent, fully aware of the market fundamentals, I *know* is overvalued? Obviously, the risk can be offset by the prospect of capital gain. But this leads us to the conclusion that, at any point in the history of a bubble, the more overvalued the currency, and the greater the probability

---

[15] Also known as 'bootstraps', 'sunspots', or 'will o' the wisp' equilibria. Note that this is another case where research on exchange rates has accompanied research on other financial assets, particularly share prices.

[16] See Section 2.5.

the bubble will burst, the more rapidly it must rise so as to compensate for the increased risk.[17]

This picture of life inside a price bubble has probably been familiar to practitioners ever since the first caveman-speculator stored food so as to gamble on an exceptionally hard winter ahead.[18] However, as the reader will by now have become aware, economists take comfort from being able to replicate the wisdom of the ages in mathematical models. In the case of the rational bubble, the comfort comes from noting that Equation 12.15, the 'market fundamentals solution' to the RE model of Section 12.2, is *not* unique, as was pointed out at the time. Consider the following:

$$s_t = \gamma (1 + b)^{-1} \sum_{k=0}^{N} \beta^k E_t z_{t+k} + B_t \qquad (12.20)$$

which simply adds on to the market fundamentals solution in Equation 12.15 a term B_t – the price bubble at time t. Now, as long as B_t has the property that:

$$E_t B_{t+1} = \beta^{-1} B_t \qquad (12.21)$$

which is a condition satisfied by a number of commonly encountered economic series, it can be shown that Equation 12.21 satisfies the original difference equation (Equation 12.11) every bit as well as the pure market fundamentals solution does.[19]

The bubble term, B_t, can be defined as simply the extent of the deviation from the market fundamental equilibrium. Unfortunately the theory has, as yet, nothing to say about *how* or *why* a bubble develops. There are two ways of looking at the role it plays. Firstly, it is sufficient that agents perceive the bubble factor to be important for it actually to be important – if it figures in their subjective model, it will find its way into the objective

---

[17] In other words, the critical question facing the investor in this type of situation is not the direction of the next major price movement, but its timing. As this author found out to his cost in 1985, even when you are right in judging a currency to be mispriced, you can still lose money if it continues to be mispriced for longer than you expected!

[18] History records a number of spectacular events that were regarded as bubbles either at the time or fairly soon after they burst, for example, the Dutch Tulip Bubble, the Mississippi Bubble, the South Sea Bubble, and more debatably, the bull markets that preceded the Wall Street crashes of 1929 and 1987.

In some cases, the bubbles were initiated by fraudsters who successfully duped irrational, or at least ill-informed, traders. However, that fact does not rule out the possibility that at some point a rational bubble mechanism may well have been at work in the market.

[19] To prove that this is true follow the same procedure as the one outlined for Equation 12.15, making use of Equation 12.21 *en route*.

Note that the analysis of bubbles exploits the well-known property of difference equations that they permit an infinite number of solutions, each being the sum of a general and a particular component.

model driving the exchange rate. Secondly, we could be said to be dealing with a variable which is unobservable to economists but observable to market agents.[20]

At any point in time, there must be some perceived probability that the bubble will burst next period. If it does burst, the exchange rate will return to the level dictated by the fundamentals. Otherwise, its movements will continue to reflect the behaviour of the bubble.

The simplest model would take the following form. Suppose the probability that the bubble, B_t, will last another period is Π and the probability it will burst is $(1 - \Pi)$. We then have the following possible outcomes for the next period, $t + 1$:

$$B_{t+1} = (\beta \Pi)^{-1} B_t \qquad \text{with probability } \Pi$$

$$= 0 \qquad \text{with probability } (1 - \Pi)$$

The reader can easily verify that this is consistent with the restriction in Equation 12.21.

In this simple case, as long as the bubble persists, the exchange rate will appreciate sufficiently enough in order to compensate a risk neutral currency holder for the possibility of loss when the bubble bursts. What this means is that, in addition to any rise justified by changes in the fundamentals, there will need to be an explosive bubble superimposed, because the greater the current divergence from equilibrium, the further the currency has left to fall, and hence the greater the prospective capital gain needs to be if the process is to be sustained.

Notice that this is more a detailed description of the phenomenon than an explanation. The literature has, as yet, little to say about what causes bubbles to start or end.[21] On the basis of casual observation, it seems that some bubbles (or apparent bubbles) are triggered by movements in the fundamentals, actual or perceived. Others seem to be spontaneous. In this respect the theory offers little enlightenment since it treats the bubble as simply a fact of life, exogenous not only to the behaviour of the market but to the fundamentals themselves. Indeed, as we can see from Equation 12.20, as long as the bubble persists it will cause the exchange rate to move, even when the fundamentals are unchanged.[22]

How will the presence of bubbles show up in the data? Obviously, the effect will be to weaken the overall link between the exchange rate and the fundamentals, even supposing that one can identify them. In terms of RE models it can be shown that ignoring the bubble term in standard

---

[20] This is not quite as implausible as it sounds, if only because there are many factors affecting exchange rates which are not included in economists' data sets because they are inherently difficult to quantify, for example political factors.

[21] Though in the example given here, it can be shown the bubble will have an expected duration of $(1 - \Pi)^{-1}$.

econometric work may well produce results that apparently contradict rationality – intuitively because a persistent positive bubble will generate a series of underpredictions in forecasts based on the fundamentals, and vice versa for negative bubbles.

Work on bubbles is still proceeding, and it is as yet difficult to say how far the facts are consistent with the theory, though some direct tests have been published. By and large, the evidence on some recent episodes (for example the 'overvaluation' of the dollar in the mid 1980s) is consistent with rational bubbles though it could also be explained, as always, by investor irrationality.

The presence of bubbles could possibly account for the failure of 'news' models to explain the variability of exchange rates. Indirect support for the view that bubbles have been at work in currency markets in recent years is provided by formal comparisons of the variability of the exchange rate, on the one hand, and the fundamentals, on the other, *excess volatility or variance bounds tests*, as they are called.

To understand how these tests are formulated, compare the following equation with Equation 12.15 in Section 12.2:

$$s_t^* = \gamma (1 + b)^{-1} \sum_{k=0}^{N} \beta^k z_{t+k} \tag{12.15'}$$

The right-hand side is simply Equation 12.15, with *actual* values of z_{t+k} replacing *expected* values. In other words, s_t^* is the level at which the exchange rate would settle if the market participants had perfect foresight. Since they cannot know the future, and have to rely on expectations, the actual exchange rate is given by:

$$s_t = E_t s_t^* \tag{12.22}$$

which is simply a tidy way of rewriting Equation 12.15, using our newly introduced definition of the perfect foresight exchange rate.

Now the only reason why the perfect foresight value of the exchange rate, s_t^*, differs from its expected value, s_t, is because of 'news' about future fundamentals. Since, under RE, 'news' items are all random their total

---

[22] There is no reason in principle why we could not respecify the simple model given here to make the probabilities depend on the market fundamentals, but not only does this complicate the analysis, it is also completely arbitrary.

There are a number of other possible extensions to the model which would make it more realistic, inevitably at the cost of some considerable complication. For example, allowing for the fact investors may be risk averse will exacerbate the explosive behaviour of the exchange rate, because an additional capital gain will be required to compensate currency holders, over and above the capital gain needed under risk neutrality. Also, the market might well perceive the chance of a crash to depend on the length of time the bubble has already run. Since the greater the probability of a crash, the more rapidly the exchange rate must increase, this modification makes the model even more explosive.

impact, as measured by the weighted sum on the right-hand side of Equation 12.15, must equally be random. It follows that we can write:

$$s_t^* = E_t s_t^* + u_t \tag{12.23}$$

$$= s_t + u_t$$

where, as we saw in Chapter 11, u_t not only has an average value of zero, it is also uncorrelated with the expected value itself. In other words, if we take the variances (see Box 12.3) of the right and left-hand sides of Equation 12.23, we derive:

$$var(s_t^*) = var(s_t) + var(u_t) \tag{12.24}$$

since we know that the covariance between s_t and u_t must be zero. As variances are always positive, this implies the following inequality test:

$$var(s_t^*) \geqslant var(s_t) \tag{12.25}$$

which states that, under RE, the variance of the actual exchange rate must be no greater than the variance of the fundamentals which drive it.

Notice this test is very general, in so far as it places no restriction on the variables to be included amongst the market fundamentals. In other words, it is not purely a test of the RE monetary model.

For technical reasons, many researchers test slightly modified versions of Equation 12.23. In any case, the result is a near-unanimous

---

BOX 12.3   Variance and covariance of random variables.

The variance of a random variable, X, is a measure of its dispersion, computed by taking the average of the squared deviations from its mean value. In general, for two random variables, X and Y, if we define:

$$Z = aX + bY$$

then it follows that:

$$var(Z) = a^2 var(X) + b^2 var(Y) + 2ab.cov(XY)$$

where $cov(XY)$ denotes the covariance of X and Y, defined as the average of the product of the deviations of X and Y from their respective means. Obviously, if $cov(XY)$ is zero, we can conclude that:

$$var(Z) = a^2 var(X) + b^2 var(Y)$$

For details, see any elementary statistics textbook.

conclusion: *exchange rate volatility is excessive relative to the volatility of the fundamentals.* In other words, the right-hand side of Equation 12.25 is unambiguously greater than the left.

To put this conclusion in perspective, it is worth pointing out that 'variance bounds' tests were originally used in research on stock market prices and dividends, with similar results: share price volatility is too great to be consistent with the degree of variation in dividends.

Notice the crucial distinction between tests in these two cases. In the case of stock prices, we can identify the fundamentals with some confidence. Under these circumstances, inequality tests are not only more informative, but can also legitimately be interpreted as tests of stock market efficiency.

In the case of the exchange rate, we can have far less confidence in our choice of fundamental variables. It follows that these tests can only throw light on the question of how far the facts are consistent with the view that exchange rates are (1) driven by a particular set of fundamentals and (2) not subject to bubbles. They are not very illuminating on the more general question of spot market efficiency.

There are a number of possible explanations of the apparent excess volatility of the major exchange rates: either currency markets are irrational, or there are significant (rational) bubbles, or important and highly volatile fundamental variables have been omitted. The latter explanation seems improbable, at least in so far as it relates to economic variables. The only variables that fluctuate anywhere near enough to overturn the main findings are financial series, like stock market prices, which are themselves excessively volatile, as has already been mentioned.[23]

However, at least one other conceivable explanation has been offered: the so-called **Peso Problem**.[24] It relates to the inherent difficulties that arise in sampling economic events, which are by their very nature once-and-for-all experiments, incapable of ever being replicated. To see what is involved, take a topical example.

Suppose, at the time of writing (mid 1989), currency markets perceive the UK authorities to be likely at some stage to give in to the mounting pressure to join the European Monetary System (EMS).[25] And suppose the market believes that accession, if and when it occurs, will be at a fixed exchange rate of £1 = DM3.00.

---

[23] An unexplored question is how far rational or irrational bubbles in one market are associated with bubbles in another.

[24] The term was coined by a researcher who took as his classic case the behaviour of the Mexican peso which, although notionally on a fixed exchange rate, traded consistently at a forward discount to the US dollar in the mid 1970s, in anticipation of a devaluation that duly materialized in 1976.

[25] Official Government policy is for the UK to accede to full membership 'when the time is right' (*sic*).

Clearly this event will be influencing market expectations at the present moment. It may be the case, for example, that the probability of accession within the next week is regarded as minute – say 0.001, or one in a thousand. On the other hand, the likelihood of accession at some point within the next 12 months may be regarded as far greater, with particularly high probability being attached to weekends when European finance ministers are due to meet. At a five-year horizon, accession will no doubt be given an even higher probability – say 40% or more, perhaps even 90%.

Now what this means is that today's spot rate of over DM3.12 to the pound will be lower than otherwise because of the (albeit tiny) probability that, during the holding period of the typical currency trader, sterling will be devalued to a new (fixed) rate of £1.00 = DM3.00. Furthermore, this cloud, however small, will cast its shadow over the forward market too, where the premium or discount will be less favourable to the pound than seems warranted on the basis of the *observable* fundamentals alone.

As can be readily seen, the result will be that models based on RE will apparently fail. In the current scenario, the otherwise 'correct' model (that is, the one that appeared to fit the facts *before* the prospect of EMS membership appeared on the horizon) will seem to overestimate the value of the pound. There are two ways of looking at the reason why the relationship between the fundamentals and the exchange rate will seem to have broken down.

The first would be to say there is a variable omitted from the list of market fundamentals: the probability of a once-and-for-all discrete change in the currency regime. The omission is not simply an oversight. We are dealing with a variable that is inherently difficult to measure – but that certainly does *not* mean it is unimportant. Indeed, it may be the case that many of the apparent departures from rationality are in reality due to unexpected shifts in unobservable or immeasurable variables.

The second is that the peso problem is also a sampling problem. In principle, just as we should expect to find approximately 50 heads in 100 tosses of a coin, so we should expect to find one example of an event like EMS accession in a thousand-week sample if, as we suppose, the probability of its occurring is really 0.001. However, if our sample period is only 500 weeks our sampling freqency may be zero leading us, mistakenly, to discount the event altogether as impossible. Indeed, the event may *never* occur. But that fact alone does not mean it was irrational to take the possibility into account – any more than we can say a man who survives a game of Russian roulette was irrational to make out his will prior to playing!

Note that there are similarities between the peso problem and the phenomenon of rational bubbles. Both, it must be emphasized, are entirely consistent with rational behaviour displayed by individual market participants. The difference is that whereas bubbles represent a divergence from the equilibrium associated with the market fundamentals, the peso problem arises out of the small probability of a large, discrete shift in the value of one or more of the fundamental variables themselves.

As a consequence, it follows that the interpretation of variance bounds tests is, or rather could be, different in the case of the peso problem from what it would be in the presence of bubbles. As we saw, the common finding that the volatility of exchange rates is greater than that of the fundamentals, could well be indicative of the presence of price bubbles. However, if over some part of our data period there was a widespread feeling that a major shift in the fundamentals could not be ruled out, it will follow that our estimate of the variance of the fundamentals will be an underestimate of the market's (rational) perception of the variance at the time.

This possibility may well invalidate our conclusion altogether: the fact that the variance bounds are breached could be a result neither of irrationality nor bubbles, but simply of the failure to take account of a significant event to which the market allocated a non-zero probability, even if it never subsequently materialized.

The peso problem is a particularly intractable obstacle to research, at least where standard econometric methods are concerned. The most hopeful approach would seem to be direct measurement of market expectations, though the relevant data has only recently become available, and, as was mentioned in Chapter 11, survey data presents researchers with a new set of methodological problems. Alternatively, there is one other way in which we could directly observe the market's assessment of exchange rate volatility: by extracting implied variances from traded options data. This approach has yet to be implemented, though at the time of writing a number of researchers are working along these lines.

12.6 Conclusions

In a sense, the conclusions reached in this chapter have been negative: the 'news' approach can explain some of the variation in exchange rates, but is ultimately defeated by their sheer volatility. The impression that the task is hopeless is reinforced by direct comparisons of the variance of exchange rates with the variance of the elements that are supposed to explain it.

Moreover, these conclusions will almost certainly be supported by research using the most recent data, when it is published. Currency markets, along with other financial markets seem to have become more volatile throughout the 1980s. In fact the trend appears to be accelerating, at least since the cataclysmic events of October 1987.

Appropriately, then, Chapter 13 will deal with a different aspect of exchange rate volatility: the risk premium and its implications.

■ **Summary**

- The 'news' approach involves relating unexpected movements in the exchange rate to revisions in the market's rational forecast of the fundamental variables. In a simple RE model this relationship will be the same as the one between the level of the exchange rate and the level of the fundamentals.

- In general, the value of a currency will depend crucially on the prospective capital gains or losses (that is, the expected rate of appreciation or depreciation) that the market expects to see accruing to holders.

- When the value of a currency depends on its expected rate of change as well as on the market fundamentals its behaviour will follow a difference equation, the solution of which relates the current level of the exchange rate to a weighted sum of current and expected future values of the fundamental variables. The weights will decline geometrically as we go forward in time, starting with a weight of unity on the current value of the fundamentals. Furthermore, the identical relationship will hold between the unexpected component of the exchange rate and the innovations (or 'news') in the fundamentals – which is the formulation known as the 'news' approach.

- There are a number of problems to be overcome in making the 'news' model operational, notably the problem of how to estimate the 'news' variables themselves. Most published work has used univariate or multivariate time series or econometric methods in order to model the fundamentals, taking the residuals as estimates of the 'news'.

- The results of implementing the 'news' approach are mixed. On the positive side the equations tend to fit reasonably well, frequently explaining a non-negligible proportion of the substantial degree of exchange rate fluctuation left undiscounted by the forward premium. On the other hand, the volatility of (unanticipated) exchange rate movements remains largely unexplained by the 'news'.

- Under RE, it ought to be the case that the variance of the observed spot rate is no greater than that of the fundamentals which determine it. Most tests suggest that the opposite is the case. In other words, the volatility of the exchange rate is greater than can be rationalized by reference to the market fundamentals.

- One possible explanation of the observed volatility could be rational price bubbles, which are said to occur when a gap opens up between the level of the spot rate and its equilibrium value, as determined by the fundamentals. Another explanation could be that agents attached a (possibly small) probability to the chance of a discrete, step change in the fundamentals, in which case the apparent, measured variance taken from the data may be an underestimate of the variance as actually perceived by rational traders (the 'peso problem').

READING GUIDE

The paper that started the 'news' literature was Frenkel (1981), though the approach was derived in some respects from one already well established in closed economy macroeconomics (for example Barro (1977)). Both papers are relatively non-technical. Other influential papers have been by Edwards (1983) and Hartley (1983).

An up-to-date (but fairly technical) survey is to be found in MacDonald and Taylor (1989), which gives a particularly good treatment of the subject matter of Section 12.5. For a discussion of some of the outstanding issues in this area, particularly the estimation problems, see Copeland (1989) and references therein.

The peso problem was first discussed by Krasker (1980). Most of the original work on variance bounds focused on stock markets (for example Grossman and Shiller (1981)), though researchers have tended to develop specialized versions of the tests to deal with exchange rates (for example Meese and Singleton (1983)). For dissenting views on volatility see West (1987) on the DM/dollar rate and Honohan and Peruga (1987), who claim the bounds are only breached if PPP is imposed.

Both bubbles and the peso problem are discussed briefly and in non-technical fashion by Dornbusch (1982). Two important early papers on the theory of bubbles (and the related question of collapsing fixed rate regimes) are to be found in Chapters 10 and 11 of Wachtel (1982), written by Flood and Garber, and Blanchard and Watson. More recently, see Diba and Grossman (1988).

As far as empirical work is concerned Evans (1986) is of interest, claiming to find a bubble in the returns to sterling holders in the early 1980s. Meese (1986) is only accessible to readers with a background in time-series econometrics. For a historical perspective on bubbles in financial markets, see Kindleberger (1978).

13

The Risk Premium

■   Introduction

We have referred to the risk premium associated with international speculation on numerous occasions throughout this book, without making any attempt to say what factors determine its size. It is now time to rectify this omission.

Unfortunately, not only is the subject a difficult one, it also involves different analytical tools from those used in the rest of the book. In particular, it relies on microeconomics – the theory of constrained choice – as well as on mathematical statistics. To make the material in this chapter as accessible as possible many complicating issues will be side-stepped. For the most part, the simplifications introduced have little effect on the central question of what determines the scale of the compensation required by a risk-averse economic agent to persuade him to speculate.

The chapter takes the following form. We start in the first section by listing a number of basic assumptions which allow us to focus on the issue at hand, without getting side-tracked into consideration of extraneous questions. Then in Section 13.2, a simplified model is analysed using the indifference curve techniques familiar from basic microeconomics. The next section, which some readers may choose to omit, goes on to analyse formally a model which, though not much more complicated, is a lot more general. Finally, as usual, the chapter closes with a brief review of the evidence on the risk premium, followed by some conclusions.

Before continuing, there are a number of preliminaries the reader is advised to undertake.

(1)   If necessary, check the definitions of risk aversion, risk neutrality, the risk premium and so on, introduced initially in Section 3.1.3.

(2)   Where necessary, readers should refresh their understanding of what is meant by an *expected value* (Section 11.1) and a *variance* (Box 12.3 of Chapter 12). The concept of *covariance* also plays an important part in Section 13.3. A brief definition will be given there to refresh the reader's memory. Explanations of all three concepts can be found in any elementary statistics textbook. (Note that the *standard deviation* is defined simply as the positive square root of the variance.)

(3)   Readers with no previous acquaintance with indifference curve analysis will find Section 13.2 heavy going. Unless, as an alternative, they can take the material in Section 13.3 in their stride, they would be best to read the chapter on indifference curves in an introductory economics textbook before proceeding.

(4)   Section 13.3 takes the theory of expected utility for granted. The Reading Guide provides references for those who wish to investigate these foundations further. However, an understanding of expected utility theory is certainly not required in order to cope with the material in this chapter.

13.1 Assumptions

The analysis in this chapter will focus on a representative economic agent ('the speculator'), whose environment is characterized by the following assumptions.[1]

(1)   There is a perfect capital market, with no transaction costs of any kind, and in particular no margin requirements for forward purchases or sales.[2]

---

[1] These assumptions, though restrictive, for the most part serve only to simplify the analysis. Most can be relaxed without weakening the conclusions very significantly (see Section 13.3.5).

[2] In principle, a forward transaction requires no advance commitment of funds. In practice however, margin calls are often required by brokers from would-be buyers of forward contracts.

(2) Only two periods are relevant to the decision: 'the present' (period 0) and 'the future' (period 1).

(3) The speculator seeks to maximize the expected value of his utility, which depends only on the amount of consumption he can enjoy in period 1, C_1. Marginal utility diminishes as consumption increases, a condition equivalent to assuming risk aversion. For simplicity we assume that no consumption takes place in period 0.

(4) There is no inflation.

(5) Other than a given quantity of wealth, W_0 (a fixed 'endowment'), the resources available for consumption in the future can only be increased by the device of speculation in forward contracts. (In other words, the possibility of buying other assets in period 0 is ruled out by assumption.)

Every pound spent on buying dollars forward costs (that is, reduces consumable resources by) $£F_0$, which is the current price of a dollar for delivery in period 1. On the other hand, it will increase consumption by $£S_1$, the spot price of dollars in period 1, when the currency is delivered and is available for exchange back into sterling on the spot market.

Net, therefore, for each pound of forward dollars purchased, future consumption benefits (or suffers) to the tune of $£(S_1 - F_0)$. If the investor spends $£A$ on forward purchases future consumption will be increased (or diminished) by $£(S_1 - F_0)A$. It follows that the total amount available for consumption will be:

$$C_1 = (S_1 - F_0)A + W_0 \tag{13.1}$$

Obviously, unless A is *zero*, C_1 will be uncertain as of period 0. Forward purchases of dollars will *increase* future consumption if the price of dollars *rises*, but will *decrease* consumption if the opposite occurs.

These assumptions will be maintained throughout the next two sections. We shall examine briefly the consequences of relaxing each of them in Section 13.3.5.

13.2 A simple model of the risk premium: mean–variance analysis

One way of representing the problem facing the currency speculator is by using the indifference curve framework familiar from the analysis of household utility maximization. In order to use that analysis, we shall have to make an additional assumption, though it will be dropped in the next section.

Specifically, let us suppose that the agent in the forward market bases his decision making solely on two parameters: the expected value of his future consumption and the risk associated with it, *as measured by its standard deviation*.

13.2.1 The indifference map

First, consider the objects of choice. In elementary microeconomics the household's tastes are defined with respect to combinations ('baskets') of two goods both of which are inherently desirable, so that more of either good is always preferable, other things being equal (that is, provided no sacrifice of the other good is required). Given that both goods are desirable, it follows that indifference curves tracing out all combinations of the two goods which yield any particular level of satisfaction will be *downward* sloping, reflecting the fact that sacrifices of one good need to be compensated by increments of the other if a constant level of utility is to be maintained.

In the present case the objects of choice on the two axes consist of one desirable characteristic, expected consumption, written *in this section only* as μ,[3] and one undesirable characteristic, risk – as measured by the standard deviation of consumption, written σ_C.[4] What will the indifference curves look like?

Consider a point on the vertical axis in Figure 13.1, like μ^0. It represents a position of no risk (no forward contracts), with a guaranteed future consumption level of μ^0. In order to draw the indifference curve through this point, we need to locate combinations of the two characteristics μ and σ_C which yield the same level of satisfaction as the certain consumption level μ^0.

Obviously, since any move away from the vertical axis involves taking on risk, the speculator will not voluntarily do so unless he is compensated – this is what is meant by risk aversion. Compensation can only take the form of higher expected consumption in the future. If the additional future expected consumption is great enough, he will willingly take on risk. The process can continue: he can be persuaded to take on even more risk by the carrot of greater expected consumption. Therefore, any combinations of μ and σ_C which yield the same utility as μ^0 must lie above and to the right of μ^0.

We conclude that the indifference curves will slope *upward* from left to right, associating *greater risk* with higher *expected values* as

---

[3] The Greek letter 'mu' is often used to denote the mean of a random variable. Here, it replaces $E(C_1)$ which is difficult to use in a diagram.

[4] This notation is logical, given that the standard deviation is the square root of the variance, which is by convention denoted σ^2. Note the subscript 'C', to allow us to distinguish between the standard deviation of consumption and the standard deviation of the future spot exchange rate, σ_s, on which, among other things, it depends.

Figure 13.1 Speculator's equilibrium in the simple model.

compensation. Furthermore, the greater the degree of risk aversion, the steeper the curves, because the greater is the compensation needed to persuade the investor to accept risk.

In addition, by an argument analogous to the one used to guarantee the convexity of indifference curves in the elementary model of household demand, it is reasonable to assume in the present case that the indifference curves will get steeper, as the compensation required per unit of risk increases with the quantity of risk already undertaken. In other words, the indifference curves will be convex from beneath, as in Figure 13.1.

Plainly, we could have used any point on the vertical axis as our starting point for drawing an indifference curve. It follows that the higher up is the indifference curve, the greater the level of utility associated with the combinations on it. Thus, combinations along the curve labelled I_2 are preferable to those on I_1, which in turn are preferable to those on I_0, and so on. The speculator's objective is obviously to reach the highest possible indifference curve.

13.2.2 The constraint: the speculative opportunity line

The constraint on the investor is derived from Equation 13.1, which showed how consumption is related to the chosen value of A, given initial wealth, W_0, the forward rate, F_0, and the outcome for the spot rate, S_1.

Firstly, consider what is implied for the *expected* value of consumption:

$$EC_1 \equiv \mu_C = (ES_1 - F_0)A + W_0 \tag{13.2}$$

because of course both the forward rate and the initial level of wealth are known as of time 0 – only the future spot rate is uncertain (see Box 13.1).

Now we need to calculate the standard deviation of consumption. The variance of consumption, σ_C^2, is simply the expected value of the squared deviation from the mean (or expected value itself):

$$\sigma_C^2 = E[(C_1 - \mu_C)^2] \tag{13.3}$$
$$= E\{[A(S_1 - ES_1)]^2\}$$
$$= A^2 E[S_1 - ES_1]^2$$
$$= A^2 \sigma_S^2$$

where σ_S^2 is the variance of the spot rate.[5] Since the standard deviation is simply the (positive) square root of the variance, this means:

$$A = \pm \frac{\sigma_C}{\sigma_S} \tag{13.4}$$

A will only be positive when the premium is positive. If the premium is negative, that is $(ES_1 - F_0) < 0$, then a positive value of A would imply a *lower* expected value of consumption than W_0, for a position involving risk. For a risk-averse agent this is out of the question. It follows that A must take the same sign as the premium, and for the purposes of the exposition here it will be assumed that both are positive.

BOX 13.1

Strictly, Equation 13.2 should read:

$$E_o C_1 \equiv \mu_C = (E_o S_1 - F_0)A + W_0$$

The subscripts on the expectations operator are suppressed throughout this chapter, however, since they always date from the first period.

---

[5] The second line of Equation 13.3 is computed simply by subtracting Equation 13.2 from Equation 13.1.

Now if we substitute for A from Equation 13.4 into Equation 13.2, we find:

$$\mu_C = \frac{\sigma_C}{\sigma_S}|ES_1 - F_0| + W_0 \tag{13.5}$$

$$= \rho'\sigma_C + W_0$$

where:

$$\rho' \equiv \frac{|ES_1 - F_0|}{\sigma_s}$$

is the risk premium normalized by the standard deviation of the spot rate.

Equation 13.5 plays the same part in the speculator's problem as the budget constraint does in the household's demand decision. It shows the trade-off between the risk and expected consumption on offer in the market, at the current level of the (normalized) risk premium.

Starting from the vertical axis of Figure 13.1, with expected consumption of W_0 achievable without speculation and hence at no risk then increased consumption can be obtained at the rate of ρ' times each additional unit of standard deviation. Speculation therefore moves the risk-return combination up a straight line with gradient ρ' and intercept W_0, like those through points H and J in Figure 13.1.

13.2.3 Equilibrium

With a risk premium of ρ'_0, the utility-maximizing combination is the familiar tangency solution at H. At this point the speculative opportunity line touches the highest possible indifference curve, so that the (normalized) market risk premium is equal to the agent's subjective marginal exchange rate between risk and expected consumption. The optimal position in forward contracts, A_0^*, can be read off in the bottom quadrant, where the straight line plots the relationship given by Equation 13.4.

Since the speculative opportunity line has gradient ρ', an increase in the normalized risk premium (from, say, ρ'_0 to ρ'_1) – whether originating in a fall in F_0 or σ_S, or rise in ES_1 – causes it to pivot upwards about the intercept W_0. Figure 13.1 shows what must be assumed to be the most likely outcome: an increase in the number of forward contracts held, from A_0^* to A_1^*.

The conclusion cannot be unambiguous, however, because a rise in ρ' makes the speculator better off, in so far as he is given the opportunity of enjoying more attractive combinations of expected consumption and risk. In response to this 'windfall gain' he may, depending on his tastes as reflected in the gradient of his indifference curves, react by settling at a point above and to the left of his original equilibrium at H. In other words, he might decide to take the benefit of the improvement in the market opportunities in the form of only a slim increase in his expected consumption and a major reduction in his risk exposure.

If the typical speculator had tastes like these, the forward market would be completely unstable.It must be assumed, therefore, that the typical agent in the forward market will tend to increase his exposure when the risk premium rises (as illustrated in the diagram at the point J) – though possibly not by very much.[6]

★ 13.3 A general model of the risk premium

The model outlined in the previous section was simplified by the special assumption that tastes were defined with respect to only two parameters of the distribution of future consumption: mean and standard deviation. While this simplification made it possible to conduct the analysis using the well-known diagrammatic apparatus of indifference curves, it had the disadvantage of being very restrictive, in ways which will be made clear later in this section.

What we shall do now is outline a model which is general enough to require only the assumptions already listed in Section 13.1. In order to do so however, we shall need to rely on algebra rather than diagrams.

13.3.1 The speculator's decision problem

The critical decision the speculator faces is how many pounds, A, to commit to forward purchases so as to maximize his expected utility. Formally, he must solve the following problem:

$$\overset{max}{A} \quad E[U(C_1)]$$

subject to the constraint that the total available for consumption in period 1 is as given in Equation 13.1, repeated here for convenience:

$$C_1 = (S_1 - F_0)A + W_0 \qquad \qquad \textbf{(13.1)}$$
$$\text{repeated}$$

Notice this is *not* the same thing as saying our speculator tries to maximize expected consumption. The solution to the problem of how to maximize expected consumption is both easy and absurd: if the risk premium $ES_1 - F_0$ is positive (negative), buy (sell) an infinite number of forward contracts, making the expected value of consumption infinite. Only for a risk-neutral agent is expected utility maximization equivalent to maximizing expected consumption – which is precisely why we conclude

---

[6] In other words, in terms of the textbook model of choice, we assume the substitution effect dominates the windfall-gain (or income) effect.

that, if the *typical* individual in the currency markets is risk neutral, the risk premium will be arbitraged down to zero.

If the typical agent is risk averse, however, increased risk will carry a utility penalty, so that there will be a subjective trade-off between risk and the expected return to speculation, as we saw in Section 13.2.[7]

13.3.2 The solution

In order to find the maximum, we need only differentiate the utility function with respect to A, which yields:

$$\frac{\partial E[U(C_1)]}{\partial A} = E\left\{\frac{\partial U}{\partial C_1}\frac{\partial C_1}{\partial A}\right\} \tag{13.6}$$

$$= E\{U'(C_1) \cdot (S_1 - F_0)\}$$

$$= E\{U'(C_1) \cdot S_1\} - F_0 E[U'(C_1)]$$

The first line comes from recognizing that the variation in expected utility arises out of the changes in C_1 induced by changes in A. Writing out the two partial derivatives explicitly (the next line), the final line follows, as long as we remember that F_0 is known, non-stochastic.

Now, for the utility-maximizing value of A – call it A^* – the derivative in Equation 13.6 must equal zero,[8] which means we must have:

$$F_0 E[U'(C_1)] = E\{U'(C_1) \cdot S_1\} \tag{13.7}$$

This is one way of presenting the solution. The left-hand side can be interpreted as the (marginal) opportunity cost (in terms of expected utility) per pound speculated in the forward market: the price of a forward dollar times the expected marginal utility of consumption. The right-hand side is the expected marginal benefit in utility terms. The solution thus fits into the familiar pattern of constrained choice, equating the marginal benefit to the marginal cost, appropriately redefined to accommodate uncertainty.

A more useful way of presenting the conclusion can be found. Start by rewriting Equation 13.7 in terms of the forward rate:

$$F_0 = \frac{E\{U'(C_1) \cdot S_1\}}{E[U'(C_1)]} \tag{13.8}$$

---

[7] The point being made here is familiar from the literature on risk bearing in general (see the Reading Guide for references).

[8] Strictly, a maximum requires not only that the first derivative be zero, but also that the second derivative be negative. The latter condition is simply the risk-aversion assumption in Section 13.1.

Now one way of presenting the definition of the covariance[9] of two random variables, X and Y, is as follows:

$$cov(X, Y) = E(XY) - (EX)(EY)$$

which in turn means that:

$$E(XY) = cov(X, Y) + (EX)(EY)$$

Using this relationship in the numerator on the right-hand side of Equation 13.8, we derive:

$$F_0 = \frac{E[U'(C_1)]ES_1}{E[U'(C_1)]} + \frac{cov[U'(C_1), S_1]}{E[U'(C_1)]} \tag{13.9}$$

$$= ES_1 + \frac{cov[U'(C_1), S_1]}{E[U'(C_1)]}$$

so that the ratio on the right is the risk premium.

In this form, the conclusion states that each agent will take a forward position such that the market risk premium is equal to the ratio of the covariance between his marginal utility and the spot rate to his expected marginal utility. As a group, speculators will drive the forward rate to a level that reflects the appropriately weighted aggregate covariance.

In equilibrium, with net demand for forward contracts equal to the supply, the market risk premium will reflect this covariance term. Intuitively, the explanation for this result is one that will look familiar to readers who have had a previous encounter with modern finance theory.

It is a commonplace of portfolio analysis that the risk associated with any particular investment can never be judged in isolation. Instead, it needs to be assessed in terms of the extent to which it increases or decreases the riskiness of the individual's position as a whole. Now it is easy to see that, at the margin, the contribution of any asset (call it the nth) to the overall riskiness of a portfolio of assets is measured by the covariance of its return with those of the other, $n - 1$. For example, in the simplest case where the initial portfolio contains only one security, buying another asset whose return mimics the first, being high in circumstances when the first is high and low on exactly the same occasions, only serves to scale up the risk. On the other hand, adding instead a second security which pays a good return in precisely the situations where the first loses money is an

---

[9] The covariance of two random variables, X and Y, is given by:

$$cov(X, Y) = E[(X - EX)(Y - EY)]$$

In other words, the expectation of the product of the deviations from their respective mean values. As the name implies the covariance is a measure of the extent to which two variables tend to move in unison. If both tend to be above (or below) their expected values at the same time, their covariance will be positive. However, if one tends to be relatively high when the other is low, the covariance will be negative.

Notice that the variance is a special case of the covariance – the variance of X is the covariance of X with itself. As such, it is always positive.

investment which reduces the overall risk of the portfolio, *even though the new security is risky when viewed in isolation.*

In the present case, holding forward contracts is a risky business in so far as the contracts tend to pay off in just those scenarios when marginal utility is high and lose money when marginal utility is low. This is because, given our assumption of risk aversion, marginal utility increases less from initially high levels than it does from low levels. Hence, the covariance term will be negative and the forward rate less than the expected future spot so as to compensate for the additional risk undertaken.

Notice that Equation 13.9 confirms the fact that there are only two very special conditions under which the risk premium will be zero. Firstly, when S_1 is not subject to uncertainty – in the jargon, when S_1 is nonstochastic – in which case, its covariance with any variable is identically zero. Secondly, when the speculator is risk neutral so that, although S_1 varies, the marginal utility, $U'(C_1)$, is constant.

13.3.3 The simple model revisited: mean-variance assumptions

This conclusion has the advantage of being general in so far as it places no restrictions whatever on the form of the utility function. But, as is often the case with very general formulations, it is awkward both to interpret and to apply for purposes of empirical research. For that reason, we now examine a special case, virtually the same as the one covered in Section 13.2.

Suppose the utility function of the typical agent takes the following form:

$$U(C_1) = \alpha \mu_c - \frac{\gamma}{2} \sigma_c^2 \qquad \alpha, \gamma > 0 \tag{13.10}$$

It must be emphasized that this formulation, known as a *quadratic utility function*, is very specialized[10] and in fact has a number of implausible features.[11]

On the other hand, it also has a number of very convenient properties. Firstly, notice that it is compatible with the simple model of Section

---

[10] The interested reader may expand the general utility function in a Taylor series about its expected value, thereby verifying that it involves all moments of the distribution of outcomes, not just the second. Imposing a quadratic utility function therefore amounts to assuming either that all higher moments of the distribution are zero (for example the normal distribution) or all higher derivatives of the utility function itself are zero. It can also be seen from the same exercise that the coefficient γ is equivalent to (minus) the second derivative of the utility function.

[11] Not least the fact that we need to impose the restriction:

$$C_1 \leqslant \frac{\alpha}{\gamma}$$

otherwise marginal utility becomes negative.

13.2, because it allows us to draw indifference curves in terms of the expected value of consumption and its standard deviation.[12] Notice that since both of its parameters are assumed positive and constant, it implies that utility increases with expected consumption and decreases with the variance.

Secondly, follow through the same procedure as in the last subsection. Maximizing $U(C_1)$ with respect to A will be found to yield the following conclusion:

$$F_0 = ES_1 - \gamma A \sigma_s^2 \qquad (13.11)$$

which says that the size of the risk premium depends on the variance of the exchange rate, the attitude to risk bearing (as measured by γ), and the size of the net forward position, A.

An alternative route to a similar conclusion involves placing restrictions on the distribution of the future exchange rate, instead of on the utility function. Thus, if the distribution is approximately normal,[13] it can be shown (see the Appendix to this chapter) that our conclusion from the general model Equation 13.9 can be rewritten as:

$$F_0 = ES_1 - \Theta \frac{A}{C_1} \sigma_s^2 \qquad (13.13)$$

where:

$$\Theta \equiv -C_1 \frac{E[U''(C_1)]}{E[U'(C_1)]}$$

is a parameter known as the **coefficient of relative risk aversion**. It is often assumed constant on the grounds that people's attitudes to risk are likely to be fairly stable, provided that we measure risk relative to the individual's initial level of wealth or consumption.

As we shall see, this is the formulation which has been used most often in empirical work. Notice that *both* quadratic utility *and* normality lead to a formulation of the demand in terms of mean and variance alone. They are alternative justifications for what is called, in the jargon of portfolio theory, the **mean–variance approach**.

---

[12] Note that, since Equation 13.10 gives utility in terms of the variance rather than the standard deviation, the indifference curves drawn with respect to the standard deviation have a non-constant gradient.

[13] For the definition of the normal distribution and a list of properties, see the references at the end of the chapter. For the moment, note that the normal distribution is for practical purposes the only distribution which is completely characterized by its mean and variance.

It should be pointed out that the future exchange rate cannot be normally distributed for a number of fairly obvious reasons, but it may approximate normality in the neighbourhood of equilibrium. Alternatively, proportionate changes in the exchange rate may be more or less normally distributed.

13.3.4 The risk premium and portfolio balance models

Much of the literature on the risk premium carries a slightly different orientation from the one in the models covered in this chapter. To see how they are related, notice first that what we have called future consumption, C_1, could equally well have been described as future *wealth*, W_1 for consistency. The speculator's problem would then have amounted to one of maximizing the expected utility of future wealth, given present wealth, W_0.

Looking back at Equation 13.12, this interpretation leads naturally to regarding the term A/C_1 as the proportion of wealth allocated to foreign assets. In fact, most of the literature treats the determination of the risk premium as a portfolio allocation problem.

Now portfolio balance models were covered at some length in Chapter 8. It is easy to see the relationship between the risk premium analysis and the asset demand equations used there – and, by the same token, the currency substitution model in Chapter 9. All we need do is solve Equation 13.12 for the desired holding of foreign assets relative to what we now identify as wealth, to give:

$$\frac{A^*}{C_1} \equiv \frac{A^*}{W_1} = \frac{1}{\Theta \sigma_s^2} \, (ES_1 - F_0) \tag{13.13}$$

In the bracket on the right-hand side we now have the risk premium, the expected return on the asset in question. So, under the restrictive conditions specified here, we have arrived at a formulation of the demand functions in Chapter 8, Equations 8.2–8.4.

One further generalization is required in order to cover the portfolio balance approach. We need to be able to cope with more than two assets (or currencies and so on). The solution is quite complicated and will not be given here. As one might expect, it turns out to involve replacing the variance of the (single) exchange rate with the multi-currency variance-covariance matrix (see the Reading Guide for details).

13.3.5 Other possible extensions

The framework for all the models considered so far in this chapter has been the highly simplified environment defined by the assumptions listed in Section 13.1. Since the published literature usually deals with a far more general setting, it is worth briefly scanning the results of relaxing some of these assumptions.

First, extending the analysis to allow consumption in period 0 as well as period 1 makes no difference whatever to our conclusions, simply because there is nothing in the speculator's decision which can have any impact on current consumption.

Second, allowing the agent to borrow or lend in domestic or foreign currency – buy or sell sterling or dollar bonds – leaves the risk premium unchanged. All it does is to generate the additional conclusion that, in equilibrium, the gap between the current forward and spot rates has to equal the concurrent interest differential between the UK and USA – the familiar covered interest rate parity condition.

As far as inflation is concerned, simply allowing for the fact that the price index may change between periods 0 and 1 leaves our conclusions unaffected, if the future price level (say, P_1) is assumed to be predictable with certainty. However, if, more realistically, we allow for the fact that P_1 itself will be a source of uncertainty, it has been shown that the risk premium becomes:

$$\frac{cov\left\{\left[\dfrac{U'(C_1)}{P_1}\right], S_1\right\}}{E\left[\dfrac{U'(C_1)}{P_1}\right]}$$

Under these more general conditions it can be seen that the risk premium will *only* be zero if the future exchange rate is known with certainty (in which case its covariance is zero, as already pointed out). On the other hand, it is no longer true that risk neutrality on its own implies a zero risk premium. The reason is that, even if the marginal utility is invariant, the covariance term will still be non-zero if there is any covariance between (the reciprocal of) P_1 and S_1.

There is one final point concealed by the simplifying assumptions made in Section 13.1. Effectively, it has been assumed that the price index relevant to the speculator's consumption is not only constant, but entirely denominated in domestic currency.

To see the implication of this consider for example the effect of an expected sterling appreciation. When consumption is exclusively domestically-produced goods priced in pounds, the *only* way the agent can benefit from the event is by selling dollars (that is, buying sterling) forward. On the other hand, if we were to allow for the fact that the relevant consumption price index ought to contain a component reflecting the value of imports priced in dollars, the sterling appreciation would be seen to bring direct benefit, in the form of the higher real purchasing power of existing wealth, W_0.

In this case, ought the rational agent to enter the forward market? Intuitively, the answer should be: not to the same extent as in the case where consumption is exclusively sterling-denominated. In fact, it can be shown that, in this more general context, the appropriate definition of the speculator's exposure to risk is the extent to which a currency's portfolio share exceeds its contribution to his cost of living.

13.4 The evidence on the risk premium

There are at least three questions about the risk premium to which one would ideally like an answer:

(1) Is there in fact a (non-zero) risk premium?
(2) If so, is it variable?
(3) If variable, is it sufficiently large and/or volatile enough to explain a substantial proportion of the fluctuations observed in floating exchange rates in recent years?

Section 11.8 covered much of the relevant background – particularly the problems faced by researchers in this area.

From the point of view of the material in this chapter, there would appear to be three possible approaches to answering the questions.

One possibility is via what were called efficiency tests in Chapters 11 and 12: using an RE substitution to replace the expected spot rate, then simply examining the forward rate forecast error for signs of systematic bias. In recent years tests like these have almost invariably produced evidence of systematic bias. As has already been pointed out, however, the weakness of this test is that, while the results are consistent with the presence of a risk-premium, they could also be explained in a number of other ways, such as non-rational expectations, for example. Even if other explanations could be ruled out it would still be true that, for technical reasons, it is extremely difficult to distinguish between a random statistical error and a non-constant risk premium.

More convincing evidence has emerged in recent years from work exploiting survey data, where expectations are measured directly from the reponses of market participants themselves. Here, as we saw in Chapter 11, the evidence suggests a substantial and variable forward rate bias, though there are reasons for supposing it cannot easily be identified with the risk premium.

There have been a number of attempts to attack the problem directly. Essentially, these involve testing equations like Equation 13.13, in other words portfolio balance equations with explicit formulations of the asset demand functions. This approach has the drawback that it relies on the mean-variance approach, with its well-known (and some would say, implausible) restrictions.[14]

---

[14] Of which there are many, both theoretical and practical. Not all, by any means, were mentioned in Section 13.3.3. Mean-variance theory has a (relatively) long and chequered history in the theory of finance, and even to some extent in the world of practical stock market analysis. In both cases disenchantment has been apparent for some years.

Many of the objections are technical. Perhaps the most serious, and convincing, is the charge that the observed distribution of returns is non-stationary, an objection which would seem to apply with even greater force to exchange rates than to share prices.

Nonetheless, the most prominent exponent of this approach, Jeffrey Frankel, has generated some extremely interesting results. He summarizes them as follows:

> '... a time-varying risk premium does not seem a promising explanation
> for any empirical findings of ... conditional bias in the prediction errors
> made by the forward rate.' (1986 p.72)

which is a conclusion based on a number of studies of different currencies.

What is particularly interesting is the reason he gives for the statement: the estimates he derives of the risk premium are simply too *small* to contribute significantly to explaining the very substantial bias in forward rate predictions. In fact, according to his estimates, a 1% increase in the supply of dollar assets relative to world wealth would raise the risk premium by only 0.02% per annum! Or, in other words, the risk premium would rise by one per cent if the share of dollar assets in the world portfolio rose by no less than 50%.

In the end, these conclusions are so unambiguous as to cast doubt on their validity, as Frankel himself has recognized:

> '... the suspicion may arise that ... mean-variance optimization is steering
> us wrong ... The hitherto persuasive argument against perfect
> substitutability has been that it requires ... highly implausible
> assumptions. But we now see that conventional estimates of risk-aversion
> and return variances imply a degree of substitutability so high that for
> some purposes it might as well be infinite.' (1986 p.72)

which is precisely why so much of the material in this book uses the working assumption of risk neutrality! The zero risk premium/perfect substitutability hypothesis is, for the moment, accepted by default.

13.5 Conclusions

In this chapter, we have shown how the risk premium is determined both in general, and in the context of a set of highly specialized assumptions (the mean-variance model). In both cases, it depends on the parameters of the probability distribution of the future exchange rate, on attitudes to risk and on the quantity of assets in existence.

Since all three are extremely difficult to measure it is perhaps hardly surprising that most of the evidence collected has been indirect, usually from efficiency tests. Much of it appeared to hint at the existence of a relatively large and highly variable risk premium. More recently, direct tests using the mean-variance framework appear to have cast doubt on that possibility, as do the results of tests using survey data.

Where does that leave us? It is quite conceivable that the mean-variance model, with all its well-known shortcomings, is the wrong one to use for direct testing, though it is hard to see an alternative that is both plausible and capable of being implemented, given the current state of the econometrician's art and the limitations of the data.

Otherwise, we are left with two alternative explanations, both uncomfortable in the extreme: *either* expectations are not rational *or* the spot and/or forward markets fail to operate properly, presumably due to some invisible trade barrier or concealed transaction cost.

■ Summary

- The context of the simple two-period model is perfect capital markets, no inflation and utility functions that depend only on the expected return and variance of return to currency speculation.

- In this setting, the optimum speculative portfolio can be derived in the standard choice-theoretic manner, that is, analogous to the consumer's equilibrium that underlies the household demand curve. The result implies that the speculator chooses a portfolio such that the market risk premium is equal to the gradient of his indifference curves. If substitution effects dominate income effects, he will take on more risk when the risk premium rises.

- In a more general model, where the investor's utility function is almost unrestricted, it is shown that the risk premium is given by the ratio of the covariance between marginal utility and the spot rate to the expected marginal utility itself. This result can be generalized further in a number of directions, for example to deal with more than two periods, inflation uncertainty, traded and non-traded goods components in the price index, and so on.

- The portfolio balance equations of Chapter 8 can be derived from the risk premium model, appropriately interpreted.

- The empirical results on the risk premium are ambiguous, to say the least, though it has to be said that this is a particularly difficult research area because of the paucity of data and the importance of unobservable parameters relating to attitudes to risk, probability distributions and investors' expectations.

READING GUIDE

For the background on the analysis of choice under uncertainty, there are many excellent textbook treatments, for example Laidler (1981) Chapter 7 (elementary) and Green (1976) Chapters 13–15 (intermediate). For an introduction to the elementary statistical concepts used here, see a statistics textbook like Mood and Graybill (1963), Wonnacott and Wonnacott (1977).

The classic references on mean–variance in general are the work of Tobin (1956) and Markowitz (1958), though the material is nowadays covered in every textbook on financial theory, for example, Sharpe (1985) or Copeland and Weston (1983). An influential application to exchange rates is that of Dornbusch (1983).

What has been called here the general model is based on Frenkel and Razin (1980). For an exhaustive (and highly mathematical) analysis of the possibilities, see Section 3 of Branson and Henderson (1985).

As far as empirical work is concerned, most of the references in Chapters 8 and 11 are relevant. However, for mean variance tests, see Frankel (1982), (1983), (1986). Other notable (though highly technical) contributions are Hansen and Hodrick (1983) and Hodrick and Srivastava (1986).

APPENDIX

This appendix demonstrates how Equation 13.12 is derived from Equation 13.9.

The proof relies on a useful theorem proved by Rubinstein (1976) which states that if two variables, x and y, are bivariate normal, then provided the first derivative of the function $g(y)$ exists, it follows that:

$$cov[x, g(y)] = E[g'(y)] \cdot cov(x, y)$$

In order to use this theorem to evaluate the numerator of the expression for the risk premium in Equation 13.9, note that if we assume S_1 is normally distributed then the same must apply to C_1, which is simply a linear transformation of S_1. We can therefore proceed to write:

$$cov\,[\,U'(C_1),\,S_1] = E[U''(C_1)]\,cov(C_1, S_1)$$

$$= E[U''(C_1)]\,cov\{[(S_1 - F_0)A + W_0],\,S_1\}$$

$$= E[U''(C_1)]A\,\sigma_s^2$$

Substituting this in Equation 13.9, we have:

$$F_0 = ES_1 + \frac{E[U''(C_1)]}{E[U'C_1)]}\,A\sigma_s^2$$

$$= ES_1 + C_1\,\frac{E[U''(C_1)]}{E[U'C_1)]}\,\frac{A}{C_1}\,\sigma_s^2$$

$$= ES_1 + \Theta\,\frac{A}{C_1}\,\sigma_s^2$$

14

A Certain Uncertainty: Non-linearity, Cycles and Chaos

■ Introduction

Uncertainty and unpredictability are unavoidable issues in any analysis of financial markets and they have been continuing themes of this book so far. In general, we have taken for granted that the two are inseparable features of systems characterized by volatility. In making this connection, we were doing no more than following standard practice not only of economists, but also of mathematicians, physicists, meteorologists, psychologists – in fact, of all those who use mathematics to model the relationship between variables over time. In the last 20 years, however, it has become clear following the work of a number of pure and applied mathematicians (see the Reading Guide) that even processes involving no uncertainty may sometimes be unpredictable, even in principle.

This chapter will attempt to explain the apparent paradox, as it relates to financial markets, and in particular to exchange rates. To achieve this, we shall cover (albeit informally) the basic results using, for the most part, graphical methods only. In the process, we start by introducing a number of essential concepts which can be used to elucidate the source and nature of the unpredictability, and its implications for empirical research and for policy.

It should be made clear at the outset that, since the mathematical developments covered in this chapter are relatively recent, and their introduction into economics even more so, some of the results are still provisional. Moreover, the significance of the topic as a whole for economics and finance is as yet undemonstrated, though it seems at this stage likely to prove momentous (at least in the view of this author).

However, it should also be plain that the material covered here involves some very advanced mathematics, much of it unfamiliar even to academic economists. For that reason, the treatment can only be sketchy, emphasizing as always the intuition behind the results and omitting a number of mathematically important concepts where they are not absolutely essential to an understanding of the argument.[1] To readers already in possession of the requisite degree of mathematical sophistication, the exposition may seem like Hamlet without the Prince, or indeed Ophelia and the King and Queen. Anyone in the fortunate position of having the mathematical tools and the time to spare is urged to follow up the references in the Reading Guide. Other readers should be aware that, if the story looks simple as told in this chapter, the unabridged version is very complicated indeed.

14.1 Deterministic versus stochastic models

So far, in Part III of this book, we have been dealing with models that take explicit account of the irresoluble uncertainty associated with exchange rate behaviour. This uncertainty was conveniently summarized by the zero-mean residual error term, denoted u_t in Chapter 11. These *stochastic* models, as they are sometimes called, involve uncertainty in a very fundamental sense, and it is important for what follows to make it clear why this is the case.

Take as an example one of the models given in Section 11.5:

$$s_t = \alpha s_{t-1} + \beta s_{t-2} + \gamma Z_t + \delta Z_{t-1} + u_t \qquad \qquad \textbf{(11.10)}$$
$$\text{repeated}$$

Now the crucial point to understand is the following. In order to forecast s_t at time $t - 1$ **with complete accuracy**, we would need to have perfect knowledge of:

---

[1] Among the notable absentees (all covered at length in the references given in the Reading Guide) are the various types of bifurcation, fractals and attractors, universality, as well as the different measures of complexity found in the literature. Moreover, all topological concepts are studiously avoided here.

(1)   the values of the parameters $\alpha, \beta, \gamma, \delta$

(2)   the values of the pre-determined variables $s_{t-1}, s_{t-2}, Z_{t-1}$ and the current value Z_t

(3)   the value of the random variable u_t

The first two types of element are, in principle at least, knowable at time $t-1$. If Equation 11.10 had no random variable in it, this knowledge would be sufficient to forecast s_t with complete accuracy. For that reason, models which contain no random terms are often called *deterministic*, that is, predetermined, and hence predictable in advance. Subject to the qualifications to be made in the remaining sections of this chapter, any inaccuracy in forecasting a deterministic model can originate only in computational errors.

However, in the presence of the random or *stochastic* component u_t, the future is unpredictable. Even in principle, the value of u_t is unknowable in advance of the time t – otherwise, it would not be a truly random innovation or 'news', as it was called at one point in this book.[2] As should be clear from previous chapters, the best that can be achieved is the forecast represented by the conditional mathematical expectation:

$$E_{t-1}s_t = \alpha s_{t-1} + \beta s_{t-2} + \gamma Z_t + \delta Z_{t-1} \qquad \textbf{(11.11)}$$
repeated

which, as we saw, will rarely be an accurate forecast, at least in the type of situations encountered in financial markets. The inaccuracy in this forecast is precisely the stochastic component, u_t, so that the greater its variance, the larger the variance of our optimal forecast error.

The point is worth stressing. Since the error in an optimal (or rational) forecast is simply the random component itself, it will mimic the properties of u_t itself. Whatever the statistical properties of u_t, for example, normality or non-normality, serial dependence or independence, constant or non-constant variance, those properties will be mirrored in the error from a forecast based on Equation 11.11 above. The prediction error in forecasting a statistical model is a random variable and can therefore be described in statistical terms.

---

[2] In Chapter 12, we examined the view that this randomness originates in news about what were called the fundamentals. For our purposes in the present chapter, it makes no difference whether this 'explanation' of the random component is correct or not. All that matters is to understand that a truly random component makes a model unforecastable.

Readers who believe that every event has a cause will want to insist that u_t must in any case reflect the influence of some other variables, whether or not we choose to label them 'fundamentals'. After all, in Einstein's famous words: 'God does not play dice'. However, as long as the omitted variables summarized in u_t are unknowable, we can regard it as having been generated by the throw of a celestial die, and in the process avoid straying on to the wilder shores of epistemology.

The distinction between deterministic, hence forecastable, and stochastic, unforecastable models was accepted more or less without question until very recently in economics, as well as in most natural and social sciences. It has deliberately been laboured somewhat here, because an understanding of the dichotomy is essential to an appreciation of the importance of what follows. As we shall see, recent research has shown that a third type of model can be formulated. The most significant feature of these new models for our purposes is that, although they involve no random component and are therefore deterministic, they are even in principle unforecastable, and in practice can only be approximately forecast over a very short horizon.

14.2 A simple non-linear model

To explain the mechanism involved, we shall employ an ultra-simple model. It must be stressed that it is being introduced purely as an example for expository purposes. There is no intention to suggest that it actually describes how exchange rates are determined. Rather, it is chosen purely as an easily manipulated example of the class of models which may give rise to the type of outcome we intend to describe.

Our starting point is to assume that the (log of the) exchange rate changes according to more or less the same mechanism used in Section 7.1 to describe the way currency speculators form their expectations:

$$\Delta s_t = \theta(\bar{s} - s_{t-1}) \tag{14.1}$$

That is to say, the change in the log price of foreign currency, Δs_t, is proportional to the previous period's gap between the actual exchange rate, s_{t-1}, and its long-run equilibrium level, $\bar{s}$. The latter is taken as given exogenously (by relative money stocks, output capacity and so forth), and for present purposes, may be regarded as constant. Note that this mechanism is meant to describe the way the actual, not the expected exchange rate moves. (It was pointed out in Section 7.3.3 that under certain circumstances, the exchange rate would indeed follow this type of path in the context of the Dornbusch model.)[3]

Now consider the term θ. As we saw in Section 7.1, it is an indicator of the speed of adjustment of the actual exchange rate to deviations from its equilibrium level: the larger the gap, the more rapid the adjustment. It was assumed to be positive; otherwise adjustment would be *away* from equilibrium, rather than towards it. Moreover, it was implicitly assumed to be smaller than one, so as to guarantee an uncomplicated path to the

---

[3] For reasons of simplicity, we ignore expectations in this chapter. In fact, as we shall see, even defining rational expectations in this context is a serious problem.

new equilibrium. However, this restriction is one we now relax. Instead, we examine the possible implications of a more complicated mechanism.

Suppose that one of the processes whereby the exchange rate adjusts is as follows. When exporters (who are, we assume, paid in foreign currency) feel optimistic about the prospects for the domestic currency, they convert their receipts as early as possible. On the other hand, when they are gloomy about the home currency, they delay conversion, and instead hold on to foreign currency deposits. Under these circumstances, the greater the volume of export receipts, the more funds available to support speculation in this way, and therefore the greater the value of θ, other things being equal.

Now, given the level of domestic and foreign prices as well as the other relevant factors, exports are likely to be an increasing function of the price of the foreign currency, s_t. As a result, we conclude that θ itself may well be an increasing function of s_t. If the relationship is linear, we can write simply:

$$\theta = \alpha s_t \qquad \alpha > 0 \tag{14.2}$$

When the domestic currency is relatively cheap (s_t high), exports are buoyant, and there is more scope for speculation against it, when it is overvalued, or in favour of it when it is undervalued. Hence, it adjusts more rapidly.

Combining Equations 14.1 and 14.2, we conclude that the exchange rate moves as follows:

$$\Delta s_{t+1} = \alpha s_t(\bar{s} - s_t) \tag{14.3}$$

which says that the exchange rate moves towards equilibrium at a rate which is greater the higher its initial level. Alternatively, we can rewrite Equation 14.3 as:

$$s_{t+1} = (1 + \alpha \bar{s})s_t - \alpha s_t^2 \tag{14.4}$$

A useful simplification follows from taking advantage of the fact that since the equilibrium exchange rate has been taken as given, we may as well specify a convenient value for it. So, by the use of an appropriate scaling factor, we can set:

$$\bar{s} = -\left(\frac{1 - \alpha}{\alpha}\right) \tag{14.5}$$

which allows us to reformulate Equation 14.4 simply as:

$$s_{t+1} = \alpha s_t - \alpha s_t^2 = \alpha s_t(1 - s_t) \tag{14.6}$$

or, for convenience:

$$s_{t+1} = f(s_t) \tag{14.7}$$

Now this is a deceptively simple equation. In fact, f is a function of the type known to mathematicians as the *logistic*, though it amounts to no more than a particular type of quadratic in s_t. Nonetheless, it turns out that this innocuous-looking equation can generate a bewildering variety of different types of path, depending on the value of α, which is known as the *tuning parameter*. In particular, values of α approaching 4 can be shown to result in time paths characterized as *chaotic*. However, as we examine the implications of successively higher values of α, many interesting and potentially important phenomena are encountered, long before we reach the point where chaos reigns.

14.3 The time path of the exchange rate

In order to examine the exchange rate behaviour implied by Equation 14.6, we first demonstrate the use of a simple diagrammatic apparatus to analyse non-linear dynamics. It then becomes possible to study the time paths implied by different values of α.

14.3.1 The phase portrait

If the notion of equilibrium is to have any meaning in the system described by Equation 14.6, then plainly it must correspond to a position such that, having arrived, s_t stays there indefinitely, unless it is disturbed again. In that sense, it must be what mathematicians call a *fixed point*.

Consider drawing a diagram with values of s_t along the horizontal axis, and s_{t+1} on the vertical. Any point in the diagram would therefore represent a combination of s_t and s_{t+1}. Where would the fixed points lie? Obviously, if any fixed points exist, they would lie along a 45° line through the origin, since it is the locus of all points equidistant from the axes, that is, all points at which $s_t = s_{t+1}$.

Now, given some positive value of α, if we plot the values of s_{t+1} corresponding to s_t, that is, the function $f(s_t)$, we generate a parabola, which is no more than the graph of a quadratic equation familiar from elementary algebra. Each point on the graph is an answer to the question: if s takes the value on the horizontal axis in one period, what value will it take in the next period? This line is known as the *phase curve* of the logistic function and the diagram is its *phase portrait*.

Before examining the general features of this parabola, it would pay to follow through its implications for the dynamic path.

Start the system off with s_t at an arbitrary value, say s_t^0 (see Figure 14.1, which is drawn for a value of $\alpha = 1.5$). As we can see from the point A on the phase curve of $f(s_t)$, starting from this initial value, the value of

Figure 14.1 Smooth convergence ($\alpha = 1.5$).

the variable next period will be s^0_{t+1}, because this is implied by the equation:

$$s^0_{t+1} = \alpha s^0_t (1 - s^0_t) \tag{14.8}$$

However, if it is s^0_{t+1} in the second period, it starts the next two-period phase at that same value. Moreover, that value can be found at the point B' on the 45° line (points labelled with a prime are on the 45° line), that is, $s^1_t = s^0_{t+1}$. Again, starting the next phase at s^1_t, the exchange rate will clearly rise to s^1_{t+1} in the subsequent period. Repeating the same logic as before, it will enter the next phase at the point corresponding to E', where $s^2_t = s^1_{t+1}$, and so on.

The usefulness of the 45° line is apparent. The path of s_t is traced out by the steps marked with arrows in the diagram, generating the points A, D, F, H ... corresponding to the sequence of values: s^0_t, s^1_t, s^2_t, ... The significance of this is that we now have a device for deriving the path of the exchange rate given only the phase diagram.[4]

---

[4]Moreover, the method is completely general, in the sense that it would work just as well with almost any other equation.

Table 14.1 Stable convergence: two examples.

t	S_t	Step size	S_t	Step size
0	0.5		0.25	
1	0.375000	0.125	0.281250	0.03125
2	0.351563	0.023438	0.303223	0.021973
3	0.341949	0.009613	0.316918	0.013695
4	0.337530	0.004419	0.324721	0.007803
5	0.335405	0.002125	0.328916	0.004195
6	0.334363	0.001042	0.331095	0.002179
7	0.333847	0.000516	0.332207	0.001111
8	0.333590	0.000257	0.332768	0.000561
9	0.333461	0.000128	0.333050	0.000282
10	0.333397	6.4E–05	0.333192	0.000141
11	0.333365	3.2E–05	0.333262	7.1E–05
12	0.333349	1.6E–05	0.333298	3.5E–05
13	0.333341	8E–06	0.333316	1.8E–05
14	0.333337	4E–06	0.333324	8.9E–06
15	0.333335	2E–06	0.333329	4.4E–06
16	0.333334	1E–06	0.333331	2.2E–06
17	0.333334	5E–07	0.333332	1.1E–06
18	0.333334	2.5E–07	0.333333	5.5E–07
19	0.333333	1.2E–07	0.333333	2.8E–07
20	0.333333	6.2E–08	0.333333	1.4E–07
21	0.333333	3.1E–08	0.333333	6.9E–08
22	0.333333	1.6E–08	0.333333	3.5E–08
23	0.333333	7.8E–09	0.333333	1.7E–08
24	0.333333	3.9E–09	0.333333	8.7E–09
25	0.333333	2E–09	0.333333	4.3E–09

Notes: AE–B means A divided by 10 to the power of B
t = time period
Initial values: $s = 0.5$ and $s = 0.25$

Table 14.1 traces out the sequence of values taken by s_t over the first 25 periods, starting from levels of 0.5 and 0.25 respectively. Thus, to six decimal places, the exchange rate settles down to its long-run level of ⅓ by the 19th period in the first case, and by the 18th period starting from 0.25. Notice the step size diminishes exponentially.

One obvious conclusion follows immediately. If, at any value s_t^*, the phase curve crosses the 45° line, the path degenerates from that point onward, because each phase starts at s_t^* and results in the same point in the next period. Formally, under those circumstances we would have: $f(s_t^*) = s_t^*$, and hence s_t remains fixed forever at the level s_t^*.

Armed with this convenient analytic tool, we can trace out the successive values taken by s_t starting from any initial value on the horizontal axis. We shall see there is a variety of different types of path the exchange rate can follow, depending on the shape of the phase portrait. In fact, the critical feature of the graph turns out to be its curvature. The greater the curvature, the richer the array of possibilities. Moreover, the degree of curvature depends on the value of the so-called tuning parameter, α.

The following properties will turn out to be crucial:

Property 1 Since the gradient of the phase curve is $\alpha(1 - 2s_t)$, it is upward-sloping (positive) as long as s_t is less than ½ and downward-sloping whenever s_t is greater than ½.

Property 2 The gradient is zero when s_t is ½. In other words, the phase curve peaks at this point.[5] Moreover, at its maximum, s_{t+1} is just $\alpha/4$, which means that the height of the curve increases with α, and reaches 1.0 when α is just 4.0.

Notice two immediate implications. When α is less than 2.0, s_{t+1} can never be greater than $\alpha/4 = ½$. Hence, if s_t starts out less than ½ (that is, to the left of the peak), it will remain there.

Property 3[6] Whatever the gradient, the fixed points where $s_t = s_{t+1}$ are at $s_t = 0$ and $s_t = (\alpha - 1)/\alpha$.

Property 4 The phase curve cuts the horizontal axis at the two points, zero and one. In other words, the positive values of s_t are restricted to the range between zero and one.[7]

Property 5 If s_t were ever to escape from the range from zero to one, it would therefore become negative. Moreover, once having become negative, the exchange rate never again becomes positive and in fact goes on diminishing without limit. In the jargon of mathematics, it tends to minus infinity.[8]

Plainly, the system's behaviour depends critically on the value of the tuning parameter. We take the different possibilities one by one, following the graphs in Figures 14.2(a) to (f). In each case, the first 50 points on the

---

[5] Both these points can be confirmed by differentiating $f(s_t)$ to give:

$$\frac{ds_{t+1}}{ds_t} = \alpha(1 - 2s_t)$$

which is obviously positive (negative) whenever s_t is less (greater) than ½, and zero when s_t is exactly ½.

[6] As can be seen by solving the equation:

$$s_{t+1} = s_t = \alpha s_t(1 - s_t)$$

to give the solutions:

$$s_t = 0 \quad \text{and} \quad s_t = \frac{\alpha - 1}{\alpha}$$

[7] Though if α is greater than four, the exchange rate can temporarily escape from these bounds. This possibility is ignored here.

[8] As the reader may verify by following the same graphical procedure as was used in Figure 14.1.

It should be remembered, incidentally, that in so far as we are modelling the log of the exchange rate, rather than a natural number, negative values are not impossible.

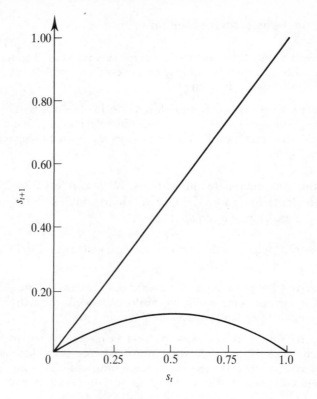

Figure 14.2(a)   The phase portrait ($\alpha = 0.5$).

time paths are displayed in Table 14.2[9] so that the interested reader can refer to the data given there for confirmation of the pattern shown in the graphs.

14.3.2 Case: $0 < \alpha < 1$

When α is between 0 and 1, the phase curve lies below the 45° line at all points (Figure 14.2(a)). The explanation can be found by looking at the data used to plot the phase curve. As can be seen from Table 14.2, when α is in this range (in the case shown here, α is 0.5), the exchange rate collapses to the fixed point at zero. Moreover, the other fixed point is negative, as can be seen from Property 3 above. More improbable still, the negative fixed point is unreachable because, by Property 5, the exchange

---

[9] Notice that the time paths in Table 14.2 all start from the initial value $s_0 = 0.25$, though we shall discuss a number of other possibilities in the coming sections. However, the graphs are only approximately scaled, so disparities between the values in the table and the phase portraits may occur as the iterations proceed.

Table 14.2 Time paths for different values of α.

t	0.5	1.5	2.75	$\alpha = \ldots$ 3.4	3.47	3.75	3.99
0	0.25	0.25	0.25	0.25	0.25	0.25	0.25
1	0.093750	0.281250	0.515625	0.637500	0.650625	0.703125	0.748125
2	0.042480	0.303223	0.686829	0.785719	0.788773	0.782776	0.751852
3	0.020338	0.316918	0.591511	0.572440	0.578137	0.637642	0.744417
4	0.009962	0.324721	0.664471	0.832158	0.846314	0.866455	0.759138
5	0.004931	0.328916	0.613111	0.474881	0.451331	0.433914	0.729562
6	0.002454	0.331095	0.652316	0.847855	0.859281	0.921123	0.787233
7	0.001224	0.332207	0.623699	0.438590	0.419584	0.272459	0.668314
8	0.000611	0.332768	0.645421	0.837178	0.845060	0.743344	0.884465
9	0.000305	0.333050	0.629345	0.463457	0.454339	0.715439	0.407725
10	0.000153	0.333192	0.641492	0.845460	0.860265	0.763448	0.963527
11	0.000076	0.333262	0.632445	0.444236	0.417125	0.677231	0.140221
12	0.000038	0.333298	0.639260	0.839427	0.843667	0.819709	0.481030
13	0.000019	0.333316	0.634168	0.458283	0.457669	0.554198	0.996064
14	0.000010	0.333324	0.637997	0.844083	0.861282	0.926485	0.015642
15	0.000005	0.333329	0.635131	0.447463	0.414579	0.255415	0.061436
16	0.000002	0.333331	0.637284	0.840616	0.842181	0.713168	0.230071
17	0.000001	0.333332	0.635671	0.455535	0.461206	0.767097	0.706781
18	0.000001	0.333333	0.636882	0.843278	0.862278	0.669971	0.826894
19	0.000000	0.333333	0.635974	0.449345	0.412079	0.829162	0.571130
20	0.000000	0.333333	0.636655	0.841276	0.840677	0.531198	0.977313
21	0.000000	0.333333	0.636145	0.454005	0.464770	0.933850	0.088468
22	0.000000	0.333333	0.636528	0.842807	0.863193	0.231653	0.321761
23	0.000000	0.333333	0.636241	0.450443	0.409775	0.667461	0.870741
24	0.000000	0.333333	0.636456	0.841650	0.839252	0.832338	0.449080
25	0.000000	0.333333	0.636294	0.453136	0.468131	0.523319	0.987155
26	0.000000	0.333333	0.636416	0.842533	0.863976	0.935461	0.050595
27	0.000000	0.333333	0.636325	0.451082	0.407800	0.226402	0.191659
28	0.000000	0.333333	0.636393	0.841864	0.838002	0.656790	0.618154
29	0.000000	0.333333	0.636342	0.452638	0.471068	0.845313	0.941798
30	0.000000	0.333333	0.636380	0.842373	0.864595	0.490345	0.218708
31	0.000000	0.333333	0.636351	0.451454	0.406234	0.937150	0.681791
32	0.000000	0.333333	0.636373	0.841987	0.836991	0.220873	0.865638
33	0.000000	0.333333	0.636357	0.452353	0.473436	0.645331	0.464072
34	0.000000	0.333333	0.636369	0.842281	0.865051	0.858296	0.992350
35	0.000000	0.333333	0.636360	0.451668	0.405079	0.456089	0.030291
36	0.000000	0.333333	0.636367	0.842058	0.836235	0.930269	0.117201
37	0.000000	0.333333	0.636361	0.452188	0.475202	0.243256	0.412824
38	0.000000	0.333333	0.636365	0.842228	0.865366	0.690310	0.967177
39	0.000000	0.333333	0.636362	0.451793	0.404281	0.801683	0.126665
40	0.000000	0.333333	0.636365	0.842099	0.835708	0.596202	0.441378
41	0.000000	0.333333	0.636363	0.452093	0.476432	0.902795	0.983788
42	0.000000	0.333333	0.636364	0.842197	0.865573	0.329086	0.063637
43	0.000000	0.333333	0.636363	0.451865	0.403758	0.827957	0.237754
44	0.000000	0.333333	0.636364	0.842122	0.835359	0.534165	0.723097
45	0.000000	0.333333	0.636363	0.452038	0.477245	0.933123	0.798909
46	0.000000	0.333333	0.636364	0.842179	0.865703	0.234018	0.641007
47	0.000000	0.333333	0.636364	0.451906	0.403426	0.672200	0.918167
48	0.000000	0.333333	0.636364	0.842136	0.835137	0.826301	0.299794
49	0.000000	0.333333	0.636364	0.452006	0.477761	0.538228	0.837571
50	0.000000	0.333333	0.636364	0.842169	0.865784	0.932020	0.542823

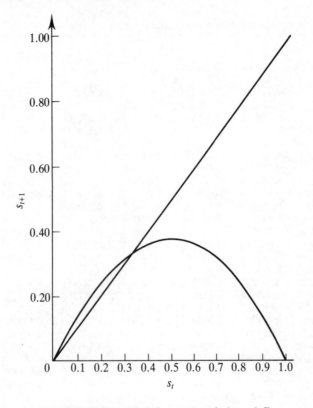

Figure 14.2(b) The phase portrait ($\alpha = 1.5$).

rate would tend to minus infinity, once having dropped below zero. The two facts taken together mean this scenario can be safely ruled out as a possible description of reality.

14.3.3 Case: $1 < \alpha < 2$

The case when α lies between 1.0 and 2.0 is somewhat uninteresting. In fact we have already more or less covered it: Figure 14.1 is simply a close-up on Figure 14.2(b). Since the non-zero fixed point is below ½ (in fact, at ⅓), the 45° line cuts the phase curve to the left of the peak, and the exchange rate converges smoothly in gradually diminishing steps. In the jargon of mathematics, convergence is said to be monotonic: that is to say, it is always moving towards equilibrium, with no detours or doubling back on itself, as can be seen from the third column of Table 14.2.

It is important for what follows to step back a moment from the dynamics of the phase portrait to examine the explanation for this

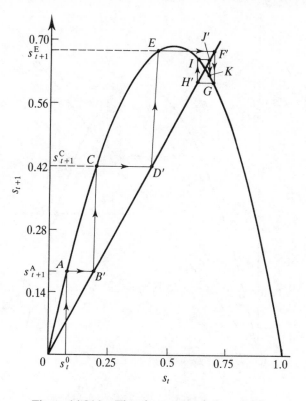

Figure 14.2(c) The phase portrait ($\alpha = 2.75$).

outcome in terms of our basic model of the exchange rate. Equation 14.3 can be rewritten as follows:

$$s_{t+1} = (\alpha s_t)\bar{s} + (1 - \alpha s_t)s_t \tag{14.9}$$

This says that next period's level of the exchange rate is a weighted average of its long-run equilibrium level, $\bar{s}$, and its current actual level, s_t, with the weights being αs_t and $(1 - \alpha s_t)$ respectively.

Notice that the term αs_t is nothing other than our more complicated version of θ, in the non-linear form we introduced in this chapter.

Now as long as α is between 1.0 and 2.0, this crucial term can be no greater than $2s_t$. Hence, when s_t is to the left of the peak (that is, less than ½), αs_t must be less than 1.0, and therefore the weights in Equation 14.9 must both lie between 0 and 1.0.

From here, the explanation is straightforward. Starting from below equilibrium, an increase in the current exchange rate will move the next period's value closer to equilibrium, by raising its weighting αs_t, and reducing the weighting on its present level, $1 - \alpha s_t$. The smooth convergence to the fixed point follows accordingly.

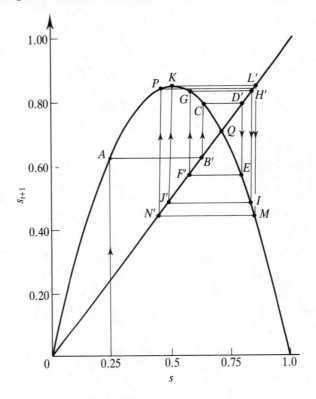

Figure 14.2(d) The phase portrait ($\alpha = 3.4$).

In fact, in this case the dynamics of the exchange rate are more or less identical to those of the linear model analysed in Section 7.3. Just as in the linear case, the greater the gap $\bar{s} - s_t$, the more rapid the increase in s_t and the higher its level in the next period. Starting at any given distance below equilibrium, it closes a proportion of the gap each period, as the fall in the value of the domestic currency induces a greater volume of exports, hence more speculation by exporters delaying repatriation of their receipts.

The important point is in the balance of these two effects. On the one hand, what we could call the linear effect inside the brackets in Equation 14.3 gradually reduces the rate of depreciation, Δs_{t+1} in subsequent periods, as the gap between the exchange rate's current level and its equilibrium diminishes. On the other hand, the non-linear effect continues to provide acceleration, as successive increases in s_t raise the value of the variable adjustment coefficient αs_t. As long as α is less than 2.0, however, the first effect predominates, and the net outcome is deceleration as equilibrium is approached.

This unexciting conclusion has been laboured because it turns out to be the key to understanding the richness of the possible outcomes in the

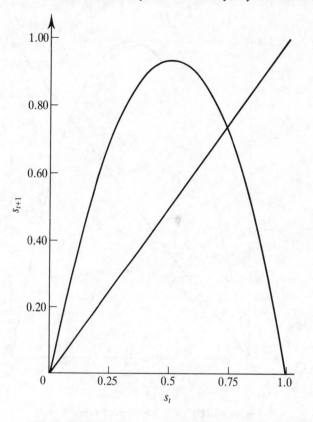

Figure 14.2(e)   The phase portrait ($\alpha = 3.75$).

more complicated (and interesting) cases to be analysed in subsequent sections.

14.3.4 Case: $2 < \alpha < 3$

The story gets monotonically more interesting as α passes the value of 2.0. In terms of the phase portrait, when α is exactly 2.0, the hump is high enough to cut the 45° line at its peak, so that the long-run equilibrium exchange rate is just ½. At any value of α higher than this, the fixed point is beyond the hump, at an exchange rate greater than ½. Though the numbers in Table 14.2 start at 0.25, a lower starting point has been chosen here, simply to make the graphics clearer.

   Suppose $\alpha = 2.75$ (Figure 14.2(c)). Starting at an arbitrary value of the exchange rate, s_t^0 the path proceeds as before towards equilibrium via the points A, B', C, D', to E, where something not seen in the previous examples occurs. When the exchange rate reaches the level at E (that is,

Figure 14.2(f)   The phase portrait ($\alpha = 4.0$).

when $s_{t+1} = s_{t+1}^E$) it starts the next two-period phase at a value which generates an overshoot to F' and hence G. Following the path on to H', I, J', K ..., the pattern is clearly cyclical. This process, often called a cobweb, takes the exchange rate beyond its equilibrium level (at G), then back below it in the next period (at I), then beyond it again (point K) and so on.

   As is clear from Figure 14.2(c), the cyclic fluctuations continue forever, with each phase taking the exchange rate back and forth around its fixed point. The important point, however, is that at each stage the exchange rate moves closer to equilibrium. In other words, the *cycle is stable*, with the swings becoming less wild as period succeeds period. In time-series terms, each succeeding peak in the two-period cycle is lower and each trough higher than its predecessor. Figure 14.3(a) plots the sequence of points in this stable cobweb against the time periods, showing clearly how the cycle converges on its long-run level, which in this case is:

$$\frac{\alpha - 1}{\alpha} = \frac{2.75 - 1.0}{2.75} = 0.64$$

Figure 14.3(a) Path of exchange rate ($\alpha = 2.75$).

The explanation for this outcome is to be found, as before, in the value of αs_t. At low levels of the exchange rate, as at points like A and C in Figure 14.2(c), this term is less than 1.0. Hence convergence proceeds gradually towards equilibrium, as in the previous case.

However, since the fixed point is at a value of s_t greater than ½, at some stage αs_t must exceed 1.0. If α is only slightly above 2.0, this situation will only occur when s_t is very close to ½, that is, just before the peak of the phase curve. The greater is α, the lower the value at which the cycle begins. For $\alpha = 2.75$, as in Figure 14.2(c), the condition is fulfilled when s_t passes 0.36 (at E).[10]

The implication of having αs_t greater than 1.0 is that the weights in Equation 14.3 are greater than 1.0 on the equilibrium and *negative* on the

[10] It should be clear that the point E is the departure point for the cycle, only for the particular path starting from the arbitrarily chosen initial value in Figure 14.2(c) (approximately 0.08), because it is the first time the exchange rate passes the 0.36 level. For another starting value, it might take fewer or more iterations. Of course, starting from an exchange rate greater than 0.36, the cyclic behaviour would start at once.

current exchange rate. That in turn means the next period's exchange rate is dragged down below its current level, but not by enough to reverse its ultimate convergence. In other words, the (albeit artificial) speculative mechanism assumed in our model makes for a progression towards equilibrium proceeding by two steps forward and one step back.

As before, the nature of the process is illustrated (for a value of α of 2.75) in Table 14.2, where it can be seen that the sequence in this case goes: 0.25, 0.52, 0.69, 0.59, 0.66, 0.61, 0.65, 0.62, 0.65, 0.63, 0.64 ... so that, by the end of ten periods, it has already settled down to a range of fluctuation of only 0.01. By the time the 50 periods shown in the table have elapsed, it has reached its steady state – at least, as close as the sixth decimal place can show. This path is shown as the time series in Figure 14.3(a).

14.3.5 Case: $3 < \alpha < 3.68$

The really interesting situations arise for values of α greater than 3.0. Consider Figure 14.2(d), drawn for an α value of 3.4. The sequence of points generated at successive stages of the process starts as though it is again following a cobweb: A, B', C, D', E .... But then F' implies a lower level of s_{t+1} than at B', so the cycle is now diverging. At the next point, G, s_{t+1} is above its level at the same phase of the previous cycle (at C).

Although we have not drawn more than two cycles, the impression of instability could be confirmed by following the process on for a few more iterations. As can be seen from the time series for this value of α (Figure 14.3(b) and the appropriate column of Table 14.2), the initial stages consist of a number of cycles of increasing amplitude. Surprisingly, however, the instability is only temporary, in the sense that, at some point, the amplitude settles down and we see that the system is ultimately characterized by a regular two-period cycle, tending neither to explode to infinity nor to implode on the fixed point (Q in the phase diagram). Thus, while the fixed point is never reached (other than fortuitously), and would in any case be unsustainable even if the exchange rate were ever to arrive there,[11] the long-run behaviour of the exchange rate follows a highly stable pattern. Once the pattern has been established, it is sustained indefinitely, in the absence of any further disturbance.

In the present case, as we can see from Figure 14.3(b), a perfect two-period cycle with absolutely constant peaks (equal to 0.84) and troughs (at 0.45) ensues after period 24. In the jargon of non-linear dynamics, the

---

[11] Readers interested in the mathematics should note that, in general terms (that is, for broader classes of functions than the logistic), the borderline between stability and instability of the fixed point is determined by the gradient of the phase curve in the region in question. If it is greater than 1.0 (in absolute terms), the fixed point is unstable. Since at the fixed point the gradient is $2 - \alpha$ in the case of the logistic function, it is unstable for values of α greater than 3.0.

Figure 14.3(b)   Path of exchange rate ($\alpha = 3.4$).

exchange rate path is said to have periodicity of two, because it is characterized by the feature that the same values recur every second period, so
that we find:

$$s_t = s_{t+2} = s_{t+4} = \cdots$$

and

$$s_{t+1} = s_{t+3} = s_{t+5} = \cdots$$

This unrealistically neat pattern turns out to be only the first of the
possibilities, however. As the value of the tuning parameter is raised,
the cycle increases in amplitude. But at a value of α of just under 3.45, the
two-period cycle becomes unstable. Instead of fluctuating between only
two values, the exchange rate begins to follow a pattern of switching
between four values, $s_t, s_{t+1}, s_{t+2}, s_{t+3}$, with $s_t = s_{t+4}$, $s_{t+1} = s_{t+5}$, $s_{t+2} = s_{t+6}$,

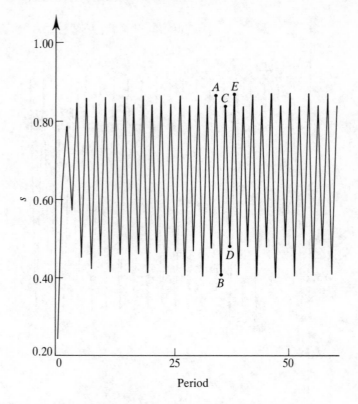

Figure 14.3(c)   Path of exchange rate ($\alpha = 3.47$).

$s_{t+3} = s_{t+7}$, the next cycle beginning again with $s_{t+4} = s_{t+8}$, and so on *ad infinitum*. This four-period cycle is illustrated in Figure 14.3(c), where the points A, B, C, D form one complete cycle consisting of a high peak (at A), followed by a low trough (B), then a lower peak (C) and finally a higher trough (at D), and back to the original level at the start of the next cycle (E).

The story does not end there, however. The process of sudden change from a stable cyclic pattern to one with a period twice as long is known as *bifurcation*, and it occurs repeatedly as the value of α is increased, with successive 8-period, 16-period, 32-period cycles establishing themselves over an increasingly narrow range of values of the tuning parameter. It is important to note that, although at each bifurcation a cycle of period n appears, and replaces the old cycle of period $n/2$, nevertheless the old cycle is, in a sense, still present. All that happens is that the lower-period cycle becomes unstable from the bifurcation point onward. In principle, therefore, it could still make an appearance, though the probability of it occurring is negligible.[12]

---

[12] In fact, zero in the limit.

The *period-doubling* pattern or cascade, as it is sometimes known, can therefore be thought of as a play, with a cast list made up of all possible periodicities. As the play progresses (α increases), all the characters ultimately make an entry on stage, though mostly in bit parts, and in strict order of appearance. As each new periodicity steps out into the limelight, the previous one steps back into the shadows stage left or right. *But it is still present, even if it is not currently playing a part in the proceedings.*

This fact has important implications in the present case, because it turns out that, in the approximate range $3.45 < \alpha < 3.68$, cycles of every period assert themselves in a predictable order, starting with all the even-number periods and finishing with odd-period cycles.[13] Eventually, by the time a cycle of period 3 is established at about $\alpha = 3.68$, all other periodicities have made their appearance and the stage is full. We are ready for the finale.

14.3.6 Case: $3.68 < \alpha < 4$

The process reaches its climax when α passes a value of about 3.68, at which point the three-period cycle ceases to be stable. From here on, the number of possibilities becomes almost endless. It is only from this point on, that the type of behaviour known as *chaos* may (or may not) be observed.[14]

---

[13] The order of appearance of the different periodicities was set out very precisely by a Russian mathematician named Sarkovskii, as follows:

$$2^0 < 2^1 < 2^2 < 2^3 < 2^4 \ldots < \ldots <$$
$$\ldots < \ldots < \ldots$$
$$\ldots 2^N.9 < 2^N.7 < 2^N.5 < 2^N.3$$
$$\ldots < \ldots < \ldots$$
$$\ldots < \ldots < \ldots$$
$$\ldots < \ldots < 2^2.9 < 2^2.7 < 2^2.5 < 2^2.3$$
$$\ldots < \ldots < 2^1.9 < 2^1.7 < 2^1.5 < 2^1.3$$
$$\ldots < \ldots < 2^0.9 < 2^0.7 < 2^0.5 < 2^0.3$$

For mathematicians, the exciting aspect of this series is that it is not peculiar to the logistic function. Its applicability is much broader. In fact, it is one of a number of so-called universal features of non-linear functions.

For our purposes, two major implications are worthy of note. First, an infinite cast of cycles with even periods makes its appearance before the first odd cycle. Second, the last cycle to appear on stage has a period of $2^0.3$, that is, just 3. Hence, by the time a 3-period cycle arises, all other periodicities have already appeared.

[14] What follows in this section is an attempt to provide the reader with an intuitive understanding of what is meant by chaos (or complexity, as it is sometimes known) and of its implications. The mathematical literature contains a number of different formal definitions of chaos, emphasizing varying aspects of the phenomenon: sensitive dependence, mixing, and so on. For an example, see Devaney (1989).

To appreciate some of the subtleties and pitfalls in this area, we need to introduce some additional mathematical concepts (as usual, in deliberately informal definitions):

An aperiodic path is one characterized by no regular cycle or pattern. Alternatively, it has a period of infinity. That is to say, it would only repeat itself after an infinite number of periods have elapsed so that the path never revisits any point it has previously visited.

It can be seen that this amounts simply to the absence of periodicity.

Much of the mathematics literature in this area is concerned with notions of measure and measurability. For this purpose, we use the following definition:

The measure[15] of an interval is equal to its length, where single points are given a length of zero.

This follows straightforwardly on the idea familiar from elementary geometry that a single point has zero length. It follows that two or more points, as long as they are isolated, also have zero length. By extension, even where we have an infinite number of isolated points, the length in this sense is still zero. We can therefore have an interval or more generally a set with an infinite number of points in it, but nonetheless with measure zero.

To appreciate the relevance of this approach, consider the following experiment. Imagine a set of measure zero, that is, containing a large number of discrete points. For example, it might be a map of the world, with the points defined by the intersections of the lines of latitude and longitude thoughtfully drawn by the publishers at, say, 100 intervals. Now suppose I were to stick a pin in the map somewhere at random. Plainly, the probability of me landing on one of the intersection points is very small. But even if I did actually appear to the naked eye to have landed precisely on the point where the 30° East line of longitude crosses the 50° North line of latitude, it is very likely that examination under a magnifying glass would show my pinhole to be both too big and too off-centre to coincide precisely with the 'true' point 30° *E* 50° *N*. In the unlikely event that I was absolutely spot on under the magnifying glass, a look through a microscope would always show I was in fact slightly off-centre to one side or the other.

In other words, the probability of my pin landing on any of the finite number of grid references marked on the atlas is zero. The obvious next step might seem to be to draw a finer grid. But a moment's consideration will bring the reader to the realization that the same argument applies again. The finer the grid, the more points there are on the map. Nonetheless, the probability of landing exactly on one of them is zero.

---

[15] Slightly more strictly, the Lebesgue measure. There are a number of other concepts of measure used in the literature which amount to more or less the same thing in the present context.

Figure 14.3(d) Path of exchange rate ($\alpha = 3.75$).

In the limit (that is, as the grid is made infinitely dense), the probability of landing on any of the points is therefore zero.

In the same way, *any property of our series which applies only to a set of measure zero will never actually be observed.* Specifically, any feature which applies only to paths starting out from a set of measure zero cannot be expected ever to be seen in practice.

Armed with these concepts, we now return to the analysis of the logistic function. Once the three-cycle has appeared, all other cycles have become unstable. In other words, they apply only over a set of initial points whose measure is zero. From this point onward, a number of possibilities appear.

First, consider Figure 14.2(e), the phase diagram drawn for $\alpha = 3.75$. Other than the fact that the hump has become even larger, there is no obvious qualitative change in the phase curve compared to lower values of the tuning parameter. But when we come to generate the exchange rate path in the usual way, we find a sequence of points meandering around the whole region from 0 to 1 with no apparent pattern.

In time-series terms, Figure 14.3(d) is typical in its eccentricity. For this value of α, it shows the first 100 periods starting with $s_0 = 0.25$. At a casual glance, it may seem to follow a somewhat erratic two-period cycle. But closer inspection shows that any pattern is illusory, with relatively high peaks separated sometimes by one lower peak, sometimes by two or three lower peaks. Moreover, even the high peaks are uneven. There are also two sequences of five or six low-volatility periods.

It is also quite easy to see how patterns might seem to be present even when they are not. From about periods 12–55, the series in Figure 14.3(d) might well appear to the observer to follow a reasonably regular (albeit high amplitude) cycle. Then sudenly it settles down for two or three periods, before regaining its former volatility over the subsequent periods. This type of behaviour seems fairly typical of chaotic processes.

14.4 Chaos

The explanation given so far of how chaotic processes arise was inevitably oversimplified, so as to remain within the limits of what could be explained with graphic methods alone. In the process, many of the more complicated aspects of non-linear equations were sidestepped or ignored altogether.

In this section, we deal with some of these issues, albeit at a superficial level. Before doing so, however, it is worth repeating that the logistic function in Equation 14.6 is only one example of the class of functions which can result in chaotic behaviour for some values of the basic parameters. A quadratic was chosen for its simplicity and for the fact it has been more thoroughly analysed than any other type of non-linear function. But there is an almost limitless number of different possible functional forms which could give rise to chaotic behaviour over some range of parameter values. In particular, there is a far richer variety of dynamic possibilities in multivariate equation systems, which some writers claim are more relevant to economics than univariate models like the logistic and tent maps.[16] These possibilities are not explored here, though they figure

---

[16] For any variable x_t, the so-called tent map (for example, Devaney (1987)) takes a form like:

$$x_{t+1} = \begin{cases} 2x_t & 0 \leqslant x_t \leqslant \dfrac{1}{2} \\[2mm] 2 - 2x_t & \dfrac{1}{2} \leqslant x_t \leqslant 1 \end{cases}$$

It also generates a chaotic time-series process, and in some respects is even easier to study than the logistic.

Figure 14.3(e) Path of exchange rate ($\alpha = 3.75$); $t = 201$ to 250.

largely in the published literature (see the Reading Guide at the end of the chapter).

Instead, we shall concentrate here on an understanding of what is meant by chaos, and on dispelling a number of common misapprehensions about its properties. The following points must be stressed:

(1) A chaotic process need not be particularly volatile. It can in fact display long periods of quiescence.

(2) By definition, an essential feature of chaotic processes is that they display sensitive dependence on initial conditions. What this means is illustrated in Figure 14.3(e). The unbroken line there plots the outcome for periods 200–250 with $\alpha = 3.75$, starting from an initial value for the exchange rate of 0.25 (as in Figures 14.3(a) to (d)), while the dotted line shows exactly the same computation, with the

sole difference that it assumes a starting value of the exchange rate of 0.249. As can be seen, not only is each series more or less indistinguishable from a completely random variable, there is also virtually no relationship between the two lines, in spite of the fact that they were both generated by exactly the same function.

It should be made absolutely clear what is so surprising about this outcome. In the first place, the fact that the graph shows the situation after 200 periods have elapsed should be seen in the right context. It certainly does not mean that the phenomenon can be dismissed as unimportant because 200 years is a long time. After all, there is no obvious translation of mathematical periods into calendar time. In financial markets, the appropriate modelling period may be as short as a single trading day, or even an hour or minute. Certainly, a 200-period horizon may be far from irrelevant for practical purposes.[17]

More importantly, however, the reader should realize that one would normally (that is, for non-chaotic series) expect to find one of the following three scenarios: either the two series should get closer together as time passes (corresponding, roughly speaking, to stability), or they should diverge to an ever-increasing degree (instability), or the difference between them should fluctuate regularly (periodic or cyclic behaviour). What is surprising is the fact that the difference between the two chaotic series in Figure 14.3(e) shows no sign of diminishing, nor of growing, nor of following any regular pattern. Quite simply, the similarity between the two seems to be temporary, with the two series sometimes being almost identical (for example, from $t = 219$ to $t = 230$), and at other times following paths which seem to bear virtually no relationship to each other.

What is so disturbing about chaotic functions is that their sensitivity is infinite, in the sense that even the smallest variation in their initial conditions results in a process that is totally transformed. Figure 14.3(f) gives another example of this effect. It graphs the time series for $\alpha = 3.99$ from $t = 101$ to $t = 200$, for processes which started at $t = 0$ from $s_0 = 0.25$ (the solid line) and from a value smaller by only 10^{-15} (the broken line). As can be seen, the two lines are sometimes close enough to be indistinguishable, but most of the time they bear little similarity to each other.

---

[17] As it happens, this particular time slice (periods 201–250) was chosen purely for practical purposes: the two graphs deviated enough to show up reasonably well in print, given the limitations of the software and hardware being used. For those interested in simply replicating these and similar graphs, all that is required is a reasonably powerful PC and one of the more sophisticated spreadsheet programs. The graphs given here were originally generated running QUATTRO-Pro under Windows on a PC with a 50MHz 80486 processor. Readers wishing to explore more sophisticated models can choose between a number of specialist maths packages available nowadays for PCs and workstations.

Key —————— $s_0 = 0.25$ −−−−−− $s_0 = 0.25 - 10^{-15}$

Figure 14.3(f) Path of exchange rate ($\alpha = 3.99$); $t = 101$ to 200.

(3) This phenomenon is sometimes known as the 'butterfly effect'. The expression derives from meteorology, where it was first investigated. It implies that even the minuscule effect on initial weather conditions of a butterfly's wings fluttering in one part of the world might be sufficient to trigger a causal chain leading ultimately to a hurricane on the other side of the world.

For our purposes, perhaps its most important implication is for forecasting. Every forecast has to have a point of departure, a starting value from which to make projections into the future. If a series is non-chaotic, we can forecast with the confidence that, at the very least, we know the current value of the variable in question. By contrast, when the function is chaotic, this confidence is likely to be misplaced, simply because, however accurately we know the current value, it will never be accurate enough to prevent possibly unlimited divergence between the forecast and actual values as time passes.

Key ——— α = 4.0   ——— α = 3.999...

Figure 14.3(g)   Path of exchange rate ($\alpha = 4.0$ vs $\alpha = 4.0 - 10^{-12}$).

Moreover, this danger would still exist even if the process generating the variable, the 'true' model, could be identified with 100% precision – which it never can be, of course.

(4)   This is not the only aspect to sensitive dependence. Chaotic functions are also sensitive to their parameter values. Figure 14.3(g) gives a simple (and extreme) example, comparing the behaviour of the logistic function with values of the tuning parameter, α, that differ by only 10^{-12}, but starting from the same initial value, $s_0 = 0.25$. It can be seen that even the tiniest error in estimating parameter values can be every bit as damaging as inaccuracies in the initial values. This is important because in the case of a variable like the exchange rate, errors in estimating model parameters are absolutely unavoidable.

(5) One possible conclusion is that forecasting is only feasible, if at all, at very short horizons. This was (and remains) the position taken by meteorologists in response to their discovery of the butterfly effect. At the risk of being defeatist, it amounts to taking a pragmatic view of the scope for forecasting: the prediction horizon is simply as long as proves practicable. Forecasts are updated as often as is necessary to preserve a specified minimal level of accuracy, without which they are completely useless.

(6) It has been stressed that tracking errors in chaotic systems, whether due to small variations in the initial conditions or in the parameter values, persist indefinitely. In that sense, there is no convergence between the series. But, on the other hand, there is no tendency to increased divergence either, at least in the sense that a chaotic function remains within certain bounds. This boundedness is a crucial feature of chaos. In the present case, it means that the exchange rate visits all points in the [0, 1] interval if we wait long enough. In other words, all values between 0 and 1 crop up eventually, but of course never recur.

This point needs emphasizing because it implies, among other things, that chaos need not necessarily be associated with excessive volatility, and certainly does not imply a tendency towards extreme values or an exceptionally broad range of fluctuation.[18]

(7) We saw that chaos can be viewed as the culmination of a sequence of changes in the cyclic behaviour of a non-linear function. In a sense, therefore, the concept of chaos is closely related to the notion of periodicity. As we saw, a one-period process repeats itself every (one) period, a two-period process is repeated every second period, and an N-period process every N periods. It is natural, therefore, to say that a process which never repeats itself has infinite period, or no period at all (hence aperiodic).

This perspective may not come naturally to readers accustomed to thinking in terms of mainstream economics and econometrics. After all, we know economic variables virtually never display an unambiguous regular cyclical pattern. In what sense is chaos any different? And, in any case, we tend to think of cycles as being the exception rather than the rule in economics. By and large, we do not expect to find a very marked periodicity (or 'seasonality') in financial variables, not least because any obvious pattern may well imply the persistence of unexploited profit opportunities. However, far more is at stake here.

---

[18] As we have seen, for all values of α less than 1.0 or greater than 4.0, the value of s_t 'escapes' to $-\infty$.

In the first place, remember we are dealing in this chapter with a deterministic model. It is one thing to say that stable patterns in the data are hidden by random disturbances, which is essentially the position taken by applied economists in normal empirical research. It is a different thing altogether to suggest there may be no underlying regularities even in the simple 'true' model.

Secondly, the concept of periodicity needs to be interpreted very broadly. It covers far more than seasonality. Essentially, by periodicity we mean to encompass any discernible pattern. An *n*-period cycle is a pattern which is replicated every *n* periods. The pattern can be as complicated as it is possible to imagine. For example, if *n* is 27, it could involve a value of 1.23 times the cycle average at the 14th period of the cycle, 0.45 times at the 15th period, 0.21 times at the 16th, and so on. As long as the next 27 periods display the same pattern, the periodicity is maintained.

In this sense, *periodicity amounts to the same thing as forecastability. An aperiodic series cannot be forecast.*[19] Putting the matter another way, a random series can be visualized as one with infinite periodicity.

For high values of *n*, and when the period in question is relatively long (that is, when we are looking at relatively low frequency data, say monthly or annual), then the periodicity may be too long for us to observe in practice. For example, in the unlikely event that there is actually a 300-year cycle in the exchange rate, it will obviously be many years (or rather centuries) before we shall be able to observe it. For practical purposes, therefore, it may make very little difference whether a series is strictly aperiodic or simply characterized by very long periodicity.[20]

On the other hand, in financial markets, a day or even an hour could be viewed as a long time in terms of the underlying behaviour patterns driving the variables. In this context, an apparently long-period cycle may be quite short in terms of observations, for example, *n* = 300 when dealing in minutes.

14.5 Evidence

The problems involved in testing for chaotic behaviour or, more generally for non-linearity in exchange rates are many, and too complicated to be

---

[19] The problem here for applied economists (like the author) is that we are accustomed to thinking of forecasting in multivariate terms, in the context of econometric models for example, with univariate forecasting as a special (and restrictive) case. However, given the processes for the exogenous variables, linear models which are complete are reducible to univariate processes, which can then be used for forecasting, at least in principle.

Note that the theory of multivariate non-linear processes is much more complicated and in any case not yet fully understood, hence the concentration here on univariate models.

[20] Notice that there is a sense in which computer random number generators can never be truly random, precisely because they must always have some periodicity, albeit an extremely long one.

explained in any detail here. Not the least of the problems (and one which has barely been addressed in the published literature) is the possibility that reality may be best described by a model which is *both* non-linear (chaotic or non-chaotic) *and* stochastic.

The next section attempts to give an intuitive outline of the major difficulties facing researchers in this area and of the solutions that have been proposed.

14.5.1 Testing problems

Faced with a block of exchange rate data, how can signs of chaotic behaviour be identified?

The starting point for testing has to be the question of linearity or non-linearity. After all, chaos is an essentially non-linear phenomenon. If a time series is linear, it cannot be chaotic. As has been shown, chaos occurs as a consequence of what might be called extreme non-linearity. Research in this area starts, therefore, from a search for evidence of non-linearity.

Now, in a sense, this work has entailed a fundamental change – a paradigm shift, as it is sometimes called – in attitudes to empirical work on financial markets. With few exceptions, previous research (including the work summarized in earlier chapters of this book) had concentrated exclusively on a search for linear relationships, usually not even allowing for the possibility of non-linearity.[21] Attention was explicitly or implicitly restricted to linear models.

For example, the whole emphasis in testing had previously been on finding *correlation* between variables: correlation between explanatory variables and the dependent variable, with success defined in terms of an absence of correlation in the residual error. However, a zero correlation coefficient between two random variables, X and Y, is evidence only that there is no *linear* relationship between them. A non-linear relationship can be present even if the correlation coefficient is zero.

What kind of tests can one use to isolate evidence of non-linear relationships between variables or, indeed, between current and past values of the same variable? As always, we avoid the technicalities, which are amply explained elsewhere (see the Reading Guide), concentrating instead on the intuition underlying the tests deployed.

Notice that in many cases the search for non-linearities is applied to the residuals from a linear model. This practice either reflects the fact that the 'true' model is presumed linear by default (that is, in the absence of

---

[21] Except for very simple forms of non-linearity, for example, log linearity and, more recently, models of variance autocorrelation, so-called ARCH processes.

convincing evidence of non-linearity), or sometimes that it is simply easier to extract any linear relationship at the outset.[22]

The tests can be divided into three broad classes:

(1)   The simplest tests are straightforward extensions of those applied to linear models. For example, correlation-based tests on a set of residuals $[u_t u_{t-1} \ldots u_{t-N}]$ can be replaced by tests on the set of squared residuals, $[u_t^2 u_{t-1}^2 \ldots u_{t-N}^2]$ The problem here, of course, is that the test will only isolate a quadratic relationship. For example, if the residuals in question are actually linked by a cubic relationship, this fact is unlikely to be revealed by a test on the squared residuals.

(2)   To remedy this defect, tests which make no assumptions about the nature of any non-linearity are required. The most commonly used tests of this general type are a class based on the notion of *correlation dimension*. The idea here is illustrated in Figures 14.4 and 14.5, which show a scatter of points s_t, s_{t+1} for two (imaginary) time series of exchange rates suspected of concealing a linear or non-linear pattern. Clearly, the series in Figure 14.4 shows little sign of any regularity. By contrast, Figure 14.5 looks highly promising.[23] What sort of test might reveal the pattern in Figure 14.5, while discounting any regularity in Figure 14.4?

In Figure 14.4, the observations are scattered in haphazard fashion around the space. Consider drawing a square of a given size, say 1cm by 1cm, somewhere in the space (the inner of the two boxes). As can be seen, in the present case there are only four points in the box.

Now draw a square with sides that are double the length, that is, 2cm by 2cm. Of course, doubling the length of the sides increases the area by a factor of four. But what happens to the number of points inside the box? Since in Figure 14.4 the points are evenly spread over the space, the number of points in the square also increases by about the same factor, from 4 to 16 or 17.

By contrast, performing the same exercise on the data in Figure 14.5 produces a very different outcome. As the length of the square's sides are doubled, the number of points increases by far less than four times. In fact, it goes from 4 to around 8 or 9 (one of the points is on the edge of the box), slightly more than double. The extent to which the number of points increases as the square is

---

[22] There seems to be no consensus in the literature about the advisability or otherwise of fitting linear time series before testing for non-linearity.

[23] In fact, Figure 14.4 consists of the output from a random number generator, whereas Figure 14.5 plots 200 iterations of the logistic with a tuning parameter of 3.75.

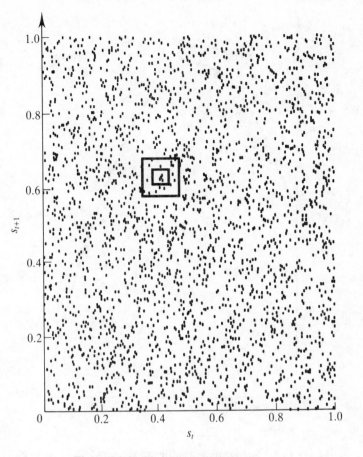

Figure 14.4 Random numbers: noise.

expanded is an indicator of how far the series deviates from a random spread. Moreover, where a non-linear relationship does exist, it can also provide some hints as to the form of non-linearity.

A number of test statistics have been developed based on generalizations of this sort of measure, although there are still a number of difficulties in applying them. The most obvious problems relate first to the distributional characteristics of the tests, particularly in view of the shortage of data points in research on exchange rates. This may seem strange to readers with a background in economics. After all, macroeconomists are accustomed to empirical research on annual or quarterly data sets, for example, GNP or the balance of payments, where 200 or 250 observations are the norm.

Figure 14.5 Scatter diagram for logistic function ($\alpha = 3.75$).

By comparison, 2000 or 3000 daily exchange rates might seem more than adequate.[24]

However, there are grounds for believing that investigating the kind of behaviour covered in this chapter requires far larger data sets than this. Some researchers have used data sets made up of 30 000 or 40 000 minute-by-minute observations, and a number of studies have been published using over a million data points.

(3) As has already been seen, chaotic series are forecastable, but only at short horizons. Because of their sensitivity to the initial conditions, forecasting errors rapidly accumulate to the point where the forecast becomes useless.

---

[24] Virtually all research on exchange rates prior to chaos (that is, almost all the work covered in earlier chapters) involved daily data, at best, and for the most part, monthly, weekly or quarterly data.

This fact suggests that tests for chaos could be based on forecastability. The problem is, of course, that the forecast used in the test could hardly presuppose any particular non-linear model. The standard techniques in the applied economist's toolbox – econometrics and time-series analysis – are ruled out in advance. However, researchers in the natural sciences are accustomed to using non-parametric methods in this kind of context, and these techniques form the basis for a number of different tests.

One frequently followed approach involves using these forecasting methods to arrive at measures of the extent to which adjacent values of the variable diverge as time passes, in other words, direct tests of sensitivity to initial conditions. These tests are based on the concept of the *Lyapunov exponent*,[25] an indicator of the speed with which adjacent points diverge. Even more than the other testing approaches, this type of work requires large data sets (an absolute minimum of 10 000 observations, in the view of some researchers) and commensurate computing power.

14.5.2 Results

Investigating non-linearity in financial markets is still in its infancy. However, at this stage a number of reasonably sound conclusions seem to have emerged. Before listing them, however, the reader should be aware of near-simultaneous developments in econometrics.

It should be pointed out that the advent of non-linear testing of the type described in the previous section coincided with an important development in mainstream time-series econometrics. As has been pointed out already in this book, the evidence suggests clearly that the volatility of exchange rates varies between periods of extreme turbulence and periods of relative calm. In other words, volatility tends to cluster, with days or weeks of high variance movements succeeding each other. Researchers in the 1980s responded to this finding by suspending the assumption of an independent, identically distributed (IID) error term. In its place, they incorporated an error term with a variance which followed an explicit time-series process. The so-called autoregressive conditional heteroscedasticity or ARCH models and its variants[26] seem to fit the facts quite well in most financial markets, including currency markets, in the sense that they improve the accuracy of the standard models.

---

[25] See the Reading Guide for explanations of this measure of sensitivity.

[26] ARCH models spawned a whole family of offspring, all known by acronyms: GARCH, EGARCH, IGARCH, and others. Interested readers can find out more by consulting any up-to-date econometrics textbook.

Against this background, non-linear research in financial markets has broadly attempted to address the questions in the following sequence:

(1) Is the original data set (the rates of return) IID? In other words, is there evidence of linear or non-linear dependence? By and large, the evidence from correlation dimension and related tests seems to point to the existence of some underlying non-linear structure, though its nature is still in some doubt.

(2) If the data are characterized by non-linear dependence, is the system chaotic? This question is extremely difficult to answer. However, the few published results of forecastability tests show little sign of chaos.

(3) Some studies appear to indicate that residuals from appropriately-specified GARCH models show little sign of any remaining non-linear dependence.[27] This would seem to suggest that GARCH models may be an adequate representation of exchange rate time series.

We await further developments on both the methodological and application fronts. In particular, there is likely to be a large volume of research emerging in the next few years deploying a battery of more advanced tests, and applying them to data observed at very high frequencies (minute-by-minute and more).

In the meantime, it should be realized that it is to some extent a matter of choice whether we think of a series as a stochastic or deterministic process. In practice, there are several reasons why both may be possible. In the first place, as has already been pointed out, if the 'true' deterministic process is of high dimension, it may be simpler to conceive of it as random. Secondly, it seems improbable that a financial series could ever be completely deterministic. Thirdly, there is a reasonably straightforward way of treating outcomes of chaotic processes as though they are random variables. It may well be that agents in financial markets form expectations as though they are operating in a truly stochastic environment. In that sense a stochastic model may well be consistent with their beliefs.

14.6 Conclusions

How should one interpret these results? To put them into context, one needs to backtrack to the questions discussed at the beginning of the chapter.

Ultimately, one cannot avoid asking what is meant by randomness. If, like Einstein, you do not believe in true randomness, in other words, if you conceive of the error term in a stochastic equation as simply a

---

[27] See especially the papers by Hsieh mentioned in the Reading Guide.

portmanteau intended to hold all the unobserved or unmeasurable variables which cannot be explicitly included elsewhere, then *other things being equal* you will always prefer a deterministic model to a stochastic model. From this standpoint, a stochastic model is simply a temporary fix, intended to do a job until a permanent (that is, deterministic) solution can be found. As such, it may work better than the best available deterministic model for the moment. But as always, that judgement is purely temporary, pending further research to take us closer to a situation where residual error terms can be suppressed.

If the empirical results so far suggest that stochastic models provide a marginally better representation of exchange rate time series than deterministic models, readers who take the Einstein line may remain unimpressed. They may demand that stochastic models substantially outperform deterministic in order to justify their inferior theoretical basis.

On the other hand, many people will find inherently implausible the idea of a deterministic model of a financial variable. From this viewpoint, randomness must be intrinsic to a price set in a market populated by human beings who are prone to moods, to illness, who react unpredictably, who are liable to spill their coffee just at the moment when important news appears on their trading screen, and so on. People who take this view will be unimpressed by models which purport to 'explain' everything, leaving no room for randomness.

There are a number of reasons why this school will carry the day for a long time to come, at least in the sense that we shall invariably have to allow for a stochastic component, even where it is superimposed on chaos. One obvious point is that, even if we believe all events can in theory be modelled (even the moment a trader spills his coffee), it is out of the question in practice to build such a 'universal' model, and will remain so for the foreseeable future. A second reason for randomness is that, for all sorts of technical reasons (not least, the limits on the size of available datasets and on the computing power to analyse them), it is at present impossible to test for chaotic processes of dimension beyond about 10 or 12. Thus, by default, the choice facing researchers lies between low dimension chaos and a stochastic model. Finally, it should be said that even if we were capable of detecting the 'true' model generating the apparently random behaviour of financial variables, the likelihood is that it would involve an extremely complicated mathematical structure. Under these circumstances, we might well end up preferring a stochastic model as a more manageable representation of reality.

Whatever answer one gives to the philosophical question of whether or not irreducible randomness exists, it has to be recognized that, empirically at least, there is a major practical difference between modelling a currency market and the type of models developed by the physicists who pioneered chaos theory.

The dilemma for economists is as follows.

On the one hand, it is every bit as important for us to know whether markets are chaotic or not, and if they are chaotic, to find the equation that describes their motion. After all, if financial markets are indeed characterized by sensitive dependence on initial conditions, the scope for butterfly effects is potentially unlimited. Moreover, the policy implications of chaos could be momentous.[28]

On the other hand, even if one believes in an ultimately deterministic truth, it is a Holy Grail which in the case of currency markets is unlikely ever to be achievable. However sophisticated and all-embracing our model, it seems we are always going to require a random term to cover the myriad of accidents and coincidences that characterize any financial market: the trader whose computer screen malfunctions or who presses the wrong key, the actual or threatened political upheaval following a scandal involving a finance minister, and so forth. Not least, we need to model a market full of traders making decisons based on the output of computer models of chaotic financial markets.

■ Summary

- An exchange rate model involving a non-linear iterative deterministic process can be analysed with the aid of a phase diagram, relating the value of the variable in any period to its level in the previous portrait.

- In the case of the simple model selected as an example, the phase portrait and the resulting behaviour depend on the value of the critical tuning parameter, which in a sense measures the degree of non-linearity (that is, the deviation from linearity) of the model.

- Depending on the value of the critical parameter, the exchange rate may follow a path that is characterized by monotonic convergence to equilibrium, or by either stable or unstable periodic oscillations around the equilibrium.

---

[28] It is not at all obvious that they point towards the need for any form of intervention by the authorities, least of all fixed exchange rates, as is sometimes assumed. After all, if the instability originates in the underlying net demand for a currency, fixing the exchange rate may prove impossible altogether. Moreover, the effect of any intervention which simply changes the 'initial values' for the demand will be unpredictable over anything longer than the very short term. The question of how to stabilize chaotic systems is yet to be answered, but it would appear that at the very least successful intervention would need to alter the parameters of the underlying system. Given the difficulties involved in simply identifying a chaotic system, this is a formidable task indeed, far beyond the competence of present-day statisticians.

- For some values of the tuning parameter associated with extreme non-linearity, the system exhibits what is known as chaotic behaviour. That is to say, it follows a path which is ostensibly random.

- Chaotic behaviour is defined by extreme sensitivity to initial conditions, so that the smallest inaccuracy in defining a starting point results in a forecast which bears less and less resemblance to the actual outcome as time passes.

- Empirical testing for non-linear dependence and more specifically for chaos in economic data is still in its infancy. The results so far are mixed. However, a number of researchers have detected some degree of complexity, especially in high frequency financial data. In general, one would have to conclude that the question of the relevance of chaos to financial markets remains an open question.

READING GUIDE

As regards the material in this chapter, it should be clear that references vary enormously in the level of mathematical sophistication required of the reader. In most cases, topology is the main barrier to entry. The majority of the readings on chaos theory are from the maths/physics/general science literature, though economics is fast catching up.

In general terms, the best casual reading on the subject is Stewart (1990), which gives plenty of background material on the major researchers in the field. Gleick (1987) is even more casual and has been a bestseller.

The most readable non-technical introductions to the material covered in this chapter are May (1976) and Baumol and Benhabib (1989), the latter written from the perspectives of economics. Two useful textbooks are by Peitgen, Jurgens and Saupe (1992), which is non-technical but gives especially good coverage of fractal geometry and Devaney (1989), which is more formal. Azariadis (1993) contains some excellent chapters on linear and non-linear dynamics, and covers a number of interesting applications in financial economics and general macroeconomics.

There are a number of useful collections of readings. Cvitanovic (1989) is a good buy for those wanting quick access to the seminal papers (mainly from the physics literature), especially those on bifurcation theory, universality and so forth. For specifically economics readings, see Anderson, Arrow and Pines (1988) and Barnett, Geweke and Shell (1989).

The literature on non-linearity and chaos in exchange rates is still in its infancy. The best starting point, however, is Brock, Hsieh and LeBaron (1991), which devotes a chapter each to stock markets and exchange rates. Hsieh (1993) looks for non-linearities in currency futures prices.

Part IV

Conclusions

The last chapter looks back at the material covered in this book and discusses where we might go from here, in particular what look the most promising avenues for future research.

15

Conclusions

15.1 Summary of the Book

15.2 Where do we go from here?

In this book, I have tried to provide the determined reader with a fair summary of the state of our existing knowledge about exchange rates and an adequate foundation for getting to grips with the original literature, if so desired. This concluding chapter will briefly survey the material in the book, then go on to consider the question: where might research go from here?

15.1 Summary of the book

In the first chapter the reader was introduced to the working of a currency market under fixed and floating exchange rates and the significance of the balance of payments was explained. As a background to the theory to follow, a brief history of the international monetary system was given, with particular emphasis on the prelude to today's floating exchange rates: the disintegration of the Bretton Woods regime.

There followed three chapters of essential preliminaries. In the first, it was shown how extending the law of one price to product markets in the open economy led to the conclusion that price levels ought to move in unison, once allowance was made for exchange rate movements. Unfortunately, however attractive it might look in theory, purchasing power parity turned out to fit the facts very poorly, if at all.

431

By contrast, extending the law of one price to the market for international securities looked more promising. Two conclusions emerged from Chapter 3. First, arbitrage ought to make the forward premium equal to the international interest differential – and, by and large, the evidence suggests it does. On the other hand, uncovered interest rate parity is much more difficult to test since it involves the unobservable *expected* rate of depreciation.

Finally in Part I, Chapter 4 extended the textbook aggregate demand and supply framework to accommodate an open economy.

The preliminaries completed, Part II examined a number of models of exchange rate determination, starting with the monetary model, a convenient benchmark for future reference. In essence it is an extension of the classical quantity theory to the open economy context. Firstly it predicts that increases in the money stock will be reflected in depreciation of the same proportion and secondly, that (real) income growth will be associated with a rising international currency value. Both results automatically flow from the fact that the model is constructed out of two building-blocks: PPP and the balance of supply and demand in the money market. Not surprisingly, given the failure of PPP to fit the facts, the monetary model also fares rather poorly in that respect.

On the other hand, the Mundell–Fleming model (Chapter 6) goes to the opposite extreme of taking the price level as constant. Since it also ignores the role of expectations its relevance to contemporary currency markets is limited, though it has been very influential, both on academic researchers and on the architects of macroeconomic policy, particularly in the UK and USA.

The Dornbusch model (Chapter 7) represents a compromise, suspending PPP in the short run but acknowledging it as undeniable in the long run. The implication turns out to be that financial markets, which are still assumed to clear instantaneously, have to *over*adjust to disturbances.

In fact, this conclusion is quite general, as was seen in the next two chapters. In particular, overshooting is a feature of portfolio balance models (Chapter 8) in which investors are seen as allocating their wealth to three broad asset categories: domestic money and bonds and foreign currency bonds. It is also an implication of currency substitution models (Chapter 9) in which investors are assumed to focus more narrowly on the choice between domestic and foreign currency balances, shifting their relative money demand in response to changes in the rate of depreciation.

Both models make strong predictions, especially with regard to the link between the current account and the exchange rate. Neither fits the facts very closely. Neither proves reliable for forecasting purposes. Part II ends with a chapter on a topic in what is sometimes called political economy: what does our understanding of exchange rates imply for the optimal size of a currency zone? In particular, what are the likely effects of the planned European Monetary Union?

In Part III, the consequences of uncertainty, which had been avoided up to this point, were confronted under three headings. Start with an equation like Equation 11.4, rewritten as follows:

$$s_t = \rho_{t-1} + f^t_{t-1} + u_t \tag{15.1}$$

Chapter 11 looked at the role of the forward rate in this equation and in the process introduced the important concepts of rational expectations and market efficiency. Chapter 12 concentrated on the innovation term, u_t, and showed that it ought to be explained by the intermittent arrival of new information – 'news' – about the fundamentals. In the next chapter, the risk premium, ρ_{t-1} was linked to the behaviour of individual decision makers faced with investment choices under conditions of uncertainty.

Examination of the evidence revealed something of a puzzle. On the one hand, unbiasedness could be ruled out with some confidence. In other words, the intercept term in Equation 15.1 was not zero. On the other hand, from several points of view, it was hard to credit that the risk premium could explain the gap between the spot and lagged forward rate. The same applied to 'news': the theory contributed to some extent to an explanation of the facts, but nowhere near enough.

The last chapter served not only to bring the story up to date in covering the most recent research topics, but also pointed to a possible reconciliation of some of the recurrent themes in the book. It was shown there that in some cases non-linear models can generate predictions for exchange rate behaviour that cover almost every variety of conceivable pattern, ranging from almost mechanical cycles to fluctuations that are virtually indistinguishable from randomness. Whether this type of model will ultimately allow us to gain more of an insight into the workings of currency markets remains to be seen.

15.2 Where do we go from here?

The reader may feel slightly cheated at the end of a book like this. After all, we do not seem to know very much about exchange rates, do we? Or, more precisely, there are lots of negative statements we can make with confidence: PPP does *not* explain exchange rate fluctuations, *nor* do money stocks, *nor* interest rate differentials ... and so on.

In the first place it should be pointed out that negative results may still be worth having.[1] Sometimes, a process of elimination is the best one can do.

---

[1] For example, at the time of writing the first edition, news had just been published of the finding by medical researchers that nitrates do *not* cause cancer, contrary to previous suspicions.

More than that, however, it has been made clear throughout the book that a major reason why most theories of exchange rate determination fail is because of their inability to explain the *volatility* we actually observe. Most of the candidate variables proposed by the different theories are simply far too stable to fit the bill.

Now volatility is a general feature of financial markets. In fact, the currency markets can appear positively tranquil by comparison with some of the more turbulent markets, such as stock markets for example.

Perhaps the very fact that turbulence is so widespread in financial markets is a clue to how we ought to think about the problem. Suppose that the factors which generate the turbulence have causes which are common to financial markets, but which are completely *independent* of events in any *specific* market. In other words, suppose that exchange rate volatility contains two components: one attributable simply to the fact that currency markets behave like the financial markets of which they are an example and another component reflecting fluctuations in the fundamentals.

Notice that this is not quite the same as what was called the 'news' approach in Chapter 12. Fluctuations due to 'news' are, by definition, the result of the behaviour of investors with rational expectations operating in an efficient market. Instead, what is being suggested here is that an underlying relationship between the fundamentals and the exchange rate – perhaps along the lines of one of the models covered in the first half of this book – may be swamped in practice by not one but *two* types of turbulence: the volatility that characterizes financial markets in general superimposed on the volatility that results from the impact of 'news'. Let us call the first type: **market volatility** and the second: **information volatility**.

Now, if there were a way of stripping out the market volatility from our observed exchange rate series, we would then be able to identify the appropriate fundamental model by fitting a 'news' model to deal with the information volatility. Unfortunately, we are as yet a long way from being able to explain market behaviour, though an increasing amount of work has been published in recent years, and the pace has accelerated in the aftermath of the 1987 stock market crashes.

It should be appreciated in this regard that the problem of explaining stock market volatility is subtly different from the problem of explaining exchange rate volatility. To see why, take the case of a share in a company whose future profits (and dividends) are known *with certainty*.[2] Ask yourself what 'model' one would use to determine the share price.

Put in this fashion the question has an obvious answer. We hardly need a 'model'. All we need do is capitalize the known future income stream. Furthermore, we have proof that this present value model is

---

[2] For those readers who find it difficult to imagine, suppose that the company simply owns a building which has been let at a fixed rent on a very long lease.

correct because there are plenty of riskless securities available (we simply call them bonds rather than shares) and, sure enough, their market price never deviates very far from their present value, once account is taken of differences in tax treatment, detailed redemption provisions and so on.

Notice the contrast with the situation in exchange rate research. Since they know the identity of the fundamental variables, stock market researchers can confidently attribute deviations from this benchmark to the effects of uncertainty. This gives them a head start over exchange rate researchers in dealing with the type of questions covered in Chapters 11 and 12 of this book. Thus, for example, their variance bounds tests on share prices have to be regarded as more conclusive than those on exchange rates.

It seems likely, therefore, that progress on the research agenda in stock markets is going to be very important in affecting our thinking about exchange rates. We have already encountered an example of this. The work on bubbles (see Section 12.5) was a response to evidence of stock market inefficiency. As was pointed out, it is a special approach, in so far as it takes market perversity for granted without trying to explain it. But attempts to explain market behaviour are being made. A number of avenues are currently being explored:

(1) *Alternatives to rational expectations*: as we have seen, the direct (or survey-based) evidence on RE is mixed. Work by Kahneman and Tversky (1979, 1982) has suggested alternatives, though their applicability to financial markets is yet to be demonstrated.

(2) *Market inefficiency*: notably, recent work on so-called 'noise trading' in stock markets (Black, 1988; Kyle, 1987). This research is very much in its infancy and in any case it is not clear that it will produce any conclusions directly applicable to currency markets. At best, it looks at the present moment as though it may serve to provide a measure of theoretical rationalization for the type of models being generated by the time-series theorists, whether stochastic or deterministic.

(3) *Non-linear time series* (that is, stochastic models) may offer some hope of 'describing' if not really explaining exchange rate movements. One reason for turning in this direction (apart from the fact that the possibilities of linear time series seem to have been exhausted) is to be found in an examination of high-frequency data: weekly, or better still daily. Two features are found to emerge. Firstly, the variance of exchange rate changes is plainly non-constant itself. Secondly, the market seems to be characterized by relatively long periods of tranquillity, punctuated by spells of turbulence.

The previous chapter looked at one approach to modelling this type of behaviour. Another approach, so-called ARCH models and their variants, involves extending standard econometric or time-series models to incorporate a non-constant error variance term. Usually, this involves a sub-model of the residual variance which is itself essentially a univariate time series (typically an ARMA(1, 1) process). The implication is that episodes of volatility tend to cluster, as a result of spillovers from previous periods. To a great extent, this sort of process seems to represent the facts about exchange rates quite well. Nonetheless, it should be clear it does little to advance our understanding of why exchange rates fluctuate.

These three developments seem to hold out the best hope of ever escaping from a situation where as soon as a model is found which appears to explain *past* movements it promptly breaks down, generating predictions that become more and more inaccurate. For the moment, we remain victims of an affliction widely recognized as:

> ' ... the Light-in-the-Refrigerator Syndrome, i.e. is the light on when the door is shut? The only way to find out is to open the door – in which case the door is not shut any more ... '[3]

In the meantime, perhaps the *worst* thing we could do would be to pretend that we know more than we actually do – an affliction which seems to affect academics occasionally and politicians, professional and amateur, very frequently – as witnessed by some of the arguments used in Britain to support the case for EMS membership.

---

[3] From: *The Complete Yes Minister: The Diaries of A Cabinet Minister*. Edited by Jonathan Lynn and Antony Jay, published by the BBC, 1984, p.22

Bibliography

Adler M. and Lehmann B. (1983). Deviations from purchasing power parity in the long run. *Journal of Finance*, **38** (5), 1471–87

Aliber R. Z. (1973). The interest rate parity theorems: a reinterpretation. *Journal of Political Economy*, **81** (6), 1451–59

Anderson P. W., Arrow K. J. and Pines D. (1988). *The Economy as an Evolving Complex System*. Reading, MA: Addison-Wesley

Artis M. J. (1984). *Macroeconomics*. Oxford: Oxford University Press

Azariadis C. (1993). *Intertemporal Macroeconomics*. Oxford, UK and Cambridge, USA: Blackwell

Baillie R. T., Lippens R. E. and McMahon P.C. (1983). Testing rational expectations and efficiency in the foreign exchange market. *Econometrica*, **51**, 553–63

Barnett W. A., Geweke J. and Shell K. (1989). *Economic Complexity: Chaos, Sunspots, Bubbles and Nonlinearity*. Cambridge: Cambridge University Press

Barro R. J. (1974). Are government bonds net worth? *Journal of Political Economy*, **82**, 1095–1117

Barro R. J. (1977). Unanticipated money growth and unemployment in the United States. *American Economic Review*, **67**, 101–15

Barro R. J. (1984). *Macroeconomics*. John Wiley & Sons

Baumol W. J. and Benhabib J. (1989). Chaos: significance, mechanism, and economic applications. *Journal of Economic Perspectives*, **3**(1), 77–105

Begg D. K. (1982). *The Rational Expectations Revolution in Macroeconomics*. Oxford: Philip Allan

Begg D. K., Dornbusch R. and Fischer S. (1987). *Macroeconomics*. Maidenhead: McGraw-Hill

Bilson J. F. (1979). Recent developments in monetary models of exchange rate determination. *IMF Staff Papers*, **26** (2), 201–23

Bilson J. O. (1981). The speculative efficiency hypothesis. *Journal of Business*, **54**, (3) 435–51

Black F. (1986). Noise. *Journal of Finance*, **41** (3), 529–43

Blanchard and Katz (1992). Regional evolutions. *Brookings Papers on Economic Activity*, 1:1992

Blanchard O. J. and Watson M. (1982). Bubbles, rational expectations and financial markets. In *Crises in the Economic and Financial Structure* (Wachtel P., ed.), pp. 295–315. Lexington: Lexington Books

Branson W. H. (1983). Macroeconomic determinants of real exchange risk. In *Managing Foreign Exchange Risk* (Herring R. J., ed.), Chapter 1. Cambridge: Cambridge University Press

Branson W. H. and Halttunen H. (1979). Asset market determination of exchange rates: initial empirical and policy results. In *Trade and Payments Under Flexible Exchange Rates* (Martin J. P. and Smith A., eds.), pp. 55–85. London: Macmillan

Branson W. H. Halttunen, H. and Masson P. (1977). Exchange rates in the short run: the dollar–Deutschemark rate. *European Economic Review*, **10**, 303–24

Branson W. H. and Henderson D. W. (1985). The specification and influence of asset markets. In *Handbook of International Economics (Volume II)* (Jones R. A. and Kenen P. B., eds.), pp. 749–93. Amsterdam: North-Holland

Brock W. A., Hsieh D. A. and LeBaron B. (1991). *Nonlinear Dynamics, Chaos and Instability: Statistical Theory and Economic Evidence*. Cambridge, MA: MIT Press

Bruno M. and Sachs J. (1982). Input price shocks and the slowdown in economic growth: the case of UK manufacturing. *Review of Economic Studies*, **49**, 679–705

Buiter W. H. and Miller M. H. (1982). Monetary policy and international competitiveness. In *The Money Supply and The Exchange Rate* (Sinclair P. J. N. and Eltis W. A., eds.). Oxford: Oxford University Press

Buiter W. H. and Miller M. H. (1983). Real exchange rate overshooting and the output cost of bringing down inflation: some further results. In *Exchange Rates and International Macroeconomics* (Frenkel J., ed.), pp. 317–68. Chicago: University of Chicago Press

Buiter W. H. and Purvis D. D. (1983). Oil disinflation and export competitiveness: a model of the Dutch disease. In *Economic Interdependance and Flexible Exchange Rates* (Bhandari J. S. and Putnam B. H., eds.), pp. 221–48. Cambridge MA: MIT Press

Calvo G. and Rodriguez C. A. (1977). A model of exchange rate determination under currency substitution and rational expectations. *Journal of Political Economy*, **85** (3), 617–26

Cassel G. (1916). The present situation of the foreign exchanges. *Economic Journal*, March

Christou C. (1992). National monetary policies and the European Monetary Union. *Greek Economic Review*, August

Chrystal A. (1977). Demand for international media of exchange. *American Economic Review*, **67**, 840–50

Copeland L. S. (1983). Public sector prices and the real exchange rate in the UK recession. *Bulletin of Economic Research*, **35** (2), 97–121

Copeland L. S. (1989). Exchange rates and 'news': a vector autoregression approach. In *Innovations in Open Economy Macroeconomics* (Macdonald R. and Taylor M. P., eds.). Oxford: Blackwell

Copeland T. E. and Weston J. F. (1983). *Financial Theory and Corporate Policy* 2nd ed. Reading MA: Addison–Wesley

Cvitanovic P. (1989). *Universality in Chaos* 2nd ed. Bristol and New York: Adam Hilger

Daniel B. C. (1982). Monetary expansion and aggregate supply in a small open economy. *Economica*, **49** (195), 267–87

Deardorff A. V. (1979). One way arbitrage and its implications for the foreign exchange markets. *Journal of Political Economy*, **87** (2), 351–64

Devaney R. L. (1989). *An Introduction to Chaotic Dynamical Systems* 2nd ed. Redwood City, CA: Addison-Wesley

Diba B. T. and Grossman H. I. (1988). Rational inflationary bubbles. *Journal of Monetary Economics*, **21**, 35–46

Dooley M. P. and Shafer J. R. (1983). Analysis of short run exchange rate behavior: March 1973 to November 1981. In *Exchange Rate and Trade Instability* (Bigman D. and Taya T., eds.), pp. 187–209. Cambridge MA: Ballinger

Dornbusch R. (1973). Devaluation, money and non-traded goods. *American Economic Review*, **63**, 871–80

Dornbusch R. (1976). Expectations and exchange rate dynamics. *Journal of Political Economy*, **84**, 1161–76

Dornbusch R. (1976). The theory of flexible exchange rate regimes and macroeconomic policy. *Scandinavian Journal of Economics*, **78** (2), 255–76

Dornbusch R. (1982). Equilibrium and disequilibrium exchange rates. In *International Financial Management: Theory and Application* (Lessard D. R., ed.), pp. 151–72. John Wiley & Sons

Dornbusch R. (1983). Exchange rate risk and the macroeconomics of exchange rate determination. In *The Internationalization of Financial Markets and National Economic Policy* (Hawkins R. G., Levich R. M. and Whilborg C. G., eds.), pp. 3–27. Greenwich Conn: JAI Press

Dornbusch R. and Fischer S. (1980). Exchange rates and the current account. *American Economic Review*, **70** (5), 960–71

Dunn R. M. (1983). The many disappointments of flexible exchange rates. *Princeton Essays in International Finance*, **154**, Princeton: University of Princeton Press

Eastwood R. K. and Venables A. J. (1982). The macroeconomic implications of a resource discovery in an open economy. *Economic Journal*, **92**, 285–99

Edwards S. (1982). Exchange rates and news : a multi-currency approach. *Journal of International Money and Finance*, **1** (1), 211–24

Edwards S. (1983). Floating exchange rates, expectations and new information. *Journal of Monetary Economics*, **11**, 321–36

Evans G. W. (1986). A test for speculative bubbles in the sterling–dollar exchange rate: 1981–1984. *American Economic Review*, **76** (4), 621–36

Fama E. F. (1970). Efficient capital markets: a review of theory and empirical work. *Journal of Finance*, **25**, 383–417

Feldstein M. (1992). Europe's Monetary Union: The Case Against EMU. *The Economist*, 13 June 1992

Fleming J. M (1962). Domestic financial policies under fixed and floating exchange rates. *IMF Staff Papers*, **9**, 369–77

Flood R. P. and Garber P. M. (1982). Bubbles, runs, and gold monetization. In *Crises in the Economic and Financial Structure* (Wachtel, P., ed.), pp. 295–316. Lexington: Lexington Books

Frankel J. A. (1979). On the Mark: a theory of floating exchange rates based on real interest differentials. *American Economic Review*, **69**, 610–22

Frankel J. A. (1980). Tests of rational expectations in the forward exchange market. *Southern Economic Journal* **46** (4), 1083–1101

Frankel J. A. (1982). In search of the exchange rate premium: a six currency test assuming mean variance optimization. *Journal of International Money and Finance*, **1**, 255–74

Frankel J. A. (1983). Monetary and portfolio-balance models of exchange rate determination. In *Economic Interdependence and Flexible Exchange Rates* (Bhandari J. S. and Putnam B. H., eds.), pp. 84–115. Cambridge MA: MIT Press

Frankel J. A. (1983). Estimation of portfolio-balance functions that are mean-variance optimizing: the Mark and the dollar. *European Economic Review*, **23**, 315–27

Frankel J. A. (1986). The implications of mean–variance optimization for four questions in international macroeconomics. *Journal of International Money and Finance*, **5**, 53–75

Frankel J. A. and Froot K. A. (1987). Using survey data to test standard propositions regarding exchange rate expectations *American Economic Review*, **77** (1), 133–53

Frenkel J. A. (1976). A monetary approach to the exchange rate: doctrinal aspects and empirical evidence. *Scandinavian Journal of Economics*, **78** (2), 200–24

Frenkel J. A. (1977). The forward exchange rate, expectations and the demand for money: the German hyperinflation. *American Economic Review*, **67** (4) 653–70

Frenkel J. A. (1978). Purchasing power parity: doctrinal perspective and evidence from the 1920s. *Journal of International Economics*, **8** (2), 169–91

Frenkel J. A. (1980). The collapse of purchasing power parities during the 1970s. *European Economic Review*, **7**, 145–65

Frenkel J. A. (1981). Flexible exchange rates, prices and the role of news: lessons from the 1970s. *Journal of Political Economy*, **89**, 655–705

Frenkel J. A. and Levich R. M. (1975). Covered interest arbitrage: unexploited profits? *Journal of Political Economy*, **83** (2), 325–38

Frenkel J. A. and Razin A. (1980). Stochastic prices and tests of efficiency of foreign exchange markets. *Economics Letters*, **6**, 165–70

Frenkel J. A. and Razin A. (1988). The Mundell–Fleming model a quarter century later: a unified exposition. *IMF Staff Papers*, **35**, 567–620

Frenkel J. A. and Rodriguez C. A. (1982). Exchange rate dynamics and the overshooting hypothesis. *IMF Staff Papers*, **29**, 1–30

Friedman M. (1953). The case for flexible rates. *Essays in Positive Economics*. Chicago. University of Chicago Press

Gleick J. (1987). *Chaos: Making A New Science*. London: Cardinal Books

Grabbe J. O. (1986). *International Financial Markets*. Holland: Elsevier

Green H. A. (1976). *Consumer Theory*. London: Macmillan Press

Grossman S. F. and Shiller R. J. (1981). The determinants of the variability of stock market prices. *American Economic Review*, **71**, (2), 222–27

Grubel H. G. (1977). *International Economics*. Homewood Ill: Richard D. Irwin

Hamburger M. J. (1977). The demand for money in an open economy: Germany and the United Kingdom. *Journal of Monetary Economics*. **3**, 25–40

Hansen L. P. and Hodrick R. J. (1980). Forward exchange rates as optimal predictors of future spot rates: an econometric analysis. *Journal of Political Economy*, **88**, 829–53

Hansen L. P. and Hodrick R. J. (1983). Risk averse speculation in the forward foreign exchange market: an econometric analysis of linear models. In *Exchange Rates and International Macroeconomics* (Frenkel J., ed.), pp. 113–52. Chicago: University of Chicago Press

Hartley P. (1983). Rational expectations and the foreign exchange market. In *Exchange Rates and International Macroeconomics* (Frenkel J., ed.), pp. 153–88. Chicago: Universty of Chicago Press

Hodrick R. J. and Srivastava S. (1986). The covariation of risk premiums and expected future spot exchange rates. *Journal of International Money and Finance*, **5**, s5–s22

Hsieh D. A. (1993). Using nonlinear methods to search for risk premia in currency futures. *Journal of International Economics*, **35**, 113–32

Hume D. (1741). Of the balance of trade. In *Essays: Moral, Political and Literary* Oxford: Oxford University Press (reprinted 1963)

Isard P. (1977). How far can we push the law of one price? *American Economic Review*, **67**, 942–48

Johnson H. G. (1967). Money in a neo-classical one sector growth model. In *Essays in Monetary Economics*, pp. 143–78. London: Unwin

Johnson H. G. (1972). The monetary approach to balance of payments theory. In *Further Essays in Monetary Theory* London: Allen & Unwin

Johnson H. G. (1977). The monetary approach to the balance of payments: a non-technical guide. *Journal of International Economics*, **7**, 251–68

Kahneman D. and Tversky A. (1979). Prospect theory: an analysis of decision under risk. *Econometrica*, **47**, 263–91

Kahneman D. and Tversky A. (1982). Intuitive prediction: biases and corrective procedures. In *Judgement Under Uncertainty* (Kahnman D., Slovic P. and Tversky A., eds.). Cambridge: Cambridge University Press

Katseli and Papaefstratiou L. T. (1979). The re-emergence of the purchasing power parity doctrine in the 1970s. *Princeton Studies in International Finance*, **13**, Princeton University

Kindleberger C. P. (1978). *Manias, Panics and Crashes*. London: Basic Books and Macmillan

Kindleberger R. and Lindert. (1978) *International Economics* 3rd edn. Homewood Ill: Richard D. Irwin

Kouri P. J. (1976). The exchange rate and the balance of payments in the short and in the long run: a monetary approach. *Scandinavian Journal of Economics*, **78**, 280–304

Kouri P. J. (1983). Balance of payments and the foreign exchange market: a dynamic partial equilibrium model. In *Economic Interdependance and Flexible Exchange Rates* (Bhandari J. S. and Putnam B. H., eds.), pp. 118–56. Massachusetts: MIT Press

Krasker W. (1980). The peso problem in testing the efficiency of forward exchange markets. *Journal of Monetary Economics*, **6**, 269–76

Kravis I. B. and Lipsey R. E. (1971). Price competitiveness in world trade. New York: Columbia University Press

Krugman P. (1992). Six skeptical propositions about EMU. *Greek Economic Review*, August

Kyle A. S. (1985). Continuous auctions and insider trading. *Econometrica*, **53**, 1315–35

Laidler D. E. (1981). *Introduction to Microeconomics* 2nd edn. Oxford: Philip Allan

Laidler D. E. (1985). *The Demand for Money: Theories, Evidence and Problems*. New York: Harper and Row

Levich R. M. (1979a). On the efficiency of markets for foreign exchange. In *International Economic Policy: Theory and Evidence* (Dornbusch R. and Frankel J. A., eds.), pp. 246–66. Baltimore Md: Johns Hopkins University Press

Levich R. M. (1979b). *The International Money Market: An Assessment of Forecasting Techniques and Market Efficiency*. Greenwich Connecticut: JAI Press

Levich R. M. (1985). Empirical studies of exchange rates: price behavior, rate determination and market efficiency. In *Handbook of International Economics* (Jones R. W. and Kenen P. B., eds.), pp. 979–1040. Amsterdam: North-Holland

Macdonald R. (1988). *Floating Exchange Rates: Theory and Evidence*. London: Unwin Hyman

Macdonald R. and Taylor M. P. (1989). Economic analysis of foreign exchange markets: an expository survey. In *Innovations in Open Economy Macroeconomics* (Macdonald R. and Taylor N. P., eds.), pp. 3–107. Oxford: Basil Blackwell

Magee S. P. (1978). Contracting and spurious deviations from purchasing power parity. In *The Economics of Exchange Rates: Selected Studies* (Frenkel J. A. and Johnson H. G., eds.)

Markowitz H. M. (1959). *Portfolio Selection: Efficient Diversification of Investments*. New York: John Wiley & Sons

Marston R. C. (1982). Wages, relative prices and the choice between fixed and flexible exchange rates. *Canadian Journal of Economics*, **15** (1), 87–103

May R. M. (1976). Simple mathematical models with very complicated dynamics. *Nature*, **261**, 459

McKinnon R. I. (1963). Optimum currency areas. *American Economic Review*, **53**, 717–65

McKinnon R. I. (1979). *Money in International Exchange* Oxford: Oxford University Press

McKinnon R. I. (1982). Currency substitution and instability in the world dollar standard. *American Economic Review*, **72** (3), 320–33

Meade J. A. (1955). The case for variable exchange rates. *Three Banks Review*, September, **26**, 3–27

Meese R. A. (1986). Testing for bubbles in exchange markets: a case of sparkling rates? *Journal of Political Economy*, **94**, (2), 345–73

Meese R. A. and Rogoff K. (1983). The out-of-sample failure of empirical exchange rate models: sampling error or misspecification? In *Exchange Rates and International Macroeconomics* (Frenkel J., ed.), pp. 67–112. Chicago: University of Chicago Press

Meese R. A. and Singleton K. J. (1982). On unit roots and the empirical modelling of exchange rates. *Journal of Finance*, **37**, 1029–35

Mood A. M. and Graybill F. A. (1963). *Introduction to the Theory of Statistics* 2nd edn., Kogakusha: McGraw-Hill

Mundell R. A. (1961). A theory of optimum currency areas. *American Economic Review*, **51**, 509–17

Mundell R. A. (1962). The appropriate use of monetary and fiscal policy under fixed exchange rates. *IMF Staff Papers*, **9**, 70–7

Mundell R. A. (1968). *International Economics*. New York: Macmillan

Mussa M. (1976). The exchange rate, the balance of payments and monetary policy under a regime of controlled floating. *Scandinavian Journal of Economics*, **78**, 228–48

Mussa M. (1979). Empirical regularities in the behaviour of exchange rates and theories of the foreign exchange market, In *Policies for Employment, Prices, and Exchange Rates* (Brunner K. and Meltzer A. H., eds.), Carnegie Rochester Conference Series (Vol. 11)

Muth J. F. (1961). Rational expectations and the theory of price movements. *Econometrica*, **29**, 315–35

Officer L. H. (1976). The purchasing power parity theory of exchange rates: a review article: *IMF Staff Papers*, **23**, 1–60

Officer L. H. (1982). *Purchasing Power Parity and Exchange Rates: Theory, Evidence and Relevance*. Greenwich Conn: JAI Press

Parkin M. P. and Bade R. (1988). *Modern Macroeconomics* 2nd edn. Oxford: Philip Allan

Peitgen H-O., Jurgens H. and Saupe D. (1992). *Chaos and Fractals: New Frontiers of Science*. New York: Springer-Verlag

Roll R. (1979). Violations of purchasing power parity and their implications for efficient international commodity markets. In *International Finance and Trade* (Sarnat M. and Szego G. P., eds.). Cambridge MA: Bellinger

Sarkovskii A. N. (1964). Coexistence of cycles of a continuous map of a line into itself. *Ukrainian Mathematical Zeitung*, **16**, 61–71.

Sharpe W. F. (1985). *Investments* 3rd edn. Englewood Cliffs NJ: Prentice-Hall

Sheffrin S. S. (1983). *Rational Expectations*. Cambridge: Cambridge University Press

Stewart I. (1990). *Does God Play Dice?* London: Penguin Books

Taylor M. P. (1987). Covered interest parity: a high-frequency, high-quality data study. *Economica*, **54**, 429–38

Taylor M. P. (1988). What do investment managers know? an empirical study of practitioners' predictions. *Economica*, **55**, (218), 185–202

Tobin J. (1958). Liquidity preference as behaviour towards risk. *Review of Economic Studies*, **25**, 65–86

Tobin J. (1965). Money and economic growth. *Econometrica*, **33**, 671–84

Tobin J. (1969). A general equilibrium approach to monetary theory, *Journal of Money Credit and Banking*, **1** (1), 15–29

Tsiang S. C. (1959). The theory of forward exchange and effects of government intervention on the forward exchange market. *IMF Staff Papers*, **7**, 75–106

Williamson J. (1983). *The Open Economy and the World Economy*. New York: Basic Books

Wilson C. A. (1979). Anticipated shocks and exchange rate dynamics. *Journal of Political Economy*, **87** (3), 639–47

Wolff C. C. (1986). Exchange rate models and innovations: a derivation. *Economics Letters*, **20**, 373–76

Wonnacott R. J. and Wonnacott T. H. (1977). *Introductory Statistics* 3rd edn. John Wiley & Sons

Appendix: List of Symbols

$\tilde{X}$ Ratio of UK to US value of variable X, X/X^* (Section 5.1).

$\overline{X}$ The equilibrium, fixed or long-run value of an endogenous variable, X. Otherwise, denotes exogenous variable (Section 5.2).

$\dot{X}$ The change in the value of the variable S per unit of time, dX/dt (Section 9.1.2).

$\dot{x}$ The rate of change (growth rate) of the variable X per unit of time, $d(\log X)/dt$ (Section 7.3).

X^* The value of the variable X for the USA (Section 2.4).

A Investor's holding of forward contracts to buy dollars (Section 13.2.2).

B The surplus on the current account of the UK balance of payments (Section 6.1.2).

D Deposit liabilities of the commercial banks (Section 4.1.2).

DC Domestic credit (bank advances) (Section 4.1.2).

f The forward premium, $F/S - 1$ (Section 3.2).

F The stock of dollar-denominated securities held by the UK private sector (Section 8.1).

F_t The forward exchange rate at time t for currency to be delivered at time $t + 1$ (Section 3.2).

FX Gold and foreign currency reserves of Bank of England (Section 4.1.2).

G Government spending on goods and services (Section 4.1.1).

K Net inflow of capital from USA into UK (Section 6.1.2).

L Lending by UK commercial banks to UK non-government sector (Section 4.1.2).

LG Lending by Bank of England to UK government (Section 4.1.2).

MB^b Monetary base in bank tills (Section 4.1.2)

MB^P Monetary base in circulation with public (Section 4.1.2).

MB Total monetary base: $MB = MB^b + MB^P$ (Section 4.1.2).

M^s The supply of money (Section 4.1.2).

M^d The demand for money (Section 4.1.2).

μ The growth rate of the UK money stock, (Section 9.1).

$$\frac{d \log M^s}{dt} = \frac{1}{M^s} \frac{d M^s}{dt}$$

μ_X The mean of a random variable, X (Section 13.2.1).

P The (product) price level in the UK economy (Section 2.3).

Q The real exchange rate, SP^*/P (Section 2.4).

r A representative UK interest rate (Section 3.1.1).

ρ The risk premium on transactions in the forward market (Section 6.7).

S Exchange rate (£ price of $) (Section 1.1).

σ_X The standard deviation of the variable, X (Section 13.2.1)

σ_X^2 The variance of the variable, X (Section 13.2.2).

V The value of UK oil revenues at any point (Section 7.4).

$\overline{V}$ The permanent-income value of UK oil revenues (Section 7.4).

W UK private sector financial wealth (Section 8.1).

Y Nominal national income (Section 4.1)

y Real national income, Y/P (Section 4.1).

Index

Page numbers in **bold** type refer to definitions.